ArtScroll History Series®

Rabbi Nosson Scherman / Rabbi Meir Zlotowitz

General Editors

The Early Acharonim

The Early

compiled and edited by
Rabbi Hersh Goldwurm

Acharonim

Biographical Sketches of the Prominent Early Rabbinic Sages and Leaders from the Fifteenth - Seventeenth Centuries

Published by

Mesorah Publications, ltd

FIRST EDITION
First Impression ... October, 1989
Second Impression ... July 2008
Third Impression ... June 2011

Published and Distributed by
MESORAH PUBLICATIONS, Ltd.
4401 Second Avenue
Brooklyn, New York 11232

Distributed in Europ by
LEHMANNS
Unit E, Viking Business Park
Rolling Mill Road
Jarrow, Tyne & Wear NE32 3DP
England

Distributed in Australia & New Zealand by
GOLDS WORLD OF JUDAICA
3-13 William Street
Balaclava, Melbourne 3183
Victoria Australia

Distributed in Israel by
SIFRIATI / A. GITLER — BOOKS
6 Hayarkon Street
Bnei Brak 51127

Distributed in South Africa by
KOLLEL BOOKSHOP
Ivy Common 105 William Road
Norwood 2192, Johannesburg, South Africa

ARTSCROLL HISTORY SERIES®
THE EARLY ACHARONIM

Typography by Compuscribe at ArtScroll Studios, Ltd.

Printed in the United States of America by Noble Book Press
Bound by Sefercraft, Quality Bookbinders, Ltd. Brooklyn, N.Y.

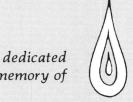

This volume is dedicated
to the memory of

Raymond and Rachel Haber

רחמים בן סטי ע״ה

כ״ד אלול תש״ך

רחל בת נזהה ע״ה

כ״ג תמוז תשכ״ה

To Raymond Haber, a good name was the most important thing —
that is how he lived and what he instilled in his children.

Born in Aleppo, Syria, he came to America at 16, working as a peddler and
opening his own business in California. He married Rachel Sutton in 1937, and
they lived in California until 1945. Then they came to New York in order to
raise their children in the religious tradition of the Syrian community.

Raymond and Rachel opened their home to scores of newcomers —
many of whom they brought to this country.
It was a tradition of goodness that they passed on to their children.

Rachel Haber's love of Torah, mitzvot, and her fellow Jews is unforgettable. As
an infant in Jerusalem she lost her mother. She revered and adored her father
and these were the feelings she brought to her husband and children.

Quietly she would collect funds for the needy.
Quietly she arranged marriages.
Quietly she helped people with personal and business problems.
Quietly she cared for the sick.
Always quietly, but with all her heart.

Raymond and Rachel were staunch supporters of the Syrian community's
first yeshivah day school — and their son was in its first class.

We, their family, whose lives were molded by their love and ideals,
dedicate this sefer to them.

תנצב״ה

~§ Table of Contents

✑ Publisher's Preface

Mesorah Publications Ltd. is proud to present *The Early Acharonim,* as the next volume in the series that began with *The Rishonim* several years ago. This book provides biographical information on the lives and times of the great Torah sages who flourished between the fifteenth and the eighteenth centuries. It was a period when the landscape of Jewish life changed radically. The Inquisition had wiped Spain and Portugal from the Jewish map. Persecution and shifting historical phenomena dimmed the other countries of Western Europe as centers of Torah greatness. From then on, the pendulum would shift to the East.

The manner of learning, too, would change, because the foundation-laying work of the *Rishonim* was over and a significant amount of the work of later generations would be based on their writings. Furthermore, the task of codifying the laws into a new framework, the *Shulchan Aruch,* had begun, and many *Acharonim* would contribute to this activity. It was during the period covered by this book that the Sephardic and Ashkenazic halachic traditions would develop.

By giving brief biographies of the greatest individuals of the period, tracing the rebbe-talmid relationships, showing their chronological development, and sketching the growth and dispersions of the various Jewish communities, this work will enrich the learning and perspectives of students of Torah. Such research was never uppermost in the mind of Torah scholars, nor should it be. However, it is helpful and enlightening in many ways, as a reading of this book will quickly demonstrate.

To help the reader gain a broad picture of the era, the book includes many maps, charts, and indices, among them an index matching authors with their most important *sefarim.* Of particular interest and importance, the book provides a historical perspective on the spread of Jewish settlement and the development of new communities.

Heretofore, works of this nature in English have been written by scholars of secular inclination. To them, great Jewish leaders were the statesmen, writers, philosophers. To the people of Torah, however, Jewish leaders are those who maintain the people's identity as the "Nation of Torah." The figures in this book are distinguished because of their contribution to Torah scholarship or their leadership of Israel in its constant struggle to maintain that identity.

This volume was compiled and prepared for publication by Rabbi Hersh Goldwurm who is respected both as a *talmid chacham* — he is the author of six volumes of the ArtScroll Mishnah Series; and as a historian — *History of the Jewish People* and *The Rishonim*. His vast knowledge, particularly of *soferim usefarim*, authors and their works, is obvious throughout this volume. A similar volume is now in preparation on the *Later Acharonim*, the leading sages from the eighteenth century onward.

Part of the material in this book is based on research generously provided by Rabbi Shmuel Teich.

Mrs. Nina Ackerman Indig's editing is meticulous and her eye for intricate details has greatly enhanced every page.

We sincerely hope that these glimpses into the lives of our great Torah personalities and their works will inspire a new generation to add its own imprint on the developing history of the Torah Nation. In our era, too, history has shifted the centers of Jewish scholarship to new lands, even new continents. In the past, *Klal Yisrael* has responded with new epochs of Torah greatness. May it do so in our time as well.

Rabbi Meir Zlotowitz/Rabbi Nosson Scherman
General Editors

Erev Succos 5750 / October 1989
Brooklyn, New York

Historical Introduction

৵৵ Foreword

In the previous volume, *The Rishonim*, which deals with the early masters (*Rishonim*), we found it advantageous to separate the listings by geographic designation (Spain, France, etc.). The political and physical conditions prevailing in the period between the tenth and fifteenth centuries (the time frame of that book) allowed for very little cross-fertilization between the scholarly communities of the various countries. Therefore, as each community developed internally, it evolved in its own distinctive style.

In the fifteenth century — the earliest dealt with in this volume — drastic changes were beginning to occur. Travel between countries was becoming less difficult and more frequent, and the invention of the printing press made the dissemination of ideas and scholarship easier by far than it had been previously. The expulsion of Spanish Jewry from its fatherland brought the exiles into actual contact with other Jews in many lands (e.g., Turkey and Italy), and the acceptance of R' Yosef Caro's *Shulchan Aruch* as 'the' authoritative code for Jewish law did much to fuse the two major branches of Jewry, unifying both within a common religious and scholarly heritage. In contrast to the period of the Rishonim, of which it is relatively simple to identify an author as a Sephardi or an Ashkenazi, it is very difficult to do so for authors of the period covered by this volume simply on the basis of the subject matter itself — the differences now being much more subtle. The separations between the two strains of Jewry became evident more in the realm of culture, lifestyle and other external phenomena, and did not affect the world of scholarship — the topic of this book — to any great extent. For this reason, in this and subsequent volumes, the sages will be listed in chronological order (according to their dates of death), disregarding their countries of origin.

Another striking phenomenon about the fifteenth century is the plethora of expulsions it brought for world Jewry. In addition to the dramatic expulsion of the Jews from the entire Iberian Peninsula, a host of smaller expulsions and persecutions were visited upon the Jews of Germany and Austria. These banishments resulted in far-reaching shifts of Jewish populations. The Spanish Jews settled mostly in the countries ringing the Mediterranean Sea, with the greatest number going to Turkey, and with sizable groups settling in Italy, Egypt, and Morocco. The German Jews emigrated in masses to the countries of Eastern Europe — Poland, Bohemia and Moravia (Czechoslovakia).

The impact these mass upheavals had on Torah scholarship is paradoxical. Both in the Sephardic and Ashkenazic groups we find an almost unprecedented sudden surge in Torah scholarship. The fundamental works in both *halachah* and *kabbalah*, which were to have the profoundest impact upon following generations of Jews, were written during this era; the *Shulchan Aruch*, under the joint authorship of R' Yosef Caro and R' Moshe Isserles, and the kabbalistic works of R' Yitzchak Luria (the Arizal), R' Chaim Vital, and R' Moshe Cordovero were composed during this period. It is as though Divine Providence, aware of the trying times Israel was to endure, had held some of the noblest spirits of the nation in reserve to ensure the continuity of Torah scholarship and observance.

In the Historical Introduction we will examine — country by country — some of the major Jewish communities and historical events as they relate to the Early Acharonim.

I. Turkey — Greece

Although Jews had been living in the Balkans and Turkey since the Second Temple Era, they had suffered greatly under the Byzantine Emperors, and the Jewish community was small and insignificant. In the fourteenth century many European Jews of Ashkenazic extraction emigrated to Greece. The Jews of Hungary (expelled in 5120/1360 by Louis the Great, king of Hungary and Poland) and the oppressed German Jews settled in Greece in significant numbers. The Jewish community on the island of Crete (Candia) seems to have been founded by these Ashkenazic émigrés. On the island of Corfu (under Venetian domination since 5146/1386) there was, in addition to the Greek Jews, a substantial Italian Jewish community.

The fourteenth century saw the emergence of a new power in the Middle East. The Turks, under Osman (5048/1288-5086/1326), had been steadily expanding their dominion into Greece and the neighboring countries, and the entity which would later be known as the Ottoman Empire was in the first phase of its formation. In 5213/1453 Constantinople — the proud capital of Byzantium, the Eastern Roman Empire — was captured by Mehmet II. He issued a proclamation welcoming all Jews to his country and took special pains to settle them in his capital, Constantinople (now Istanbul). When the Spanish Jews were expelled from their homeland in 5252/1492, and later from Portugal in 1497, Bayezid II opened the portals of the Ottoman Empire to them. They settled there in great numbers, especially in Constantinople, Salonica, and Smyrna, eventually becoming the dominant strain in the Jewish community.

The old Jewish community had possessed some scholars of note, notably R' Moshe and R' Eliyahu Capsali, and R' Eliyahu Mizrachi (who was greatly involved in the rescue and resettlement of the immigrants) in Constantinople; R' David HaKohen in Corfu; and others. The new arrivals soon founded yeshivos and communities of their own. Among them we find such men of distinction as R' Yosef Caro, who wrote most of his monumental *Beis Yosef* in Adrianople (Edirne, Turkey), R' Yaakov ibn Chaviv and his son R' Levi, R' Yosef Taitatzak, and many others. Other ethnic strains of the Jewish community are also well represented in the annals of Torah scholarship. The names of R' Yosef ibn Lev and R' Binyamin Zev (both Greek) and a host of others are well known to every student.

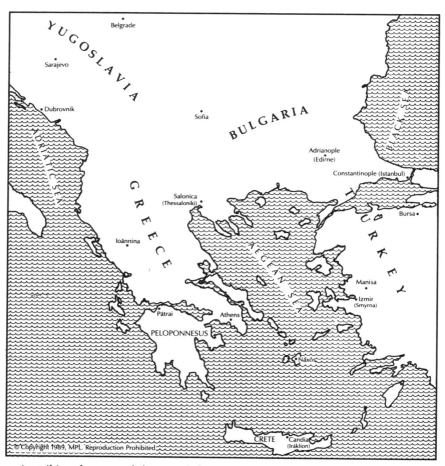

A striking feature of the Torah literature of this age is the richness of its responsa literature, including the space it devotes to the resolution of financial and marital disputes, and the great debates, regarding difficult halachic cases, among the Torah giants of the generation. It is clear that the Jews enjoyed much judicial autonomy and that great power was wielded by the Torah sages.

In 5276-77/1516-17 Selim I conquered Syria and *Eretz Yisrael*, and a wave of emigration to the Holy Land began. For centuries thereafter the Turkish communities — especially that of Constantinople — enjoyed a special relationship with the communities of *Eretz Yisrael*; in times of trouble Constantinople would be the first address towards which they turned. A number of the scholars of *Eretz Yisrael* served as rabbis of the Turkish capital, most notably R' Yosef Trani (Maharit).

During the first two centuries of the Ottoman Empire the Jews enjoyed substantial influence at Court. Many of the Sultans had private physicians who were Jewish, and who used their position to better the lot of their co-religionists. Jewish power reached its zenith during the reigns of Suleiman the Magnificent (5280/1520-5326/1566) and Selim II (5326/1566-5334/1574). When the Venetian Republic (in 5310/1550) imprisoned the extremely wealthy Marrano, Dona Gracia Mendes, on charges of judaizing, her kinsman (who was later to become her son-in-law) Don Yosef Nasi appealed to the Sultan via intermediaries, pointing out the financial advantages to his empire should the banking house of the family, and its assets, be moved from Venice to Turkey. Because of the intervention of the court physician Moses Hamon, the Sultan sent a special ambassador to Venice to negotiate for Dona Gracia's release. The extremely capable Yosef was introduced to Suleiman and gradually began to win the Sultan's confidence. Yosef backed the interests of Suleiman's older son, Selim, against those of the younger, Bayezid. Upon Bayezid's defeat, Yosef was admitted into the inner circle of advisors to Sultan Selim II, and given the region of Tiberias (desolate since the time of the Crusaders) for redevelopment as a Jewish region. In order to give the area an economic base, mulberry trees were planted for the purpose of raising silkworms. Many of the Jews in the Papal States, who were chafing under the cruel and tyrannical rule of Pope Paul IV, settled in Tiberias; an entire town emigrated en masse and settled there. The banishment of the Jews from the Papal States in 5329/1569 further strengthened the resettlement. The local yeshivah received its financial support from Dona Gracia Mendes. When Selim II ascended the throne, Yosef's fortunes reached a high point: the Sultan elevated him to the nobility and appointed him Duke of Naxos and the Cyclades (a group of islands in the Mediterranean). Don Yosef was responsible for much of the delicate maneuvering of Turkey's international politics, and nearly involved it in a war against Spain. He was also largely responsible for Turkey's declaration of war against Venice in 5331/1571, and the resultant conquest of Cyprus. (The ramifications of this action still play a role in today's international politics.) In the field of Torah scholarship, Don Yosef and his mother-in-law were instrumental in bringing R' Yosef ibn Lev to Constantinople, and were responsible for the finances of his yeshivah. They founded a printing press using Hebrew letters at the Nasi estate of Belvedere, in Constantinople, and sponsored the publication of many important works.

Many other Jewish notables were influential in the Turkish court after Yosef Nasi. The wealthy ibn Yaish family, possessing a strong tradition of scholarship, supported a yeshivah and were the gracious patrons of R' Yosef Trani for decades. In general, the Turkish Jews of the sixteenth and seventeenth centuries were the most prosperous Jewish group in Europe and Asia, and Jewish scholarship thrived in this tranquil and relatively free atmosphere.

II. Eretz Yisrael

The fortunes of *Eretz Yisrael* were closely related to those of Turkey. The Jewish communities of the Holy Land had been destroyed by the Crusaders, and made only a halting recovery under the subsequent rule of the Egyptian Mamelukes. R' Ovadyah Bertinoro, who settled in Jerusalem in 5240/1480, wrote that its population consisted of seventy families, most of them very poor. Elsewhere the situation was not better. In 5376-77/1516-17 the Ottoman Sultan Selim I conquered *Eretz Yisrael* and ushered in a new era. The exile of the Spanish Jews spurred a great wave of immigration to the Holy Land, and substantial communities were founded, especially in Jerusalem, Hebron, and Safed (*Tzfas*).

The latter town emerged as the principal Jewish settlement in the land, counting more than seven hundred Jewish families among its inhabitants (more than a third of the total population), according to mid-sixteenth-century government statistics. Safed became one of the most important centers of Jewish learning. It was able, in the middle of the sixteenth century, to boast as residents R' Yosef Caro (author of the *Shulchan Aruch*), R' Moshe Cordovero and R' Yitzchak Luria (both famous for their fundamental works on the *kabbalah*), R' Moshe Alsheich (the master of the Biblical sermon), R' Moshe Trani, and a veritable host of other well-known scholars of classic stature. This was the zenith of Safed's classic period. Directly preceding this period, R' Yaakov bei Rav had been Safed's spiritual leader, and had launched his unsuccessful attempt to revive the ancient institution of *semichah*. Toward the end of the century, a series of economic and political misfortunes were visited upon Safed. Its Jewish population slowly declined, and its importance as a center of scholarship waned. Its significance as a center of textile production dwindled, and the Sultans adopted a policy of laxness regarding the administration of these territories, leaving the inhabitants open to the persecution of lawless local strongmen.

At this juncture, Jerusalem began to assume more and more importance. Jerusalem and the surrounding area (including Hebron) constituted a separate administrative state in the Ottoman Empire. Because of the weak control exercised by the central government in Constantinople, local rulers were quite free to exploit their populations at whim. The rulers of Jerusalem taxed the Jewish community at such a high rate that it was virtually impossible for its inhabitants to remain there. It was only because of their devotion to the Holy City, and with the help of their brethren in the Diaspora, that the community was kept up. R' Betzalel Ashkenazi, author of *Shittah Mekubetzes*, settled in Jerusalem in 5348/1588, and tried to help the unfortunate community. He traveled to the Diaspora to raise funds in order to put the city on a secure financial basis. Early in the seventeenth century (5381/1621) R'

Aleppo

Euphrates River

SYRIA

Damascus

Acre · Safed
Haifa · Tiberias

JERUSALEM

· Gaza

MEDITERRANEAN SEA

ISRAEL

IRAQ

Tigris River

· Baghdad

MIDDLE EAST

Yeshayah Horowitz, the venerated rabbi of Prague and author of *Shelah* (*Shnei Luchos HaBris*), insisted on settling in Jerusalem; his presence as *rav* of the Ashkenazic community gave new strength to the settlement. However, in 5385/1625, the avaricious Mohammed ibn Farukh became pasha of the Jerusalem area and added his voracious demands to the exorbitant taxes already sapping the economic viability of the congregation. During the summer of the following year, ibn Farukh went on a voyage and left the administration of his state in the hands of his brother-in-law, Othman Aga. This petty official outdid the venal example of his predecessor and immediately commanded the elders of the Jewish community to pay him a large sum of money. When they answered that the treasury had already been emptied by the previous pilferings of ibn Farukh, and the expected income of the community for many years had already been appropriated for the payment of debts and interest, the ruler became enraged. He ordered his police to arrest the leaders of the community, and threatened to kill them. R' Yeshayah fled after being ransomed. Others remained in prison and underwent various tortures until an order was received from Damascus deposing Othman. Ibn Farukh soon returned and continued to oppress the Jewish population with the utmost brutality. By the time he was deposed in the winter of 5486/1626, the community was ruined financially and many of the inhabitants had left.

Slowly Jerusalem recovered, and by the middle of the century it had become a center of Torah scholarship, with a number of yeshivos. Chida relates that during R' Moshe Galante's tenure as spiritual leader of Jerusalem, there were eighty-seven outstanding sages in the town. The fledgling Ashkenazi community received a short-lived reenforcement with the arrival of R' Yehudah Chassid and his group (see *The Later Acharonim*), but this ill-fated attempt at settlement ended with the decimation of the Ashkenazi community due to a plague circa 5480/1720. This was a blow from which Jerusalem would not recover until the end of the nineteenth century.

During the period immediately following the Spanish exile, the Jewish masses exhibited an unusual expectation for the imminent Messianic redemption. The great suffering of Jews throughout

The Semichah Debate

the world — especially the exile of the Spanish Jews in 5252/1492, the virtual imprisonment of the unfortunate Marranos in the country of their birth, and the geo-political upheaval caused by Turkey's aspirations for world dominion through the downfall of Christian Europe — was regarded as a harbinger of better days being ushered in. A genuine yearning for penance manifested itself, which, it was hoped, would accelerate the course of events leading to the Redemption — and no doubt many of the erstwhile Marranos searched for a method by which to purge the sins of their youth.

One of the various proposals towards this end, which caused a vigorous and sometimes almost virulent debate among the leading sages of the generation, was the controversy surrounding the proposed renewal of the institution of *semichah*. According to Torah law, many judicial functions — among them the power to inflict corporal punishment — require that the court be composed of judges duly accredited with the so-called *semichah* ordination. The cardinal facet of the *semichah* is the conferring of the title 'Rabbi' upon the candidate, by a scholar possessing ordination, as part of an unbroken chain of ordinations reaching back to Moses himself, who in turn had been 'ordained' to serve as a judge by G-d. The ordination was valid only if conferred in *Eretz Yisrael*, and it had become obsolete during the persecutions of the Romans in the fourth and fifth centuries. If the *semichah* were renewed, a penitent might then present himself to a duly ordained tribunal, confess his more grievous sins, accept the punishment of *malkus* (lashes) and consequently be freed of his sins according to the Talmudic dictum that [even] those guilty of offenses liable to punishment by *kares* (spiritual excision) are exonerated if they have had the punishment of *malkus* administered to themselves (*Makkos* 13b). Besides, it was argued, the advent of the Messiah should be preceded by the appointment of duly ordained judges, as prophesied by Isaiah (1:26): *And I shall restore your judges as of yore . . . and afterward you will be called the city of righteousness*. Towards these ends R' Yaakov bei Rav, venerated rabbi and *rosh yeshivah* of Safed, proposed (c. 5298/1538) that the scholars of Safed, then the overwhelming majority of sages in *Eretz Yisrael*, confer *semichah* upon him (R' Yaakov bei Rav), whereupon he would be empowered to ordain others. The proposal was based upon a novel ruling by Rambam (*Hil. Sanhedrin* 4:11) that even an unordained assembly comprised of all the sages of *Eretz Yisrael* had the powers of a duly ordained *Sanhedrin*, and could confer ordination. The assembled sages unanimously and enthusiastically agreed to the proposal and ordained R' Yaakov, who then ordained a group of scholars.

There are conflicting reports about the identities of the ordained sages. R' Yaakov bei Rav himself (at the end of the responsum printed in *Teshuvos Ralbach*) writes that he ordained the four greatest sages of Safed. This has been assumed to refer to R' Yosef Caro, R' Moshe Trani, R' Yisrael de Corial, and R' Avraham Shalom. R' Gedalyah ibn Yachyah reports (in *Shalsheles HaKabbalah*) that ten sages were ordained, most of them not well known. Chida reports (in *Shem HaGedolim*) that he saw a document signed by R' Moshe Alsheich in which that great sage attests that he ordained R' Chaim Vital with the 'power of the *semichah*' he himself had received from R' Yosef Caro. R' Yaakov bei Rav's grandson, R' Yaakov Abulafia, is referred to as 'HaRav HaMusmach', as is his son, R' Chaim Abulafia (see *Shem HaGedolim*). The latter may be the last *musmach*.

The first ordination was conferred, in writing, upon R' Levi ibn Chaviv (Ralbach), the rabbi of the small Jerusalem community and one of the outstanding scholars of the period. However R' Levi, upon receiving the ordination (he had not been present at the ordination assembly), refused to accept it, arguing that the entire process was invalid and had no real basis in *halachah*. He pointed out that Rambam himself had not given a final ruling on his novel concept but had, uncharacteristically, added 'and the matter needs study.' Besides, the ordination was invalid even according to R' Yaakov's understanding of Rambam's view, for the latter had stipulated that *all* of the *Eretz Yisrael* sages must consent, implying that in this matter a majority opinion was not sufficient. In this case, since the sages of Jerusalem had not consented, and did not entertain the prospect of consent in the future, the ordination was invalid by any standard. R' Yaakov bei Rav answered R' Levi's objections, but R' Levi was not satisfied with the reply. The matter was debated back and forth a few times without any clear result; R' Levi refused to retract his opposition and R' Yaakov refused to declare his ordination invalid. Nevertheless, R' Levi's refusal to agree put a damper upon the *semichah* enthusiasm, and with the passage of time the proposed renewal withered away. R' David ibn Zimra, one of the foremost Torah personalities of that illustrious generation, who officiated as rabbi of Cairo at the time of the debate, remarks in his Rambam commentary: 'Based on this passage the sages of Safed and the greatest among them attempted to renew the *semichah* but they could not accomplish this because of the objection of the *chacham* of Jerusalem. They asked my opinion and that of my colleagues while I was yet in Egypt and we did not agree. I elaborated in a responsum to disprove their view and [to show] that they did not read the words of our teacher [Rambam] with sufficient care ...' Significantly, none of the prestigious disciples of R' Yaakov bei Rav, most notably R' Yosef Caro and R'

Moshe Trani (Mabit), allude in the slightest way to the reinstitution of the semichah, confirming most eloquently with their silence R' Levi ibn Chaviv's position.

III. Italy

With the advent of the era of the Acharonim the Jewish community of Italy was greatly strengthened in numbers. The southward migration of German Jews and their settlement in the northern provinces had already begun in the fifteenth century. These German Jews formed their own congregations in many places and so there evolved a unique Italian nusach Ashkenaz. Many of the Spanish exiles settled in Italy, among them such men of stature as *Don Yitzchak Abarbanel. These Sefardim became a dominant force in Jewish Italy, and the Sefardic customs in prayer — nusach Sefard — was practiced in Italy alongside the old Italian (or Roman), and German rites. Later on a significant number of Marranos settled there.

The islands of Sicily and Sardinia were Spanish possessions in the fifteenth century, and the edict of expulsion (5252/1492) was applied to their Jewish populations as well (1492). Later the duchy of Naples — Southern Italy — was acquired by the Spanish crown and the Jews were expelled from there too (5270-5300/1510-41). The focus of Jewish life was now confined to central and northern Italy.

The introduction of the printing press revolutionized Jewish learning: Whereas heretofore only a limited number of copies of a work could be made severely curtailing its circulation, thousands of copies could now be made. Italy became the 'cradle' of Jewish typography, and retained a leading position in the field of Hebrew printing for many centuries. The first printed editions of the Talmud, Mishnah, Mikraos Gedolos, Tur, Shulchan Aruch were produced there. This great availability of scholarly works made Italy a flourishing center of Jewish learning. Many communities supported their own yeshivos, and among the rabbis of the towns were some of the greatest Jewish scholars of the time.

The beginning of the sixteenth century and the concomitant Catholic reaction to the Reformation brought with it a wave of persecutions and anti-Jewish legislation by the Papacy. These laws had the force of law in the Papal states (central Italy), and were copied in many other provinces.

Various popes during the sixteenth century issued anti-Semitic decrees. In 5314/1553, Pope Julius III ordered all copies of the Talmud confiscated and burned. The order was strictly and scrupulously enforced, and the damage it caused to Jewish learning can hardly be imagined. Paul IV (5315-9/1555-9) ordered that all Jews be contained in the Ghetto and severely curtailed their economic activities; the only business he allowed them was the selling of rags.

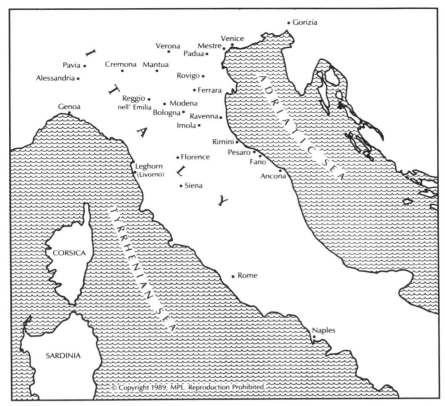

Gorizia
Venice
Verona Mestre
Padua
Pavia   Cremona Mantua
Alessandria   Rovigo
Ferrara
Reggio   Modena
Genoa   nell' Emilia Bologna
Ravenna
Imola
Rimini
Florence   Pesaro
Fano
Leghorn
(Livorno)   Ancona
Siena

ADRIATIC SEA

CORSICA

TYRRHENIAN SEA

Rome

Naples

SARDINIA

© Copyright 1989, MPL. Reproduction Prohibited.

He ordered that 25 Marranos residing at Ancona (in the Papal states) be burned at the stake (see *R' Yehoshua Soncin). Pius V (5326-32/1566-72) and Clement VIII (5352-65/1592-1605) banished the Jews from the Papal states except for the cities of Rome and Ancona. It is difficult to understand how Italian Jewry survived this excessive persecution, but survive it did, no doubt to the chagrin of its oppressors. In spite of the oppressive climate in which they lived, Italian Jews flourished in the sixteenth and seventeenth centuries, both economically and spiritually.

IV. Poland and Lithuania

The modern reader finds it difficult to grasp the scope of the political entity called Poland. History has so often favored that country with partition that one has to specify the geographical reality of the Poland being discussed. During the period dealt with here, we will refer by the name Poland to the country as it was constituted prior to its first partition in 5532/1772; thus, even some territory included in the modern U.S.S.R. is here called Poland. The

Map labels: BALTIC SEA, Nieman, Kaidan, Vilna, LITHUANIA, Lida, Grodno, Nieman, Vistula, Tiktin, Amstibovi, Bialystok, Brisk-Dakau, Mezeritch, P, Posen, O, L, Warsaw, Bug, Brisk, POLESIE, Lenshitz, A, Mezeritch Podl., Lissa, N, Kalish, D, Krotoshyn, Piotrków, Zwolen, Lublin, VOLHYNIA, Chelm, Ludmir, Lutsk, Chmielnik, Apta, Shebreshin, Zamosht, Dubno, Ostroh, Pintchow, Shidlow, Belz, Kremenitz, Vistula, Cracow, Reisha, Zolkiew, Podayetz, PODOLIA, Premysl, Lemberg, Brezan, Satanow

© Copyright 1989, MPL. Reproduction Prohibited.

Ukraine, Volhynia, and Podolia were all within the boundaries of Poland during this period. In its broadest sense the term Poland also includes Lithuania, since the duchy of Lithuania was a political subdivision of Poland during most of the period under discussion.

The Jewish settlement in Poland claimed for itself great antiquity, but its population was very sparse before the thirteenth century when Boleslav, Duke of Greater Poland (the region around Posen [Poznan], in northwestern Poland), officially admitted them to his duchy (5024/1264). Casimir III (the Great) permitted them to settle throughout the kingdom (5094/1334). It was probably during the fourteenth and fifteenth centuries that the great immigration of Ashkenazic Jews to Poland took place. The first well-known Talmud scholar who resided permanently in Poland is R' Moshe Mintz (5175/1415-5245/1485) who served as *rav* of Posen. Very little is known about the scholars who laid the groundwork for Torah scholarship in this country, and mostly all we have are random references in the works of such greats as Maharshal, Rama, and others. The names of R' Yechiel Luria (Maharshal's great-grandfather), reputedly first *rav* of Brisk (fifteenth century); R' Kalman Vermaisa, *rav* of Lemberg from 5278/1518 to 5320/1560; R' Asher and R' Moshe Storch, and R' Yitzchak Shapira, rabbis in Cracow in their time; and even the famous R' Yaakov Pollak and his celebrated disciple R' Shalom Shachna of Lublin — all these mean very little to the modern Torah scholar. However, R' Yaakov Pollak is credited with the introduction of a novel method of Talmud exposition — *pilpul* — which became very popular in the Polish yeshivos.

The yeshivos of the early period (up to the Cossack revolution in 5408/1648) played a great role in Jewish life, and great prestige was attached to the post of *rosh yeshivah*. The posts of *rav* and *av beis din* were not, as a rule, identical with that of *rosh yeshivah*. Thus we find R' Yom Tov Lipman Heller (author of *Tosefos Yom Tov*) leaving the rabbinate of Ludmir in 5404/1644 in order to serve as *rosh yeshivah* in Cracow during the tenure of R' Yehoshua ben Yosef (the *Pnei Yehoshua*) in the rabbinate.

The relationship between the rulers and the Jews was, compared to conditions elsewhere in Europe, a good one, and the Jews enjoyed relative prosperity and peace. It seems that they were allowed a great amount of autonomy, and the *kahal* (communal organization), with its leaders and the rabbinate, had considerable power. The *kehillos* (at the behest of the king) organized themselves in regional confederations which were united under one umbrella organization embracing all of Poland, called the 'Council of Four Lands' (*Vaad Arba Aratzos*). The lay leaders and members of the rabbinate who belonged to this organization would meet at periodic intervals, discuss common problems, and promulgate enactments (*takanos*) which would be binding on the populace.

At first only three regions belonged to the Council — Greater Poland (Poznan and the surrounding area), Lesser Poland (Cracow and its surroundings), and Red Russia (Eastern Galicia) — and it was called the Council of Three Lands. Later, Volhynia and Lithuania joined and it became the Council of Five Lands. In 5383/1623 Lithuania seceded from the Council and founded its own Council of the Land (or *Vaad HaMedinah*). Thenceforth the organization was known as the Council of Four Lands until its dissolution in 5524/1664 by Stanislav Augustus, the last king of Poland.

The fifteenth and sixteenth centuries were formative years for Polish Jewry, and for European Jewry in general. During this period the *Shulchan Aruch* was codified and its wide acceptance by the scholarly community was effected. The *roshei yeshivah* charted the course which Talmud scholarship was to take over the next few centuries, and such works as *Chidushei Halachos* by Maharsha put an indelible stamp on the thought processes of generations of students to this day. During the latter part of this period, when the acceptance of the *Shulchan Aruch* as the ultimate authority was no longer an open question, the interpretation of this halachic codex began to occupy the focus of the scholarly community. In a short period the classic commentaries of the *Shulchan Aruch* were written and fixed in their places of honor alongside the *Shulchan Aruch*, thereby gaining everlasting status in the annals of *halachah*.

The Cossack revolt in 5408/1648, with its attendant massacre of the Jewish masses and destruction of entire Jewish communities, had a deep impact on the course of Torah scholarship. The old orderly and structured *kehillah* and its institutions were shattered. The big and prestigious yeshivos were closed, and learning began to assume an individualistic character. Youths would learn in the local *beis hamidrash*, largely unaided, and yeshivos, where they existed, were small study groups assembled by the local *rav* or any other scholar. Nevertheless, Torah scholarship somehow managed to thrive, and great Torah personalities emerged in whose works we search in vain for mention of their mentors. The yeshivos made their comeback only in the nineteenth century, when they began to flourish again in Lithuania, and later in Poland.

The Cossack Revolt

The southern area of Poland — known today as the Ukraine — was the frontier which separated that country from the Turks and the Tatars to the south and east. This region is largely a plain and therefore provides no natural barrier. The country was sparsely populated with runaway serfs who had escaped from their masters in the north. At the end of the fifteenth century the Polish government organized these wild tribesmen into military companies for the purpose of border defense; they were thenceforth called 'Cossacks' (from a Turkish word meaning 'free men, adventurers'). The Cossacks were ethnically related to the Russians and belonged to the Russian Orthodox Church.

As Poland expanded into the fertile Ukraine and its lords took possession of its plains, the Ukrainian peasants were heavily taxed and exploited by their Polish overlords. The ill feeling between the two classes was exacerbated by the religious and ethnic enmity fostered by both groups. Very often Jews would administer the Polish landlords' estates. The Jews became identified with the oppressors, especially so when they were responsible for the collection of the exorbitant taxes. The ill will generated by this was augmented by the hatred borne by the peasants against the Jews because of their race and religion. Nonetheless, in the early revolts of the Cossacks (5351-53/1591-93; 5390/1630) the Jews were not singled out as targets for revenge. In a later abortive revolt (5397/1637) some two hundred Jews were killed. In 5408/1648 a Cossack leader, Bogdan Chmielnicki, forged an alliance with the Tatars of Crimea and raised the banner of revolt throughout the Ukraine. In the initial battle the Cossacks defeated the Poles. Chmielnicki allowed his bandits to pillage, rob and murder at will. The victory-crazed Cossacks — egged on by Greek Orthodox priests who urged them to put the infidels, both Jews and Catholics, to the sword — ranged over the Ukraine, bringing with them rapine and desolation. The Jews were given the choice to convert or be killed; since they largely refused the first option they were massacred by the thousands. Men, women and children were subjected to the most gruesome tortures and death. On 20 Sivan the Cossack bands took the town of Nemirov in the Ukraine by treachery and butchered its six thousand Jews, among them the aged and revered *rav* of the town, R' Yechiel Michel.

In the year 5411/1651 the Poles finally defeated Chmielnicki, but this did not end the unrest; rather, it hastened the demise of the Polish republic. The Cossacks formed an alliance with Russia, Poland's old enemy, and began the thirteen-year war which would ultimately result in the dismemberment of Poland a century later. In 5414-15/1654-55 the Cossacks, together with their Russian allies, mounted an attack on Lithuania. Wherever their troops reached they proceeded to butcher the Jewish population with great cruelty. When the Cossack hordes reached Vilna, the center of Jewish life in Lithuania, Duke Radzivil fled together with his army, leaving the city defenseless: 'On Wednesday, 23 Tammuz 5415/1655 almost the entire [Jewish] community fled the town. Those who had prepared horses and wagons for themselves loaded them with their wives and children, along with some belongings; and those that had not prepared fled on foot, taking their belongings and small children on their shoulders' (R' Moshe Rivkah's in his preface to *Be'er HaGolah*). The Cossacks killed 45,000 people on this day and burned Vilna for seventeen days. Meanwhile the Swedes, under Charles X, taking advantage of Poland's weakness, swooped into the embattled country from the north and conquered significant portions of it. The fleeing Jews suffered heavily from this further escalation of warfare. An eyewitness, R' Moshe Rivkah's, reports: 'When we came to the province of Zamut [Zhmud, in the northwest corner of Lithuania], close to the border of Prussia, the verse (*Amos* 5:19): *Just as a man who flees before a lion and meets a bear ...* was fulfilled with us. There too, the sword of the Swedish monarch's army followed us. They flayed us with big levies every day' (preface to *Be'er HaGolah*).

Thus ended a glorious era for Polish Jewry. It would be a long time until the Jews would re-establish themselves and their communal organization in that country.

V. Austria

The Jews of Austria had suffered greatly during the period of unrest and persecution following the Black Plague (14th century). Many Jews were burned at the stake in the environs of Vienna and the rest were expelled from the city — their property confiscated — in 5180/1420. Subsequently, Austrian Jewry experienced a short revival when R' Yisrael Isserlein (author of *Terumas HaDeshen*) headed a yeshivah at Wiener Neustadt and was recognized as the spiritual leader of all Austrian Jews. However, the Emperors would periodically order partial expulsions. In the period following the massacre of the Jews in Poland during the Cossack insurrection, many Polish Jews settled in Vienna, among them many prominent *rabbanim*. However, because of the implacable enmity of the clergy, the situation quickly deteriorated. In

5430/1670 all the Jews were expelled from Vienna, where virtually all Austrian Jews resided; this edict remained in force until 5608/1848. A few privileged Jews, having connections with the Habsburg emperors, were given special permission to live in Vienna.

VI. Germany

The history of the Jewish community in Germany from the Crusades on is one of almost constant pain and persecution. Heavy taxation kept the Jews constantly on the verge of financial ruin. At times they would fall prey to widespread violence. Roving bands of peasants, egged on by fanatical Jew-haters and incited by the hostile clergy, periodically decimated entire regions. During the Black Plague (5108/1348-5110/1350) the Jews suffered doubly. The plague took its toll of them too (although not as heavily as from the general population). In addition to this they were persecuted by crazed mobs who accused the Jews of causing the plague by poisoning the wells; it is said that 300 communities were destroyed at this time. Many Jews emigrated to the East, settling in Poland where, at that time, the situation was much more favorable for Jews.

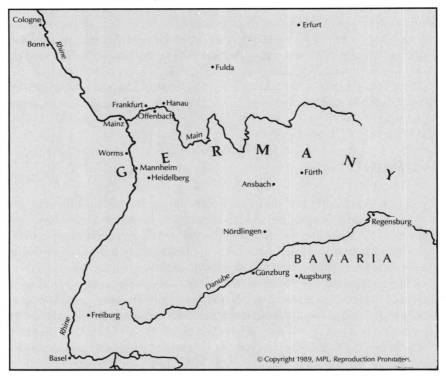

© Copyright 1989, MPL. Reproduction Prohibited.

An additional impetus to the eastward emigration was provided in the fifteenth century by a seemingly unending chain of expulsions. Principality after principality expelled its Jews. Most of these expulsions were, however, short-lived, and the Jews were allowed to return after staying away for a short period. The weakness of the German empire during that era contributed to this state of affairs. Each principality was allowed to do with its Jews as it pleased, in spite of the fact that the Jews were considered the personal property of the king, according to medieval law. The empire's lack of central authority also had a salutary effect on Jewish affairs. Because of the central government's weakness, a general expulsion was impossible.

The constant persecutions and expulsions left their mark. The massive eastward migration of Jews shifted the center of Jewish population from Central Europe to Poland, and gradually the Jews living in the Slavic East assumed the position of dominance in Jewish scholarship.

Conversely the East would now begin to supply some of the spiritual needs of the West. Many of the big cities in Germany appointed *rabbanim* from the East to fill their rabbinates. A shared heritage of customs common both to Eastern and Western Europe, the same code of laws (the *Shulchan Aruch*), a similar outlook on Judaism, acceptance of the same halachic authorities (*poskim*), similarity in language (Yiddish), and a shared historic identity as Ashkenazic Jews — all of these factors helped to blur some of the external differences between these two branches of Ashkenazic Jewry, and allowed for free cross-fertilization in matters of Torah scholarship and the spirit of the Jewish religion.

VII. Bohemia

Bohemia (פיהם, Peim, or ביהם, Beim, in Jewish literature), the westernmost province of modern Czechoslovakia, can boast of Jewish settlements probably rivaling those of Germany in antiquity. In the era of the *Rishonim* a number of Jewish scholars are known to have been from Bohemia. The *Tosafist* *R' Yitzchak ben Yaakov, known as *Ri HaLavan,* and his brother the well known traveler *R' Pesachyah of Regensburg, were from Prague. The *Tosafists* *R' Eliezer ben Yitzchak and *R' Yitzchak ben Mordechai; *R' Yitzchak ben Moshe, author of the halachic work *Or Zarua*; and *R' Avraham ben Azriel were originally from Bohemia. The Jews of Bohemia suffered greatly from the political and religious unrest of the fourteenth and fifteenth centuries, and a number of massacres were perpetrated upon them. Animosity against the Jews peaked in the sixteenth century, when they were expelled from a number of cities and massacred in a number of others. They were expelled from Prague and all of the crown cities in 5301/1541 and again in 5317/1557. Some of the Jews later returned, but many emigrated to Poland

and other countries. In Cracow, Poland the Bohemian emigrés were numerous enough to form their own congregation. At the end of the century all the Bohemian Jews were centered in Prague and a few other communities. Under the reign of Rudolph II (5336-72/1576-1612), Bohemian Jewry experienced a period of prosperity and tranquility which was matched by a spiritual renaissance. Compared to his predecessors, this Emperor was sympathetic to his Jewish subjects, and protected them. He granted an unprecedented interview to the acknowledged Jewish spiritual leader, *R' Loewe (Maharal) of Prague.

VIII. Moravia

Moravia (מעהרן, Maeren, in Jewish literature), a province in central Czechoslovakia (bordered on the west by Bohemia), did not produce any scholars of note during the *Tosafist* era, although it is certain that Jews lived there during this period. One can assume that the Jewish settlement there was sparse and small in number. Moravia had no big cities like Prague where Jewish life could flourish. *R' Yisrael Brunna (d. c. 5240/1480) is probably the first well known scholar to have served there as a rabbi. Like their Bohemian brethren, the Moravian Jews, too, suffered expulsions, and the royal cities were forbidden to them. Following the Chmelnicki massacres in Poland (5408-09/1648-49) and the expulsion of Jews from Vienna (5430/1670), a substantial number of Jews, among them some outstanding Torah scholars (e.g. *R' Shabsai HaKohen, the *Shach*), settled in Moravia.

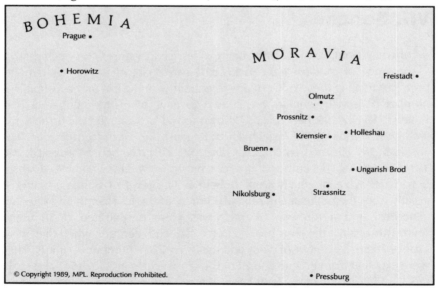

The Early
Acharonim

R' Yitzchak de Leon

רַבִּי יִצְחָק דִי לִיאוֹן

d. Spain, 5251/1491

R' Yitzchak was a disciple of *R' Yitzchak Kanpanton (the *Gaon* of Castille), and a colleague of *R' Yitzchak Abohab II. He headed a large academy and had many disciples. *R' Yosef Caro quotes a segment of *R' Yaakov ibn Chaviv's commentary on *Tur* in which R' Yitzchak is given the accolade 'the great lion', and R' Yosef Caro himself dubs him our 'great teacher.' He is not to be confused with a scholar having a similar name, *R' Yitzchak Leon ibn Tzur, who authored the apologetic work *Megillas Esther* defending Rambam's *Sefer HaMitzvos*.

None of R' Yitzchak's works have been published, but a responsum attributed to him has been preserved in the collection *Shivah Einayim* (Leghorn, 5505/1745). The responsum deals, in part, with the role that *minhag* (custom) plays in deciding points of *halachah* (law).

This collection also contains a responsum by a disciple of R' Yitzchak, defending his mentor's ruling. The great reverence in which R' Yitzchak was held is evident from this responsum, in which R' Yitzchak is referred to as 'a man of G-d.'

According to *Sefer Yuchasin*, R' Yitzchak was also a miracle worker and lived to a ripe old age.

R' Yitzchak Abohab II

רַבִּי יִצְחָק אַבּוֹהָב (הַשֵּׁנִי)

b. Toledo, Spain, 5193/1433
d. Oporto, Portugal, 5253/1493

R' Yitzchak was a pupil of *R' Yitzchak Kanpanton, the *Gaon* of Castille. He served as rabbi of Toledo, where he headed a Talmudic academy. Among his disciples were *R' Yaakov bei Rav, *R' Avraham Zacut, author of *Sefer Yuchasin*, and *R' Yitzchak Abarbanel. *R' Yosef Caro (*Beis Yosef, Orach Chaim* 168) refers to him with the accolade 'the light of the Jewish Diaspora.'

After King Ferdinand and Queen Isabella announced the decree of expulsion against all Spanish Jewry in 5252/1492, R' Yitzchak was part of a delegation of Jewish notables who appealed to King John II of Portugal for permission for the Jews to settle in Portugal. His request was granted and many Jews relocated in Oporto and other towns where they were received with favor.

R' Yitzchak's works include *Nehar Pishon* (Constantinople, 5298/1538), a book of sermons; a super-commentary on *Ramban's Bible commentary, titled *Peirush al Peirush HaRamban al HaTorah* (Constantinople, 5285/1525); a commentary on the *Tur*, quoted frequently in *Beis Yosef*; and *chidushim* on the Talmud. The *chidushim* to *Maseches Beitzah* were first published together with *Teshuvos Maharam Galante* (Venice, 5368/1608), later under the misleading name *Chidushei Galante* (Wilhermsdorf, 5476/1716), and finally as *Chidushei R' Yitzchak Abohab* in *Shitas HaKadmonim* on *Beitzah* (Jerusalem, 5719/1959). A collection of halachic correspondence between him and R' Nissim Benveniste has been preserved in the anthology *Shivah Einayim* (Leghorn, 5505/1745). His super-commentary on *Rashi's Torah commentary, and his responsa, have not been preserved.

R' Yitzchak Aramah

רַבִּי יִצְחָק בֶּן מֹשֶׁה עֲרַאמָה

b. Spain, c. 5180/1420
d. Naples, Italy, 5254/1494

R' Yitzchak held various rabbinic positions, his first being in Zamora, northern Spain (probably his birthplace), where he also headed a Talmudic academy. He then accepted the position of rabbi and preacher at Tarragona, and later at nearby Fraga, in the province of Aragon. Finally, he accepted the post of rabbi in Calatayud, where he also headed a rabbinical academy until the expulsion of the Jews from Spain in 5252/ 1492.

R' Yitzchak's fame rests upon his *Akeidas Yitzchak* (Salonica, 5282/1522), also called simply *Akeidah*. (The author is usually referred to as 'the *Baal HaAkeidah*' — the author of the *Akeidah* — or, simply, as 'the *Akeidah*'.) This work is a commentary on the Torah in the form of sermons emphasizing deep and penetrating philosophical thought. It had a profound influence on the works of *hashkafah* (perspective) of later generations; according to *Chida, "virtually all such succeeding works drank from the reliable waters of *Akeidah*."

R' Yitzchak also composed a similar commentary on the five *Megillos* (Venice, 5333/1573), and *Chazus Kashah* (Sabbionetta, 5312/1552), a treatise on religious philosophy. In this work, R' Yitzchak provides us with a short, systematic exposition of his philosophical system. Its avowed purpose is to attack the views held by the philosophers 'of the day'; specifically, the Aristotelian concept that the world is infinite in time. It discusses the relationship of philosophical ideas to the Torah, and contains many rebuttals to the attacks of Christianity on Judaism. He also authored *Yad Avshalom* (Constantinople, 5312/1552), a commentary on *Proverbs*. However, the work on *Megillas Esther* which is printed with the prevalent editions of *Akeidas Yitzchak* is not his but that of his son, R' Meir Aramah; R' Yitzchak's commentary was printed earlier in Constantinople (5278/1518) as *Peirush*

Megillas Esther. Only the preface and the beginning of the sermon on *Esther* printed with the prevalent editions of *Akeidas Yitzchak* belong to R' Yitzchak. How and why this strange hybrid of a commentary was put together can only be guessed at.

Because of the format of his work, R' Yitzchak allows himself at times to interpret the verses of the Torah in an allegorical manner, but he stresses that he does not intend the allegorical interpretation to supersede the plain meaning. Rather, he holds that in addition to its plain meaning, the Torah also contains secondary meanings which may be arrived at by means of allegory; he cites the *Zohar* as the basis for this position. R' Yitzchak cites the *Zohar* frequently, and in this he parallels the works of his contemporary, *R' Yitzchak Abarbanel.

Throughout his works, the author stresses the ascendancy of the Torah over philosophic precepts or concepts deduced by logic; reason must subjugate itself to Divine knowledge as manifested in the Torah (see e.g. *Chazus Kashah* ch. 9ff).

In consistency with this view he asserts that only those concepts which have their basis in the Torah are to be counted as (עִקָּרִים) — beliefs fundamental to Judaism. Ideas which are based on human reason — even if correct — are not fundamentals, since one need not resort to the Torah to establish them. Thus, the existence of G-d, His indivisible nature, and that He is incorporeal are not fundamentals of Judaism, just as acceptance of the world's existence, or the rational nature of man also are not — albeit they are surely true. The Torah is the essence of Judaism. Aptly, the *Baal HaAkeidah* demonstrates that each of the six festivals symbolizes one of the six concepts he considers to be fundamentals (*Shaar* 67).

It is ironic that the closing of the philosophic phase of Spanish Jewry should be overseen by two personalities — R' Yitzchak Aramah and R' Don Yitzchak Abarbanel — whose basic thought framework was rooted in medieval philosophy, and whose arguments against it were derived from the very system they were attempting to topple.

The *Baal HaAkeidah's* son, R' Meir Aramah (d. Salonica, 14 Nissan 5282/ 1522), followed in his great father's tradition. He served as *rav* of the Aragonese community in Salonica and was respected as a halachic authority by the *gedolim* in his generation. *R' Yosef Caro cites R' Meir's custom regarding the recitation of the *Hallel* and its benedictions during the *Pesach Seder* (*Beis Yosef Orach Chaim* §486; see *Shulchan Aruch* there §480), and *R' Shmuel de Medina cites one of his rulings (*Teshuvos Maharashdam, Choshen Mishpat* §299). R' Meir also carried on his father's legacy in the field of Bible commentary. He wrote extensive commentaries to sections of the Bible: *Urim VeTumim*, commentaries to the Biblical book *Isaiah, Jeremiah,* and miscellaneous comments to Biblical verses (Venice, 5363/ 1603); *Meir Iyov* on *Job* (Salonica, 5277/1513); *Meir Tehilos* on *Psalms* (Venice, 5350/1590), as well as the commentary to *Esther* mentioned earlier. R' Meir's son, R' Yaakov Aramah, was a scholar of renown, and his grandson, R' Asher HaKohen ibn Ardut, a colleague of *R' Chaim Shabsai and *rosh yeshivah* of the Aragonese community of Salonica, was one of the great Torah scholars in his generation (see *R' Aharon Perachyah).

R' David ben Avraham Aramah, the youthful twenty-year-old author of a work on the *Rambam* (Salonica, 5305/ 1545), was probably related to the *Baal* *HaAkeidah,* but the exact nature of the kinship is not known.

R' Moshe Capsali

רַבִּי מֹשֶׁה בֶּן אֵלִיָּהוּ קַאפְּשָׁאלִי

b. Candia, Crete, c. 5170/1410
d. Constantinople (now Istanbul), Turkey
c. 5260/1500

R' Moshe received his initial education from his father, R' Eliyahu, a scholar of repute. Afterwards he continued his rabbinical training at the Talmudic academies of Germany, where he studied under R' Moshe Landau (the father of *R' Yaakov Landau, author of *Sefer HaAgur*). He then returned to his homeland and was active in the communal life of his town; many *takanos* enacted in Candia are attributed to him. Later in his life (probably before the conquest of Constantinople by the Turks in 5213/ 1453) he settled in Constantinople. When Constantinople fell to the Turks, the Sultan, Mehmet II, appointed R' Moshe Chief Rabbi of Turkey, and recognized him as the legal representative of the Jewish community, on a par with the Orthodox Patriarch and the Mufti. The Sultan held the rabbi in great reverence, and occasionally consulted with him on matters of state. On one occasion his advice antagonized the Janissaries (the Sultan's private elite army). Upon the death of Mehmet II the Janissaries mutinied (in 5241/1481). They attempted to assassinate R' Moshe, who had been forewarned and narrowly escaped death.

In his function as representative of the Jews, it was R' Moshe's obligation to collect the taxes for the Sultan. His authority on internal matters was virtually absolute; he was empowered to appoint rabbis and judges, and to impose penalties.

In spite of his exalted position, R'

Moshe led an ascetic life, fasting often, and sleeping on the ground. His consuming interests were the study of Torah and its dissemination, and the betterment of the lives of his brethren. In the period following the Spanish expulsion (5252/1492), he used his considerable influence to persuade the Sultan to allow the Spanish Jews admission to Turkey. He, along with his colleague *R' Eliyahu Mizrachi, was very active in collecting funds to be used to ransom the exiles and to aid in their resettlement in Turkey.

He also found time to teach Torah. R' Eliyahu HaLevi is reputed to have boasted that he was only the 'smallest of his (R' Moshe's) disciples' (Preface to Zekan Aharon).

Although extremely modest and humble, R' Moshe displayed his full authority regarding communal and religious matters, often taxing wealthy businessmen for charitable purposes when they were unwilling to give charity according to their means.

Due to his unbending, authoritative conduct, which in reality was the basis for strengthening Torah observance throughout Turkey, R' Moshe was also the subject of opposition from those whose wrath he had incurred with his decisions. Thus it occurred that upon deciding a halachic ruling regarding the laws of marriage, one of R' Moshe's enemies distorted the facts and reported the incident to *Maharik, who denounced R' Moshe and ordered the Turkish community to remove him from office. R' Moshe, however, sent to Maharik a clear and sharp accounting of the events and the reasons for his decision. In addition, *R' Yehudah Mintz, the venerated rav of Venice who had studied together with R' Moshe in Germany during his youth, *R' Yaakov Margolies of Nuremberg, and other well-known Ashkenazic Torah sages rebuked Ma-

harik for his attack on R' Moshe. Before his death, Maharik sent his son, R' Peretz, to R' Moshe to implore his forgiveness, as he realized the facts of the case had been distorted when reported to him. R' Moshe gladly accepted the apology.

R' Moshe answered many inquiries, but only a few of his responsa have been preserved (Sinai, 3d yr., vol 5). After his death, the post of Chief Rabbi of Turkey was filled by R' Eliyahu Mizrachi.

R' Eliyahu ben Elkanah Capsali, who wrote Seder Eliyahu Zuta (Jerusalem, 5736-37/1976-77), a history, was the grandson of R' David Capsali, R' Moshe's brother.

R' Yosef Chayon

רַבִּי יוֹסֵף בֶּן אַבְרָהָם חִיּוֹן

b. Lisbon, Portugal, c. 5185/1425
d. Constantinople (now Istanbul), Turkey
16th century

R' Yosef was considered one of the leading rabbinical figures of Portugal and had many disciples who revered him greatly. Among his pupils were *R' Yosef Yaavetz and *R' Yitzchak Abarbanel. The latter is said to have addressed many inquiries to R' Yosef, who answered him in a work entitled Maggid Mishneh, which has not been preserved.

R' Yosef authored a commentary on tractate Avos entitled Milei DeAvos (Constantinople, 5339/1579), and a commentary on Psalms (Salonica, 5282/1522). His commentaries on Jeremiah, Ezekiel, the Twelve Minor Prophets, Proverbs, and Song of Songs remain unpublished.

R' Shlomo ibn Verga

רַבִּי שְׁלֹמֹה אִבְּן וִירְגָה

b. Spain, 15th century
d. Turkey, 16th century

R' Shlomo fled Spain during the Spanish expulsion, and found refuge in

Portugal, where he was forced for a time to live as a Marrano. When, in 5266/1506, the Marranos were given permission to leave Portugal, R' Shlomo settled in Turkey.

His chief accomplishment is his historic chronicle *Shevet Yehudah* (Adrianople? c. 5311/1551). The work contains reports of sixty-four religious persecutions recorded throughout the centuries, besides accounts of many religious disputations, and descriptions of Jewish customs in different countries.

R' Shlomo incorporated into his chronicle some material written by R' Yehudah ibn Verga, presumably an ancestor of the author. R' Yehudah is reported (in *Shevet Yehudah*) to have been a kabbalist and miracle worker, and a story in the *sefer* records how he miraculously saved the Jews in a town close to Seville. R' Yehudah lived during the period when the Inquisition had already begun to function in Spain (5241/1481). He maintained close contact with the Marranos, encouraging them to observe their Jewish religious practices secretly. The office of the Inquisition attempted to arrest R' Yehudah in order to obtain information concerning the Marranos but having become aware of their intentions, R' Yehudah fled to Portugal, where he lived for some years until he was located by the Inquisition. Upon his arrest he was tortured to reveal the identities of the Marranos; however, his lips remained sealed until he expired under torture.

R' Shlomo's son, R' Yosef ibn Verga (died between 5314/1554 — 5319/1559), was a respected Talmudic scholar in Turkey. He put the finishing touches on his father's work, adding material which he gathered from first-hand sources. His work *She'eiris Yosef* (Adrianople, 5314/1554), on the methodology of the Talmud, is a classic on this topic and served as a source for many distinguished works following it, such as *Shelah* and others.

R' Yehudah Chayat

רַבִּי יְהוּדָה בֶּן יַעֲקֹב חַיָּיט

Late fifteenth and early sixteenth centuries
b. Spain
d. Italy

R' Yehudah was forced to flee his birthplace in 5252/1492 during the Spanish expulsion. He settled in Portugal, only to be driven away once again during the expulsion of the Jews from Portugal in 5257/1497. He was twice captured at sea by pirates, and finally redeemed by the Jewish community of Italy, where he lived until the end of his days.

At the request of *R' Yosef Yaavetz and other Torah greats of the period, R' Yehudah composed *Minchas Yehudah* (Ferrara, 5318/1558), a commentary on the kabbalistic work *Maareches HaElokus* which is attributed to *R' Peretz HaKohen. Although designed as a commentary, this work is a classic of kabbalistic literature in its own right, and is acclaimed by the greatest kabbalists — among them *R' Moshe Cordovero.

R' Yaakov Margolies

רַבִּי יַעֲקֹב מַרְגָּלִית

d. Nuremburg, Germany, 18 Shevat 5261/1501

Very little is known about R' Yaakov's life. He was regarded as one of the Torah greats of his generation by *R' Yosef Colon and *R' Yehudah Mintz, who address him with great reverence in their responsa. The former addresses R' Yaakov with the accolade, 'a godly man . . . the head of the Diaspora . . .' (*Teshuvos Maharik* §26).

R' Yaakov was an expert on the laws of *gittin* and *chalitzah,* and a manual (*Seder*

HaGet) which he composed on these laws is quoted extensively by Rama in *Darchei Moshe* to *Tur Even HaEzer* and in *Shulchan Aruch*.

R' Yaakov's sons were also eminent scholars. R' Yaakov's *Seder HaGet* was compiled by R' Isaac Margolies, his son, who was a *rav* in Prague and died there on 24 Adar II 5285/1525.

A complete edition of *Seder HaGet*, containing various versions of this important work, was recently published by Mechon Yerushalayim (Jerusalem 5743/1983). The second part — *Seder Chalitzah* — has as yet not been published.

At the end of his life R' Yaakov was involved in two wide-ranging controversies, one regarding his disciple *R' Yaakov Pollak, and the other in reference to a decision rendered by *R' Avraham Mintz. (See *R' Yaakov Pollak.)

There was also at this time a R' Yaakov Margolies in Regensburg (Ratisbon), and historians are at odds as to whether or not he is the same person as the subject of this article.

R' Yochanan Aleiman

רַבִּי יוֹחָנָן בֶּן יִצְחָק אַלֵימַאן

b. Italy, c. 5195/1435
d. Italy, c. 5265/1505

R' Yochanan earned his living as a teacher to the children of the wealthy, in whose homes he also resided and where composed his works. He is reported to have instructed the famous theologian, Count Pico della Mirandola, who was a strong proponent of *kabbalah*.

R' Yochanan's most extensive work, *Chai HaOlamim* (not printed), takes an ethical approach towards attaining complete devotion to G-d, which is the ultimate goal of perfection. He also authored *Einei HaEidah* (unpublished), an allegoric Torah commentary; *Cheishek Shlomo*, a philosophical commentary on

Song of Songs, part of which — the extensive introduction entitled *Shaar HaCheishek* — has been published (Leghorn, 5550/1790). Another part of the introduction, named *Shir HaMaalos LeShlomo*, expands on the magnificent qualities of King Solomon; the commentary itself, and a kabbalistic work of R' Yochanan's are also unpublished.

R' Yosef Yaavetz

רַבִּי יוֹסֵף בֶּן חַיִּים יַעֲבֵץ

b. Spain or Portugal, c. 5195/1435
d. Mantua, Italy, 5267/1507

R' Yosef was an articulate preacher and a prolific author. He sojourned for some time in Lisbon where he became acquainted with *R' Yosef Chayon and *Don Yitzchak Abarbanel and was influenced by them, both in person and by their writings. During the expulsion of the Jews from Spain in 5252/1492, R' Yosef shared the unfortunate fate of his brethren. He first sailed to Sicily and later went to Mantua, where he was warmly received. There he devoted his energy to consoling and giving spiritual direction to the Spanish exiles who were arriving in Italy in great numbers.

A strong opponent of philosophy, he turned to the Talmud and *kabbalah* for all authentic religious instruction. The author of an important kabbalistic work, *R' Yehudah Chayat, relates that R' Yosef's encouragement was a factor in the writing of his *Minchas Yehudah*. R' Yosef stressed that strong belief and study of the Torah and Talmud were the heart of Judaism. During the time of the Spanish persecutions, he pointed out, the enlightened philosophers, who had arrived at their religious convictions through a philosophical approach, were among the first to abandon the religion of their forefathers; while the common and uneducated Jews sanctified G-d's name with their wealth and lives.

R' Yosef's works deal with ethics and religious dogma, and include the following: *Or HaChaim* (Ferrara, 5315/1555), against the pursuit of philosophy; *Yesod HaEmunah* (ibid.), an essay on the fundamental beliefs of Judaism; and *Maamar HaAchdus* (Ferrara, 5314/1554), in which he disputes *Rambam's designation of thirteen concepts as the fundamentals of Judaism. R' Yosef also disputes the assertions of *R' Chisdai Crescas and *R' Yosef Albo on this matter. According to R' Yosef Yaavetz there are three fundamental beliefs: (1) the unique oneness and unity of G-d; (2) his providence over the created world; (3) the eventual perfection of the universe in that the entire Creation will come to realize the true conception of G-d and be led to serve Him. These fundamentals are elaborated on at length in this essay. Further works include a commentary on tractate *Avos* (Constantinople, 5313/1533); a commentary on *Psalms* (Salonica, 5341/1571); and *Chasdei Hashem* (Constantinople, 5293/1533), meditations on G-d's providence and love for his creatures. One of the prominent chassidic masters, R' Hirsh Elimelech Shapira of Dinov (author of *Bnei Yisaschar*), wrote a commentary (*Mayan Ganim*) on R' Yosef's *Or HaChaim* (Zolkiew, 5608/1848). R' Yosef Yaavetz's works enjoyed great popularity among preachers, and he earned for himself the distinction of being known as 'the *chassid* Yaavetz'.

R' Yosef's son, R' Yitzchak, who published many of his father's works, was a prominent rabbi in Salonica, and his great-grandson (a grandson of R' Yitzchak), R' Yitzchak ben Shlomo, is the author of the extensive commentary *Toras Chessed* on most of *Kesuvim* (Belvedere, 5357/1597).

R' Yehudah Mintz

רַבִּי יְהוּדָה בֶּן אֱלִיעֶזֶר הַלֵּוִי מִינְץ

b. Germany, c. 5168/1408
d. Padua, Italy, 5268/1508

Chief Rabbi of the Ashkenazic community in Padua for forty-seven years, R' Yehudah was considered the leading halachic authority of Italy in his later years. R' Yehudah was a pupil of his relative, *R' Asher Enshchen, and a cousin of *R' Moshe Mintz, with whom he carried on a halachic correspondence. He is highly lauded by *R' Eliyahu Mizrachi (*Teshuvos R' Eliyahu Mizrachi*, ch. 56) and *Maharshal (*Teshuvos Maharshal*, ch. 6) for his halachic acumen, and for the ordinances which he instituted in Padua.

R' Yehudah headed a yeshivah in Padua, and many of the Italian rabbis of his era were his disciples. He was succeeded in his post by his son R' Avraham, a greatly revered scholar, and, upon the latter's demise (5285/1525), by his disciple and the son-in-law of R' Avraham, *R' Meir Katzenellenbogen, popularly known as Maharam Padua. Most of R' Yehudah's writings were destroyed shortly after his death, but sixteen of his responsa and a short treatise on the laws of *get* (divorce) and *chalitzah* (release from the obligation of levirate marriage) were printed together with *Teshuvos Maharam Padua* (Venice, 5313/1553). Many of R' Yehudah's descendants were numbered among the prominent rabbis of Italy.

R' (Don) Yitzchak Abarbanel

רַבִּי (דוֹן) יִצְחָק בֶּן יְהוּדָה אַבַּרְבְּנֵאל

b. Lisbon, Portugal, 5197/1437
d. Venice, Italy, 5268/1508

R' Yitzchak was a scion of one of the oldest and most respected Sephardic families, which traced its lineage to the royal house of King David. His grandfather, R' Shmuel Abarbanel, had served as an advisor to the king of Castille and was an admirer of *R' Menachem ben Zerach. R' Menachem was appointed rabbi of Toledo through R' Shmuel's influence, and dedicated his work Tzeidah LaDerech to him. R' Yehudah Abarbanel, son of R' Shmuel and father of R' Yitzchak, served as financial advisor to the king of Portugal.

R' Yitzchak studied Talmud and halachah under *R' Yitzchak Abohab II and *R' Yosef Chayon, and was probably influenced by the latter's inclination towards the kabbalah. He was also an avid student of Jewish religious philosophy and had a thorough knowledge of the writings of the Spanish and Provencal scholars in this field. At an early age he began to compose works on some of the most profound problems in Jewish philosophy, such as prophecy and Biblical interpretation. However, he was forced to interrupt his literary career after King Alfonso V of Portugal appointed him treasurer, and his time was consumed by the political affairs of the country.

Abarbanel's benevolence knew no bounds, and many times he was called upon to use his wealth and influence for the good of his brethren. On one occasion, when the Jewish inhabitants of a town in Morocco were captured and put up for sale as slaves, he gave a considerable sum from his own fortune, and arranged for the collection of the remaining funds needed for ransom. Upon the death of King Alfonso in 5241/1481, R' Yitzchak was accused by the late king's son and successor, John II, of participating in a conspiracy. Warned in time, R' Yitzchak fled to Castille in Spain, settling in Toledo.

In his new home, R' Yitzchak returned to his first love, writing, and in the course of a short period produced extensive commentaries on the books of Joshua, Judges, and Samuel. He had already begun to comment on Kings when he was called to serve the monarchs of Castille and Aragon. Who knows what treasures of thought and exegesis were denied to Israel because of Don Yitzchak's financial genius!

Indeed, his literary output during this period was astounding, even if one does not take into consideration the emotional and physical turmoil R' Yitzchak was undergoing at that time. He began the commentary on Joshua on 10 Cheshvan 5244/1484, and completed it on the twenty-sixth of that month — within a span of sixteen days! The commentary on Judges was written between Rosh Chodesh Kislev and the twenty-fifth of that month, while the much longer commentary on Samuel took two and a half months to write — from 1 Teves to 13 Adar.

It was at this time that King Ferdinand and Queen Isabella of Aragon and Castille called upon R' Yitzchak to serve as treasurer of their joint kingdoms. Under his management revenues increased, and the monarchs were extremely satisfied with him. When Ferdinand invaded and conquered the Moslem kingdom of Granada (see Historical Introduction to The Rishonim), R' Yitzchak advanced considerable sums of money to the government.

R' Yitzchak remained in this post until the edict calling for the expulsion of the Jews from Spain was issued in 5252/1492. When the expulsion order became known, R' Yitzchak attempted to negotiate with the monarchs and offered them a bribe to revoke their harsh decree. When they refused his offer, he took up the wandering staff along with the rest of his persecuted brethren, and left Spain.

R' Yitzchak settled in Naples, Italy,

where he utilized the short period of time during which he was unencumbered by service to royal masters to render service to the Supreme King — and completed the commentary to *Melachim* (*Kings*), which he had begun eight years earlier. He finished this work on the eve of *Rosh Hashanah* of 5253/1493.

When the city was taken by the French in 5255/1495, R' Yitzchak followed the young King Alfonso to Messina (Sicily), and then went to Corfu. Here Don Yitzchak was rewarded with an extraordinary stroke of heavenly providence. An extensive work on *Deuteronomy*, composed by R' Yitzchak in his youth while yet in Portugal, had been lost when he fled that country, and had been presumed destroyed together with other writings. Miraculously, this work was returned to R' Yitzchak while he was in Corfu. He used his stay in Corfu to add to this work. It was at first published separately as *Mirkeves HaMishneh* (Sabbionetta, 5311/1551), but was later included in all editions of the Torah commentary.

Abarbanel then went to Monopoli (in Southern Italy), and lastly settled in Venice in 5263/1503. It was during this period that he completed many unfinished works of previous years and composed many new works.

Abarbanel's literary output was voluminous and multi-faceted, but most of it can be grouped under three classifications: (a) Biblical exegesis; (b) philosophy; and (c) writings about the Messianic period. He authored commentaries on the Torah (Venice, 5339/1579), the *Early* and *Later Prophets* (Pesaro, 5280/1520), and *Daniel* (*Maayenei HaYeshuah*; Ferrara, 5311/1551).

Two of Abarbanel's works which concentrate on the Messianic hope are *Mashmia Yeshuah* (Salonica, 5286/1526),

which elaborates on the Biblical passages relating to the Messiah, and its companion work *Yeshuos Meshicho* (Tarnopol, 5572/1812), dealing with references to the Messiah in the Talmud and *midrash*. In these treatises, as well as in his work on *Daniel*, Abarbanel boldly attacks the christological implications read into the texts by theologians, and discusses at length such Christian concepts as the anti-christ. One is surprised both at Abarbanel's boldness, and by the fact that these works were allowed to be published in the Christian Europe of those times. On the other hand, Abarbanel is unique among Jewish Bible commentators in that he does not hesitate to quote the comments of Christian exegetes such as Jerome, Nicholas de Lyre, and others, sometimes even accepting their views.

A striking feature of Abarbanel's works, which paradoxically both contributed to their popularity but also somewhat detracted from it, is their comprehensiveness. One can expect to find in them, on any topic, a comprehensive digest of the views of scholars preceding Abarbanel, in addition to the author's own view, detailing the arguments for and against each position. Abarbanel's commentaries strongly stress the conceptual aspect of Scripture, dwelling at length on questions of fundamental beliefs relating to the commentary. However, his commentaries were greatly lengthened by these incursions into the realm of *hashkafah* (outlook) and this aspect tends to discourage many a casual reader. Abarbanel prefaced his commentaries with introductions dealing with matters germane to the discussed text in general, such as its authorship, sequence, etc. Some of these introductions are quite extensive and can be considered as separate treatises; his introduction to *Parashas*

Bereishis contains a lengthy discussion about the meanings of the basic terms used in the Torah's Creation narrative, such as the terms *bara* (created), and *shamayim* (heavens).

Abarbanel's basic thought framework was the philosophical system developed by Spanish Jewish philosophers. However, he objected to the tendency to read philosophical concepts into the Scripture text. Thus he rejected the interpretation adopted by many medieval Jewish commentators that the four terms used in the first two verses of the Torah (heavens, earth, water and void) refer to the four fundamental elements (*yesodos*), or that the Torah refers to the creation of formless matter (חוֹמֶר הַיּוּלִי) which preceded the world as we know it. Here and there he interjects sporadic references to the *Zohar* and to the 'True Wisdom' — i.e., the *kabbalah*. However, in general, he refrains from drawing upon the esoteric lore and keeps these references to a minimum. Abarbanel endorses the belief in the transmutation of souls (*gilgul*), although he admits that it cannot be proven but must be accepted on the basis of tradition.

In general it may be said that Abarbanel tends to favor the traditionalists and to reject ideas rooted in speculative philosophy. Thus he tends to favor *Ramban where the latter differs from *Rambam, and, in many places, denounces *ibn Ezra and *Ralbag in strong terms.

One of Abarbanel's works is *Rosh Amanah* (Constantinople, 5266/1506), in which he reviews the Thirteen Principles of Faith as enumerated by Rambam, and defends him against the arguments of *R' Yosef Albo, *R' Chisdai Crescas II and others who said that Rambam's *Ikkarim* (principles) were not fundamental to the Jewish faith. Abarbanel's main defense is that the word *ikkar* as used by

the Rambam refers, not to tenets underlying the entire religion, but rather to important dogma which must be held by every Jew. His defense of Rambam's articles of faith notwithstanding, Abarbanel insists that Rambam's compilation of fundamental beliefs is postulated on the idea that in Torah, as in scientific and philosophic disciplines, certain ideas are central to the whole and are thus termed 'fundamentals'. However, in Abarbanel's own opinion, the very idea of fundamental beliefs is foreign in concept to Judaism. Since the teachings of the Torah have been revealed by G-d himself, they are therefore all of equal value, thereby negating a system of principles.

Abarbanel's philosophical works include *Ateres Zekeinim* (Sabbionetta, 5317/1557), a philosophical commentary on *Exodus* 23:20; *Shamayim Chadashim* (Rodelheim, 5588/1828), to prove the creation of the heavens *ex nihilo*; *Mifalos Elokim* (Venice, 5352/1592), on the same topic; *She'eilos R' Shaul HaKohen* (Venice, 5334/1574), responses to the philosophical queries of R' Shaul HaKohen of Candia; a commentary to Rambam's *Moreh Nevuchim* (*Guide for the Perplexed*; Prague, 5591/1831); *Nachalas Avos* (Constantinople, 5265/1505), a commentary on tractate *Avos;* and *Zevach Pesach* (Constantinople, 5265/1505), a commentary on the Passover *Haggadah*. This last work is very popular, and an abridgment, *Tzli Eish,* was written by *R' Yehudah Aryeh de Modena (Venice, 5369/1609). Another abridgment, *Kitzur Abarbanel* on *Avos* and the *Haggadah*, was composed by R' Yaakov Hertzkes (Lublin, 5365/1605); this version has recently been reprinted. The short commentary *Tzli Eish* has been reprinted numerous times, and the long commentary was a basic text for all of the classic commentators after Abarbanel. Maharal of Prague, although he rarely refers to Abarbanel by name, clearly carries on a running polemic with him in his *Gevuros Hashem*.

A commentary by R' Yitzchak pertaining to a halachic difficulty in Rambam's *Mishneh Torah* is cited by *R' Yosef Caro in *Kessef Mishneh* (*Berachos*, ch. 3), and in *Beis Yosef* (*Orach Chaim* 168).

R' Avraham Saba

רַבִּי אַבְרָהָם בֶּן יַעֲקֹב סַבַּע

b. Spain, c. 5200/1440
d. c. 5268/1508

R' Avraham was a disciple of *R' Yitzchak de Leon, who also instructed him in *kabbalah*. Following the Spanish expulsion of 5252/1492, R' Avraham sought refuge in Portugal. Five years later, after the Portuguese expulsion, he made his way to Fez, Morocco — but only after he had lost his two young sons to forced conversion. There R' Avraham was received with great honor, and he instructed the community in the ways of Torah.

R' Avraham had composed many works during his sojourn in Portugal, among them a Torah commentary and a commentary on the five *Megillos*. However, King Emanuel issued a decree outlawing possession of Jewish literature, and R' Avraham was forced to bury his precious manuscripts under an olive tree in Lisbon, never to see them again. In Fez he resumed his literary career and produced his famous Torah commentary, *Tzror Hamor* (Venice, 5282/1522), a homiletic interpretation interspersed with kabbalistic comments. An upgraded edition, emended on the basis of manuscripts and early prints, has been published recently (v. I: Jerusalem, 5745/1985). This commentary is a reworking from memory of a book he had written in Portugal and been forced to bury. His *Eshkol HaKofer* is a commen-

tary on the books of *Esther* (Drohobycz, 5664/1904) and *Ruth* (Bartfeld, 5668/1908). Many historical particulars pertaining to the Spanish exile are scattered throughout these *sefarim*. His kabbalistic treatise *Peirush Esser Sefiros* remains unpublished. The other works mentioned in R' Avraham's *sefarim*, *Tzror HaKessef* (a comprehensive treatise of *halachos*), and commentaries on *Avos* and on the other three *Megillos*, have been lost.

*Chida (*Shem HaGedolim*) records a tradition that towards the end of his life R' Avraham set out for Italy. At sea a terrible storm threatened the entire ship with destruction. The passengers, having observed R' Avraham's saintliness during the trip, begged him to entreat G-d to avert the impending disaster. R' Avraham replied that he would grant their request on the condition that should he die aboard ship, his body would be taken to a Jewish community for burial. The captain assured R' Avraham that his request would be fulfilled, and the latter prayed until the sea was restored to calm. A few days later, on the eve of *Yom Kippur*, R' Avraham passed away at sea. Complying with his promise, the captain brought R' Avraham's body to the port of Verona, Italy, where the Jewish community buried it with great honor.

It is assumed that *R' Yosef Caro's father-in-law, R' Yitzchak Saba, was R' Avraham's son.

R' Yoel ibn Shuiv

רַבִּי יוֹאֵל אִבְּן שׁוּעִיב

b. Spain
d. Salonica, Turkey (now Greece)
c. 5270/1510

R' Yoel ibn Shuiv spent his youth in Aragon (Spain), but sometime after 5229/1469 he settled in Tudela (in the then-independent kingdom of Navarre, now a province in Northern Spain). In 5255/1495, R' Yoel again took the wanderer's staff in hand, and moved to Salonica, Turkey. (No doubt he was afraid that Navarrese Jewry would suffer the same fate as the Spanish Jews.) There he served as rabbi and preacher to one of the Spanish congregations.

His works include *Olas Shabbos* (Venice, 5337/1577), sermons on the Torah; *Nora Tehillos* (Salonica, 5329/1569), a commentary on *Psalms*; a commentary to *Job* titled *Ein Mishpat*, quoted in his other works; and a commentary on *Lamentations* (Salonica, 5281/1521), which was subsequently published together with R' Avraham Galante's *Kinas Sesarim* under the title *Kol Bochim* (Venice, 5349/1589). Comments by 'ibn Shuiv' in a commentary on *Song of Songs* by R' Avraham ben Yitzchak HaLevi (Sabbionetta, 5319/1559) have been assumed to come from a work by R' Yoel, but it has recently been demonstrated (Preface in the Jerusalem reproduction of *Drashos ibn Shuiv* [Cracow, 5333/1573]) that they rather belong to an esteemed member of the ibn Shuiv family preceding R' Yoel by many generations — *R' Yehoshua ibn Shuiv.

R' Yoel's son, R' Shmuel (d. Salonica, 22 Tammuz 5288/1528), was also a scholar of note, and served as a *rav* in the Aragonese community in Salonica. A small portion of R' Yoel's work on *Lamentations* was, in fact, written by R' Shmuel.

R' Avraham Chayon

רַבִּי אַבְרָהָם בֶּן נִסִּים חַיּוּן

b. Portugal
d. Constantinople (now Istanbul), Turkey
c. 5270/1510

A pupil of *R' Yosef Chayon, R' Avraham was forced to leave his native

Portugal in 5257/1497 due to the edict of expulsion, and found refuge in Constantinople. His work *Amaros Tehoros* (Constantinople, 5276/1516) deals with ethics and repentance.

R' Ovadyah Yarei of Bertinoro

רַבִּי עוֹבַדְיָה יָרֵא בֶּן אַבְרָהָם מִבְּרְטִינוֹרָא

b. Italy, c. 5200/1440
d. Jerusalem, Eretz Yisrael, before 5276/1516

R' Ovadyah was probably born in the small town Bertinoro (between Cesena and Forli in Northern Italy), hence his cognomen: he is popularly referred to as 'the Bartenura'. R' Ovadyah was a disciple of *R' Yosef Colon (Maharik). R' Ovadyah is mentioned in a responsum of his mentor (*Teshuvos Maharik*, §70), and an additional responsum addressed to a 'R' Ovadyah' (*Teshuvos Maharik HaChadashos*, §23) was probably written to 'the Bartenura'. After serving as rabbi in various Italian communities (lastly in Citta di Castello in central Italy), he set out for the Holy Land in 5246/1486. His journey, which lasted two years, took him through many Jewish centers, and in Salerno and Palermo he spent some time disseminating Torah knowledge among the inhabitants.

Arriving in Jerusalem in the spring of 5248/1488, R' Ovadyah found the community in a deplorable condition. Most of the inhabitants were poor, and iniquitous officials tyrannized the population. R' Ovadyah's strong personality and great reputation as a scholar led to his being accepted as spiritual head of the community. His main concern was to establish a yeshivah in which the younger generation would be able to pursue Talmudic and halachic studies. He succeeded in obtaining money for the poor from his connections in Italy, and he also helped abolish many unjust taxes which the Arab pashas had imposed upon the Jewish populace. *R' David ibn Zimra (*Teshuvos HaRadvaz* §1180), states that R' Ovadyah was famous for his knowledge, and head of all the rabbis of Jerusalem.

In 5250/1490 he officiated for a short span of time as *rav* of the fledgling Jewish community of Hebron, but even at this time he considered himself an inhabitant of Jerusalem.

R' Ovadyah's dream of establishing a Talmudic academy was realized after 5252/1492 when many Spanish refugees reached the Holy Land. Because they were superior in learning to the native inhabitants, the Spanish Jews were immediately interested in securing a place of learning for their young men, and R' Ovadyah's academy grew steadily.

R' Ovadyah is most famous for his *Mishnah* commentary (Venice, 5309/1549), printed in most standard editions. His commentary became so attached to the *Mishnah* that it has become the unquestioned primary commentary to the *Mishnah* and is comparable in this aspect to *Rashi's commentary on the Talmud. The commentary is based primarily on the commentaries of Rashi and *R' Shimshon of Sens (Rash MiShantz), the commentary of *Ramban to *Zeraim* and *Taharos*, and *Rosh (notably to *Maseches Shekalim*).

R' Ovadyah's other works are *Amar Nakeh* (Pisa, 5570/1810), a supercommentary to Rashi's Torah commentary; and some *piyutim* (liturgical compositions). He also composed annotations to the *chidushim* of his master, Maharik, which have not been published.

A kabbalistic commentary on the book of *Ruth* (Venice, 5345/1585), printed under the names *Peirush Bertinoro* and *Mikraei Kodesh*, is not by the R' Ovadyah under discussion, but by his nephew R' Ovadyah ben Zecharyah Hamon of Bartenura.

The letters which R' Ovadyah addressed to his family and friends are of great historical interest. They contain first-hand information concerning the social, economic and intellectual conditions of the Jews in Sicily, Greece, Egypt and *Eretz Yisrael*, including customs and geographical data. Some of his letters have been published under the name *Darchei Tziyon* (Kolomea, 5646/1886).

R' Avraham Zacut

רַבִּי אַבְרָהָם בֶּן שְׁמוּאֵל זָכוּת

b. Salamanca, Spain, c. 5200/1440
d. Damascus, Syria, c. 5275/1515

R' Avraham Zacut (sometimes pronounced Zacuta) was descended from a prominent family which had come to Spain after the expulsion of the Jews from France in 5066/1306. His ancestor, R' Moshe Zacut, was a disciple of R' Yehudah ben Asher (a direct descendant of *Rosh); and R' Shmuel of Valencia (one of the greatest Talmudic scholars in pre-expulsion Spain) was his relative. R' Avraham testifies about his ancestors that 'They all stood steadfast in the religious persecutions of Castille (in the year 5151/1391) in the service of G-d and His Torah.' The renowned kabbalist *R' Avraham ben Eliezer HaLevi (author of *Maamar Mesharei Kitrin*) was his brother-in-law.

R' Avraham was a disciple of his father R' Shmuel and of *R' Yitzchak Abohab II, and he also pursued the study of mathematics and astronomy. His mastery of astronomy was so thorough that he was appointed an instructor at the University of Salamanca. He designed an improved astrolabe, innovating the process of making it of copper instead of wood, as was the mode of the day. His astronomical tables were considered to be the most accurate in that era, and were used by Columbus on his voyages. Indeed, they saved his life on one occasion. On his third expedition to America, Columbus was faced with starvation when the Indians on the island of Hispaniola (Haiti and the Dominican Republic) refused to sell him food. Columbus made use of the fact that Zacut's tables forecast a lunar eclipse on February 29, 1504, and cowed the Indians with his threat to obliterate the moon. Columbus' notes on the margin of his copy of Zacut's tables are yet extant.

After the Spanish expulsion of 5252/1492, R' Avraham fled to Portugal, where he was appointed court astronomer to King John II, and to his successor Emanuel I. Before Vasco da Gama embarked on his famous voyage to India he consulted R' Avraham, who provided his newly perfected astronomical tables for the voyage.

In 5257/1497 the Jews were expelled from Portugal, and R' Avraham once again set sail, this time for North Africa. After many hardships, including being taken captive twice, R' Avraham finally arrived in Tunis. It was there that he wrote his most important work, *Sefer Yuchasin* (Constantinople, 5326/1566), a chronicle of Jewish history from the creation of the world until his own day.

R' Avraham did not find peace in Tunis either. He later emigrated to Turkey, and then to Damascus where he resided until his death.

R' Avraham's complete mastery over the vast sea of the Talmud and *midrash* is clearly evident in his comprehensive treatment (in *Sefer Yuchasin*) of all the *Tannaim* and *Amoraim* mentioned in the *midrash* and Talmud. All the *Tannaim* and *Amoraim* are listed in alphabetical order, with references to the places in the Talmud and *midrashim* where information concerning them is found. *R' Yechiel Halperin's masterful work on this topic, *Seder Tannaim VeAmoraim*, is arranged in the form of additions to and notes on R' Avraham's material. R' Avraham's interpretation of a passage of Talmud is cited favorably by *R' Levi ibn Chaviv (Ralbach) in a responsum.

R' Avraham did not live to see his *Sefer Yuchasin* in print. The *sefer* was printed first in Constantinople (5326/1566) by R' Shmuel Shulam, who made extensive changes and added important sections to it. In the second printing (Cracow, 5341/1581), more additions (including some glosses attributed to *Rama) were made. A critical edition, based on manuscripts and the first edition, and containing *R' Yaakov Emden's glosses and other additions, was printed in Edinburgh (5617/1857). Additional material which had been deleted by R' Shmuel Shulam, probably because it might have offended the authorities, was subsequently found and published by R' A.C. Freiman in his preface to the Frankfurt am Main (5685/1925) and Jerusalem (5723/1963) editions of *Sefer Yuchasin*.

R' Avraham's major treatise on astronomy, containing his tables, is extant in many manuscripts and was printed by the University of Strassburg in 1918. This work was translated into Latin and Spanish and printed at least two times during Zacut's lifetime. R' Avraham also prepared a thoroughly revised edition of the *Aruch* containing many of his own comments and additions. A partial copy of this was yet extant at the beginning of this century (see Preface to *Aruch HaShaleim*).

R' Yaakov ibn Chaviv

רַבִּי יַעֲקֹב בֶּן שְׁלֹמֹה אִבְּן חָבִיב

b. Zamora, Spain, c. 5205/1445
d. Salonica, Turkey (now Greece), c. 5276/1516

R' Yaakov was a disciple of R' Shmuel of Valencia. At the time of the expulsion from Spain he fled to Portugal, where he experienced the same misfortunes that befell his unfortunate fellow Jews in that land. His beloved young son Levi, already showing promise as a great Talmudic scholar, was snatched from him and forcibly baptized. R' Yaakov succeeded in freeing his son and together they fled the country. He found refuge in Salonica where he remained until the end of his days, spreading Torah knowledge among the inhabitants.

R' Yaakov's greatness was soon recognized by the local scholars and he was appointed to lecture in the yeshivah of the native Jews. Upon the arrival of numerous Spanish refugees, a separate Spanish *kehillah* (*Kehal Geirush*) was formed, with R' Yaakov as its *rav*. He was greatly respected by the *rabbanim* of the old Turkish communities, i.e. *R' David HaKohen, *R' Yosef ibn Lev and *R' Shmuel de Medina, who quote his opinions in their responsa with reverence. The latter quotes his view concerning the leniencies allowed by the old communities in regard to the inspection of a slaughtered animal's lungs. The old communities conducted themselves in this regard as did the *Ashkenazim*, whose custom is more lenient concerning this matter. R' Yaakov held that the *Sephardim* could accept this leniency, which ran counter to their custom, because of the dictum that one should conduct oneself according to the 'custom of the place'. The custom of Salonica incorporated this leniency until modern times.

In Salonica a wealthy scholar, Don Yehudah Benveniste, offered R' Yaakov hospitality, and also gave him access to his extensive library. It was in Don Yehudah's home that R' Yaakov composed his monumental work, *Ein Yaakov* — a compilation of all the aggadic material found in *Talmud Bavli* and *Talmud Yerushalmi*. He also composed a commentary on this work adapted from the most popular commentators, such as *Rashi, *Tosafos (some of the Tosafos quoted by him are not in our editions), *Ramban, *Rashba, *Ritva, and many others, including original interpretations.

Although the work follows the sequence of the Talmudic tractates, R' Yaakov also intended to add an index dividing the material into twelve principal subjects, such as Torah, kindness, peace, etc., in order to aid the reader to easily find the topic of his choice. He also planned an index with references grouped according to the weekly Torah portions.

Ein Yaakov became a very popular work, and immediately upon its first printing (Salonica, 5276/1516) it became an important textbook used mainly by the working class who did not have the time and ability to delve into halachic and Talmudic intricacies. It was published numerous times since then. Many commentaries were written on the *Ein Yaakov*, among them *Iyun Yaakov*, *Ben Yehoyada*, and additions and a commentary under the name *HaBoneh* (the Builder) by *R' Yehudah Aryeh de Modena.

R' Yaakov did not live to complete the entire work. He died after the volume containing *Seder Zeraim* and *Seder Moed* had been printed, and the remainder was published after his death by his son, the celebrated *R' Levi ibn Chaviv. The latter, however, did not find his father's notes to the remaining four *sedarim*, nor was he able to collect the *aggados* in *Yerushalmi*. (It seems it was difficult to obtain copies of this Talmud; see R' Yaakov's comments printed at the end of *Seder Nashim* in the Vilna edition.) The promised index was never printed, either.

R' Yaakov is also the author of a

commentary on *Tur Orach Chaim* and *Yoreh Deah*, which is quoted in *Beis Yosef*.

R' Eliyahu Mizrachi (Ra'am)

רַבִּי אֵלִיָּהוּ בֶּן אַבְרָהָם מִזְרָחִי (רא"ם)

b. Constantinople (now Istanbul), Turkey
5210/1450
d. Constantinople (now Istanbul), Turkey
5285/1525

Also known simply as 'The Mizrachi', R' Eliyahu was a disciple of R' Eliyahu HaLevi (*HaZakein*) of Constantinople and *R' Yehudah Mintz of Padua. During his early years R' Eliyahu served as a *dayan* and teacher in Constantinople. In 5260/1500, after the death of *R' Moshe Capsali, R' Eliyahu Mizrachi was appointed Chief Rabbi of Turkey, and the Sultan accorded him the same authority which had been given to R' Moshe Capsali, and supported his enactments and rulings concerning the Jewish community.

R' Eliyahu was very active in organizing people and collecting money to aid in the absorption of the many Jewish refugees who had been expelled from Spain in 5252/1492. He relates in a responsum (*Teshuvos R' Eliyahu Mizrachi* §66; not in all editions) that for a greater part of a year he neglected his manifold communal responsibilities as *dayan* and *rosh yeshivah*, and devoted his time to alleviating the plight of the refugees. He was therefore greatly hurt when the good he had done was not remembered by its recipients. R' Gershon Mizrachi, R' Eliyahu's son, was the victim of a rumor that he had made a verbal declaration acknowledging Mohammed as 'the prophet'. In Moslem countries this is tantamount to a formal conversion, and R' Gershon's life was in danger if he did not actualize his declaration by adopting the practice of the Moslem religion. He fled to the Mediterranean island of Naxos to escape persecution by the authorities. The local Jews — erstwhile refugees — revived the libel, further endangering R' Gershon.

R' Eliyahu writes: 'For I rendered much good to them [the Spanish exiles] . . . I suffered with them close to a year's [time] gathering funds . . . I was drawn into great controversies with all of the communities . . . and put many rich householders under the ban because they did not contribute the amounts I requested of them . . . I put myself in danger because of my constant pain and aggravation . . . Because of them I neglected my studies and researches for close to a year.'

One of R' Eliyahu's well-known pupils was R' Eliyahu HaLevi (died c. 5300/1540), author of the collection of responsa *Zekan Aharon* (Constantinople, 5494/1734), noted *payetan*, and successor to R' Eliyahu in the Constantinople rabbinate; *R' David Conforte in *Korei HaDoros* conjectures that this student of the Mizrachi was a grandson of the Mizrachi's mentor, R' Eliyahu HaLevi HaZakein. Two of the Mizrachi's other pupils were R' Tam ibn Yachya, author of the responsa collection *Ohalei Tam* (in the collection *Tumas Yesharim*; Venice, 5380/1620); and *R' Avraham ibn Yaish.

Besides his Talmudic and halachic knowledge, R' Eliyahu was also proficient in mathematics and astronomy, and instructed students in these fields.

R' Eliyahu had a fruitful literary career, the most famous of his works being his super-commentary to *Rashi's Torah commentary, *Beur LePeirush Rashi al HaTorah* (Venice, 5287/1527), thereafter known simply as *The Mizrachi*. This erudite and learned work strives to locate the Talmudic and midrashic sources for Rashi's comments, answers most arguments of *Ramban against

Rashi's interpretation, and attempts to resolve all difficulties connected to Rashi's commentary. Most of what has been written on Rashi since the Mizrachi's time is based on his classic commentary, and some works have been written as super-commentaries to it. *R' Shmuel Eidels (Maharsha), in his chidushim to the Talmud, comments at length on the Mizrachi wherever applicable. The work has been reprinted numerous times, and at least one abridgment of this lengthy work has been published (Kitzur Mizrachi or Minchas Ani by R' Yitzchak HaKohen of Ostroh, Prague 5364/1604).

R' Eliyahu also wrote Tosafos al Smag (Constantinople, 5280/1520), chidushim on Sefer Mitzvos Gadol by *R' Moshe of Coucy, and responsa, one part printed under the name Teshuvos She'eilos R' Eliyahu Mizrachi (Constantinople, 5321/1561), and additional responsa in a collection called Teshuvos Mayim Amukim (Venice, 5407/1647) which also contains responsa by *R' Eliyahu ibn Chaim.

R' Eliyahu achieved proficiency in the sciences as well, and wrote extensively on mathematics, astronomy, and philosophy. His short treatise on mathematics, Sefer HaMispar (Constantinople, 5294/1534), was later abridged and printed together with a Latin translation (Basel, 5306/1546). A commentary to Ptolemy's classical al-Magest (astronomy), and a commentary to one of the works of the Arab philosopher al-Ghazali (mentioned in *R' Moshe Almosnino's Me'ametz Ko'ach), were never published.

In the time of R' Eliyahu there was a substantial Karaite community in Turkey, and there was considerable contact between it and the Rabbanite community. Many Rabbanite scholars instructed the Karaites in the sciences and even in Hebrew grammar and Scripture.

Some of the community leaders who opposed this practice got together and declared a ban of excommunication upon those who engaged in this practice. R' Eliyahu, however, opposed the ban, pointing out that some of the greatest scholars and pious men of previous generations had taught Karaites, and that the community leaders lacked the authority to impose their will upon the majority which opposed it (Teshuvos R' Eliyahu Mizrachi, §57).

R' Eliyahu's conclusions are based on purely halachic considerations, and his ruling should not be seen as tendentious — showing feelings of leniency toward the Karaites — as some scholars have argued. When he was asked about intermarriage between Rabbanites and Karaites, he condemned such marriages in the strongest terms, again basing his ruling on convincing halachic considerations (op. cit. 58). The opposition to kabbalah imputed to him on the basis of a superficial reading of one of his rulings (op. cit. §1) also has no foundation; in that responsum, too, R' Eliyahu arrives at his conclusion guided solely by halachic considerations.

R' Avraham ben Eliezer HaLevi

רַבִּי אַבְרָהָם בֶּן אֱלִיעֶזֶר הַלֵּוִי

b. Spain, c. 5200/1440
d. Jerusalem, Eretz Yisrael, c. 5288/1528

R' Avraham was a brother-in-law of *R' Avraham Zacut, and a disciple of R' Yitzchak Gakon, one of *R' Yitzchak de Leon's students. After the expulsion of the Jews from Spain in 5252/1492 he sojourned in various countries, passing through Italy, Greece and Turkey. Eventually he made his way to Egypt, and from there to Eretz Yisrael. He settled in Jerusalem and was appointed one of the deans at the Talmudic academy sponsored by R' Yitzchak HaKohen Sholal, the illustrious *naggid* (official representative of the Jews) of Egypt.

R' Avraham began his literary career while yet in Spain, where he wrote his first work, *Mesoras HaChachmah,* an explanation of the ten *Sefiros* (emanations) and other kabbalistic subjects. (This work has been published in a scholarly journal.) R' Avraham's fame rests upon the only work he published, *Maamar Mesharei Kitrin* (Constantinople, 5270/1510). In this short treatise, R' Avraham sets forth his interpretation of the verses in *Daniel* which foretell the date of the Messiah's coming. R' Avraham saw in the conquest of Constantinople in 5213/1453 by the Turks a harbinger of the Messianic age and the beginning of the downfall of Rome, and foresaw the year 5290/1530 as the year of the Messiah's coming.

R' Avraham composed many other kabbalistic works which remain unpublished. Some scholars erroneously attributed *Sefer HaZikaron,* a supercommentary on *Rashi* (Leghorn, 5605/1845), to the R' Avraham HaLevi who is the topic of this article, whereas it was really authored by a contemporary of his — R' Avraham Bukrat HaLevi.

R' Avraham was very preoccupied with hastening the redemption, and therefore sent constant letters to all countries outside the Holy Land exhorting the Jews to repentance; some of these letters have been published in various journals.

R' Yaakov Pollak

רַבִּי יַעֲקֹב בֶּן יוֹסֵף פּוֹלַק

d. Lublin, Poland, 5290/1530

As indicated by his surname, R' Yaakov was probably born or raised in Poland. Very little is known about his life with certitude; even his father's name and date of death are open to doubt.

Nonetheless, it is evident from the writings of the greats of following generations that R' Yaakov's personality dominated Torah study in the Polish yeshivos of his day, and that his method of *pilpul* served as an inspiration to thousands of Talmud students for generations. So strong was this influence that in spite of the protestations of many Torah giants against this system of learning they were unable to eradicate it, and admitted that they themselves had been constrained to offer discourses utilizing the very method they decried. Clearly we have in front of us a dominant figure in Torah scholarship: strong minded, independent, and original.

R' Yaakov was a disciple of *R' Yaakov Margolies of Nuremberg, and together with his master's son, R' Isaac Margolies, he headed a prominent yeshivah in Prague, where he also served as rabbi.

As already mentioned, R' Yaakov Pollak introduced a new method of Talmudic study known as *pilpul,* or *chilukim.* It is virtually impossible today, due to the dearth of original examples (R' Yaakov and his disciple *R' Shalom Shachna did not publish any of their discourses), to have a clear and definitive concept about this learning method. The designation *pilpul* given it by contemporaries and later generations is a generic term applicable to any type of involved Talmudic discourse, and is used to describe even the discussions of the *Amoraim* themselves. From the protestations of succeeding generations against R' Yaakov's type of *pilpul*, we can surmise that it was a complicated, convoluted approach to the Talmud, using linguistic inferences to draw artificial conclusions, and deriving premises using certain standard methods of text examination peculiar to this style of learning, the validity of which were disputed by the opponents of this system. A conclusion, no matter how flimsily drawn, would be used to prove yet another concept, heaping premise upon premise, until the lecturer proved the point which was the central theme of his discourse. The end result was a magnificently constructed edifice of elaborate and far-fetched conclusions, intellectually stimulating because of its ingenuity, but weak in its construction; for each facet of the argument, if examined closely, could not withstand scrutiny. Indeed, it was charged that the conclusions were preconceived, and that the proofs were artificially manufactured, 'tying thread to thread' until a seemingly strong rope was formed, connecting matters having no real connection. Even its supporters admitted to the shortcomings of the method, and defended it only for its use in 'sharpening' the minds of the young students, and stimulating them to intensive study. None of the rabbis used this method to arrive at halachic conclusions in their responsa, and it was restricted to discourses in the yeshivah.

R' Yaakov Pollak was involved in one of the great halachic controversies of his time, as follows: In approximately 5250/1490 (or 5260/1500), R' Yaakov's widowed mother-in-law had given one of her daughters, who was still a minor, in marriage to R' David Zehner, a promising Talmudist. Later, regretting this step, as R' David was much older than his bride, the mother asked him to consent to a divorce, which he refused to do. Upon the advice of R' Yaakov the marriage was annulled by a declaration of *miun* (unwillingness). [According to Talmudic law, a minor orphan, married to someone based on the consent of her mother or brother, has the right to void their act before reaching her majority by a declaration of dissatisfaction with the match, and does not need a divorce.] Following the annulment, all the local rabbis and scholars rose in protest against R' Yaakov, as *R' Menachem of Merseburg, a recognized authority who had lived more than half a century before, had expressly forbidden the use of *miun* for fear that it would lead to many family and halachic problems. Among R' Yaakov's foremost opponents was his mentor, R' Yaakov Margolies of Nuremberg, who declared a ban upon him as long as he persisted in his decision. R' Yaakov paid no heed to these threats and permitted his sister-in-law to remarry without a bill of divorce. This stirred up a tremendous fury in the rabbinic world. The greatly revered *R' Yehudah Mintz of Padua was consulted, and he wrote a responsum which strongly censured R' Yaakov Pollak and advised him to go to the grave of R' Yaakov Margolies (who had died in the interim) to ask his forgiveness (*Teshuvos Mahari Mintz,* §13). Significantly, *Rama (*Darchei Moshe Even HaEzer* and *Shulchan Aruch* 155:21) cites R' Yaakov's ruling, accepting it in spite of the overwhelming protest against it. This is evidence of the great regard in which Rama held R' Yaakov, the teacher of Rama's own mentor and father-in-law *R' Shalom Shachna of Lublin.

Due to the bad feelings in Prague, R' Yaakov decided to return to his native Poland and accepted the post of rabbi of Cracow. His reputation preceded him, and he was warmly received and revered by his countrymen. There he established a large yeshivah and was virtually the founder of Talmudic learning in Poland. Thousands of pupils studied under him, among them such outstanding scholars as R' Shalom Shachna of Lublin. In Cracow, too, R' Yaakov became embroiled in a bitter controversy with *R' Avraham Mintz of Padua, which resulted in much acrimony and in declarations of excommunication from both sides.

After living over twenty years in Cracow, R' Yaakov journeyed to *Eretz Yisrael* and spent some time in Jerusalem. On his return trip he stopped in Turkey where he became acquainted with *R' Avraham Treves, and gave an approbation to, his *sefer*, *Birkas Avraham*.

Upon his return to Poland, he took up residence in Lublin where, according to legend, he died on the very same day as his opponent, R' Avraham Mintz. It is told that in spite of the great reverence in which R' Yaakov was held, his grave was surrounded by a fence, and would not be approached closely, in deference to the ban which had been pronounced upon him. Some scholars have, however, expressed doubt about the veracity of this story.

R' Yaakov refused to leave any written works, as his modesty would not permit him to become the halachist for future generations. Rather, he preferred that each authority decide the law according to his own deductions. His teachings remained in the minds and hearts of his pupils and influenced the Talmudic and halachic methods of many generations to come.

R' David HaKohen (Radach)

רַבִּי דָּוִד בֶּן חַיִּים הַכֹּהֵן (רַדַּ"ךְ)

d. Adrianople (Edirne), Turkey
c. 5290/1530

R' David was a disciple of *R' Yehudah Mintz. Although he carried on an extensive halachic correspondence with his contemporaries, among them *R' Eliyahu Mizrachi, *R' Yosef Taitatzak, *R' Yaakov ibn Chaviv, and *R' Moshe Alashkar, only thirty-three (very lengthy) responsa were published (Constantinople, 5298/1538). The manuscript from which this work was published was nearly destroyed in a fire. Its miraculous

survival may have provided the impetus for the author's son, R' Chaim HaKohen, to publish the *sefer*. This work gained acceptance as a halachic classic and is cited by later *poskim*.

R' David is known for his stringent view in regard to the halachic status of the Marranos. He emphatically states in his responsa that all Marranos having the opportunity to escape from their native countries and move to Turkey, where they could return to Judaism freely, but do not do so due to their prosperous positions, are to be designated halachically as apostates.

R' David Vital, author of *Kesser Torah* on the *mitzvos* (Constantinople, 5298/1538), was R' David's disciple and son-in-law.

R' Avraham Mintz

רַבִּי אַבְרָהָם בֶּן יְהוּדָה מִינְץ

d. Padua, Italy, 5288/1525

The son of *R' Yehudah Mintz, R' Avraham succeeded his father as rabbi of Padua, and was a recognized Talmudist and halachist. He added comments to his father's *Seder Gittin*, which is printed together with the responsa of R' Avraham's son-in-law, *Maharam Padua (Venice, 5313/1553).

*R' Gedalyah ibn Yachya (*Shalsheles HaKabbalah*) relates that R' Avraham got embroiled in a halachic controversy with *R' Yaakov Pollak concerning the adjudication of a complicated monetary case. The case involved two Jews in Bologna and more than a hundred *rabbanim* wrote opinions about it. R' Avraham and R' Yaakov Pollak took opposite stands on this matter, and the exchange of letters between them became very heated. R' Gedalyah relates that he heard that these *gedolim* died both on the same day.

R' Yosef ibn Zaiach (or Zaiat)

רַבִּי יוֹסֵף בֶּן אַבְרָהָם צַיָּאח (צְיּוּת)

Damascus, Syria, d. after 5291/1531

R' Yosef served as rabbi of Jerusalem, but due to pressure from the Turkish government he was forced to flee to Damascus, where he also retained a rabbinical post. From time to time R' Yosef would return to Jerusalem for short periods, and it was in Jerusalem that he completed his kabbalistic works, *Avnei HaShoham* and *She'eiris Yosef*, which were never published. R' Yosef was a noted halachist who received inquiries from Syria, Egypt and *Eretz Yisrael*. His volume of responsa, which was not published, contained over six hundred replies to halachic inquiries. Some of his decisions have been published in the works of his contemporaries, e.g. *R' Yosef Caro (Avkas Rochel §10, 54, 115, 116, 139, 186, 188, 189) who refers to him with great reverence (see *Teshuvos R' Yosef Caro* §7), *R' Moshe Trani, *R' Levi ibn Chaviv, and *R' Moshe Alsheich. Two responsa by him appear in the anthology *Shivah Einayim* (Leghorn, 5505/1745).

R' Shlomo Molcho

רַבִּי שְׁלֹמֹה מוֹלְכוֹ

b. Portugal, c. 5260/1500
d. Mantua, Italy, 5292/1532

Raised as a Marrano, R' Shlomo served as a secretary at the royal court in Lisbon, under the name Diogo Perez. In 5285/1525, the mysterious adventurer David HaReuveni arrived in Portugal and was received at the royal court with diplomatic courtesy. David claimed to be the brother of Joseph, the king of an alleged war-loving Jewish tribe living in the 'East'; David presented himself as the commander of his country's armed forces. He offered the crowned heads of Europe a pact wherein he bound himself to aid them to wrest the Holy Land from the Moslems. David was cordially received by the Pope, and his proposal was given serious consideration. His appearance in Portugal so inspired R' Shlomo that he decided to return completely to the Jewish fold, and had himself circumcised. Fearing danger as a result of this act, David HaReuveni sent him to Turkey. In Salonica, R' Shlomo came under the influence of *R' Yosef Taitatzak and *R' Yosef Caro and delved deeply into the mysteries of *kabbalah*. One must marvel at R' Shlomo's intellectual qualities, for in a short while he was able to master this aspect of Torah to the extent that people thronged to hear his discourses.

R' Shlomo thereafter ascended to *Eretz Yisrael* and spent some time in Safed, where he was engaged to be married. In about 5290/1530 he arrived in Italy, preaching about the coming redemption and exhorting the masses to repentance. Among his listeners were high-ranking members of the Catholic clergy, who were also very inspired by his fiery sermons and accurate predictions. He accurately predicted the flooding of Rome in 5290/1530 and an earthquake in Portugal in 5291/1531. He was even granted an audience by Pope Clement VII, who was very fond of him and granted him complete safety in Rome. However, R' Shlomo was reported to the Inquisition as being a Christian apostate, not a Jew, and was immediately incarcerated in the Inquisition prison. Through the intervention of the pope himself, he was secretly freed and told to flee Rome.

R' Shlomo next appeared before Charles V, Emperor of the Roman Empire, who granted him an audience — and then issued an order for him to be delivered to the Inquisition at Mantua, where he was given the choice of accepting the Christian religion or facing death. R' Shlomo sanctified G-d's name and was burned at the stake.

R' Shlomo's memory was venerated by succeeding generations and especially by his contemporary, R' Yosef Caro. In the latter's work *Maggid Meisharim*, R' Shlomo is referred to as 'Shlomo, my chosen one'. He left two kabbalistic works, *Sefer Drashos R' Shlomo Molcho*, which was later known as *Sefer HaMefoar* (Salonica, 5289/1529), and *Chayas Kaneh* (Amsterdam, 5420/1660).

R' Binyamin Zev

רַבִּי בִּנְיָמִין זְאֵב בֶּן מַתִּתְיָהוּ

d. Greece, c. 5300/1540

Although a merchant by trade, R' Binyamin Zev was also a member of the Yeshivah of Arta (in the province of Epirus, in southwestern Greece) and is chiefly known through his halachic disputes with many of his contemporaries. His collection of responsa, entitled *Binyamin Zev* (Venice, 5299/1539), contains four hundred fifty responsa on the most diverse subjects. It was not received too well by some prominent Polish and Italian rabbis of the era, namely *Maharshal and *Maharam Padua, but he is cited by later authorities and by his contemporary *R' Moshe Isserles, thereby winning for himself a permanent place in the annals of *halachah*.

His son-in-law, R' Shmuel Kalai, author of responsa *Mishpetei Shmuel* (Venice 5360/1600), was a disciple of *R' David HaKohen, and a prominent rabbi in Greece.

R' Moshe Alashkar
(Maharam Alashkar)

רַבִּי מֹשֶׁה בֶּן יִצְחָק אַלְאַשְׁקָר

b. Spain, c. 5220/1460
d. Jerusalem, Eretz Yisrael, c. 5302/1542

R' Moshe was a pupil of R' Shmuel of Valencia. Following the Spanish expulsion of 5252/1492, R' Moshe experienced great perils: he was taken prisoner by pirates and faced the fate of being drowned. After much suffering he escaped from his captors and found refuge in Tunis, North Africa. R' Moshe resided in Tunis for some years. He lived in Greece for a while and later in Cairo, Egypt.

Cairo had become the home of many Spanish refugees, who in a short time had acquired influence surpassing that of the original Jewish inhabitants. R' Moshe was elevated to an important rabbinical post as *dayan* in Cairo, and much honor was bestowed on him due to his great learning.

R' Moshe was considered a leading halachic authority and many rabbinical leaders of the day sent him their inquiries, among them *R' Eliyahu Mizrachi, *R' David HaKohen, *R' Yaakov bei Rav, and *R' Levi ibn Chaviv. His responsa (Sabbionetta, 5314/1554) are among the classics of halachic literature. His responses are replete with quotations from the writings of the *geonim*, which would otherwise have been lost.

An expert in the Arabic tongue, R' Moshe translated a number of *Rambam's responsa from Arabic into Hebrew. These would otherwise have been unknown to Talmudic scholars until modern times.

Although R' Moshe was himself a devotee of the *kabbalah*, as indicated in his poetry, he nevertheless was a great admirer of Rambam and defended his views on matters of faith against the attacks of *Sefer HaEmunos* of *R' Shem Tov ibn Shem Tov I (*Teshuvos Maharam Alashkar* §117).

R' Moshe also authored a commentary on *Tur Orach Chaim* entitled *Geon Yaakov*, mentioned by *Chida but, unfortunately, not preserved. He also composed a commentary on tractate *Avos* which is cited numerous times by *R' Shmuel de Uzeda in his *Midrash Shmuel*, and a super-commentary to *Rashi's Torah commentary. Both of these works have not been published.

R' Avraham of Prague

רַבִּי אַבְרָהָם בֶּן אַבִיגְדוֹר מִפְּרָאג

d. Prague, Bohemia (now Czechoslovakia) 5303/1543

Some confuse R' Avraham with his namesake, the son of the famed kabbalist *R' Avigdor Kara (to whom the authorship of *Sefer HaKaneh* and *Sefer HaPliah* is attributed), but they are not the same in spite of the similarity of the names, for the kabbalist R' Avigdor Kara died (9 Iyar 5199/1439) long before this R' Avraham (who is cited by *Rama as R' Avraham of Prague) was born. He served as rabbi of Prague for many years, after *R' Yaakov Pollak departed for Poland. One of his disciples was R' Avraham, *R' Mordechai Yafeh's father.

R' Avraham's works include notes on *Tur* (printed partially in *Tur*, Augsburg, 5300/1540, and other editions); and a super-commentary on *Rashi's Torah commentary (unpublished). He also composed a *selichah* (penitential hymn) titled *Anah Elokei Avraham*, but this is thought by some to be authored by the other R' Avraham, the son of the kabbalist R' Avigdor Kara.

R' Yaakov bei Rav

רַבִּי יַעֲקֹב בֶּן מֹשֶׁה בֵּי רַב

b. Maqueda, Spain, 5235/1475
d. Safed, Eretz Yisrael, 1 Iyar 5306/1546

A disciple of *R' Yitzchak Abohab II, R' Yaakov resided in Spain until the expulsion of 5252/1492. After the expulsion he fled to North Africa, where he was enthusiastically received in recognition of his extensive erudition. He was appointed rabbi of Fez, Morocco at the tender age of eighteen, even though the community comprised some five thousand souls, including some prominent scholars. He later stayed for some time in Tlemcen (Algeria) from where he eventually made his way to *Eretz Yisrael* and settled in Jerusalem. There he established a flourishing yeshivah, but was forced to disband it (c. 5280/1520) because of a famine. R' Yaakov then went to Egypt. In Cairo he re-established his yeshivah and served on the *beis din* of the *naggid*, R' Yitzchak Sholal, with whom he formed a close personal relationship. There he continued to spread Torah knowledge, and many disciples gathered around him. He soon returned to *Eretz Yisrael* (no later than 5284/1524) and settled in Safed (Tzfas), where he established a yeshivah which attracted some of the greatest scholars of the generation. *R' Yosef Caro, *R' Moshe Trani (Mabit), and many other luminaries considered themselves his disciples.

In Safed (5298/1538) R' Yaakov decided to re-establish the *semichah* ordination. *Semichah* had been in effect in a continuous line from Moses until it was disrupted when the yeshivos of the *Amoraim* in *Eretz Yisrael* were forced to close during the persecution of the Romans in the fourth century. The *semichah* had to be conferred in *Eretz Yisrael*, by a sage who was himself ordained, and once it had been discontinued, it could not be reinstituted. The *semichah* conferred upon its recipients the right to officiate as judges in all types of adjudication, including cases of capital and corporal punishment. [The ordination practiced in our times is only an affirmation of the recipient's proficiency in *halachah*, and is valid only for adjudicating cases for which a bona-fide judge is not required.]

R' Yaakov's stated intention in restoring the *semichah* was to enable penitents, specifically some of the Spanish Jews who had masqueraded as Christians, to achieve full atonement. *Rambam (*Hilchos Sanhedrin* 17:7) rules that the punishment of *malkus* (lashes) serves in lieu of the awesome *kares* (spiritual excision), so that one who has committed a sin punishable both with *kares* and *malkus* can have the decree of *kares* lifted when he has been punished with *malkus*. Thus, R' Yaakov reasoned, penitents could achieve full atonement for their more serious transgressions if there were a *beis din* which was authorized to administer this punishment.

He based his reasoning on a statement of Rambam (*Mishneh Torah Hilchos Sanhedrin* 4:11) that if all scholars residing in *Eretz Yisrael* would consent to ordain one in their midst with judicial power, this would be considered a valid *semichah,* and then he, in turn, would have the power to ordain others. R' Yaakov renewed the *semichah* chain in 5298/1538, having himself officially ordained after obtaining the unanimous consent of all the scholars of Safed. R' Yaakov then, in turn, ordained four of the most illustrious scholars of Safed, namely: R' Yosef Caro, R' Moshe Trani, R' Yisrael de Corial, and R' Avraham Shalom.

R' Yaakov also sent a letter of ordination to *R' Levi ibn Chaviv, Chief Rabbi of Jerusalem, but the latter refused to accept it, declaring the entire *semichah* program invalid. R' Levi argued that R' Yaakov's interpretation of Rambam was faulty, that Rambam had not meant to make a definitive ruling; hence one could not draw conclusions from the ruling. Besides, even according to R' Yaakov's understanding, the reinstitution of the *semichah* was conditional upon the consent of *all* the scholars, and therefore was invalid inasmuch as the Jerusalem scholars had not been consulted.

A major controversy now arose between the supporters of the renewal of *semichah* and their antagonists, involving many rabbinical authorities, including *Radvaz, who sided with R' Levi ibn Chaviv. The dispute grew, but soon after R' Yaakov had ordained the above-mentioned scholars, he was forced to flee Safed as a result of a libel spread against him regarding some financial matter. He found refuge in Damascus where he spent some time.

Because of the opposition to the reinstitution of *semichah,* the enthusiasm of its backers also flagged, and very few *semichos* were conferred. R' Yosef Caro ordained *R' Moshe Alsheich, who in turn ordained *R' Chaim Vital. *R' Yaakov Abulafia (whose mother was a daughter of R' Yaakov bei Rav), and his son R' Chaim Abulafia the Elder, are referred to as having *semichah,* as well as R' Yaakov ben Avraham bei Rav II, a grandson of R' Yaakov bei Rav. The greatest proof of the lack of enthusiasm for the *semichah* is that R' Yaakov's greatest disciples, R' Yosef Caro and R' Moshe Trani, make no mention of it in their works. R' Yosef Caro remarks a number of times in his *Shulchan Aruch* that we do not have *semichah* in our days. R' Yaakov himself realized that his idea had failed, and wrote a letter expressing his disappointment that he had not been able to fulfill this *mitzvah.* He stressed his pure motives in the matter, insisting that 'The good G-d knows that my entire intention was only for the sake of Heaven.'

Among R' Yaakov's works were a commentary to Rambam's *Mishneh Torah* (till the end of *Zeraim*), wherever the commentary *Maggid Mishneh* is not extant. A work called *Beis Yaakov*, containing at least substantial portions of this work, has appeared in our times in an edition of *Mishneh Torah* (ed. Pardes, Jerusalem, 5717/1957). A selection of his responsa, *Teshuvos Ri bei Rav,* appeared in Venice more than one hundred years after his demise (5423/1663). To this work his *chidushim* to *Maseches Kidushin* were appended. Additional *chidushim* to *Kidushin* were printed in recent times (Jerusalem, 5700/1940), and a new edition based on a manuscript has appeared (Jerusalem, 5741/1981). Additional responsa are to be found in the works of his disciples and contemporaries (*Teshuvos Mabit, Teshuvos Ralbach, Teshuvos R' Eliyahu Mizrachi, and Avkas Rochel*). R' Yaakov's comments to *Tur* are mentioned in *Beis Yosef.* A collection of commentaries to the *Later Prophets* (R' David ibn Hin, *Likutei Shoshanim;* Venice, 5362/1602) cites commentaries by R' Yaakov bei Rav. Some of his comments to the book of *Ruth* are cited in the *peirush* by R' Ovadyah (ben Zecharyah) Hamon of Bertinoro (Venice, 5345/1585).

R' Yosef Taitatzak

רַבִּי יוֹסֵף בֶּן שְׁלֹמֹה טַאִיטַאצָק

b. Spain, c. 5225/1465
d. Constantinople (now Istanbul), Turkey
c. 5306/1546

R' Yosef was already an adult and an accomplished scholar when he was forced to flee Spain with his father and brother during the expulsion in 5252/1492. The family settled in Salonica where his father, also a recognized Torah scholar, was one of the leaders of the nascent Sephardic community; the father — R' Shlomo Taitatzak — died there.

R' Yosef headed a yeshivah in Salonica which attracted some of the finest minds of Turkish Jewry. Soon he was acknowledged as one of the greatest Torah sages of the generation. *R' Shmuel de Medina (Maharashdam) and *R' Yitzchak Adribi considered themselves his disciples. *R' Yosef Caro acknowledged his authority and published some lengthy disputations he had with R' Yosef Taitatzak in his *Beis Yosef (Yoreh Deah* 201, *Even HaEzer* 17).

For a short period he lived in Serres (a town north of Salonica), where he established a yeshivah, but soon he returned to Salonica. At the end of his life he settled in Constantinople, where he died.

R' Yosef was an accomplished kabbalist, and he led an ascetic life. It is related that with the exception of the nights of the Sabbath and festivals, for forty years R' Yosef never slept in a bed, but on a box with his feet on the ground. He would arise precisely at midnight to mourn the destruction of the Temple and immerse himself in Torah study. No one knew of his practice except his wife, who revealed it after his death (*Reishis Chachmah, Shaar HaKedushah*, ch. 7).

In *Shem HaGedolim*, R' Chaim Y.D. Azulai (Chida) refers to a letter by R' Yosef (which was printed in *She'eiris Yehudah*) in which R' Yosef states that eighteen hours of his day were taken up with learning and teaching his disciples, and that he took care of his mundane needs during the remaining six hours. Chida also reports that R' Yosef received instruction in Torah from a heavenly voice — a *maggid* — and that his grandfather, R' Avraham Azulai, preserved in his writings a lengthy segment of the discourses which were the result of the *maggid's* teachings.

In addition to his vast erudition in religious areas, R' Yosef was adept in astronomy and astrology, and may have been proficient in other secular disciplines as well. The historian Meir Benayahu reports the existence of a manuscript containing R' Yosef's comments on astrology (Preface to *Piskei HaGaon Maharit*).

R' Yosef also maintained close contact with *R' Shlomo Molcho, who corresponded with him and was a guest at his home in Salonica in 5289/1529.

R' Yosef's works include *Ben Poras* (Venice, 5359/1599), a short commentary on *Ecclesiastes; Lechem Sesarim* (Venice, 5368/1608) on *Daniel* and the five *Megillos;* comments on tractate *Avos* (unpublished), and halachic responsa quoted in works of his contemporaries and disciples (see *Binyamin Zev,* 7-9, and others). According to R' Yitzchak Adribi, R' Yosef also authored a commentary on *Rif's *Sefer HaHalachos.*

R' Yosef's *chidushim* appear in several publications. A collection of *chidushim* on various *masichtos* of the Talmud, named *Otzar HaShittos,* has recently been published (Jerusalem, 5739/1979). It contains *chidushim* by various Turkish *rabbanim* of the era following the Spanish expulsion. Many *chidushim* of R' Yosef's are contained in this work. Meir Benayahu has collected all of the responsa by R' Yosef found in the works of his contemporaries and in manuscripts and published them as *Piskei HaGaon Maharit* (Jerusalem, 5747/1987). In addition, some of R' Yosef's *chidushim* were printed in *She'eiris Yehudah* (Salonica, 5360/1600) by his grand-nephew, R' Yehudah Taitatzak.

Some other members of R' Yosef's family were also prominent scholars. We have already mentioned his father, R' Shlomo. His brother R' Shmuel (died in Salonica, 5322/1562) was an accomplished scholar; M. Benayahu collected his rulings and appended them to R' Yosef's responsa as *Piskei Mar Shmuel.*

R' Shmuel's son R' Yaakov was a *rosh yeshivah* in Salonica, and his grandson R' Shmuel (II) was *rav* of Magnesia (Manisa), Turkey, and was already highly regarded when he died at the young age of thirty-nine (c. 5341/1581). The brother of R' Shmuel (II), R' Yehudah Taitatzak, printed R' Shmuel's *chidushim,* together with those of his great-uncle R' Yosef, in *She'eiris Yehudah.* These, too, were appended to *Piskei HaGaon Maharit.*

R' Eliyahu Bachur

רַבִּי אֵלְיָהוּ בֶּן אָשֵׁר בָּחוּר

b. Neustadt, Germany, 5228/1468
d. Venice, Italy, Shevat 5309/1549

R' Eliyahu was born in Germany, and because of this is many times referred to as R' Eliyahu Ashkenazi, the German. Like many German Jews of his time, he emigrated to Italy in order to escape the persecution and oppression which was the lot of German Jewry. In 5264/1504 he was teaching Hebrew language and grammar in Padua. To assist his students he wrote notes, called *nimukim,* to the grammatical work of *R' Moshe Kimchi, *Darchei Lashon HaKodesh* (also called *Sefer Mehalech Shevilei HaDaas*). The manuscript was given for transcription to a man named Binyamin ben Yehudah who published it in Pesaro (5268/1508) as his own work. The plagiarist had interspersed the work with remarks from other works and thus the first edition of this book differed in many vital points from the author's original, and contained many errors. These mistakes did not prevent the book from gaining popularity, and it became the manual of choice for both Jewish and Christian Hebrew-language students. In 5306/1546 R' Eliyahu published a corrected version of the book in Venice, at the insistence of his friends, and after nearly forty years the work was finally attributed to its rightful author. R' Eliyahu gained a reputation as one of the foremost Hebrew grammarians and his lucid, unencumbered, and concise style endeared him to all students of Hebrew. The Renaissance brought with it a renewal of interest in the classical languages — Hebrew included — and R' Eliyahu's works were in great demand among the Christian intelligentsia.

R' Eliyahu's activities in Padua were interrupted in 5269/1509, when the city was taken and sacked by the combined armies of Emperor Maximilian I of Germany, Louis XII of France and other members of the League of Cambrai. R' Eliyahu, having lost all his possessions, was forced to seek a new place to live. He went to Venice, but finding no means there by which to earn a livelihood, continued on to Rome. Here Cardinal Egedius di Viterbo, who was studying Hebrew, offered to maintain R' Eliyahu and his family in exchange for Hebrew lessons. R' Eliyahu spent thirteen years at the palace of the cardinal, translating Hebrew texts for him and composing many grammatical works.

The cardinal was a well-rounded scholar, and R' Eliyahu benefited scholastically from Viterbo's knowledge of Greek; he cites the learned cardinal's comments many times in his works. R' Eliyahu admits that one of his works — Mesores HaMesores — was written at the suggestion and inspiration of the cardinal. R' Eliyahu was widely criticized for giving instruction in Torah to Gentiles and he felt compelled to justify himself before the public. In a lengthy preface to his Mesores HaMesores, R' Eliyahu defends his actions based on three considerations: (1) his poverty virtually put him in a position where he was permitted to transgress the prohibition, based on the dictum 'The saving of a life supersedes [most of] the laws of the Torah';

(2) many prominent men before him had instructed Gentiles; and (3) the prohibition referred mainly to the transmission of the secrets of the kabbalah and other secrets of the Torah (cf. She'eilos UTeshuvos Be'er Sheva in Be'er Mayim Chaim §14). It is of interest, however, that the manuscript from which the kabbalistic work Sodei Razya (by *R' Elazar Rokeach of Worms, Kolomei, 5696/1936) was printed was copied by R' Eliyahu for Cardinal Egedius.

It was during this period that R' Eliyahu composed Sefer HaBachur (Rome, 5278/1518), his classic grammatical work. That same year he published grammatical tables of verbs for beginners, entitled Luach BeDikduk HaPoalim VeHaBinyanim; and Sefer HaHarkavah, a work on unusual words in the Bible. In 5280/1520 he published Pirkei Eliyahu — a sequel to Sefer HaBachur.

However, in 5287/1527, R' Eliyahu's serenity was once again disturbed when the armies of Emperor Charles V conquered Rome, and R' Eliyahu lost his property and most of his manuscripts. He returned to Venice, where the printer Daniel Bomberg engaged him as a proofreader in his Hebrew publishing house. There, once again, he found pupils — both Jews and non-Jews — interested in studying the Hebrew language; among them was the French ambassador, Georges de Selve. R' Eliyahu resumed his literary activity and published Mesores HaMesores (Venice, 5298/1538) on the intricacies of the mesorah (lit. tradition) — the system which is used to ensure the proper spelling and punctuation of the Bible. In the preface to this sefer R' Eliyahu presented his assertion that the punctuation marks used to indicate the vowels are not of Sinaitic origin and had been introduced by the Tiberian Massoretes in post-Talmudic times. This raised a great controversy in rabbinic circles and R' Eliyahu's view was not accepted (see *R' Azaryah min HaAdomim, *Imrei Binah*, ch. 57). In the same year he published *Tuv Taam* (Venice, 5298/1538) about the system of cantillation (*taamim*) used in reading the Bible.

R' Eliyahu's reputation spread, and he was offered various prestigious teaching positions in Christian universities. However, he was not interested in being a professor of Hebrew at those institutions, and, furthermore, refused to live in any city — such as Paris — where his fellow Jews were not welcome.

In 5300/1540, after Bomberg's printing firm had ceased to exist, R'Eliyahu accepted an invitation from another Christian printer, Paul Fagius, to supervise his publishing house in Isny, Germany. There R' Eliyahu published *Sefer Tishbi* (Isny, 5301/1541), a dictionary containing 712 (the numerical equivalent of *Tishbi*) previously undefined words used in the Talmud, the *midrash*, and in colloquial speech; and *Sefer Meturgeman* (Isny, 5301/1541), a concordance and dictionary of Aramaic words found in the various *targumim*. In the latter two works, R' Eliyahu sometimes used German or Yiddish translations, making this probably the first instance of the use of Yiddish in a book intended for scholars. Another work of his is *Shemos HaDevarim* (Isny, 5302/1542).

After returning to Venice in 5304/1544, R' Eliyahu published for the first time a correct edition of his notes (*nimukim*) to the *Michlol* and *Sefer HaShorashim* of *Radak (Venice, 5306/1546). His *Sefer HaZichronos,* a concordance of the words in the Bible, remains in manuscript; an excerpt from it was printed, together with a French translation (Frankfurt am Main, 5635/1895). R' Eliyahu's works enjoyed great popularity during his lifetime and the period following it; some of them were printed in many editions. He was especially appreciated by Gentile Hebraists, and many of his works were translated into Latin and other languages. Part of a scholarly correspondence between R' Eliyahu and Sebastian Munster, a Hebraic scholar and pupil of R' Eliyahu who translated many of his works into Latin, was published in an edition of *Radak* to *Amos* (Basel, 5291/1531) under the name *Michtav MeEliyahu*. *R' Yosef Tumim remarked on the importance of R' Eliyahu's works in a letter printed in the preface to his *Pri Megadim* to *Shulchan Aruch, Orach Chaim,* and expressed his view that every child should be familiarized with *Sefer Meturgeman and Sefer Tishbi.*

R' Eliyahu also bears the perhaps dubious distinction of being the first to print secular material in Yiddish and thus to be the father of Yiddish literature. He wrote *Bava D' Antone* (Isny, 5301/1541) — a paraphrase of a popular Italian chivalric novel about the knight Sir Bevois of Hampton — which was later printed as *Bove Buch* (thus originating the Yiddish expression 'Bube Maisse'). He also wrote other less-known compositions in Yiddish.

Another facet of R' Eliyahu's work in Yiddish is his translation of sections of the *Tanach* — the first Yiddish translation of Scripture. This includes his translation of Torah, the five *Megillos* and the *haftaros* (Constance, 5304/1544); *Psalms* (without Hebrew text; Augsburg, 5305/1545); and *Shmuel Buch* (probably a paraphrase of the Biblical book of Samuel; Augsburg, 5304/1544).

Many of R' Eliyahu's works are punctuated and their punctuation differs in many places from the punctuation prevalent today. This assumes special significance in light of his assertion (preface to *Meturgeman*) that the punctuation of the *targumim* is not to be relied upon.

R' Meir ibn Gabbai

רַבִּי מֵאִיר בֶּן יְחֶזְקֵאל אִבְּן גַּבַּאי

b. Spain, c. 5240/1480
d. first half of sixteenth century

A victim of the expulsion from Spain when yet a boy, R' Meir and his family finally found safety in Egypt, where he spent the rest of his life.

R' Meir authored popular kabbalistic works: *Tolaas Yaakov* (Constantinople, 5320/1560), a kabbalistic interpretation of the prayers (composed at the age of twenty-six); *Avodas HaKodesh* (Mantua, 5305/1545), an introduction to the *kabbalah*, which became a recognized classic and elaborates on the fundamental ideas of the 'secret lore', the differences between its approach and that of such rationalists as *Ralbag and others, and the fallacies of the rationalist system; and *Derech Emunah* (Constantinople, 5320/1560), a treatise which was written in response to the questions by R' Meir's disciple, R' Yosef HaLevi, on the con-cept of the ten *sefiros* (divine emanations).

R' Yosef Korkos

רַבִּי יוֹסֵף קוֹרְקוֹס

Eretz Yisrael, late 15th — early 16th century

A native of Spain, at the time of the expulsion in 5252/1492 R' Yosef fled to Egypt, where he studied as an associate of *Radvaz. From there he made his way to *Eretz Yisrael*.

A contemporary of *Radvaz, R' Yosef corresponded with him on many halachic topics. He is best known for his commentary on *Rambam's *Mishneh Torah*, which is known to scholars primarily through the extensive quotes from it in *R' Yosef Caro's *Kessef Mishneh*. This commentary, which originally

encompassed (at least) the divisions *Zeraim, Avodah, Korbanos* and *Taharah* of Rambam's code, has been preserved only partially. Only the commentaries to *Zeraim* (Smyrna, 5317/1557) and *Avodah* (in the Schulsinger edition of *Rambam*, New York, 5707/1947) have been published. Extensive quotes from the work on *Korbanos* have been published (ibid.) as well as a collection of responsa dealing with difficult passages in Rambam's *Hilchos Shabbos* (in R' Chaim Y.D. Azulai's *Teshuvos Chaim Shaal*, Leghorn, 5555/1795; and in the said edition of *Rambam*). A commentary on *Maseches Kesubos* (*Shas El HaMekoros*, Jerusalem) has been attributed to him. *R' Yosef Caro and *R' Moshe Trani mention him in their responsa with great reverence and recognition, and some of his responsa have been printed in the former's *Avkas Rochel*. A lengthy responsum by R' Yosef is cited by Radvaz in his *Teshuvos* (§340).

R' Avraham ibn Yaish

רַבִּי אַבְרָהָם אִבְּן יָעִישׁ

Constantinople (now Istanbul), Turkey,
c. late 15th — early 16th century

R' Avraham was driven from his native Portugal during the expulsion of 5257/1497, and settled in Constantinople. His halachic decisions were widely respected and a number of his responsa are included in the responsa of *R' Eliyahu Mizrachi.

R' Levi ben Yaakov ibn Chaviv (Ralbach)

ר' לֵוִי בֶּן יַעֲקֹב אִבְּן חָבִיב (רַלְבַּ"ח)

b. Zamora, Spain c. 5245/1485
d. Jerusalem, Israel c. 5305/1545

R' Levi was the son of a famous father, *R' Yaakov ibn Chaviv, the author of *Ein Yaakov*. R' Levi was born in Spain before the expulsion and, like many others, his family fled to Portugal when the edict of expulsion was implemented. Soon the situation of the Jews in that unfortunate country also deteriorated, and tens of thousands of children were torn from their parents' arms and forcibly baptized (see The Rishonim, p. 27). R' Levi managed to escape from Portugal together with his father and settled in Salonica.

Various writers have misread a passage in R' Levi's writings in which he speaks about his sojourn in Portugal and concluded erroneously that R' Levi was forcibly converted to Christianity in his youth, a misconception which should be corrected here. During a heated halachic debate in which R' Levi took part, his opponent made a veiled remark which alluded to something in R' Levi's past. R' Levi responded to the hint in a forthright manner, '. . . for even if they did change my name during the period of conversion, I did not change. He who tests hearts and investigates thoughts knows that I always feared Him. Though I did not have the privilege to sanctify His name, nevertheless my heart trembles within me from before His wrath. Moreover, at the time I had not yet reached the age of culpability in His Court of Justice [i.e., he was less than twenty years old]' (Kuntres HaSmichah in Teshuvos Ralbach). Even if 'change of name' is a figure of speech denoting conversion, it must in this case refer to a facet of conversion not requiring the person's participation [e.g., a forcible sprinkling of baptismal water]; R' Levi clearly says that he himself did nothing and that others 'changed his name'. It is also very possible that R' Levi merely had a Christian name assigned to him while hiding from the Portuguese authorities.

In Salonica R' Levi studied under his father and under some other scholars and was acknowledged as an outstanding halachic authority while he was yet very young. *R' Eliyahu Mizrachi respected him greatly and relied on his halachic acumen to such a degree that he would endorse R' Levi's decisions almost without reading them (Kuntres HaSmichah in Teshuvos Ralbach). When his father died (5276/1516) without having completed the Ein Yaakov, R' Levi finished the work. As his reputation grew, his influence in the community of Salonica also grew and his opinion was sought on most communal matters. He officiated as the head of the local yeshivah and taught many distinguished disciples. *R' Shmuel de Medina and *R' Yissachar Susan considered themselves his disciples.

In approximately 5282/1522, R' Levi decided to go to Eretz Yisrael. He visited Jerusalem for a short while but, for reasons unknown, left the city to return two years later. In his responsa, R' Levi indicates that, while on his way to Eretz Yisrael, he stayed for a while in Allepo where he lectured to the local Torah scholars. He also resided for some time in Safed, where he met *R' Yaakov bei Rav for the first time. These two outstanding Torah scholars had a number of heated debates concerning halachic matters (Teshuvos Ralbach §105). In one particularly acrimonious exchange concerning the validity of a get (bill of divorce), R' Levi debated R' Yaakov bei Rav's disciple *R' Moshe Trani who argued on behalf of his mentor (op. cit. §129 ff.). R' Levi eventually (c. 5284/1524) returned to Jerusalem where he was soon acknowledged as the chief rabbi and leader of the Holy City.

Upon arriving in Jerusalem he began to interest himself in halachic matters having special relevance to Jerusalem. Thus he established the proper procedure for observing Purim on Shabbos (op. cit. §32). [In Jerusalem Purim is observed on 15 Adar which can occur on Shabbos. 14 Adar, which is the general date for Purim, cannot occur on Shabbos]. Of special importance is his responsum about the correct year in which the shemittah is to be observed (op. cit. §143).

In Jerusalem R' Levi was to take part and play the dominant role in an historic halachic controversy whose outcome had far-reaching consequences. R' Yaakov bei Rav, the leading Torah authority of Safed, which was at the time the most prestigious community in Eretz Yisrael, made an attempt (in 5298/1538) to re-establish the institution of semichah (see Historical Introduction and *R' Yaakov bei Rav). The Torah scholars of Safed, most of whom considered themselves R' Yaakov's disciples, embraced the proposal enthusiastically, and the semichah was to be re-established again by universal acclamation after a thousand year hiatus. The fervor surrounding the imminent re-establishment had a Messianic tinge to it, since it was essential, in the view of its proponents, that the semichah be re-established before the advent of the Messiah. After *R' Yaakov bei Rav had been crowned with the semichah, the sages of Safed wrote to R' Levi, outlining the basis for their action and proposing to ordain R' Levi as well. However, R' Levi refused to be swept up in the enthusiasm, and notwithstanding his virtual isolation in the scholarly world, courageously took a strong stand against the ordination, refusing it for himself and refuting the proofs advanced as a basis for the re-establishment of the semichah. Ultimately, R' Levi's view was tacitly acknowledged by the scholarly world, and the semichah idea quietly withered away.

The only thing we have of R' Levi's Torah legacy is the compilation of his responsa, She'elos U'Teshuvos R' Levi ibn Chaviv [or She'elos U'Teshuvos Ralbach] (Venice 5325/1565). This work contains, besides the author's halachic correspondence, a number of chidushim to Rambam's Mishneh Torah, and miscellaneous chidushim to the Talmud; most of the chidushim to Hilchos Kiddush HaChodesh now appear in the prevalent editions of Mishneh Torah.

In addition to his greatness in Torah, R' Levi was also proficient in astronomy. His chidushim to the parts of Mishneh Torah which relate to this science have already been mentioned; a lengthy essay on an astronomic matter which has relevance to Torah appears in the She'elos U'Teshuvos (§145). Very revealing is his responsum on a matter touching on kabbalah -- the concept of gilgul neshamos (metempsychosis). After admitting that he was not adept in the kabbalah, 'because..one must receive [instruction in the kabbalah] from a teacher who himself has received, and in our days and our country there were not many people who were expert in it,' he nevertheless gives his opinion about the specific concept of gilgul neshamos. The Jewish sages of the post-Talmudic era, he writes, can be divided into two groups. There are those who examine matters of religion with human reason and [therefore] involved themselves with secular philosophy. It is difficult for these sages to accept the concept of gilgul neshamos. However, there is a much larger group of sages who approach such matters with faith, and all in this group have written that the belief of gilgul neshamos is a true belief and that it is a fundamental tenet (ikar); we are all obligated to follow the view of the latter group. However, he admonishes that things of this nature should be discussed in writing only and not in public (§8). At the end of the volume is the *Kuntres HaSmichah* which relates the abortive attempt to re-institute the *semichah* and presents the arguments for and against it. This is the most important source for our knowledge of this controversy.

R' Ovadyah Sforno

רַבִּי עוֹבַדְיָה בֶּן יַעֲקֹב סְפוֹרְנוֹ

b. Cesena, Italy, c. 5230/1470
d. Bologna, Italy, c. 5310/1550

R' Ovadyah, aside from being a proficient Torah scholar and halachic authority (see *Teshuvos Maharam Padua*, §48-49), was also a physician and educated in secular subjects. During his sojourn in Rome, where he studied medicine and other disciplines, he instructed the humanist scholar Johann Reuchlin in the Hebrew language and grammar. Reuchlin is well remembered in Jewish history for his firm and impassioned defense of the Talmud — at great cost to himself — against the calumnies of the apostate Pfefferkorn and his supporters and fellow agitators in the monkish orders of Germany. R' Ovadyah lived in Rome for a long time and is mentioned by David HaReuveni as one of the local rabbis who came to visit him when he stayed in Rome (5284/1524). Later he settled in Bologna where his younger brother R' Chananel, who was very close to R' Ovadyah, lived. There R' Ovadyah supported himself by practicing his profession — medicine— and at the same time officiated as a *dayan* in the local *beis din*. He was active in communal affairs and was instrumental in the opening of a printing establishment in Bologna, where he published his work *Or Amim*.

R' Ovadyah is well known for the Torah commentary which bears his family name — *Sforno* (Venice, 5327/1567) — and which is still very popular with students and educators. He also composed commentaries to *Song of Songs* and *Ecclesiastes* (printed together with the commentary on *Chumash*); a commentary to *Job* titled *Mishpat Tzedek* (printed together with *Oheiv Mishpat* by *Rashbatz; Venice, 5350/1590), wherein Job is portrayed as a traditionalist, a man whose belief is based on tradition, who is called upon to answer the intellectual onslaughts upon his faith by rationalists and adherents of philosophy; and a commentary to *Psalms* (Venice, 5346/1586). Fragments of a commentary to *Jonah, Habbakuk* and *Zachariah* have been preserved in *Likutei Shoshanim* by R' David ibn Hin (Venice, 5362/1602). His commentary to *Avos* is printed in the edition of *Machzor Roma* with *Kimcha D'Avishuna* (Bologna, 5301/1541). R' Ovadyah's commentaries are distinguished in their terseness, lucidity, and adherence to plain meaning, together with short comments on the philosophical and ethical implications of the text. A short treatise outlining the philosophical framework of R' Ovadyah's thought, aptly called *Kavanos HaTorah*, is appended to his Torah commentary. In it he dwells upon the purpose of the narratives in the Torah, some of the *chukim* (precepts whose purpose is not fathomable), and, at great length, upon the Tabernacle (*Mishkan*) and its particulars. All of these works (except for the commentary on *Avos*) were published posthumously.

The only work of R' Ovadyah's which was published during his lifetime is *Or Amim* (Bologna, 5297/1537). In this treatise R' Ovadyah sets out to answer the philosophical questions raised against the Torah by Jewish and Gentile scholars. He especially addresses himself to reconciling Torah with Aristotelian thought where possible and refuting those of its tenets which are incompatible with Torah thought, and to demon-strating their untenability. *Or Amim* was probably also intended for Gentile read-ership — as implied by its name — and R' Ovadyah personally prepared a Latin translation of it which he sent to Henri II of France. (It was published as *Lumen Gentium* in Bologna in 5308/1548.) R' Ovadyah seems to have had a special relationship with this monarch who ap-parently had a taste for scholarship, for R' Ovadyah also sent him his commen-tary to *Song of Songs* together with a letter of dedication.

A critical annotated edition of all of R' Ovadyah's writings has been prepared by R' Z. Gottlieb and published by Mossad HaRav Kook in two volumes (Jerusalem, 5740/1980), together with a collection of letters shedding light upon many facets of R' Ovadyah's life.

R' Avraham Treves

רַבִּי אַבְרָהָם בֶּן שְׁלֹמֹה טְרֶיוִיש

b. Italy, 5230/1470
d. Jerusalem, Eretz Yisrael, c. 5312/1552

R' Avraham was a descendant of *Rashi and a relative of *Maharik. He was also known as R' Avraham Tzarfati (the French), presumably because he was of French extraction. In his youth he was an instructor of Talmud in the little town of Rubico near Ferrara. There, he reports in the preface to *Birkas Avraham*, he had a vision in which a sage, who presumably was the prophet Elijah, re-vealed himself and discussed a problem in that week's *sidra* with him.

R' Avraham traveled through Turkey and Greece, spending several years in Constantinople and Salonica and be-coming acquainted with the great schol-ars of those places. He maintained halachic correspondence with many of the leading scholars of the day, among them *R' Eliyahu Mizrachi and *R' Yosef

Caro, who laud him for his erudition and saintliness. In Salonica he was warmly received by *R' Yaakov ibn Chaviv, who solicited his opinion on a difficult hala-chic problem concerning a *heter agunah*, i.e., establishing the death of a man who had disappeared, in order to allow his widow to remarry.

R' Avraham relates an interesting episode in connection with this halachic query. On 25 Nissan 5265/1505, while en route to deliver his affirmative reply to the *rabbanim*, R' Avraham fell into a swiftly running river near Skopje (now Yugoslavia) and was dragged down-stream by the current. His companions gave him up for dead. Later he was pulled out of the water by two Gentiles. After vomiting great amounts of water and bile, R' Avraham recovered, to the wonder of his two rescuers. He at-tributed his miraculous rescue to the merit of the *heter agunah* which he was about to deliver, and commemorated the day with a fast for the rest of his life (Preface to *Birkas Avraham*).

R' Avraham authored *Birkas Avraham* (Venice, 5312/1552), a halachic treatise. In it he defended the custom then current in Ashkenazic communities that the *chazzan* recite the *berachah* of *Al Netilas Yadayim* for the congregation together with all the other *berachos*, instead of each congregant reciting it when he washed his hands. R' Avraham prided himself that, in the course of his lengthy discussion, he was able to clarify three hundred additional halachic prob-lems. A glowing *haskamah* (approbation) to this *sefer*, with an accolade to its author by R' Yosef Caro and many other rabbis of his time, appears in its preface.

In his later years R' Avraham settled in Jerusalem. Halachic decisions by him appear in the responsa of his contempo-raries. An exchange of opinions between him and R' Yaakov ibn Chaviv and his son *R' Levi ibn Chaviv appears in the latter's responsa, *Teshuvos Ralbach* (1-2); with *R' Yaakov bei Rav and R' Yosef Caro in *Avkas Rochel* (11-14, 33-35); and with R' Eliyahu Mizrachi in *Teshuvos R' Eliyahu Mizrachi* (74-76).

R' Yitzchak Leon ibn Tzur

רַבִּי יִצְחָק לֵיאוֹן בֶּן אֱלִיעֶזֶר אִבְּן צוּר

Italy, 16th century

R' Yitzchak is the author of *Megillas Esther* (Venice, 5352/1592), a popular commentary on *Sefer HaMitzvos* of *Rambam. It mainly seeks to answer the critical comments (*hasagos*) of *Ramban to that work. Although some later authorities have expressed reservations about the excellence of this work (see e.g. *Shach, Choshen Mishpat* 28:14), his *Megillas Esther* still retains its place as the foremost commentary on the *Sefer HaMitzvos,* and has been printed in most editions of this *sefer.* Subsequent editions of *Megillas Esther* delete some extraneous material found in the first edition.

A pamphlet containing a decision by R' Yitzchak and other contemporary Italian rabbis, entitled *Psak R' Yitzchak Leon . . .,* was published in Rome (5306/1546). In this responsum R' Yitzchak mentions that his residence was in Ancona.

R' Eliezer ben Shlomo ibn Tzur, R' Yitzchak's father, was also a scholar.

R' Yosef (Yoselman) Loanz of Rosheim

רַבִּי יוֹסֵף (יוֹסְלְמַן) בֶּן גֵּרְשׁוֹן לוֹאַנְץ

b. Germany, c. 5240/1480
d. Rosheim, Alsace (now France), 5314/1554

One of the greatest advocates Jewry ever possessed, R' Yoselman set out upon this course of life during his early years. In 5270/1510 he was appointed *parnes u'manhig* (guide and leader) of the Jewish communities of lower Alsace, and was given the right to issue enactments for the Jews of his district and bans against refractory members. He also had the responsibility to defend individuals and communities against oppression, and, if necessary, to appeal to the governor and to the emperor. In this capacity R' Yoselman appeared several times before the emperors Maximilian I and Charles V. Soon after Charles V ascended the throne in 5280/1520, R' Yoselman procured a letter of protection from him for the whole of German Jewry. He also successfully interceded several times with the emperor's brother, King Ferdinand, in favor of the Jews of Bohemia and Moravia.

In 5285/1525 R' Yoselman succeeded in protecting the Jewish populace of Alsace against aggression by the hordes of peasants who had participated in the Peasants' Revolt. In 1524-26 the peasants of Southern Germany rose up against the upper classes and the Catholic clergy. As usual in such upheavals, the Jewish population of the affected areas suffered heavily from the excesses of the frenzied mob.]

In his memoirs R' Yoselman records many cases of persecution against the Jews of Germany, and tells how they were many times forced to become martyrs for their faith. Three of R' Yoselman's uncles died 'for the sanctification of His Name'. He relates how he defended the Jews before the authorities, sometimes endangering his very life for their sake. He also defended the Jews against the attacks of Martin Luther, founder of the Protestant faith and one of the most vile enemies of the Jews.

An eminent Torah scholar whose every spare moment was devoted to study, R' Yoselman also found time to put his thoughts to paper. *R' Yosef Yospa Han

Norlingen quotes from R' Yoselman's writings twice in his *Yosef Ometz* (Frankfurt am Main, 5483/1723). One of these quotes (perhaps from the lost first part of *Sefer HaMiknah*) opens a window for us into the souls of Jews like R' Yoselman, and is fit to be quoted here: "If, G-d forbid, one is put to the test because of some sin, he should be assured that G-d will strengthen his heart to endure pain which is even greater than [the pain of] death . . . and Rif [probably R' Peretz in his glosses to Tashbeitz] writes that if a person, man or woman, concentrates on the Great Name . . . to sanctify it, he is assured that he will withstand the test and not feel the pain . . . as it is known . . . that many give themselves over to be burned and are killed for the 'sanctification of His Name' and do not cry out 'Oy' nor 'Avoy' . . . As I the writer have witnessed . . . that when they went to be killed they accepted the 'yoke of the kingdom of Heaven' with great love, even though they suffered great pain and lived yet for ten days and nights . . . What I have witnessed I have written with certitude . . :." (*Yosef Ometz* §482).

R' Yoselman authored *Sefer HaMiknah*, an ethical and philosophic work which has recently been published (Jerusalem, 5730/1970). This work is divided into two parts. The first, which has only been partially preserved, deals with ethics, concentrating on the evil caused by informers (to the government). This was a topic too well known to R' Yoselman, having interceded many times with the authorities not to act on information communicated by (Jewish) informers. Even what remains of this chapter is of great historical interest. R' Yoselman gives many actual examples of the harm caused by informers; some of the cases cited were witnessed by R' Yoselman himself. The second part is a

novelty, for here R' Yoselman, an Ashkenazic Jew, shows himself to be an adherent of the philosophy of Sephardic Jewry. In the main, this part is a review of *Derech Emunah*, by R' Avraham Bibago.

R' Yoselman's memoirs survived all these decades, and were published in a scholarly journal. A number of full-length biographies have been written about this fascinating personality, and a gripping fictionalized account of his life has been created by Rabbi Marcus Lehmann (*Rabbi Joselman of Rosheim*).

R' Yehoshua Boaz Baruch

רַבִּי יְהוֹשֻׁעַ בּוֹעַז בֶּן שִׁמְעוֹן לְמִשְׁפַּחַת בָּרוּךְ

b. 5278/1518
d. Italy, c. 5315/1555

Almost nothing (except that his family had been exiled from Catalonia) is known about R' Yehoshua Boaz's life, but his contribution to Jewish learning is inestimable. Every day the Talmudic student encounters him on the pages of the *Gemara* and benefits from his improvement of the Talmud texts.

Observing that there were many diverse opinions regarding *halachah*, and no general rule used in decision-making, R' Yehoshua Boaz planned the compilation of two works: *Sefer HaTaamim*, also named *Sefer HaPeshutim*, containing the basic source material necessary for arriving at an intelligent assessment of the *halachah* (e.g., the pertinent passages of the *Gemara*, *Rif*, et al. — all in concise form); and *Sefer HaMachlokes*, containing all the halachic material around which controversies had arisen, in order to aid the student in ascertaining the majority opinion. *Chida reports that he saw the manuscript of the first work. Much of the material in the second was incorporated into *Shiltei HaGiborim*, R' Yehoshua's work on *Rif* and *Mordechai* which is printed in all prevalent editions of *Rif.*

R' Yehoshua's zeal to simplify the study of the Talmud, and the opportunity afforded him by his association with the publishing houses in Italy, led him to introduce some important features into the printed editions of the Talmud which remain part of it to this day.

R' Yehoshua Boaz provided the Talmud with a reference apparatus which greatly facilitates its study. He provided references for all the Biblical verses mentioned in the Talmud. These references were printed in the margin of the Talmud under the name *Torah Or*. He also compiled *Mesores HaShas,* references to parallel Talmudic texts in which a particular passage occurs (actually R' Yehoshua upgraded an already printed *Mesores*); and *Ein Mishpat,* references to the halachic conclusions reached by *Rambam, Smag,* and *Tur,* based on the Talmudic discussions. The latter two works were also printed in the margin of the Talmud page and are printed in every subsequent edition. He also compiled a halachic index to the Talmud named *Chikur Halachah,* arranged according to the system of Rambam's *Mishneh Torah,* which was printed (once) in the Sabbionetta edition of the *Rif* (5315/1555). He introduced the division of *Rosh* and *Mordechai* into numbered paragraphs so that these important *poskim* could be referred to accurately. Heretofore, references to these *poskim* had been by chapter only, making it difficult to find the cited passage.

In Sabbionetta, in 5313/1553, R' Yehoshua Boaz undertook to direct the publication of a new, improved edition of the Talmud with many important features, but only one tractate, *Kidushin,* was published. Shortly after the publication of this volume, Pope Julius III pronounced a ban on the Talmud (2 Elul 5313/August 12, 1553), and further publication of the Talmud in most of Italy was halted (see also *R' Meir Katzenellenbogen).

R' Yehoshua died — still a young man — during the publication of the Sabbionetta edition of the *Rif.*

R' Shlomo Sirilio

רַבִּי שְׁלֹמֹה בֶּן יוֹסֵף סִירִילְיוֹ

b. Spain, c. 5245/1485
d. Jerusalem, Eretz Yisrael, 5318/1558

R' Shlomo left his native Spain as a child with his parents, due to the expulsion in 5252/1492. The family settled in Salonica, where R' Shlomo received his education.

In 5292/1532 R' Shlomo emigrated to *Eretz Yisrael,* first settling in Safed and later in Jerusalem, where he spread Torah knowledge to his disciples.

R' Shlomo composed a comprehensive commentary on *Seder Zeraim* and *Maseches Shekalim* of *Talmud Yerushalmi,* being the first published commentator to undertake such a task. The commentary on *Berachos* was first published by R' Meir (Marcus) Lehmann in Mainz (5635/1875), and later in some editions of *Talmud Yerushalmi.* The entire commentary to *Zeraim* was published in a series of volumes together with *Emunas Yosef* by R' Yosef Dinkeles (Jerusalem, 5694-5727/1934-1967). The commentary to *Shekalim* was published (Jerusalem, 5718/1958) together with *Har Ephraim* by R' Ephraim Garbus. R' Shlomo also composed a short treatise on the laws of *shechitah* and *bedikah* entitled *Hilchos Shechitah UBedikos* (Constantinople, 5291/1531). *R' Shmuel de Medina (*Teshuvos Maharashdam, Yoreh Deah* §40) relates that R' Shlomo attempted to introduce in Safed some leniencies in regard to *bedikah* which were practiced in Salonica, but was opposed by *R' Yaakov bei Rav.

He also compiled a Talmudic text, culled from various Talmudic sources, to tractate Ediyos, which has no Talmud, and composed a commentary on this text. *Chida, who mentions this work, considers it a rare accomplishment of the highest caliber. This work, as well as the commentary to Zeraim, is cited often by *R' Shlomo Adeni in his commentary (Meleches Shlomo) on Mishnayos. According to some sources, R' Shlomo Sirilio succeeded *R' Levi ibn Chaviv in his post as rabbi of Jerusalem.

R' Shalom Shachna of Lublin

רַבִּי שָׁלוֹם שַׁכְנָא בֶּן יוֹסֵף מלוּבְּלִין

d. Lublin, Poland, 1 Kislev 5319/1558

R' Shalom Shachna was one of the most prominent disciples of *R' Yaakov Pollak, and he continued the process of Talmudic development in Poland inaugurated by his master.

After R' Yaakov Pollak's death in 5290/1530, R' Shalom Shachna was appointed his successor as rabbi of Lublin and head of the great Talmudic academy founded by R' Yaakov. The epitaph engraved on R' Shalom's gravestone states that he stood at the head of a yeshivah for forty years without being paid at all for his efforts. R' Shalom Shachna followed his master's method of study, termed, chilukim or pilpulim; this was a very ingenious and intricate manner of study (see *R' Yaakov Pollak). Thousands of students flocked to R' Shalom Shachna and he thus headed one of the greatest yeshivos to ever exist in Poland. Among his most prominent pupils was *Rama (R' Moshe Isserles), who later became R' Shalom Shachna's son-in-law.

R' Shalom Shachna was revered as the greatest scholar of his day in all of Poland, according to the historian *R'

David Ganz. Rama, in his notes to Yesod Olam, states that all the great Polish rabbinical scholars of the following generation were disciples of R' Shalom Shachna.

Like his master R' Yaakov Pollak, R' Shalom Shachna did not write any works. His son revealed that the reason for this was the great modesty of his father, who wished not to be relied upon in the halachic decisions of future generations (Teshuvos Rama §25).

After his death, R' Shachna's post as rabbi and rosh yeshivah in Lublin was filled by his son R' Yisrael, a celebrated Talmudist. A lengthy responsum by him is included in Teshuvos Rama (§25).

R' Kalman Vermaisa (of Worms)

רַבִּי קַלְמָן ווירְמַייזָא

d. Lemberg (Lvov), Poland (now Russia)
2 Iyar 5320/1560

R' Kalman was one of the first prominent rabbinical figures to spread Talmudic study in Poland. Serving as rabbi of Lemberg for forty-two years, he saw virtually thousands of students pass through his yeshivah. A responsum by him is printed in Teshuvos Rama (§15), followed by a responsum by his son-in-law, R' Elazar ben Mano'ach. *R' Yosef Katz refers to both R' Kalman and his son-in-law as 'the sages of our generation' (Teshuvos She'eiris Yosef §1). R' Moshe ben Elazar Isserles (Rama's nephew and grandson of Maharshal) mentions R' Kalman as one of the authorities who praised Maharshal's Yam shel Shlomo, and refers to him as 'a sage presiding over the yeshivah, the splendor of Israel and its pride, its king and lord, his eminence the gaon — R' Kalman Vermaisa' (Preface to Yam shel Shlomo, Chulin).

R' Meir Katzenellenbogen (Maharam Padua)

רַבִּי מֵאִיר בֶּן [שְׁמוּאֵל] יִצְחָק קַצֶנֶלְנְבּוֹיגֶן (מַהֲרַ"ם פַּדוּבָה)

b. Prague (?) Bohemia, (now Czechoslovakia) 5242/1482
d. Padua, Italy, 10 Shevat 5325/1565

In his youth R' Meir studied under *R' Yaakov Pollak, and later he traveled to Italy and studied under *R' Yehudah Mintz. The latter's son and successor, *R' Avraham Mintz, was so impressed by the young student that he chose him to be his son-in-law.

Upon the death of R' Avraham Mintz in 5285/1525, R' Meir was appointed his successor and became Chief Rabbi of Padua, a position he held until his death.

R' Meir maintained a halachic correspondence with *R' Ovadyah Sforno, *R' Moshe Alashkar, R' Eliyahu ben Elkanah Capsali, *R' Yochanan Treves and, especially, *Rama, the latter also being a relative. His responsa (Teshuvos Maharam Padua, Venice, 5313/1553) were printed together with what remained of the responsa of R' Yehudah Mintz, including some notes by R' Avraham Mintz on the laws of divorce and chalitzah. Some of R' Meir's responsa also appear in the responsa of his kinsman, R' Moshe Isserles. Both Maharshal and Rama regarded R' Meir as one of the greatest scholars of the age.

R' Meir's notes on the Rambam were published in the edition of the Mishneh Torah which was printed in Venice by Aloisio Bragadini in 5510/1550. In the same year a competitor — Marco Guistiniani — printed a competing edition of Rambam and found it necessary to print in his edition a selection of Maharam's notes, to which a comment had been added minimizing the scholarship of these notes and belittling their (unnamed in this edition) author. *Radvaz wrote a detailed critique of these notes in his responsa (§1613-81), but was probably unaware of their author's identity.

The consequences of this incident transcended the monetary squabble between the two Gentile publishers. R' Meir, who was a partner to Bragadini in this edition of Rambam, turned to R' Moshe Isserles in Cracow to render his opinion on the matter. Rama (Teshuvos Rama, §10) responded with a beautifully argued responsum containing many novel points. Rama argued that although Guistiniani was a Gentile he was compelled to follow Jewish law in this regard, and that he was to be restricted to selling his edition only after R' Meir had sold all the copies of his edition. Finally, Rama pronounced a ban [cherem] on Guistiniani's edition as long as the conditions stipulated in the verdict had not been fulfilled.

This did not end the matter. Guistiniani appealed to the ecclesiastical powers and the matter was brought before the pope. Testimony was given by apostates, among them Solomon Morano, the grandson of *R' Eliyahu Bachur, that the texts printed by Bragadini contained calumnies against the Christian religion and its founder. As a result of this, in 5313/1553 Pope Julius III issued a law against the printing or possession of the Talmud.

A comment by R' Meir on a quote from the Talmud cited in Yalkut Shimoni was published in the edition of that work printed in Venice (5326/1566) and subsequent editions. A tract (unpublished) dealing with kabbalistic matters was in the possession of the proofreader of the edition of Sefer HaKaneh printed in Prague (5370/1610), and is ascribed by him in his comments to a R' Meir of Padua, but it has been shown that probably this does not refer to R' Meir Katzenellenbogen.

R' Meir is one of the signers of a far-reaching rabbinic enactment (takanah) signed in Padua in the year 5314/1554, forbidding the publication of any work without the approbation of recognized rabbinic authorities. This led to the establishment of the familiar custom, honored all over the Jewish world, to garner haskamos from prominent rabbis prior to the publication of a sefer.

R' Yehoshua Soncin

רַבִּי יְהוֹשֻׁעַ שׁוֹנְצִין

d. Constantinople (now Istanbul), Turkey
5329/1569

R' Yehoshua served as rabbi of the Majorcan community of Constantinople. He authored Nachalah LeYehoshua (Constantinople, 5491/1731), responsa and chidushim on tractates Eruvin and Shevuos.

One of those responsa is the prime source for a historical event and sheds much light on the complexity of the issues faced by Jewish leaders at that time. The Jewish community in the important mercantile center, Ancona, was predominantly comprised of Marranos who had escaped from Spain and Portugal. This thriving town was then within the borders of the Papal States. When the infamous Paul IV assumed the papacy he directed the brunt of his anti-Jewish persecution at the unfortunate Marranos, whom he proclaimed to be apostatizing Christians subject to the strictures of the Inquisition. Many of the Jews converted to Christianity, but twenty-three held to their faith steadfastly and were publicly burned. The Jews in Turkey, especially the influential Spanish and Portuguese communities, were outraged at these developments, and they endeavored to place a ban on trade with Ancona. This ban, if approved by the rabbis, would have effectively destroyed the trade of Ancona, and established its competitor city, Pesaro, as a prime port of trade with Turkey. R' Yehoshua, however, vigorously opposed the ban on the grounds that it would harm the Jews remaining in Ancona, as well as endanger the other Jews in Italy.

*R' Chaim Benveniste, author of Knesses HaGedolah, was a descendant of R' Yehoshua.

R' Moshe Cordovero (Ramak)

רַבִּי מֹשֶׁה בֶּן יַעֲקֹב קוֹרְדוֹבֵּירוֹ (רמַ"ק)

b. 5282/1522
d. Safed, Eretz Yisrael, 23 Tammuz 5330/1570

Ramak studied Talmud and halachah under *R' Yosef Caro, and at the young age of twenty was ordained by *R' Yaakov bei Rav with the newly re-established semichah.

R' Moshe studied kabbalah at a young age under his brother-in-law, *R' Shlomo Alkabetz. He became the most recognized kabbalist of Safed and had many renowned disciples, among them *R' Eliyahu de Vidas, author of the ethical classic Reishis Chachmah, and *R' Avraham Galante.

Ramak authored a classic work on the fundamental concepts of the kabbalah, entitled Pardes Rimonim (Salonica, c. 5340/1580). Because of its great importance, this work was summarized by two of the greatest kabbalists of R' Moshe's generation. *R' Menachem Azaryah of Fano, a great admirer of Ramak, wrote a partial condensation called Pelach HaRimon (Venice, 5360/1600), and Ramak's disciple *R' Shmuel Galiko wrote Assiss Rimonim (Venice, 5361/1601), a condensation of the entire work. Ramak's other works are Or Ne'erav (Venice, 5347/1587), an introduction to the study of kabbalah; Sefer Gerushin (Venice, 5361/1601), kabbalistic interpretations on verses of the Torah composed during pilgrimages to the grave sites of the *Tannaim* and *Amoraim* during periods of self-imposed exile; *Tomer Devorah* (Venice, 5348/1588), an ethical and inspirational treatise which was reprinted numerous times; *Elimah Rabasi* (Brody, 5641/1881) on kabbalistic terminology; *Shiur Komah* (Warsaw, 5643/1883), expositions of kabbalistic topics; *Tefillah LeMoshe* (Premysl, 5652/1892), a commentary on the *siddur*; and *Or Yakar*, a voluminous commentary on the *Zohar*. *Chida (R' Chaim Y.D. Azulai) relates that R' Menachem Azaryah of Fano paid Ramak's widow a small fortune to have *Or Yakar* copied. This work remained unpublished for centuries, probably because of its great size, but (most of it) has appeared in recent times. To date, fourteen folio-sized volumes of this work have been published (Jerusalem, 5722-46/1962-86), with three volumes covering the commentary to the *Tikunei Zohar Chadash* (Jerusalem, 5732-35/1962-65).

He also wrote a kabbalistic commentary to the *piyut Atah Konanta* which describes the Temple service of the *Kohen Gadol* on *Yom Kippur* (said by the Sephardic and Chassidic congregations in the *Mussaf* of *Yom Kippur*), published (Venice, 5347/1587) as *Peirush Seder HaAvodah*; *Zivchei Shelamim* (Lublin, 5373/1613), commentaries on the prayers of *Rosh Hashanah* and *Yom Kippur*; *Maamar Nichbad VeYakar* (Lvov, 5549/1789); and *Derishos BeInyanei HaMalachim*, published in the first edition of R' Reuven Margolies' *Malachei Elyon* (Jerusalem, 5705/1945).

R' Moshe also authored commentaries on the Torah and *Sefer Yetzirah,* which were not published.

In Ramak's works the tendency to explain and elucidate the fundamentals of the *kabbalah* in rationalistic terms is very prominent, and the philosophical theories of earlier Jewish thinkers are often discussed in depth.

After Ramak's death, the *kabbalah* of the hitherto almost unknown *R' Yitzchak Luria (the Arizal) gained ascendancy, and there was a tendency to discredit Ramak's works. R' Menachem Azaryah of Fano warned against this tendency and asserted that the study of Ramak's works had not lost its validity (Preface to *Pelach HaRimon*).

Ramak was greatly revered by his contemporaries, and R' Yitzchak Luria testified to seeing a pillar of fire proceeding before the coffin at his funeral (see *Kesubos 17a*).

R' Menachem HaBavli

רַבִּי מְנַחֵם בֶּן מֹשֶׁה הַבַּבְלִי

d. Hebron, Eretz Yisrael, c. 5331/1571

Leaving his native Bagdad with his father and brothers, R' Menachem settled in Safed and was a reputable halachist. A responsum by him is printed in *Teshuvos R' Yosef Caro (Dinei Gittin §14).*

R' Menachem authored *Taamei HaMitzvos* (Lublin, 5331/1571) on the reasons for the commandments, with kabbalistic overtones; this is quoted in *Shelah* and other works. In some editions of this work, the author has erroneously been listed as R' Menachem HaBavli Recanati, confusing the author with the great thirteenth-century author *R' Menachem Recanati who also wrote a work titled *Ta'amei HaMitzvos*. In his introduction, R' Menachem relates that he also composed a much longer work on the reasons for the commandments, entitled *Taamei HaMitzvos HaAruchos;* however, this work has not been preserved.

R' Menachem left Safed, the most populous city of *Eretz Yisrael* during that time, in order to reside in Hebron, the resting place of the Patriarchs. In the introduction to his *sefer* he stipulates that all income derived from its sales should be used to construct a wall around the Jewish quarter in Hebron for protection from its enemies.

R' Moshe Isserles (Rama)

רַבִּי מֹשֶׁה בֶּן יִשְׂרָאֵל אִיסֶרְלִיש (רְמָ"א)

b. Cracow, Poland, c. 5290/1530
d. Cracow, Poland, 18 Iyar 5332/1572

R' Moshe was born into one of the most prestigious families in Cracow. His father, R' Yisrael Isser ben Yosef, was himself a *talmid chacham* of note (Rama mentions him several times in his *Darchei Moshe*), an extremely successful businessman noted for his philanthropy and a lay leader (*parnes umanhig*) of the Cracow Jewish community, which was one of the most respected in sixteenth-century Europe. Reb Moshe's cognomen, Isserles, is merely an allusion to his father's middle name, Isserl (a common nickname for Yisrael). R' Yisrael's father, R' Yosef, and the latter's father-in-law, R' Moshe Auerbach, were all lay leaders (*parnassim*) of the *kehillah*, and R' Yisrael's mother, Gittel, was especially prominent for her philanthropy. Rama's maternal grandfather, R' Elazar Shrentzel, was a son-in-law of R' Yechiel Luria, first rabbi of Brisk, and grandfather to *R' Shlomo Luria and *Maharam Padua. Rama's brother, R' Elazar, was a son-in-law of R' Shlomo Luria, and his sister, Miriam, was married to R' Pinchas Horowitz (d. Cracow, 17 *Teves* 5378/1618), a noted scholar and *rosh yeshivah*.

R' Moshe studied under *R' Shalom Shachna of Lublin, the foremost *rosh yeshivah* in Poland. His master was so fond of him that he took him as his son-in-law. Shortly after his marriage, the young R' Moshe was appointed as a rabbi in Cracow, an astoundingly prestigious post for so young a man. In a responsum, dated 5310/1550, Rama was asked by his aged and venerable kinsman Maharam Padua to rule on a sensitive case regarding the publication of *Rambam's *Mishneh Torah* (see *R' Meir Katzenellenbogen).

In the year 5312/1551-52 misfortune stalked R' Moshe. On 10 Teves his mother, Dinah Malkah, died; on 11 Sivan his twenty-year-old wife — Golda, daughter of R' Shalom Shachna — followed; and on 27 Sivan, Drezl, his aged maternal grandmother, passed away. To perpetuate their memory Rama's father built a synagogue which came to be known as 'The Rama's *Shul*'. R' Moshe married the daughter of R' Mordechai Katz, a respected member of the Cracow community; she was also the sister of *R' Yosef Katz, author of *Teshuvos She'eiris Yosef*.

Rama established a Talmudic academy in Cracow, where he delivered his brilliant discourses, and also supplied the students' material needs.

Among Rama's better-known disciples were *R' Mordechai Yafeh, author of *Levush*, who defended the rulings of his mentor often in his works; *R' Yehoshua Falik HaKohen, author of *Sefer Me'iras Einayim* (*Sma*); *R' David Ganz, famed historian and astronomer; *R' Hirsh Shor, one of the teachers of *R' Yoel Sirkis (the *Bach*); *R' Binyamin Solnik, author of *Masas Binyamin*; *R' Menachem Tiktin; and R' Avraham Horowitz, the father of *R' Yeshayah Horowitz (author of *Shelah*).

Rama was recognized as a halachic authority while still a young man. He carried on an extensive halachic correspondence with his older contemporaries, such as Maharam Padua, *R' Yosef Caro, and *Maharshal. Rama's writings, as far as they are known to us, do not betray that he was an enthusiast of the intricate *pilpul* method of study (see *R' Yaakov Pollak) prevalent in Poland at that time, and rather stressed the halachic aspect of Talmudic study, preferring the more apparent meanings of the texts.

In addition to Talmud and *halachah*, Rama immersed himself in the study of medieval Jewish philosophy and *kabbalah*, believing that the two systems were compatible and the supposed differences between them were a mere matter of semantics. The keen interest in philosophy shown by students in Polish yeshivos in the period preceding the Cossack pogroms of 5408/1648 and 5415/1655 (as related by *R' Chaim Yair Bacharach in *Teshuvos Chavos Yair*) may perhaps be attributed to Rama's interest in this subject. His disciple R' Avraham Horowitz composed a commentary (*Chessed L'Avraham*) to Rambam's philosophical introduction to his commentary on *Avos* (*Shemonah Perakim*), and R' Mordechai Yafeh wrote comments to Rambam's *Moreh Nevuchim* (*Levush Pinas Yikras*). Rama's elder contemporary, R' Shlomo Luria, strongly took him to task for his interest in secular studies — especially philosophy — and took the opportunity to point out grammatical errors in a responsum written by R' Moshe, adding sarcastically that R' Moshe would have spent his time more profitably by concentrating on the study of Hebrew grammar instead of on the works of the Greek (Aristotle). Rama answered his kinsman with great respect but did not defer to his views. He attributed his purported mistakes in grammar to established usage — which was indeed at variance with Biblical usage — not to rank ignorance. Rama also evinced a keen interest in astronomy and history, and by his personal example probably influenced his disciple R' David Ganz to immerse himself in these studies.

Rama's fame rests upon his works, especially his annotations to R' Yosef Caro's *Shulchan Aruch*. Being that R' Yosef Caro adopted the practices of the Sephardic communities, his code was not usable for Ashkenazic Jewry until Rama added his supplement, called *Sefer HaMapah*, consisting of notes inserted into the text (Cracow, 5331/1571). This work established Rama as the pre-eminent halachist for all of Ashkenazic Jewry, who accepted the *Shulchan Aruch* — as modified by these notes — as the penultimate code of law. Where there is conflict between R' Yosef Caro and Rama, the Ashkenazim generally follow Rama's decision. But the accomplishments achieved by Rama with these notes transcended the parochial needs of Ashkenazic Jewry. His notes elevated R' Yosef Caro's *Shulchan Aruch* from an individual expression of halachic view, to the level of an authoritative halachic codex worthy of use by all of Jewry. It is probably this unique aspect of this joint work which contributed greatly to its eventual universal acceptance and thus transformed the *Shulchan Aruch* from a mere halachic compendium into the ultimate *halachah* authority. On a spiritual level Rama's role may perhaps be compared to that of *Beis Hillel* in the *Mishnah*, whose rulings, the Talmud states, were accepted because of their humility. It surely was Rama's humility which induced him to express his opinions in the form of glosses to a contemporary work rather than opt for personal accomplishment in the form of an original, individual work. The very name he gave his glosses demonstrates this spirit. They are aptly named *Sefer HaMapah* (the covering); they are merely the cloth which covers the 'set table' (*Shulchan Aruch*) and lends it grace.

Rama's rulings are heavily based on the opinions of the Tosafists and later

German and French scholars, including the rulings of scholars preceding him only by a generation or two. In this he differed from Maharshal who favored an original approach to *halachah*, based mainly on the interpretation of the Talmudic texts. He also differed from R' Yosef Caro, not in his basic approach to *halachah*, for the latter, too, leaned on the rulings of earlier authorities, but in his choice of authorities: R' Yosef Caro's *Shulchan Aruch* is based almost exclusively on the views of *Rif, Rambam and *Rosh, with heavy emphasis on Rambam. Another distinctive feature of Rama's approach is his reverence for time-hallowed custom, and he warns to be careful not to disparage Jewish customs, 'for they were not instituted for naught'. He also made extensive use of the rule that in cases involving substantial monetary loss (*hefseid merubah*) more lenient views may be followed.

Rama also authored *Darchei Moshe*, short comments on *Tur* and *Beis Yosef*, which formed the basis for his glosses on *Shulchan Aruch*. The author had originally envisioned this as an encyclopedic work, elaborating on all the conflicting views regarding any matter touched upon in *Tur*, and concluding with the final *halachah*. He had already completed the part on *Orach Chaim* when R' Yosef Caro published his commentary (*Beis Yosef*) to *Orach Chaim* and *Yoreh Deah* (Venice, 5310-5311/ 1550-1551). Rama realized that he had been pre-empted, shortened his work and completed it in the form of a complement to *Beis Yosef*. Rama never saw this work published; it was printed in a truncated form together with the *Tur* (Berlin, 5462-63/1702-03) and is today a standard feature of that work. The work as it was abridged by Rama was published (without *Tur*) on *Orach Chaim*

(Fuerth, 5520/1760), and *Yoreh Deah* (Sulzbach, 5452/1692) accompanied by notes called *Orach Mishor* by R' Yochanan Kremenitzer (author of a work by the same name on tractate *Nazir* and *Rambam Hilchos Nezirus*). *Darchei Moshe* on *Choshen Mishpat* has been ‚published recently (Jerusalem, Vol. I, 5739/1979; Vol. II, 5442/1982).

Another of Rama's major works is *Toras Chatas* (Cracow, 5329/1569), a codex on dietary laws modeled on *R' Yitzchak of Duren's *Shaarei Dura*. Rama's colleague, *R' Chaim ben Betzalel, severely criticized *Toras Chatas* in his *Vikuach Mayim Chaim* (Amsterdam, 5472/1612). In his preface R' Chaim lists his general arguments against *Toras Chatas*. Among the reasons is a flat rejection of the entire trend to present *halachah* in codex form. *Halachah* has to be rooted in solid Talmudic scholarship and its codification leads to the temptation to dispense with the arduous task of studying the texts and to rely only on the authority of the codifier. Besides, Rama had considered only the Polish customs, which even at that early date differed substantially from the usage in Germany. R' Yosef Shaul Nathanson wrote a refutation of R' Chaim's arguments called *Toras Moshe*, published with *Vikuach Mayim Chaim* (Zolkiew, 5619/ 1859, in *Chamishah Sefarim*). The *Toras Chatas* too was accepted as an authoritative work and is discussed extensively by *Shach* and other commentators to *Shulchan Aruch Yoreh Deah*. Extensive commentaries were composed to it: *Minchas Yaakov* by *R' Yaakov Reisher (Prague, 5449/1689); *Damessek Eliezer* by R' Eliezer ben Yehoshua of Shebreshin (Wilhermsdorf, 5478/1718), and others. An extensive commentary — *Toras HaAsham* by *R' Yom Tov Lipman Heller — has recently been published (Jerusalem, 5737/1977).

Besides his halachic works, Rama wrote *Mechir Yayin* (Cremona, 5319/ 1559), an allegorical exposition on the Book of *Esther*. Rama wrote this work in the year 5316/1556 when he fled Cracow because of a plague and found himself alone and without *sefarim* in nearby Shidlow on Purim. In order to participate in the rejoicing even under these unfortunate circumstances, Rama conceived the novel idea to write a commentary on *Esther*, which he presented to his father in lieu of *mishlo'ach manos*. He also wrote *Toras HaOlah* (Prague, 5330/ 1570), a philosophical explanation of the Temple and its sacrifices. In this work, Rama mentions his commentary to the aggadic portions of the Talmud, which had not been published.

Rama's responsa (Cracow, 5400/ 1640) contain one hundred thirty-two halachic communications, some of them by his colleagues. His commentary to the *Zohar*, cited by *R' Eliyahu Loanz in his (manuscript) commentary (*Aderes Eliyahu*) to *Zohar*, has remained unpublished. R' Eliyahu's work was seen by *Chida and *R' Ephraim Zalman Margulies.

An excerpt from his *chidushim* to Talmud is printed in tractate *Bava Metzia* of the Talmud edition printed in Amsterdam in 5404-05/1644-45.

Rama also wrote notes to many works, among them historical notes to Chapter 18 of part IV in *Yesod Olam* (in most editions of *Sefer Yuchasin*); *R' Eliyahu Mizrachi's super-commentary on Rashi, printed in some of the editions of the *Chumash* with *Ha'ameik Davar* (by Netziv); *Mordechai* (in the printed editions); and on R' Yonah's *Issur VeHetter HaAruch* (*Yad Rama*, Lvov, 5626/1866). He also annotated Rambam's *Moreh Nevuchim* (*Guide for the Perplexed*) and *R' Yaakov Weil's *Shechitos UBedikos*.

R' Chaim Michel (*Otzros Chaim*) reports that Rama wrote a commentary on the Hebrew translation of a medieval work on astronomy. This work was intended to instruct beginners in this discipline, and remains unpublished.

A unique facet of Rama's accomplishments was his expertise as a scribe. Rama obtained a special authoritative *tikun* (manual for writing Torah scrolls) from Safed through the services of R' Yosef Caro, and wrote a Torah scroll following its instructions. It is said that it contained twenty-four variations from most other scrolls in Eastern Europe. This scroll, which existed up to World War II, was deposited in 'The Rama's *Shul*' and would be read from on selected occasions.

The reverence for Rama is attested to by the yearly pilgrimages to his grave on his *yahrzeit*, which are observed to this day, and Jewry's appreciation for his accomplishments is fittingly summed up in the inscription which appears on his tombstone: "From Moshe (Rambam) to Moshe (Rama) there was no one like Moshe."

R' Yitzchak Luria Ashkenazi, The Ari

רַבִּי יִצְחָק בֶּן שְׁלֹמֹה לוּרְיָא (אַר״י - אֱלֹקִי ר' יִצְחָק) אַשְׁכְּנַזִי

b. Jerusalem, Eretz Yisrael, 5294/1534
d. Safed, Eretz Yisrael, 5 Av 5332/1572

Most eminent of all the kabbalists, R' Yitzchak was born in Jerusalem and descended (at least on the paternal side) from Ashkenazim, as attested by his surname (Luria = Lorraine) and the denomination 'Ashkenazi', appended to his name. This is also confirmed by his disciples.

Losing his father while yet an infant, he moved from Jerusalem with his mother to her brother's estate in Cairo, Egypt. There the Ari received his formal

Talmudic instruction from *Radvaz and *R' Betzalel Ashkenazi. At a young age he was recognized as an accomplished Talmudist and halachist.

In 5289/1549, the Ari married his uncle's daughter and continued his studies undisturbed, as his uncle provided generously for all his needs. Following his marriage, the Ari spent six years of intensive study with R' Betzalel Ashkenazi, and collaborated with him in the compilation of *Shittah Mekubetzes* on *Maseches Zevachim*.

After this period, the Ari began to immerse himself in the study of *kabbalah*. He would spend the weekdays in a house near the Nile, where he would pray and study in complete solitude, and return home for Shabbos, when he would converse only in the holy tongue. His saintliness was obvious to all who saw him, and all were awed by his appearance.

The Ari attained great heights in the comprehension of the *kabbalah*, and surpassed his predecessors. Elijah the Prophet would instruct him in the sacred teachings of *kabbalah* and reveal to him previously unknown mysteries. It was Elijah who revealed to him that he was to ascend to *Eretz Yisrael* and settle in Safed, where he was to transmit all his teachings to *R' Chaim Vital, as he was soon to depart from the world.

The Ari arrived in Safed in 5330/1570 and immediately went to the home of *R' Moshe Cordovero, the recognized head of the kabbalistic school. However, R' Moshe died shortly after the Ari's arrival, and the Ari eulogized him in glowing terms.

After the death of R' Moshe Cordovero, the Ari was recognized as the greatest kabbalist of his generation and also as a holy man with the power to perform miracles, read a person's thoughts, and predict the future.

In keeping with Elijah's instructions, the Ari occupied himself primarily with instructing R' Chaim Vital. R' Chaim invited other disciples to join their studies, even though the Ari was displeased with this type of publicity. More than once, the Ari rebuked R' Chaim for involving other disciples in their studies, and warned that he would regret this action; but R' Chaim, wishing to share knowledge with his colleagues, persisted in this practice. It was said that the Ari's early death at the age of only thirty-eight was due to the fact that he was induced by R' Chaim Vital to reveal sublime secrets to the latter's colleagues who were not yet worthy of hearing them.

Except for a few notations, the Ari left no writings, because, when he began to lecture on a topic, there was such a flow of wisdom that it was simply impossible for him to commit it all to writing. This was so not only when he taught *kabbalah*; even in Talmudic study he would offer six different lectures each day on a particular topic, which also were not written. Much of his great legacy was preserved by R' Chaim Vital, most of whose numerous works represent the lectures he had heard from the master.

The Ari lies buried in Safed. His tomb remains a holy shrine for pilgrimage to this day.

R' David ibn Zimra (Radvaz)

רַבִּי דָוִד בֶּן שְׁלֹמֹה אִבְּן זִמְרָא (רַדְבַּ"ז)

b. Spain, c. 5240/1480
d. Safed, Eretz Yisrael, 5333/1573

R' David arrived in Safed as a child after the Spanish expulsion. According to some, his parents first stayed in Fez, Morocco, before settling in Safed. In Safed he became acquainted with R' Yosef Iscandari when he (R' David) was thirteen years old. (R' Yosef was not his mentor as supposed by some writers; see *Teshuvos Radvaz* §596.) *Chida reports that (probably in Safed) Radvaz studied under R' Yosef Saragossi, "a rabbi who was accustomed to miracles". [R' Yosef Saragossi was presumably from a Spanish family which had settled in Sicily. A descendant of R' Yosef relates that his grandfather was exiled from Sicily (in 5252/1492) and that he sanctified *Hashem's* Name in public. R' Yosef settled in Cairo and later in Safed.] It appears that at this period of his life R' David left Safed. It is not known where he spent the interim years before settling in Egypt. Perhaps he spent this part of his life in Jerusalem. R' David was a diligent student and in a few years was known far and wide as an accomplished rabbinic authority.

Radvaz emigrated to Egypt in about 5274/1514, and settled in Cairo. In a short time he was recognized as Chief Rabbi of Egypt, a post which he held for forty years. He did not, however, earn his livelihood from the rabbinate, but engaged in business, becoming a wealthy and benevolent merchant.

Radvaz was also very active in the communal affairs of the various Egyptian congregations, settling their disputes and grievances. He also introduced important enactments in the religious life of Egypt. Among these was abolishing the custom of using the Seleucid era as the basis for determining the year used as the date on bills of divorce or of sale. This practice, known as *minyan shtaros,* had been in use in the East since the times of Alexander the Great. It was discontinued in *Eretz Yisrael* upon the establishment of the Hasmonean kingdom, but persisted in the rest of the East even after the Hellenistic empires founded by Alexander's successors had disintegrated (see *Avodah Zarah* 10a). In Egypt, *minyan shtaros* was used until it was abolished by Radvaz.

Radvaz headed a large academy in Cairo comprising many disciples, among them *R' Betzalel Ashkenazi, *R' Yitzchak Luria (the Ari *HaKadosh*), and *R' Yaakov Castro.

In 5313/1553, Radvaz returned to *Eretz Yisrael* and settled in Jerusalem. Observing the dire straits of the community, he abolished the old practice under which Torah scholars were obligated to pay only half the amount of taxes as non-scholars, and made everyone pay equally. Continuously worsening economic conditions, and the fact that the pasha had cast his eye on Radvaz's wealth, forced Radvaz to leave Jerusalem and settle in Safed.

There he finally found peace and was greatly honored and revered by the local *beis din* and by *R' Yosef Caro, because of his great erudition and his advanced age. In decisions signed by the entire *beis din,* R' Yosef Caro would honor Radvaz and let him sign first (*Avkas Rochel* §140, 187).

Radvaz's works include his extensive responsa (7 volumes were published in various places and, later, all together in Warsaw [5643/1883] in two volumes, and an additional volume of responsa was published recently [Bnei Brak, 5735/1975]); *Magen David* (Amsterdam, 5473/1713), a kabbalistic treatise on the alphabet; *Metzudas David* (Zolkiew, 5622/1862), a kabbalistic exposition of the six hundred thirteen commandments; *Migdal David* (Lemberg, 5643/1883), a kabbalistic commentary on *Song of Songs;* *Klalei Gemara* (in *Meharerei Nemeirim,* Venice, 5359/1599), *chidushim* on the Talmud quoted in *Shittah Mekubetzes;* and a commentary on *Rambam's *Mishneh Torah* wherever there is no *Maggid Mishneh.* Of this, *Yekar Tiferes* (on *Haflaah* and *Zera'im*) was published in

Smyrna (5517/1757), in the Rambam edition of Warsaw (5642/1882) and in later standard editions; on *Kedushah* and *Shoftim* (ibid.); *Hilchos Shluchin Ve-Shutfin* and *Avadim* in *Rambam*, Shulsinger edition (New York, 5706/1946), and on *Sefer Avodah* (ibid.). A selection of Radvaz's responsa pertaining to difficult passages in *Rambam's code was compiled by R' B. Zuckerman and printed in the Shulsinger edition of the code. R' David also composed a lengthy poetic treatise, *Kesser Malchus*, an imitation of ibn Gabirol's *Kesser Malchus* utilizing the concepts of the *kabbalah* (printed in *Or Kadmon*, Venice, 5463/1703).

R' Shlomo Luria (Maharshal)

רַבִּי שְׁלֹמֹה בֶּן יְחִיאֵל לוּרִיָא (מַהַרְשַׁ"ל)

b. Brisk (Brest-Litovsk), Poland (today Russia)
c. 5270/1510
d. Lublin, Poland, 12 Kislev 5334/1573

Maharshal was descended from a prominent rabbinical family which traced its genealogy to *Rashi, and was related to many of the prominent rabbis of his era, among them *R' Moshe Isserles and *R' Meir Katzenellenbogen. In his youth he studied under his father, R' Yechiel, and under his maternal grandfather, R' Yitzchak Kloiber. He became the son-in-law of R' Kalman Haberkasten — *rosh yeshivah* in Lvov and Ostroh — and when his father-in-law left Ostroh (to settle in Jerusalem), R' Shlomo succeeded him in his post. He served as rabbi and *rosh yeshivah* in Brisk, Ostroh, and finally (c. 5329/1569) in Lublin, where he officiated as *rosh yeshivah* while R' Yisrael, son of *R' Shalom Shachna, served as rabbi.

Some of the greatest scholars of his generation considered themselves his disciples: *R' Mordechai Yafeh and *R' Yehoshua Falik HaKohen (both of whom also studied under *Rama); *R' Chaim ben Betzalel, brother of *Maharal of Prague; and, according to a tradition preserved by R' Meir Perles in his biography of Maharal of Prague (*Megillas Yuchasin*, Warsaw, 5624/1864), Maharal himself studied under Maharshal.

Maharshal's approach to *halachah* was unique in his generation in that he refused to accept the views of the old masters without first tracing each subject to its source in the Talmud and commentaries and proceeded from there to ascertain the correct view. Independent and strong-minded, Maharshal did not hesitate to disagree with *R' Yosef Caro and even *Rambam in instances where, in his opinion, they had not penetrated the essence of the subject in making their decisions.

Maharshal opposed the method of *pilpul* used in the Polish yeshivos of his day (see *R' Yaakov Pollak); rather, he preferred the method of seeking to comprehend the plain meaning of the Talmudic discussions. He was especially interested in determining the correct text of the Talmud and *poskim*, and criticized R' Yosef Caro for basing many decisions on inaccurate texts. His *Chachmas Shlomo* is testimony to the pains he took to establish the correct version in the Talmud and its principal commentaries — Rashi and Tosafos — from existing manuscripts and from the context itself.

Maharshal was also very critical of R' Yosef Caro for the method of compromise he used in deciding the *halachah*, i.e., recognizing three authorities, *Rif, Rambam, and *Rosh, and in any controversy between the three deciding in favor of the majority. Maharshal opposed, firstly, the designation of only these three as authorities, and the complete disregarding of any other halachic opinions, especially those of the Tosafists; and secondly, not basing the decision on an independent evaluation of the merits of each opinion, measured by the criterion of its plausibility as a true interpretation of the Talmudic texts.

Maharshal's most important work was *Yam shel Shlomo*, a monumental Talmud commentary implementing the above-mentioned method of Talmudic analysis. It is essentially a collection of discourses or essays on the halachic points in each passage of Talmud, listing all the important opinions with a discussion about their compatibility with the Talmud text, and Maharshal's halachic conclusion based on the foregoing discussion. Originally composed for sixteen tractates, only seven have been preserved: *Bava Kama* (Prague, 5378/1618); *Chullin* (Cracow, 5395/1635); *Yevamos* (Altona, 5500/1740); *Beitzah* (Lublin, 5396/1636); *Kiddushin* (Berlin, 5526/1766); *Gittin* (Berlin, 5521/1761), and *Kesubos* (Warsaw, 5610/1850). His glosses on the Talmud with Rashi and *Tosafos,* entitled *Chachmas Shlomo*, are today included in every edition of the Talmud. Many of the entries in this work are unintelligible today because of the liberties publishers have taken in truncating them, and because many of Maharshal's proposed emendations have become the standard text. Maharshal criticized vehemently the emendations introduced in the (partial) Talmud edition published in Lublin (5319-28/1559-68), although these were based on the notes of the venerated *R' Shalom Shachna of Lublin and his son R' Yisrael.

Maharshal also authored responsa (Lublin, 5335/1575); *Yerios Shlomo* (Prague, 5369/1609), a super-commentary on Rashi's commentary to Torah, with remarks on *R' Eliyahu Mizrachi's commentary; *Amudei Shlomo* (Basel, 5360/1600), a commentary on *Smag;* and *Ateres Shlomo* (Lublin, 5358/1598), a commentary on *Shaarei Dura.*

Maharshal also wrote liturgical poems for the Sabbath, together with his own commentary on these poems (printed together with the laws and interpretation of *Birkas HaMazon* by R' Nassan Shapira under the title *Birkas HaMazon UZemiros* [Lublin, 5335/1575], and as *HaZemiros* [Lublin, 5356/1596]); *Menoras Zahav Tahor* (Prague, 5341/1581), a kabbalistic interpretation of *Psalm 67,* its arrangement in the form of a *menorah,* remarks about the significance of this psalm, together with prayers to be said with it, and a diagram in the form of a tree (*ilan*) showing the configuration of the kabbalistic *sefiros* (emanations). This work was later published with a commentary by *R' Meir Popperos (Shklov, 5545/1785).

A strong and independent personality, Maharshal had many halachic controversies with his contemporaries. His criticism of R' Shalom Shachna's emendations to the Talmud has already been alluded to. Besides .this, he did not hesitate to voice his objections to the intricate method of *pilpul* which was the hallmark of R' Shalom's yeshivah, thereby creating friction between the students of the two yeshivos. In his responsa Maharshal alludes, with chagrin, to the anguish caused by the 'disciples of the elder sage and his son.'

Rama was an exception to Maharshal's critical assessment of his colleagues; Maharshal was unstinting in his praise of this young kinsman. However, his friendship and love for Rama did not deter him from criticizing him for studying philosophy and secular subjects. He also castigated him severely for not using proper grammar in his writings (*Teshuvos Rama* §6). In their later years, the friendly relationship between those two great sages became strained because of Rama's criticism of Maharshal's decisions in matters of *issur v'hetter.*

Although Rama did not refer to him by name, Maharshal resented the strong and continuous criticism directed at him in Rama's *Toras Chatas* and castigated his younger kinsman in his *Yam shel Shlomo* to *Chullin*.

Maharshal was an extremely humble person. *Chida relates that even as the rabbi of such outstanding communities as Ostroh and Lublin, Maharshal did not hesitate to appoint a preacher whose duty it was to reproach him for any wrongdoing and preach to him on the ways of the righteous, and whenever this preacher would enter his home, the eminent Maharshal would immediately sit before him in a most humble manner and listen to his exhortation as would any common person.

Maharshal's enigmatic view on the use of the *Zohar* as a source of *halachah* illustrates his independence of thought and uncompromising devotion to the truth as he saw it. Maharshal was a devoted follower of the *kabbalah* and ranked the *Zohar* on the same level as other midrashic literature. He reproached his colleague Rama for dividing his attention between the *kabbalah* and philosophy (see *Teshuvos Rama* §6). Nevertheless, when he was asked to rule upon the question of whether the *tefillin* should be fastened to the arm while sitting, in accordance with the *Zohar*, Maharshal adamantly refused to entertain such a notion, citing the example of the sages of previous generations who had not changed their custom to accord with the *Zohar* in this matter, nor in the matter of putting on *tefillin* on the intermediate days of *Yom Tov* (*chol ha'moed*; *Teshuvos Maharshal* §98).

The story is related that once while Maharshal was in the midst of writing his *Yam shel Shlomo*, he had only a small candle, enough to burn for half an hour. Chagrined, he sat down and commenced to write rapidly in order to accomplish as much as possible. A miracle occurred: Maharshal continued writing throughout the entire night, and the candle did not extinguish itself until the break of dawn. Maharshal saw in this a sign that G-d was pleased with his work and hinted at this incident in his introduction to *Yam shel Shlomo* on tractate *Chullin*.

One of Maharshal's disciples, *R' Moshe Mos, wrote a very popular work titled *Matteh Moshe* (Cracow, 5351/ 1591) on the laws of everyday life and the festivals, which is replete with descriptions of the customs of his mentor.

R' Yosef ben Yehoshua HaKohen

ר' יוֹסֵף בֶּן יְהוֹשֻׁעַ הַכֹּהֵן

b. Avignon, France, Teves 5257/1496
d. Italy (?), after 5334/1574

R' Yosef's father, R' Yehoshua HaKohen, was a Spanish Jew who, upon the expulsion of Spanish Jewry from Spain, settled in Avignon, where he married his cousin Dulca; there his son Yosef was born. When Yosef was five years old the family moved to Genoa (Italy) where he spent his childhood years. In c. 5275/ 1515 the Jews were expelled from Genoa and Yosef's family settled in the small town of Nova, north of Milano. There Yosef was married in the year 5277/1517. Like many Italian Jews, he took up medicine as a profession by which to earn his livelihood. In 5298/1538 he returned to Genoa to practice as the official doctor of the town. However, twelve years later R' Yosef left Genoa because of competition and jealousy from other doctors. He settled in Voltaggio (north of Genoa) where he continued to practice his profession. In 5328/1568 he settled in Monferrato (northwest of Genoa) where he probably died. It was there that he finished his work *Emek*

HaBacha in 5335/1575 — when he was already 78 years old.

R' Yosef had a keen interest in history, and expended considerable effort to collect historical data and to compile it. He was especially interested in the martyrology of world-wide Jewry, and makes it a point to highlight Jewish suffering in his works. He authored *Divrei HaYamim LeMalchei Tzarfas UBeis Ottoman HaTogar* (lit. *A History of the Kings of France and [of] the Turkish Ottomans*; Sabbionetta, 5314/1554), a world history with special emphasis on the histories of France and the Ottoman Empire; and *Emek HaBacha* (Vienna, 5612/1852), a chronological recountal of Jewish suffering. This work has great importance for Jewish history, especially for its reports of Jewish persecution in Italy during the lifetime of R' Yosef. Among the sources upon which he drew was a similar work in Portuguese by a contemporary Marrano author, *Consola-cam as Tribulacoes de Israel*, by Samuel Usque (Ferrara, 5313/1513).

A collection of (personal) letters by R' Yosef has recently been published under the name *Igrono shel R' Yosef HaKohen Baal Emek HaBacha* (Jerusalem, 5746/1986).

R' Yosef Caro

רַבִּי יוֹסֵף בֶּן אֶפְרַיִם קָארוֹ

b. Toledo, Spain, 5248/1488
d. Safed, Eretz Yisrael, 13 Nissan 5335/1575

As a child, R' Yosef fled with his family to Constantinople, Turkey, because of the Spanish expulsion of 5252/1492. There he received his Talmudic training from his father, R' Ephraim, and his uncle, R' Yitzchak Caro. From Constantinople he moved to Adrianople (Edirne), Turkey, and finally made his way to *Eretz Yisrael*, where he arrived about 5295/1535. In the introduction to

Kesser Torah by R' Shmuel de Avila (Amsterdam, 5485/1725), a document is reproduced which contains a rabbinic decree published in Egypt in the year 5269/1509, and which is signed by a R' Ephraim Caro. If we are to assume that this signature belongs to R' Yosef Caro's father, we may then assume that it was during this period that R' Yosef Caro studied under R' Yaakov bei Rav (who was in Egypt at this time), and it is due to this period of instruction that he calls R' Yaakov 'my teacher' (cf. *Shem HaGedolim*).

Immediately upon arriving in Safed, R' Yosef was appointed a member of the *beis din* of *R' Yaakov bei Rav and enthusiastically supported the latter, whom he regarded as his teacher, in his endeavors to restore the ancient institution of *semichah* (authoritative rabbinical ordination and jurisdiction). R' Yosef was one of the four scholars who received *semichah* from R' Yaakov. Even after R' Yaakov's death, R' Yosef tried to carry on the *semichah* tradition by ordaining his pupil, *R' Moshe Alsheich, but he finally gave up his endeavors, convinced that he could not overcome the bitter opposition to the *semichah* revival. Significantly, he does not mention the attempt to revive the *semichah* in *Beis Yosef*, *Shulchan Aruch*, or *Kessef Mishneh*.

Upon the death of R' Yaakov bei Rav in 5306/1546, R' Yosef assumed the leadership of the Safed *beis din*. This *beis din* was probably the one held in the highest regard throughout the world at that time, and its opinion was sought on difficult issues by rabbis from all over. Even the eminent *R' Moshe Isserles, who lived in faraway Poland, turned to R' Yosef for his opinion on a difficult matter and addressed him in terms approaching awe (see *Teshuvos Rama* §47-48).

R' Yosef's imprint on shaping *halachah* is indisputable, as his works became the authoritative halachic code used to decide any point of Jewish law to this day. While still residing in Turkey, R' Yosef began his commentary to the *Turim* of *R' Yaakov ben Asher, and he worked on it for approximately twenty years. This commentary traces each ruling in *Tur* to its Talmudic source, cites all other opinions relevant to each ruling, and concludes with a decision.

R' Yosef completed this commentary in 5302/1542, and named it *Beis Yosef*. He then spent twelve years reviewing the work and adding supplementary notes (see his note at the end of *Beis Yosef* on *Choshen Mishpat*). During this time he also began to publish it: *Orach Chaim* (Venice, 5310-11/1550-51); *Yoreh Deah* (Venice, 5311/1551); *Even HaEzer* (Sabbionetta, 5313/1553); and *Choshen Mishpat* (Sabbionetta, 5319/1559). This commentary was warmly received. Within a few years the entire work had to be reprinted because of the great demand for it (Venice 5324-27/1564-67), and no less a personage than *R' Meir Katzenellenbogen of Padua took part in its redaction.

After having published the entire *Beis Yosef*, R' Yosef compiled a synopsis and index for it entitled *Shulchan Aruch* (Venice, 5325/1565), wherein only the halachic decisions are cited, broken down into simple paragraphs, without recourse to the sources and reasons behind the decisions. The purpose of this work, as outlined by R' Yosef in his preface, was twofold: (a) *To guide the student in deciding which view to accept as practical halachah.* R' Yosef set down as a guiding principle the tenet that out of the multitude of *poskim* three were the most authoritative: *Rif, *Rambam, and *Rosh. In most cases the *halachah* would be decided according to the majority view of any two of these, but in many cases Rambam's view was ac-

cepted even against the majority; (b) *to facilitate the memorization of the halachos.* R' Yosef divided the *Shulchan Aruch* into thirty sections so that the student who reviewed one section per day would go over the entire code once every month.

This work succeeded probably beyond the greatest expectations of the author, as it was to become the official code of Jewish law for all subsequent generations. Ironically, the success of this work probably prevented the realization of the author's plan for its constant review. As the *Shulchan Aruch* gained acceptance, commentaries and super-commentaries were compiled upon it, making speedy review impossible, and in subsequent generations new attempts were made to shorten the way to the final *halachah*. Among these are *Shulchan Aruch HaRav, Chayei Adam* and *Kitzur Shulchan Aruch.*

The *Shulchan Aruch* did not become the cornerstone of *halachah* without some opposition. Ashkenazic halachists protested that it did not take into consideration the views and customs of the Tosafists and many other Ashkenazic authorities, usually deciding in accordance with the Sephardic authorities, especially Rif and Rambam. Still another critique regarded the danger of deciding *halachah* without having knowledge of the Talmudic discussions on the point in question. Among the opposition stood *Maharshal; *R' Mordechai Yafeh, author of *Levush;* and *Maharam Lublin.

However, the *Shulchan Aruch* won acceptance by the Ashkenazic community through *R' Moshe Isserles (Rama), who added glosses to both *Beis Yosef* and *Shulchan Aruch,* subscribing to the customs of Ashkenazic Jewry. This definitely enabled the *Shulchan Aruch* to emerge as a universally acceptable work. Eventually many commentaries appeared on the *Shulchan Aruch* — *Magen Avraham, Turei Zahav, Shach,* and *Be'er HaGolah,* to mention just a few — and these helped R' Yosef Caro's work gain greater popularity than any other work since the Talmud.

R' Yosef Caro authored another monumental work, a commentary on Rambam's *Mishneh Torah* entitled *Kessef Mishneh* (Venice, 5334-35/1574-75), which has been published in almost every edition of Rambam.

As head of the Safed *beis din,* R' Yosef's opinion was frequently sought on complicated halachic questions. Some of his responses dealing with laws pertaining to *Even HaEzer* were published by his son Yehudah as *She'eilos UTeshuvos R' Yosef Caro* (Salonica, 5358/1598). Selected *chidushim* on *Gittin, Kiddushin,* and *Kesubos,* which had been delivered by R' Yosef as lectures in his yeshivah, were included in this volume. Additional responsa were published two centuries later under the title *Avkas Rochel* (Salonica, 5551/1791). These collections of responsa also include responsa by other scholars of the generation, and, in many cases, those dissenting with R' Yosef's view.

R' Yosef was an extremely saintly person: humble, devout, gentle and ascetic. He was a kabbalist and was intimate with his contemporary, the famed kabbalist, *R' Shlomo Alkabetz, who probably instructed him in the *kabbalah.* R' Yosef also had a heavenly spirit called a *maggid* (preacher) who would make himself known only by his voice, instruct R' Yosef in kabbalistic interpretation, and encourage him in his righteous endeavors. The interpretations on verses of the Torah as heard from the *maggid* were written down by R' Yosef and form the text of *Maggid Meisharim* (Part I: Lublin, 5406/1646; Part II: Venice, 5416/1656).

After the publication of *Beis Yosef,* R' Yosef continued his attempts to perfect the work by adding glosses which were later published in a separate volume under the title *Bedek HaBayis* (Salonica, 5365/1605); these were incorporated into subsequent editions of *Beis Yosef* itself. R' Yosef also wrote a supercommentary on *Rashi's and *Ramban's Torah commentaries, mentioned in his son's introduction to *She'eilos UTeshuvos R' Yosef Caro,* but over the centuries it was lost. R' Yosef Caro also authored a compilation of general rules pertinent to the study of the Talmud (*Klalei HaTalmud,* printed together with *Halichos Olam,* Venice, 5358/1598). His comments to the Torah, *Pirkei Avos,* and *Song of Songs* appear in the anthology *Or Tzaddikim* (Salonica, 5559/1599).

*Chida relates that when *Beis Yosef* first appeared, R' Yosef's contemporary, *R' Yosef ibn Lev of Constantinople, forbade his disciples to use the work. He claimed that it would reduce the students' familiarity with the Talmud, as previously a student of *Tur* needed to possess total command of the Talmud in order to trace each statement to its Talmudic source, while now one could rely upon the information supplied in *Beis Yosef.* He had sixty disciples, each a specialist in a particular Talmudic tractate, and during his lecture on *Tur,* R' Yosef ibn Lev, who had complete mastery of the Talmud, would call upon the student in whose tractate the source of a statement was to be found and ask him to recite it for all to hear. If a student failed to identify the source, R' ibn Lev himself would recite the correct answer. It once occurred, during such a session, that not one pupil could indicate the source of a statement in *Tur,* and even R' Yosef ibn Lev was for the first time at a loss, and was unable to locate the origin of a particular law. He ordered the *Beis*

Yosef brought, and therein found the correct Talmudic source. R' Yosef ibn Lev then proclaimed that he saw in this a sign from Heaven that Beis Yosef was to be used as a standard halachic code, and immediately permitted his disciples to study the work.

As already mentioned, both R' Yosef's father, R' Ephraim Caro, and R' Yosef's uncle, R' Yitzchak Caro, were scholars of note. R' Yitzchak authored Toldos Yitzchak (Constantinople, 5278/1518), a popular commentary to the Torah which has been reprinted many times. *R' Yaakov Rabino cites this work extensively in his Tzenah URe'enah. In this work, R' Yitzchak cites both his brother, R' Ephraim Caro, and their father — after whom the author of the Beis Yosef was named — R' Yosef Caro. R' Yitzchak was also an eminent posek whose views are cited a number of times in his nephew's Beis Yosef. Two responsa to a query put to him by R' Yosef Caro are printed in the latter's Avkas Rochel (§47-48). Another lengthy responsum [to the question of whether yibum or chalitzah is preferable] is printed at the end of Teshuvos Beis Yosef.

R' Elisha Galiko

רַבִּי אֱלִישָׁע בֶּן גַּבְרִיאֵל גָּאלִיקוֹ

d. Safed, Eretz Yisrael, c. 5336/1576

A member of *R' Yosef Caro's beis din in Safed, R' Elisha composed commentaries, interspersed with kabbalistic interpretations, to Song of Songs (Venice, 5347/1587); Esther (Venice, 5343/1583), and Ecclesiastes (Venice, 5337/1577). He headed a large yeshivah in Safed.

R' Yochanan Treves

רַבִּי יוֹחָנָן בֶּן יוֹסֵף טְרֵיוֵיש

b. Italy, c. 5250/1490
d. Italy, 5337/1577

Scion of a prominent French rabbinical family which traced its genealogy to *Rashi, R' Yochanan was an expert halachist. Although not wishing to accept a full rabbinical position, he served as a posek and rav in the homes of the elite, who in those days employed their own rabbis on their estates to look after their halachic needs. He also worked as an editor in the Bomberg printing firm in Venice, editing halachic works.

R' Yochanan is best known for his work Kimcha DeAvishona (Bologna, 5300/1540), a commentary on the Machzor Roma. He also composed a commentary on the laws of slaughtering in the Mordechai, which was lost. Some of his halachic responsa is cited in the works of his contemporaries, among them *Rama and the *Beis Yosef (see Yoreh Deah 403).

R' Nassan Nata Shapira I

רַבִּי נָתָן נָטָע בֶּן שִׁמְשׁוֹן שַׁפִּירָא (הָרִאשׁוֹן)

d. Horodna (Grodno), Lithuania
1 Iyar 5337/1577

Rabbi of Horodna, R' Nassan Nata composed Mevo She'arim, a commentary on Shaarei Dura (Cracow, 5334/1574), and Imrei Shefer (Cracow-Lublin, 5357/1597), a super-commentary on *Rashi's Torah commentary. A different version of this work, titled Beurim or Beurim LeMaharan, was printed in Venice in 5353/1593, prior to the publication of Imrei Shefer. In the preface to Imrei Shefer, R' Nassan's son avers that the Beurim is a fraud and that a ban was placed on it. R' Nassan also wrote a commentary on Birkas HaMazon, printed in a sefer called Zemiros (Lublin, 5355/1595), which contains table liturgy by *Maharshal, and other related matter. His glosses to Tur have been printed in the Jerusalem (5717/1957) edition of that work. His grandson, *R' Nassan Nata

Shapira II, quotes him frequently in *Megalleh Amukos*.

R' Azaryah min HaAdomim (de Rossi)

ר' עֲזַרְיָה בֶּן מֹשֶׁה מִן הָאֲדוֹמִים

b. Mantua, Italy, c. 5271/1511
d. Bologna (?) Italy, 5338/1578

According to an old tradition, the family de Rossi was brought to Italy by Titus after his victory over Jerusalem.

R' Azaryah combined Talmudic erudition with a great proficiency in the Latin and Greek classics, as well as in the writings of medieval Christian scholars. In his works he draws upon Jewish, Christian, and secular sources. De Rossi resided in Bologna and Ferrara, and was present in Ferrara during the terrible earthquake on 17 Kislev (Nov. 18) 5331/1570. He and his family narrowly escaped death during that catastrophe, and he devoted a section of his *Meor Einayim* to a narration of it.

R' Azaryah is known for his controversial work *Meor Einayim* (Mantua, 5333-35/1573-75). This *sefer* is divided into three parts: I. *Kol Elokim*, a report on the earthquake which hit Ferrara in 5331/1570, including an essay on the natural and supernatural causes of natural catastrophes; II. *Hadras Zekeinim* — a translation (the first in Hebrew) of the epistle of Aristeas which contains the narrative about the Septuagint (translation of the Torah into Greek by seventy-two sages in Egypt during the reign of Ptolemy Philadelphus [3476-3515/285-246 B.C.E.]), a partial description of the Temple in Jerusalem, and the answers given by the Sages to some philosophical questions; III. *Imrei Binah* — the most extensive part of this work. It contains an examination of the writings of Philo, a Jewish philosopher who lived in Alexandria in the first century C.E.; a comparison of the Septuagint (the Greek translation of the Bible) in its prevalent version with the reports about it in the Talmud; inquiries into the Talmudic chronology of the first and second Temples, comparing the traditional dates with those given by secular writers; inquiries into the calendar systems in use among Jews in the Talmudic era, i.e., the Seleucid calendar (*minyan shtaros)* and the now-prevalent custom of dating events from Creation; a dissertation on the priestly vestments as described in the works of Philo, Josephus Flavius, the Epistle of Aristeas and Christian writers; and comments on some wondrous *aggados* in the Talmud and *midrashim*.

De Rossi's inquiries led to many conclusions which contradict the tradition of the *Tannaim* and *Amoraim*; he maintained that this was permissible in the realm of history and other areas not pertaining to *halachah*. R' Azaryah's views raised a great furor in the Italian community of his day, and two prominent rabbis — R' Moshe Provencal of Mantua and R' Yitzchak Finzi of Pesaro — wrote letters protesting the author's views, and refuting his assertions. R' Moshe Provencal's criticism reached R' Azaryah while the book was yet in proof form, so he printed it and his rejoinder as an appendix to the book. Various local *batei din* banned the book, some restricting the ban to people under the age of twenty-five, while others prohibited even having the book in one's house. Some of the extant copies of the *Meor Einayim* have written dispensations by local *batei din* attached to them, allowing the owner to keep the book.

News of the controversial *sefer* even reached *Eretz Yisrael*, and *Chida reports that in Safed a general ban (*cherem*) against it was drawn up and was to be signed by *R' Yosef Caro, but he died before signing it. The *Maharal of Prague, upon reading this sefer, was outraged that the rabbis of Italy had allowed its publication, and he wrote a lengthy critique of the sefer in his Be'er HaGolah. Nevertheless, some later sages, among them Chasam Sofer, and two of Maharal's pupils, *R' David Ganz (Tzemach David) and *R' Yom Tov Lipman Heller, cite Meor Einayim, if only to refute its views. R' Azaryah later wrote another work, Matzreif LaKessef (Edinburgh, 5614/1854), defending his views.

Meor Einayim regained popularity in modern days, when the Maskilim misrepresented R' Azaryah as a progressive Jew, a denomination R' Azaryah would surely have resented.

R' Yosef ibn Lev (Mahari ibn Lev)

רַבִּי יוֹסֵף בֶּן דָוִד אִבְּן לֵב
(מַהַר"י אִבְּן לֵב)

b. Monastir (Bitola), Turkey (now Yugoslavia)
c. 5260/1500
d. Constantinople (now Istanbul), Turkey
c. 5340/1580

In his home town, R' Yosef studied under his kinsman, R' Yitzchak ben Tzaddik ibn Lev. Later (c. 5293/1533) he settled in Salonica, where he filled the post of dayan while *R' Yosef Taitatzak was still alive.

R' Yosef was an extremely strong and outspoken personality, not fearing to enforce his halachic decisions even upon the most wealthy and influential members of the community. Unable to witness wrongdoing, he especially sought the vindication of the poor and the weak, often incurring the wrath of the wealthy class who were wont to unconscionably persecute the lower class. This character trait led to his departure from Salonica to Constantinople in 5305/1545.

*R' David Conforte (Korei HaDoros) relates the following about R' Yosef's departure from Salonica, which he heard from the sages of Salonica: R' Yosef got into a heated debate over a point of halachah with another scholar (R' Shlomo ibn Chason). The debate transcended the usual bounds of dialogue as the two sides angrily abused each other. After this incident a plague broke out in Salonica, and R' Yosef fled to a neighboring village. There his gifted twenty-eight-year-old son, R' David ibn Lev, was killed. Ostensibly, this was seen as a heavenly punishment for the unbounded strife between Torah scholars, and R' Yosef decided to leave Salonica permanently for Constantinople.

A different version is given in a postscript to a machzor printed in those days, as reported in Shalsheles HaKabbalah and by R' David Conforte: A disgruntled individual who had lost a lawsuit loudly complained to R' Yosef on the streets of Salonica. Unsatisfied with the response he got, he approached R' Yosef and slapped him. Apparently because of the culprit's financial or political power, no one dared to protest against this public humiliation of an outstanding talmid chacham. R' Yosef, appalled at such apathy in the face of public desecration of the Torah, rent his clothing and loudly proclaimed his dismay. That same night a fire broke out in a store close to the area where this incident had occurred. The fire raged on until it had destroyed five thousand houses in the Jewish section and claimed two hundred lives. After the fire, pestilence broke out, claiming yet more lives — and R' Yosef left the town.

An interesting sequel to this story is related in a letter by the venerated rav of Oshmine and Slonim, known affectionately as R' Mordechai Oshminer (author of Hadras Mordechai, Vilna, 5659/1899), to his colleague R' Pinchas, *rav* of Antipole. The venerated *rav* had seen a recurring dream on the most auspicious nights of the year — twice on *Yom Kippur*, on *Shmini Atzeres*, and on *Simchas Torah* — in which an awe-inspiring sage had appeared bearing a mysterious message from Heaven. Finally on *Simchas Torah* the sage revealed his message. He was R' Yosef ibn Lev himself, and he informed R' Mordechai that he was a descendant of the Jew who had humiliated R' Yosef in such an audacious manner centuries ago. That grave sin had been "emblazoned on the bones" of its perpetrator, who could not find peace until his sin had been atoned for. It was incumbent upon R' Mordechai to do penance for his ancestor's sin by acquiring a copy of R' Yosef ibn Lev's works, and studying them daily for a period of four years until he would commit them to memory. Upon his inquiry as to where these works could be obtained, the heavenly visitor had informed R' Mor-dechai that his colleague, R' Pinchas, had a copy in his library. The letter ends with an exhortation to R' Pinchas to send the requested work forthwith. (The letter is published in V. 2 of *She'eilos UTeshuvos R' Yosef ibn Lev*; Jerusalem, 5720/1960.)

R' Yosef next took up residence in Constantinople, and was appointed to head the great yeshivah which was sponsored by the wealthy and influential Dona Gracia Mendes. There he disseminated advanced Talmudic and halachic knowledge to hundreds of disciples until his last days.

R' Yosef was recognized as an outstanding and independent-minded halachist, and answered inquiries from far and wide. He corresponded with R' Yosef Taitatzak, *R' Shmuel de Medina and *R' Yosef Caro, and was considered the equal of the latter in Talmudic scholarship. *Chida reports that three scholars of that generation named Yosef were capable of authoring a work of the magnitude of *Beis Yosef* on the *Turim*: R' Yosef Caro, R' Yosef Taitatzak, and R' Yosef ibn Lev. Ironically, Chida relates that R' Yosef ibn Lev opposed the use of the *Beis Yosef* by his disciples on the grounds that reliance on it would tend to diminish the need for independent and individual Torah scholarship (see *R' Yosef Caro).

His responsa, *She'eilos UTeshuvos R' Yosef ibn Lev* (V. 1-4: Constantinople, 5320-57/1560-97), also contains his *chidushim* to many tractates, together with those of his son, R' David.

However, *R' Shlomo HaKohen reports that whatever appears over R' David's name in V. 1 (according to *R' Chaim Shabsai, also in V. 2; see *Shem HaGedolim*) is really of R' Yosef's authorship. Nevertheless, there is no question about R' David's ability as a scholar. The epitaph on R' David's tombstone contains the encomium "The lion of the group, filled with wisdom."

R' Moshe Trani (Mabit)

רַבִּי מֹשֶׁה בֶּן יוֹסֵף טְרָאנִי (מַבִּי"ט)

b. Salonica, Turkey (now Greece) 5260/1500
d. Safed, Eretz Yisrael, 21 Nissan 5340/1580

R' Moshe was a descendant of *R' Yeshayah of Trani I and II. He received his initial instruction from his uncle, R' Aharon Trani, an eminent scholar who was nicknamed R' Aharon *Baal Tosafos* because of his great erudition and sharpness. R' Aharon emigrated from Trani (in southern Italy) to Turkey in 5257/1497. At the age of eighteen his pupil and kinsman — R' Moshe Trani —

emigrated to Safed and became one of the most prominent disciples of *R' Yaakov bei Rav. In 5298/1538, R' Moshe was ordained by his master with *semichah* (see **Historical Introduction**) and appointed as a member of the prominent *beis din* (judicial court) of Safed. After the death of *R' Yosef Caro in 5335/1575, R' Moshe was recognized as the supreme head of this *beis din*.

Mabit (Moshe ben Yosef Trani) was a recognized halachist and carried on extensive correspondence with the authorities of his day, among them *Radvaz, *R' Betzalel Ashkenazi, *R' Moshe Alsheich, and others. He replied to halachic inquiries and his collection of responsa, *Teshuvos Mabit* (Venice, 5389-90/1629-30), contains eight hundred and six replies in three parts.

R' Moshe carried on an extensive correspondence with R' Yosef Caro on various halachic problems. Some of these halachic debates were very heated, resulting in some ill feeling between these two Torah greats. However, R' Moshe's son, *R' Yosef Trani (Maharit), relates in his biographical comments (printed in *Teshuvos Maharit HaChadashos*, Jerusalem, 5738/1978), that his father visited R' Yosef Caro during the latter's sickness and that R' Yosef blessed him on his deathbed.

Mabit also authored *Kiryas Sefer* (Venice, 5313/1553), a paraphrase of *Rambam's *Mishneh Torah,* giving the source of each law, and determining whether it is a rabbinical enactment or Torah commandment; *Beis Elokim* (Venice, 5336/1576), an ethical and philosophical treatise; and *Iggeres Derech Hashem* (Venice, 5313/1553), an ethical treatise written in 5306/1546, during the ravages of an epidemic.

Two of R' Moshe's sons were well-known *rabbanim*. The elder, R' Shlomo, was a *rav* in Cairo, and the younger, who was born to R' Moshe in his old age, was the illustrious *R' Yosef Trani.

R' Yitzchak ben Shmuel Adribi

ר׳ יִצְחָק בֶּן שְׁמוּאֵל אַדְרִבִּי

b. Turkey or Greece, c. 5270/1510
d. Salonica, Turkey (now Greece)
7 Iyar c. 5340/1580

A disciple of *R' Yosef Taitatzak, R' Yitzchak, was appointed to the post of *rav* in the Lisbon (Portuguese) Congregation in Salonica at a very young age. Later he served the Shalom Congregation in Salonica (c. 5309/1549), and was one of the most important *poskim* in his generation. He corresponded with his contemporary, *R' Shmuel de Medina, on halachic problems, and occasionally collaborated with him in the adjudication of halachic cases.

Thus, in 5333/1573, R' Yitzchak joined Maharashdam in signing a declaration of *cherem* against a functionary of Don Yosef Nasi named Daud. Daud had accepted bribes from the French and accused Don Yosef of treason. [The French were at this time embroiled in a personal confrontation with Don Yosef. The latter had loaned the huge sum of 150,000 thalers to the French government while he was still masquerading as a Christian. The French now refused to pay the debt, on the grounds that the loan made by a Christian bank was not owed to the 'Jewish' bank. Sultan Suleiman himself had written to the French king, bidding him to discharge the debt. After the passage of many years the debt had still not been paid, and the new Sultan, Selim II, authorized Don Yosef to detain and confiscate any French ships sailing in Turkish waters. Don Yosef proceeded to detain a French vessel docking at Alexandria. The French retaliated through their ambassador at Constantinople, who secured Daud's cooperation by means of a substantial bribe.] At this time Don Yosef was still at the height of his influence at the Sultan's court, and easily disproved Daud's false charges. The *rabbanim* pronounced a *cherem* upon the slanderer. Daud repented, and even got Don Yosef to request the removal of the ban. But the *rabbanim* refused, even though the plea to do so came from such an influential person — who also happened to be the hurt party in this case.

Maharashdam favorably mentions verbal exchanges of opinions he had with R' Yitzchak (see e.g. *Teshuvos Maharashdam, Choshen Mishpat* §22). At times, however, Maharashdam and R' Yitzchak disagreed vehemently in their rulings and became entangled in controversy with each other (see e.g. *Teshuvos Maharashdam, Choshen Mishpat* §40, 294; *Divrei Rivos* §328).

R' Yitzchak authored *Divrei Rivos* (Salonica, 5342/1582), responsa and *chidushim;* and *Divrei Shalom* (Salonica, 5340/1580), thirty sermons (in which commentaries by R' Yosef Taitatzak are mentioned) along with some commentaries to *Avos* and *Tehillim*.

R' Moshe Almosnino

רַבִּי מֹשֶׁה בֶּן בָּרוּךְ אַלְמוֹשְׁנִינוֹ

b. Salonica, Turkey (now Greece)
c. 5270/1510
d. Constantinople (now Istanbul), Turkey
c. 5341/1581

A gifted orator and author, R' Moshe was elected rabbi of the *Neveh Shalom* community of Spanish Jews in the city of Constantinople in 5313/1553, and of the *Livyas Chen* congregation in 5320/1560.

R' Moshe authored *Pirkei Moshe* (Salonica, 5323/1563), a commentary on tractate *Avos; Yedei Moshe* (Salonica, 5332/1572), a commentary on the five

Megillos; Me'ametz Ko'ach (Constantinople, 5342/1582), sermons; *Tefillah LeMoshe* (Salonica, 5343/1563), dissertations according to the weekly portions of the Torah; and a homiletic work, written in Spanish and dedicated to R' Yosef Nasi, duke of Naxos (see **Historical Introduction**), whose Hebrew title is *Hanhagas Chaim* (Salonica, 5324/1564).

R' Moshe was a proficient halachist, and his decisions are cited in the works of his contemporaries, such as *Maharashdam.

In 5326/1566 he successfully represented his brethren at an audience with Sultan Selim II, petitioning for the confirmation of their civil rights, which was granted at his sixth session with the Sultan.

R' Shlomo Alkabetz

רַבִּי שְׁלֹמֹה בֶּן מֹשֶׁה הַלֵוִי אַלְקַבֵּץ

b. Salonica, Turkey (now Greece)
c. 5265/1505
d. Safed, Eretz Yisrael, c. 5344/1584

R' Shlomo was a disciple of *R' Yosef Taitatzak. About 5295/1535 he emigrated to *Eretz Yisrael* and settled in Safed, where he concentrated on the study of *kabbalah*. He soon became known as one of the greatest kabbalists. His brother-in-law *R' Moshe Cordovero was his disciple in *kabbalah,* and *R' Yosef Caro was also among those who attended his lectures.

R' Shlomo is most famous for his beautiful and inspiring *piyut* (liturgical hymn) *Lechah Dodi,* incorporated into both the Ashkenazic and Sephardic *siddurim* as part of the services ushering in the Sabbath.

R' Shlomo composed numerous homiletic and kabbalistic works, mostly commentaries to Biblical books. Among his works are: *Manos HaLevi* on the book of *Esther* (Venice, 5345/1585), which was originally written in 5289/1529 and sent by R' Shlomo to his future father-in-law as a Purim gift; *Ayeles Ahavim* (Venice, 5312/1552) on *Song of Songs*; *Shoresh Yishai* (Constantinople, 5321/1561) on *Ruth*; and *Bris HaLevi* (Lemberg, 5623/1863), a kabbalistic commentary on the *Haggadah*. His unpublished works include: *Divrei Shlomo*, a commentary on the Twelve Minor Prophets (*Trei Assar*); *Ne'im Zemiros* on *Psalms*; a Torah commentary; *Pitzei Ohev* on *Job*; *Beis Hashem*; *Beis Tefillah* on the prayers; and other works, including *Lechem Shlomo*, which are mentioned in his *Ayeles Ahavim* but remain unpublished. Comments by R' Shlomo are also found in the kabbalistic commentary to *Ruth* entitled *Peirush Bartenura* (see *R' Ovadyah Bertinoro), and a sermon by him is printed in *Maamar Shivrei Luchos* by *R' Menachem Azaryah of Fano (Safed, 5624/1865).

Although R' Shlomo was one of the outstanding kabbalists of the generation, his works on *Megillos Esther* (*Manos HaLevi*) and *Ruth* (*Shoresh Yishai*) do not reflect this. Rather, they are written for the average layman, in a style popular during that era, and these two works have not lost their wide appeal to this day. R' Shlomo first presents the difficulties in the verse to be discussed, cites numerous solutions already advanced by earlier and contemporary scholars to resolve the problem, and then gives his own view on the matter. His outlook relies primarily on the views expressed by our Sages in the Talmud, *midrashim*, *targumim* and *Zohar*, and rejects commentaries based solely on rationalism or even textual analysis if they contradict the view of the Sages. He goes to lengths to demonstrate the correctness of the Talmudic Sages' exegeses. It is no doubt this quality which has endeared R'

Shlomo's commentaries to generations of Jews.

R' Shimon Labia

רַבִּי שִׁמְעוֹן לָבִּיא

b. Spain, c. 5250/1490
d. Tripoli, Libya, c. 5344/1584

As a young child, R' Shimon was forced to leave the country of his birth when all the Jews were expelled from Spain in 5252/1492. Eventually he settled in Fez (Morocco) where he grew up and spent the major part of his life. In the year 5309/1549, R' Shimon left Morocco with the intention of settling in the Holy Land.

On his journey to *Eretz Yisrael*, R' Shimon, stopping over in Tripoli, observed the degenerated state of Torah knowledge and the lax religious observance of the Jewish populace. Considering the situation carefully, he decided to give up his cherished dream of living in *Eretz Yisrael*, and chose rather to remain with the spiritually unfortunate Jews of Libya and to return them to the right path. He succeeded in attaining this objective, but never was able to reach his original destination.

R' Shimon authored an extensive commentary on the *Zohar* entitled *Kessem Paz*. The commentary was never printed in its entirety. Only the commentary to *Genesis* was published, in two volumes (Leghorn, 5545/1785). R' Shimon draws on the works of the earlier kabbalists, such as *Ramban, *Rabbeinu Bachya ben Asher, and others. The Arizal's system was as yet unknown to him. R' Shimon also authored the *Bar Yochai* hymn sung on *Lag B'Omer* in memory of the *Tanna*, R' Shimon bar Yochai. He is reputed to have been close to one hundred years old at his death.

R' Yissachar Susan

רַבִּי יְשָׂשכָר בֶּן מָרְדְּכַי דִּידִיע סוּסָאן

b. Fez, Morocco, c. 5270/1510
d. Safed, Eretz Yisrael, c. 5345/1585

As a youth, R' Yissachar studied under his father, who was a scholar. At a young age he went to settle in *Eretz Yisrael*. Arriving there in about 5287/1527, R' Yissachar settled in Jerusalem and studied under *R' Levi ibn Chaviv. He also lived in Safed for a period of time and studied together with the select group of scholars residing in that city.

R' Yissachar composed *Ibur Shannim UTekufos*, which is into two parts: the first, *Tikkun Yissachar*, containing the schedule for the reading of the Torah portions each Shabbos, along with their respective *haftaros;* and the second, *Pe'ulas Yissachar*, containing rules for arranging the calendar.

R' Yissachar was motivated to undertake this work by the fact that in 5299/1539 he traveled extensively in Turkey, and was chagrined to observe the difficulties the scholars of each community had with editing the calendar for the year, as their reference books were insufficient for helping them in this task. He therefore compiled this work and left it with his friends in Turkey, who published it in its original form (Salonica, 5324/1564) without first consulting him. Upon seeing the printed work, he was chagrined that this unedited first draft had been published. He then improved the work and published it himself in Venice (5339/1579) under the title *Ibur Shannim UTekufos*.

This work is invaluable for the information it contains about the customs of the Jewish communities of that period. Ironically, it is the first source to mention the custom to eat fruit on the fifteenth of *Shevat. Tikkun Yissachar* mentions this as a custom practiced by *Ashkenazim*, and the Ashkenazic commentaries to the *Shulchan Aruch* found no printed source for their custom besides that in the work of this Moroccan rabbi (see *Magen Avraham* 131:15). This rare work has recently been republished.

R' Eliezer Ashkenazi

רַבִּי אֱלִיעֶזֶר בֶּן אֵלִיָּהוּ אַשְׁכְּנַזִי

b. Turkey (?) 5273/1513
d. Cracow, Poland, 22 Kislev 5346/1585

R' Eliezer was probably born in Turkey to an Ashkenazic family. There he studied under *R' Yosef Taitatzak in Salonica.

R' Eliezer served as rabbi in Egypt from 5298/1538 until 5321/1561 and became widely known for his erudition. He was, however, compelled by unexplained circumstances to leave Egypt, and went to Cyprus, filling a rabbinical position in Famagusta. A few years later, in 5331/1571, when the Turks captured Cyprus, R' Eliezer moved on to Italy. He first settled in Venice, but was forced to leave because of a disagreement with *R' Shmuel Yehudah Katzenellenbogen. He then went to Prague, where he lived for about a year, and returned to Italy to take up the rabbinate of Cremona.

About his stay at Famagusta we have a first-hand report from the traveler R' Eliyahu of Pesaro, who sojourned in Cyprus in the years 5324/1564. In a letter, he describes R' Eliezer in glowing terms which bring the stature of this Torah giant to life. He relates how he found at Famagusta one of the great people of the era: "The glory of the generation who is now fifty years old . . . He is conversant in twelve languages . . . and a scholar in many subjects, a very wealthy man . . . From the day I left Venice until now I have not encountered such an awesome man of G-d . . . I plan to settle here for two years in order to learn Torah from him . . ." (*Otzar Masa'os*).

In 5338/1578, R' Eliezer traveled to Poland and took up the rabbinical post of Posen, but in 5344/1584 resigned the position and took up residence (as a private person) in Cracow, where he remained until his death.

R' Eliezer's chief work is *Maasei Hashem* (Venice, 5343/1583), a commentary on the historical occurrences mentioned in the Torah, which also includes a complete commentary on the *Haggadah*. The commentary resembles *R' Yitzchak Abarbanel's commentaries both in form and content. Like Abarbanel, R' Eliezer prefaces his commentaries with a long list of difficulties encountered in the text, and critiques on the commentaries of his predecessors. His ideological framework is strongly based on *Ram-bam's *Moreh Nevuchim*, tempered with a tinge of *kabbalah*. This work, especially the section on the *Haggadah,* is one of the classics in Torah commentary, and is used extensively by later authorities. *R' Yosef Shlomo Delmedigo (Yashar) of Candia said about this work (in his *Novlos Chachmah*) that one 'should read it from beginning to end.'

R' Eliezer also authored *Yosef Lekach* (Cremona, 5336/1576), a commentary on *Esther*. Part of the first edition was dedicated to R' Yosef Nasi, Duke of Naxos (see **Historical Introduction**). R' Yosef Shlomo Delmedigo (there) reports that R' Eliyahu wrote a super-commentary to *Ramban's commentary on the Torah which is comparable to *R' Eliyahu Mizrachi's commentary on *Rashi*.

R' Eliezer maintained halachic correspondence with *R' Yosef Caro, *Rama, *R' Yosef Katz (*She'eiris Yosef* §19) and *Maharshal, and responsa by him can be found in *She'eilos UTeshuvos Rama* (§96), and in the rare pamphlet *Hatzaa al Odos HaGet* (Venice, 5326/1566), about a controversial divorce. A number of *selichos* by R' Eliezer can be found in various collections of prayers.

R' Gedalyah ibn Yachya

רַבִּי גְּדַלְיָה בֶּן יוֹסֵף אִבְּן יַחְיָא

b. Imola, Italy, c. 5286/1526
d. Alessandria, Italy, c. 5347/1587

R' Gedalyah was descended from an eminent family originating in Portugal, which boasted many great men in its ranks. R' Gedalyah's father, R' Yosef ben David ibn Yachya (5257-5299/1497-1539), was an eminent disciple of R' Yehudah Mintz; he headed a yeshivah in Imola, Italy, and authored a commentary to the five *Megillos* and *kesuvim* entitled *Peirush Chameish Megillos UKesuvim* (Bologna, 5298/1538), and an ethical-philosophical work, *Torah Or* (Bologna, 5298/1538). R' Gedalyah's grandfather, R' David ben Yosef ibn Yachya, was the *rav* of the Portuguese community of Naples (Italy) for twenty-two years until the dissolution of the Jewish communities of the area because of its annexation by Spain in 5295/1495. R' Gedalyah lauds his grandfather profusely for his scholarship in Torah and philosophy and mentions that he studied under him. He also studied under *R' Meir Katzenellenbogen in Padua and *R' Ovadyah Sforno in Bologna, and probably under his father. However, his principal teachers were R' Yaakov Finzi of Reccanata and the brothers, R' Yisrael and R' Avraham of Ravigo.

Not very much is known about R' Gedalyah's life. He was born in Italy and lived in various cities of this country. In his writings he intimates that he changed his living place very often. Once in his works he refers to Pope Pius V's ban on moneylending by Jews (5327/1567), followed by the expulsion of the Jews from the smaller towns in the Papal States (5329/1569). R' Gedalyah suffered a significant financial loss and had to leave his place of abode and travel from city to city. Towards the end of his life he settled in Alessandria (Northern Italy), where he afficiated as *rav,* and where he lived until his death.

R' Gedalyah was well versed in the Bible and Talmud and composed about twenty works. The only work which was preserved was *Shalsheles HaKabbalah* (Venice, 5347/1587), in which his other books are enumerated.

Shalsheles HaKabbalah is a historical work, arranged chronologically, beginning with Adam and extending to his own era. It has a second part which contains dissertations on a variety of subjects, for example: *derushim* about the heavenly bodies, about conception and gestation, the soul, magic, the origin of the diverse languages, et al.

R' Gedalyah's contribution to the literature of historiography is severely criticized by later authorities, notably *R' Chaim Yosef David Azulai (Chida), for his lack of critical judgment and accuracy. Nevertheless, his work remains a valuable source for the history of the era in which he lived.

R' Chaim ben Betzalel

רַבִּי חַיִּים בֶּן בְּצַלְאֵל

b. Posen (Poznan), Poland, c. 5275/1515
d. Friedberg, Germany, 7 Sivan 5348/1588

R' Chaim was an older brother of *Maharal. He studied under *R' Shalom Shachna of Lublin and *Maharshal, and was on intimate terms with his colleague, *Rama.

In 5295/1535, R' Chaim came to Worms, Germany, where his uncle, R' Yaakov ben Chaim, served as rabbi. R' Chaim opened a yeshivah and began disseminating Talmudic knowledge among the young students. Upon his uncle's death about fourteen years later,

R' Chaim was appointed to succeed him as Chief Rabbi of Worms. Not long after this he was offered the rabbinate of Friedberg (near Frankfurt am Main) where he officiated as *rav* until his death.

R' Chaim authored *Iggeres HaTiyul* (Prague, 5365/1605), miscellaneous interpretations to Biblical, Talmudic and midrashic passages; and *Sefer HaChaim* (Cracow, 5353/1593) on *mussar;* both works were written during the plague which ravaged Friedberg in 5338/1578. Being confined to his home for nearly two months, and unable to concentrate on complicated Talmudic discourse because of the worrisome situation, R' Chaim composed these ethical treatises which have been acclaimed as masterpieces throughout the generations.

His halachic work *Viku'ach Mayim Chaim* (Amsterdam, 5472/1712) is a criticism of Rama's *Toras Chatas* on the dietary laws. R' Chaim, in general, disapproved of short codes, inasmuch as they tend to discourage the student from independent Talmudic investigation.

R' Chaim was a careful grammarian and advocated the study of Hebrew language and grammar. To this he dedicated an entire textbook entitled *Eitz Chaim,* which was not published. His super-commentary to *Rashi's Torah commentary, titled *Be'er Mayim Chaim,* has recently been published (Vol. I: Brooklyn, 5725/1965; Vol. II: London, 5729/1969; Vol. III: London, 5731/1971).

R' Avraham de Boton

רַבִּי אַבְרָהָם בֶּן מֹשֶׁה דִי בּוֹטוֹן

b. Salonica, Turkey (now Greece), 5305/1545
d. Salonica, Turkey (now Greece), 5348/1588

A disciple of *Maharashdam, R' Avraham served as rabbi of the Puglia (Italian) community in Salonica until he died during a plague when he was forty-three. In spite of his young age, *R' Avraham corresponded in *halachah* with such greats as *R' Moshe Trani. Among his better-known disciples was *R' Shabsai Yonah.

R' Avraham gained world acclaim with his *Lechem Mishneh* (Venice, 5369/1609), a very important and comprehensive commentary on *Rambam's *Mishneh Torah,* republished with almost every edition of Rambam's work and considered a classic in this field.

R' Avraham was also a halachist, and his second work, *Lechem Rav* (Ismir, 5420/1660), includes some of his responsa. His Talmudic *chidushim* on tractate *Bava Kamma* have been published in *Meharerei Nemeirim* (Venice, 5354/1594), but his *chidushim* to other tractates remain unpublished.

R' Avraham's three sons were all distinguished scholars. His son R' Meir is the author of a volume of responsa called *She'eilos UTeshuvos R' Meir de Boton* (Ismir, 5440/1680).

R' Avraham Galante

רַבִּי אַבְרָהָם בֶּן מָרְדְּכַי גַּלַאנְטִי

d. Safed, Eretz Yisrael, 5348/1588

R' Mordechai, the progenitor of the Galante family which boasts many illustrious members, was a Spanish exile who had settled in Rome. *Chida (*Shem HaGedolim*) relates that R' Mordechai's family name had been Angel, but that because of his handsome appearance he was nicknamed *Galante Homo* by the Roman nobility with whom he had business connections. His comeliness caused him to be put in a trying situation in which he successfully underwent an extreme spiritual and physical ordeal. To celebrate this accomplishment his children adopted the name Galante.

R' Avraham was a disciple of his older brother, *R' Moshe Galante. While yet in their youth, both brothers left their

native Rome and emigrated to *Eretz Yisrael*. There R' Avraham immersed himself in kabbalistic studies under *R' Moshe Cordovero, whom he considered his greatest master.

R' Avraham composed a commentary on *Zohar* entitled *Yare'ach Yakar,* a condensation of R' Moshe Cordovero's commentary *Or Yakar,* which has come down to us in its abridged form in *Zaharei Chammah* of *R' Avraham Azulai; *Zechus Avos* (Bilgorai, 5671/1911), a kabbalistic commentary on tractate *Avos;* and *Kinas Sesarim* (Venice, 5349/1589), a kabbalistic interpretation to *Lamentations* printed in the collection *Kol Bochim.*

According to *Chida, R' Avraham was a man of means and financed the construction of the building in Meron which houses the tombs of R' Shimon bar Yochai and his son, R' Elazar.

R' Shmuel de Medina (Maharashdam)

רַבִּי שְׁמוּאֵל בֶּן משֶׁה דַּי מֶדִינָה (מַהֲרַשְׁדַ"ם)

b. Salonica, Turkey (now Greece), 5266/1506
d. Salonica, Turkey (now Greece), 5350/1590

R' Shmuel was a pupil of *R' Levi ibn Chaviv and *R' Yosef Taitatzak. He served as rabbi in many Turkish communities and had countless disciples, among them *R' Avraham de Boton, author of *Lechem Mishneh*. R' Shmuel's halachic decisions were in great demand, and numerous inquiries were sent to him. He was considered one of the outstanding Talmudic scholars in an extraordinary era.

During his lifetime, Maharashdam's responsa were published in Salonica (5341-42/1581-82) as *Piskei R' Shmuel de Medina.* After R' Shmuel's death, the responsa were republished by his son as *She'eilos UTeshuvos Maharashdam*

(Salonica, 5354-58/1594-98). This version contained substantial additions, and was rearranged according to the order of the *Tur*. Close to one thousand (963) decisions were included in the second edition. In addition, thirty of his sermons were published under the title *Ben Shmuel* (Mantua, 5382/1622). *Chida reports that he saw Maharashdam's *chidushim* to many *masichtos* in manuscript.

R' Yehudah Muscato

רַבִּי יְהוּדָה בֶּן יוֹסֵף מוּסְקָאטוֹ

b. Osimo, Italy, c. 5280/1520
d. Mantua, Italy, c. 5350/1590

In addition to considerable learning in Talmud and *halachah*, R' Yehudah also possessed a thorough knowledge of Greek and Arabic philosophy and was fluent in several languages. In Mantua he was close to the circle of the two Provencal brothers — R' Moshe, who was the rabbi of the city, and R' David — both of whom were also educated in secular disciplines. *R' Azaryah min HaAdomim seems to have been a close friend of his, and mentions that he showed R' Yehudah several passages of his *Meor Einayim* before it was published. He preached regularly in his home town of Mantua, and served as a model to the Italian *darshanim* (preachers) who followed him. His sermons are collected in *Nefutzos Yehudah* (Venice, 5349/1589), and are a significant contribution to homiletic literature.

R' Yehudah's fame, however, stems from his excellent commentary to *R' Yehudah HaLevi's *Kuzari*, entitled *Kol Yehudah* (Venice, 5354/1594). This commentary, which is considered the best one on the *Kuzari*, elaborates at length on all of the philosophical themes mentioned by R' Yehudah HaLevi, drawing on his own thorough knowledge of Greek and Arabic philosophy and science, and on all of the subtle nuances in the language of the *Kuzari*.

R' Yissachar Ber HaKohen

רַבִּי יְשָׂשכָר בֶּער בֶּן נַפְתָּלִי הַכֹּהֵן

b. Shebreshin, Poland
d. Hebron, Eretz Yisrael, c. 5350/1590

R' Yissachar (who was known as Berman Ashkenazi) is famous for his running commentary on the entire *Midrash Rabbah*, entitled *Matnos Kehunah* (Cracow, 5347/1587). He also authored *Mareh Kohen* (Cracow, 5349/1589), an index of Biblical verses found in the *Zohar*. *Chida (*Shem HaGedolim*, v. 2, s.v. *Rabbah*) and *R' David Conforte report that R' Yissachar emigrated to *Eretz Yisrael* and is buried in Hebron, near the grave of *R' Eliyahu de Vidas.

R' Yosef Katz

רַבִּי יוֹסֵף בֶּן מָרְדְּכַי גֶּרְשׁוֹן כַּץ

b. Cracow, Poland, c. 5270/1510
d. Cracow, Poland, 3 Shevat 5351/1591

R' Yosef, who was a brother-in-law of *Rama (Rama's second wife was his sister), held the position of *rosh yeshivah* in Cracow for over fifty years. He engaged in extensive halachic correspondence, and inquiries poured in from such distant localities as Italy and Turkey. The venerable *R' Shlomo Luria, in one instance, requested his opinion on a halachic disagreement he had with R' Yitzchak Betzalel's, and R' Yosef did not hesitate to state his strong disagreement with Maharshal's viewpoint. Interestingly, Maharshal does not refer to R' Yosef in terms of an older *gaon* writing to a young contemporary (as he does in his correspondence with Rama), but as to an equal. R' Yosef was definitely older than Rama, and signed before him in a joint responsum printed in *Teshuvos Rama*.

Nevertheless, he refers to his younger brother-in-law's glosses on *Shulchan Aruch* in a number of instances, and treats them as an authoritative halachic source. His collection of responsa, *She'eiris Yosef* (Cracow, 5350/1590), also contains notes on *Mordechai* which were omitted in subsequent printings of the work.

In 5331/1571, R' Yosef published the halachic work *Agudah* by one of the early Ashkenazic masters (*R' Alexander Zusslein HaKohen). He corrected the text, and added references, short explanatory comments (in parentheses), and a preface. He reports that he was able to find only one copy of this important work in Poland and considered it a great privilege to preserve it for posterity. He expressed his hope that the sainted author would come to greet him in the 'world to come' in recognition of his labor.

R' Shlomo ben Yehudah Leib

רַבִּי שְׁלֹמֹה בֶּן יְהוּדָה לֵיב

b. Lublin, Poland
d. Lublin, Poland, 5351/1591

Known as R' Shlomo R' Leibush, or alternatively, 'der yunger R' Shlomo' (the young R' Shlomo) to differentiate between him and *R' Shlomo Luria, he was rabbi of some of the most prestigious communities in Poland — Lemberg, Posen, and finally (5347/1587), his home town, Lublin. He also served as a *rosh yeshivah* in Cracow; that is where the *Shelah studied under him. R' Yehudah Leib, his father, was also an outstanding scholar and *rosh yeshivah* in Lublin. R' Shlomo's contemporaries refer to him with great reverence. He was noted both for his great erudition and his character, and is consistently referred to as 'HaChassid' (the truly pious).

R' Shlomo was a disciple of *Maharshal and possibly also of *R' Shalom Shachna of Lublin, and one of the leading members of the Council of Four Lands (see **Historical Introduction**). His yeshivah produced many disciples; most notable among them were the *Bach and the *Shelah. Upon the latter he had a tremendous influence; the *Shelah* refers to his mentor very often, attaching great importance to his customs. Through the agency of his venerated pupil, many of R' Shlomo's customs have become widely accepted, for example, the custom of removing the *tefillin* from the head with the left hand in order to show that one does not want to get rid of the *tefillin* quickly, and that of not making *kiddush* on the first day of *Shavuos* before it is definitely night.

R' Shlomo did not publish any works, and for centuries his name has been perpetuated only in the works of his distinguished disciples. Recently a volume containing some of his rulings and responsa has been published under the title *Piskei UShe'eilos UTeshuvos Maharash MeLublin* (Brooklyn, 5748/1988), based on a manuscript work and quotations in the works of his disciples. A short treatise entitled *Seder Gittin*, on the complicated rules for spelling personal names in *gittin* (bills of divorce), which gives rulings by R' Shlomo, his disciples and his contemporaries, is also contained in this volume.

R' Betzalel Ashkenazi

רַבִּי בְּצַלְאֵל בֶּן אַבְרָהָם אַשְׁכְּנַזִי

b. Eretz Yisrael, c. 5280/1520
d. Jerusalem, Eretz Yisrael, c. 5352/1592

R' Betzalel is generally regarded as a Sephardic scholar — and rightly so — for he grew up and spent his life among Sephardim. However, by birth he was an Ashkenazi, and as reported on the title page of his volume of responsa (in the first edition), his father's brother was 'the greatest rabbi in Ashkenaz — R' Yitzchak Betzalel's'. This is probably the great scholar by the same name — an antecedent of the *Turei Zahav* — who was *rav* of Ludmir during this period and is mentioned in the responsa of *Maharshal and *Rama.

At an early age, R' Betzalel left *Eretz Yisrael* together with his family and emigrated to Egypt. He studied under *Radvaz (in Egypt) and R' Yisrael de Corial (in Safed). R' Betzalel attained such great heights in Torah knowledge that when Radvaz emigrated to *Eretz Yisrael,* R' Betzalel succeeded him as Chief Rabbi of all Egyptian Jewry.

R' Betzalel, besides being an acknowledged leading halachist, was also involved in the communal affairs of Egyptian Jewry.

After some time (c. 5348/1588), R' Betzalel returned to his native *Eretz Yisrael,* and settled in Jerusalem. There he administered the communal affairs of both the Sephardic and Ashkenazic communities. In this capacity he traveled on several occasions to surrounding countries — Egypt, Syria, and Turkey — in order to raise funds.

R' Betzalel's fame rests upon his monumental work — *Shittah Mekubetzes,* or *Asifas Zekeinim* — which is a compilation of the *chidushim* of many of the great *Rishonim* (early commentators) on many tractates of the Talmud. Many of the original manuscripts of these older commentators have since been lost and are known to us only through R' Betzalel's work. This work has been published on the following *masichtos*: Beitzah (Constantinople, 5491/1731; together with *She'eilos UTeshuvos Nachalah LiYehoshua)*; Kesubos (Constantinople, 5498/1738); Nazir (Leghorn, 5534/1774); Bava Kamma (Amsterdam, 5512/1752); Bava Metzia (Amsterdam, 5481/

1721); *Bava Basra* (Leghorn, 5534/1774); additions to *Bava Basra* (together with *Yad Ramah;* Salonica, 5551/1791); *Nedarim* (Berlin, 5620/1860); *Sotah* (with *Bris Yaakov*; Leghorn, 5560/1800); on *Berachos* (in *Berachah Meshuleshes;* Warsaw, 5624/1864); *Zevachim, Menachos, Chullin, Temurah* and *Bechoros* in *Mizbe'ach Kaparah* (Leghorn, 5570/1810).

However, some of these *shittos* were not authored by R' Betzalel, and his authorship of some others is doubtful. The title *Shittah Mekubetzes* given to the works on *Berachos* and *Beitzah* is simply a misnomer; these works are not a collection of the writings of earlier commentators on these tractates, but rather a collection of independent works by authors whose identity has not been established with any degree of surety. The work on *Berachos* has been attributed, variously, to *Ritva or to his father R' Avraham Asevilli (see *Ginzei Rishonim, Berachos*). The work on *Beitzah* has been speculatively assigned to a pupil of *R' Nissim Gerondi. A question was raised about R' Betzalel's authorship of the *shittos* on *Nedarim* and *Nazir,* and *Chida reports that he heard from a prominent person that the *shittos* on *Nazir* and *Bava Basra* were authored by *R' Aharon Lapapa, but this assertion has been disputed by later scholars. Chida reports he saw R' Betzalel's *shittos* on tractates *Shevuos* and *Gittin;* these are apparently lost.

R' Betzalel's glosses on the margin of his copy of the Talmud to most of *Seder Kodashim* have been published in the Vilna edition of the Talmud; they include the material printed in *Mizbe'ach Kaparah*. These glosses are extremely important for the study of this *seder* which was largely neglected by the earlier commentators, for R' Betzalel emended the text of the Talmud, *Rashi,* and

Tosafos by comparison to manuscript versions of these works, and added extracts from unpublished Tosafos, such as Tosefos Sens (Shantz), Chitzoniyos and other collections of Tosafos, as well as other early commentators.

R' Betzalel was also known as a halachist and he replied to many halachic inquiries. His responsa, She'eilos UTeshuvos R' Betzalel Ashkenazi, were published during his lifetime (Venice, 5350/1590). Among his disciples were *R' Yitzchak Luria (the Ari HaKadosh), and *R' Shlomo Adeni, the commentator to the Mishnah and author of Meleches Shlomo.

R' Moshe Alsheich

רַבִּי מֹשֶׁה בֶּן חַיִּים אַלְשֵׁיךְ

b. Adrianople (Edirne), Turkey, c. 5268/1508
d. Safed, Eretz Yisrael, Elul 5353/1593 ?

R' Moshe was born into a family of Spanish exiles living in Adrianople, and learned under *R' Yosef Caro while the latter yet resided in Adrianople. R' Moshe later moved to Salonica and studied under *R' Yosef Taitatzak. R' Moshe arrived in Eretz Yisrael as a young man, and spent most of his life in Safed. There he was ordained by R' Yosef Caro with the semichah ordination instituted by *R' Yaakov bei Rav (see Historical Introduction), and served as a dayan in the great beis din of Safed.

Although R' Moshe devoted the major part of his time to the study and teaching of Talmud, and to the adjudication of cases of law and halachic rulings — fulfilling his obligations as a dayan — he nevertheless found time to concentrate on Biblical studies, preparing sermons for the community which he would deliver on Shabbos. He was a gifted preacher and his sermons were eagerly anticipated. From these sermons he developed his popular Torah commen-

tary entitled Toras Moshe, or, as it is usually referred to in awed reverence of the author — Alsheich HaKadosh (the holy Alsheich). He published the first part, on Genesis, in Constantinople (Belvedere, 5355/1595), explaining in his introduction that since many other preachers had adopted his sermons as part of their own, compounding their theft by missing important points in his thinking, he felt compelled to publish this work to end this practice. After R' Moshe's death, his son R' Chaim published the entire commentary (Venice, 5361/1601).

R' Moshe also authored commentaries on other books of the Bible, his first published work being Chavatzeles HaSharon, a commentary on Daniel (Constantinople, 5323/1563). His other works are: Maros HaTzovos on the Early Prophets (Venice, 5361/1601); Romemos Keil on Psalms (Venice, 5365/1605); Rav Peninim on Proverbs (Venice, 5352/1592); Chelkas Mechokeik on Job (Venice, 5263/1603); Shoshanas HaAmakim on Song of Songs (Venice, 5351/1591); Devarim Tovim on Ecclesiastes (Venice, 5361/1601); Devarim Nichumim on Lamentations (Venice, 5361/1601); Masas Moshe on Esther (Prague, 5377/1617, with Shoshanas HaAmakim); Einei Moshe on Ruth (Venice 5361/1601); and a commentary, also called Maros HaTzovos, to most of the Later Prophets except Ezekiel (Venice, 5367/1607). Part of R' Moshe's work on Tehillim (on the first forty-one psalms) was published in Constantinople, without the author's consent, as Tapuchei Zahav (Kuru Gishmu, 5353/1593). His commentary to midrash, a work called She'arim, which contains dissertations on matters central to Judaism, and his commentaries to selected Talmudic passages (sugyos) were never published.

Although R' Moshe was a kabbalist, his commentaries hardly betray this fact, and center primarily on homiletic themes, stressing ethical and inspirational lessons which may be gleaned from the various Biblical texts. However, the thought framework underlying R' Moshe's homilies is often anchored in the cement of the *kabbalah*. R' Moshe Alsheich's popularity as a *darshan* was not restricted to his own generation and locale. His works became the building blocks for generations of preachers for their sermons, and for centuries the multitudes were reared on the "Holy Alsheich." However, the sheer length of the Alsheich's works made them inaccessible to the average person, and this was in spite of the author's protestations that the limited time available to him precluded him from elaborating on his themes! Efforts were made to shorten his *Toras Moshe* and to present his thoughts in digest form. Abridgments were made of the commentary to the *Chumash* (two), the five *Megillos, Psalms,* and *Proverbs*. Because of the Alsheich's popularity, selections were made from his writings and arranged as commentaries to *Maseches Avos* and *Haggadah shel Pesach*. R' Moshe's halachic responsa, containing one hundred forty replies, was published after his death (Venice, 5365/ 1605).

On 1 Av in the year 5350/1590, the eighty-two-year-old R' Moshe left *Eretz Yisrael* to raise funds for the Jewish community in Safed, which had been impoverished due to a widespread famine. He managed to return to his beloved Safed (summer of 5353/1593), and died shortly thereafter.

His best-known disciple was *R' Chaim Vital, who also instructed his teacher in some of the intricacies of the Arizal's *kabbalah*.

R' Shmuel Yafeh Ashkenazi
רַבִּי שְׁמוּאֵל בֶּן יִצְחָק יָפֶה אַשְׁכְּנַזִי
b. Bursa, Turkey, c. 5285/1525
d. Constantinople (now Istanbul), Turkey
19 Elul 5355/1595

R' Yitzchak, R' Shmuel's father, was a distinguished *talmid chacham* and businessman of Ashkenazic lineage who resided in Bursa, Turkey. His gifted son, R' Shmuel, studied under R' Yitzchak ben Tzaddik ibn Lev (a relative of *R' Yosef ibn Lev, who is mentioned in the latter's responsa), who headed a yeshivah in Bursa at that time.

In the year 5309/1549, R' Shmuel traveled to Constantinople for the purpose of marriage, and also to learn in the yeshivos there; this city would become his permanent place of residence. Eventually he was appointed rabbi in one of the communities of Constantinople — probably in the Ashkenazic one. R' Shmuel also headed a yeshivah, and the study and teaching of Talmud and *halachah* occupied most of his time and energy. However, in his capacity as rabbi, R' Shmuel undertook the responsibility of reaching his congregation through sermons, which he preached every Sabbath and on the Festivals. He was an excellent *darshan,* and chose the vast midrashic literature, especially Midrash Rabbah, as his source.

Unable to find a suitable midrashic commentary, R' Shmuel set about composing his own, and after many years of labor he produced a voluminous commentary on *Midrash Rabbah* which includes the Pentateuch and five *Megillos*. R' Shmuel titled his commentary *Yefeh To'ar,* and the first volume, on *Bereishis Rabbah* (Venice, 5366/1606), appeared after his death. Next appeared his work on *Vayikra Rabbah* (Constantinople, 5408/1648), and then one on *Shemos Rabbah* (Venice, 5417/1657). The commentaries to *Bamidbar Rabbah* and *Devarim Rabbah* remain unpublished.

His commentaries on *Midrash Rabbah* to the Books of *Ruth, Esther,* and *Lamentations* were titled *Yefeh Anaf* (Frankfurt an der Oder, 5456/1696), and *Yefeh Kol* was written on *Midrash Shir HaShirim Rabbah* (Ismir, 5499/1739). His works, although not widely studied because of their length and rareness, are probably considered to be the commentaries par excellence on the *midrash*. A condensation of this work is printed in the Romm edition of *Midrash Rabbah* (Vilna, 5638/1878).

R' Shmuel also composed a commentary on the *aggadah* of *Talmud Yerushalmi*, entitled *Yefeh Mareh* (Venice, 5350/1590); and *Yefeh Einayim* (Venice, 5391/1631), sermons and notes to *R' Eliyahu Mizrachi's commentary on *Rashi*. His unpublished works include his responsa, *Beis Din Yafeh; Yafeh LaBedikah,* a reference work for the topics to be found in the *aggados* in *Yerushalmi* and *midrash;* a commentary on *Koheles Rabbah;* and *Yefeh Nof* on *Midrash Shmuel.* Some of his halachic decisions are cited in the responsa of *Maharashdam and *Maharit, and a responsum dealing with determining the correct year for the *shemitah* has been published in the periodical *Moriah* (9th yr, #11).

R' Avraham Menachem Rappo of Porto

רַבִּי אַבְרָהָם מְנַחֵם בֶּן יַעֲקֹב הַכֹּהֵן רַפָּא מְפּוֹרְטוֹ

d. Porto, Italy, 18 Cheshvan 5357/1596

The progenitor of the famous Rappaport rabbinical family, R' Avraham spent his youth in Venice, absorbing both Talmudic and secular studies. He studied Hebrew grammar under *R' Eliyahu Bachur.

R' Avraham composed a Torah commentary entitled *Minchah Belulah* (Verona, 5354/1594). His sermons and responsa were not published.

The name Rappaport is popularly supposed to be a contraction of רפָּא פּוֹרְט (*rofei port*), physician of Port(o). More probably the word רפָּא is the German word Rappe (Raabe), meaning raven, which seems to have been the German surname of R' Avraham. At the end of his preface to *Minchah Belulah*, R' Avraham refers to himself as מִבְּנֵי הָעוֹרְבִים, 'of the children of the ravens'. His family coat of arms, which appears at the end of this *sefer*, has a pair of hands raised in priestly blessing (symbolizing the author's *kehunah* status) and a raven.

The *kehunah* status of the Rappaport family was considered by many *gedolim* to be unquestionable, and often an effort is made to obtain a *kohen* from this family for the *mitzvah* of *pidyon haben.*

R' Matisyahu Delacrot

רַבִּי מַתִּתְיָהוּ בֶּן שְׁלֹמֹה דֶּלַקְרוֹט

Poland, 16th century

In his youth, R' Matisyahu traveled to Italy, where he immersed himself in the study of *kabbalah* and also in the sciences and philosophy. Upon returning to his native Poland, he began instructing disciples in *kabbalah*. Among his pupils was *R' Mordechai Yafeh, who had the highest regard for R' Matisyahu.

R' Matisyahu wrote commentaries to many kabbalistic works; including R' Yosef Gikatilia's *Shaarei Orah* (Cracow, 5354/1594), *R' Menachem Recanati's Torah commentary, and R' Peretz HaKohen's *Maareches Elokus;* the last two commentaries are unpublished. R' Matisyahu also authored a commentary to *Mareh HaOfanim,* an astronomical work

(Ofenbach, 5480/1720; with *Tzuras HaAretz*), and wrote *Tzel HaOlam* (Amsterdam, 5493/1733), on various scientific matters.

His son, R' Yosef, was rabbi of Shebreshin (Poland), and author of *Chidushei R' Yosef* (Lublin, 5360/1600), chidushim on tractate *Eruvin*.

R' Eliyahu de Vidas

רַבִּי אֵלִיָהוּ בֶּן מֹשֶׁה דֵּי וִידַאשׁ

b. Safed, Eretz Yisrael, 16th cent.

d. Hebron, Eretz Yisrael, late 16th century

A disciple of *R' Moshe Cordovero, R' Eliyahu is the author of the celebrated classic *Reishis Chachmah* (Venice, 5339/1579), one of the most popular and revered *mussar* works.

R' Eliyahu, in his work, stresses the Biblical, Talmudic and midrashic sources, feeling that the mere words of these sources are more influential in motivating a person and molding his character and aspirations than are works based on philosophical reasoning. However, R' Eliyahu drew freely from the ethical works of his predecessors, notably *Chovos HaLevavos* and the works of *Rabbeinu Yonah of Gerona.

R' Eliyahu's use of quotations and ideas from the *Zohar* ushered in a new genre of *mussar* works using the *kabbalah* as part of their ideological framework. At the end of his work R' Eliyahu saw fit to include a summary of selected topics which are treated at length in *Menoras HaMaor* by *R' Yisrael al-Nakavah. Thus, until this monumental work was first published in modern times (Vol. 1-4: New York, 5689-92/1929-32), *Reishis Chachmah* preserved the only published remnant of the former work. The last two sections of the *sefer* contain two small midrashic anthologies and are a rich collection of ethical sayings originating from the Tan-

naim and *Amoraim*. *Reishis Chachmah* rapidly became a very popular work and some of the outstanding sages of later generations greatly appreciated it and encouraged its study. *Chida (*Shem HaGedolim*) urges that every person set aside a daily period of study in *Reishis Chachmah*.

Because of its popularity, the need for a shortened version was soon felt. R' Eliyahu himself prepared an abridged version titled *Totza'os Chaim*, with the addition of some kabbalistic *kavanos* pertaining to the daily prayers (Constantinople, 5345/1585). Other abridgments are *Tapuchei Zahav* by R' Yechiel Mille (Mantua, 5383/1623), and *Reishis Chachmah HaKatzar* by R' Yaakov Poyeto (Venice, 5360/1600). This last work was completed in the year following the initial publication of *Reishis Chachmah*. The abridgments, especially the latter one, also enjoyed great popularity and were reprinted numerous times.

R' Shmuel Galiko

רַבִּי שְׁמוּאֵל גַּאלִיקוֹ

Safed, Eretz Yisrael, 16th century

A disciple of *R' Moshe Cordovero, R' Shmuel viewed his master's work *Pardes Rimonim* as the most thorough exposition of kabbalistic literature. However, due to its lengthy style it was difficult to follow. Therefore, in order to make the work more accessible, R' Shmuel composed *Asis Rimonim* (Venice, 5361/1601), an abridged version of *Pardes Rimonim*. *R' Menachem Azaryah of Fano, who owed his initial introduction to *kabbalah* to this work (which he used prior to its publication), published a second, improved edition of this work with additions of his own (Mantua, 5384/1624).

R' Aharon of Pesaro

רַבִּי אַהֲרֹן מִפִּיסָארוֹ

Pesaro, Italy
Second half of 16th century

R' Aharon is primarily known for his popular work *Toldos Aharon* (Freiburg, 5343/1583), notes on the Bible containing references to passages of the Babylonian Talmud. The author published a revised edition of his work to the *Chumash* and five *Megillos* containing additional references to *Zohar*, *Akeidas Yitzchak* and *Ikkarim* (Basel, 5351/1591). The work was later printed in the margin of many editions of the Bible with additional references to the *Talmud Yerushalmi* (compiled by R' Yaakov Sasportas and named *Toldos Yaakov*). R' Aharon's work was upgraded a century later by R' Aharon ben Samuel from Posen (Poland) with references to many more sources (*Midrash Rabbah, Tanchuma*, etc.) and published in Frankfurt an der Oder (5451/1691); a revised edition named *Beis Aharon* with many additional references was published by R' Avraham David Lavaut (Vilna, 5641/1881).

R' Aharon of Pesaro was a rich, greatly respected and influential man who owned a significant library. He was the driving force behind the publication of *R' Yitzchak Abarbanel's *Mirkeves HaMishneh*, his commentary to *Deuteronomy* (Sabbionetta, 5311/1551), and is described in the publisher's preface to this work as 'a prince and grandee in Israel.'

R' David ben Avraham Shemaryah

רַבִּי דָּוִד בֶּן אַבְרָהָם שְׁמַרְיָה

Salonica, Turkey (now Greece)
Second half of 16th century

R' David is best known for his abridged version of the *Zohar* which he entitled *Toras Emes* (Salonica, 5364/1604), including a short commentary and translation of the difficult words in the *Zohar*, entitled *David HaKattan*.

R' Shmuel Yehudah Katzenellenbogen

רַבִּי שְׁמוּאֵל יְהוּדָה בֶּן מֵאִיר קַצֶּנֶלֶנְבּוֹיגֶן

b. Padua, Italy, 5281/1521
d. Venice, Italy, 6 Nissan 5357/1597

The son of *R' Meir of Padua (Maharam Padua), R' Shmuel became a recognized halachic authority during his youth and was appointed a member of the Venice *beis din*. R' Shmuel Yehudah also maintained an active halachic correspondence with the Polish rabbinical authorities *Rama and *Maharshal.

From the year 5326/1566 until his death, R' Shmuel Yehudah served as Chief Rabbi of Venice, where he headed a prominent Talmudic academy. Aside from a few scattered responsa which appear in the works of his contemporaries, he also authored a work comprising twelve philosophical dissertations containing some eulogies on contemporary rabbinical figures, among them a eulogy on his relative, Rama. The book was published in Venice in 5354/1594 as *Drashos R' Shmuel Yehudah*, or *Shteim Esrei Drashos*. In one of the editions (Warsaw, 5636/1876) the work was misnamed *Drashos Mahari Mintz*, and it is this edition which has been reproduced a number of times.

R' Shmuel Yehudah sent his son, R' Shaul Wahl, to study in the famous yeshivos of Poland. According to one source, he studied under Maharshal in Brisk d' Lita (Brest-Litovsk). A well-known legend relates that R' Shaul became very popular with the princes and officers, whom he advised on strategic problems, as well as problems involving difficult mathematic calculations. According to Polish law, the government was not to remain overnight without a monarch and when, upon the death of the old king, the nobles were unable to agree on a successor, R' Shaul was elected to the office of King for one day. Some speculate that his surname, Wahl, is an allusion to this story (*wahl* means election in Yiddish).

R' Menachem of Tiktin (Maharam Tiktin)

רַבִּי מְנַחֵם דָּוִד בֶּן יִצְחָק מִטִיקְטִין
(מַהֲרַ"ם טִיקְטִין)

Tiktin, Poland, 16th century

A disciple of *Rama, R' Menachem composed glosses on *Sefer HaHalachos* of *Rif and on *Mordechai*, which are now included in the collection of notes called *Chidushei Anshei Shem* and printed in the standard editions of the *Rif* and *Mordechai*. He wrote notes on the Torah commentaries of *Rashi and *Ramban, notes on the prayers, and a commentary on the *Zohar*, all mentioned in his son's introduction to the glosses, but unfortunately not preserved.

R' Menachem should not be confused with R' Meir HaLevi Horowitz of Tiktin who is also known as Maharam Tiktin. Besides the difference in the first name, the latter Maharam Tiktin lived about one century after the former.

R' Elazar Azkari

רַבִּי אֶלְעָזָר בֶּן מֹשֶׁה אַזְכָּרִי

b. Constantinople (now Istanbul), Turkey
5293/1533
d. Safed, Eretz Yisrael, 5360/1600

R' Elazar was born in Constantinople to a family of Spanish refugees. He was a disciple of R' Yosef Sagis, and maintained a halachic correspondence with *R' Moshe Trani and his son, *R' Yosef Trani. After spending his youth in Con-

stantinople, R' Elazar emigrated to Safed, and his love for *Eretz Yisrael* knew no bounds.

R' Elazar was a kabbalist and well respected by the *Ari. He was of very saintly character and composed many lofty and beautiful poems depicting the yearning of the soul to cleave to G-d. The best known of these is the popular poem, *Yedid Nefesh*.

R' Elazar authored a monumental ethical work, entitled *Chareidim* (Venice, 5361/1601), elaborating on those *mitzvos* of the Torah which are in effect during the post-Temple era, but stressing, in addition to their halachic aspect, their ethical and religious dimension. This work received wide acclaim and was republished many times. It may be ranked with such popular and outstanding ethical works as *Menoras HaMaor*, *Reishis Chachmah* and *Kav HaYashar*. R' Elazar is also the author of a small *sefer* on ethics called *Divrei Kevushim* (Pietrkov, 5671/1911). He also composed a commentary to *Yerushalmi* of *Masichtos Berachos* (printed in some editions) and *Beitzah* (New York, 5727/1967). His commentary to *Lamentations* is cited in *Kol Bochim*, but has not been preserved. Fragments from his commentary to *Yerushalmi* of *Sedarim Zeraim* and *Moed* are cited in *Meleches Shlomo* on *Mishnah*.

R' Yaakov Abulafia

רַבִּי יַעֲקֹב אַבּוּאַלַפְיַע

d. Safed, Eretz Yisrael, c. 5360/1600

R' Yaakov was a disciple of his maternal grandfather, *R' Yaakov bei Rav, who ordained him with the *semichah* ordination (see **Historical Introduction**). He served as rabbi of Gallipoli, Turkey, and from there obtained the rabbinate of Damascus, where he headed a large yeshivah.

*Chida reports that R' Yaakov authored numerous responsa and that his decisions were sought far and wide, but none of his works were published. Shortly before his death he returned to his native Safed. He lies buried near the tomb of his grandfather.

R' Menachem de Lonzano

רַבִּי מְנַחֵם בֶּן יְהוּדָה דֵּי לוֹנְזַאנוֹ

16th and beginning of 17th centuries

Originally from Italy or Turkey, R' Menachem came to Jerusalem as a child with his parents. Because of economic and other considerations, R' Menachem was forced to make extensive trips throughout Turkey, Italy and Syria.

R' Menachem was by nature quick to learn languages, and he made use of these travels to perfect his knowledge of Arabic and Greek. He utilized his gift of linguistics later to compose his *Maarich* (in his *Shtei Yados*; separately, Leipzig, 5613/1853), an appendix to *R' Nassan ben Yechiel's *Aruch*. As he professes in the preface to this work, it is impossible to know the exact meaning of some of the unusual words in the Talmud and *midrashim* without a thorough knowledge of the languages from which most of the words are derived, namely Latin, Greek and Arabic. The author of *Aruch* was proficient, he says, in Latin, leaving the exact definitions of terms derived from Greek and Arabic to him — R' Menachem. During his travels he was also able to amass a large collection of Torah scrolls — upon which he later based his investigations of the *Mesorah* and of rare *midrashim*.

R' Menachem's great facility with words and his thorough knowledge of Hebrew grammar enabled him to compose some of his *sefarim* in the metered rhyme which had been made popular by the early Spanish poets. However, his outspokenness, and the sometimes blunt language he used to attack opinions with which he disagreed, caused R' Menachem much anguish during his lifetime and may have diminished his fame in later generations. He did not even shrink from criticizing the *kabbalah* of the *Arizal and *R' Chaim Vital, refusing to accept the great master's almost unquestioned authority in this field.

R' Menachem authored a compendium of works titled *Shtei Yados* (*Two Hands*), comprised of ten works and corresponding to the ten fingers of the two hands. He published part of this compendium (Venice, 5378/1618), containing one 'hand' comprised of five of his own original works, which he called *Yad Ani* (*The Pauper's Hand*). This consists of *Or Torah*, an authoritative analysis of the *mesorah, parshiyos stumos* and *pesuchos,* and other matters pertaining to the writing of Torah scrolls; *Maarich,* additions to the *Aruch; Avodas Mikdash,* a step-by-step description of the Temple service, in rhyme, together with prayers and other liturgy; *Derech Chaim,* daily laws, ethics, and exhortations (*mussar*) to better oneself, in rhyme; *Tovah Tochachas,* ethics and exhortations, in rhyme, together with *Totza'os Chaim* by R' Moshe ben Nesanel ibn Shlomo, a similar work. Regarding the second 'hand', *Yad Melech* — containing rare *midrashim* selected for publication by R' Menachem — only one 'finger' of this collection was printed (together with the above-mentioned first part of *Shtei Yados*): *Aggadas Bereishis.* Some of these works were subsequently republished separately, and a summary of *Or Torah* named *Orei Or* is to be found in *Bnei Yonah* by *R' Yonah Landsofer (Prague, 5562/1802).

The other four 'fingers' would have

been improved editions of (a) *Tanna D'bei Eliyahu;* (b) *Avos D'Rabbi Nassan* with *Maseches Derech Eretz* and *Osiyos D'Rabbi Akiva;* (c) *Sefer HaTashlumin,* which would contain passages missing from the standard editions of *Midrash Rabbah, Tanchuma,* and *Sifra,* together with *Pirkei Gan Eden* and *Eitz HaChaim* (a midrash); and (d) *Midrash Agur.* Due to lack of funds R' Menachem did not complete the publication of the second 'hand'. It seems, though, that R' Menachem published, or at least began to publish, an edition of a *midrash* titled 'Baraysa D'Rabbi Eliezer bno shel R' Yosse HaGlili UMidrash Agur (Safed, 5347/1587). Only a title page and part of R' Menachem's preface have survived, but the entire *midrash* was printed three and a half centuries later (New York, 5694/1934) as *Mishnas R' Eliezer.* (The first two chapters are printed in most copies of *Talmud Berachos* as *Shloshim UShtayim Midos shel R' Eliezer bno shel R' Yosse .*)

A short treatise containing R' Menachem's comments on the sections of *Zohar* known as *Idra Zuta* and *Sifra D'Tzniusa* under the name of *Omer Man* was published in Vilna (5643/1883), and *Sefer Maasiyos,* an anthology of stories from the *Yerushalmi* and *midrashim* (Husyatin, 5663/1903), and comments on the *Yerushalmi* (Warsaw, 5696/1936) were also published. His work criticizing R' Chaim's Vital's *kabbalah,* and comments on *Levush* (by *R' Mordechai Yafeh) were never published. (The latter work is cited by *R' Nassan Shapira III in *Matzas Shemurim,* and excerpts from the former are printed in R' E. Rivlin, *HaTzaddik R' Yosef Zundl MiSalant*). A halachic responsum by R' Menachem is printed in the collection *Tziyon ViYerushalayim* (R' Yitzchak Badhav, Jerusalem, 5658/1898).

R' Shlomo HaKohen (Maharshach)

רַבִּי שְׁלֹמֹה בֶּן אַבְרָהָם הַכֹּהֵן (מַהַרְשַׁ"ךְ)

b. Salonica, Turkey (now Greece)
c. 5290/1530
d. Salonica, Turkey (now Greece)
c. 5362/1602

A disciple of R' Yosef Firman, R' Shlomo was a recognized halachic authority in Turkey and served as rabbi of Salonica. His responsa are contained in four volumes (I: Salonica, 5346/1586; II: Venice, 5352/1592; III: Salonica, 5354/1594; IV: Salonica, 5412/1652), which include *chidushim* on *Hilchos Gerushin* of *Mishneh Torah* and the Talmud.

*Chida (*Shem HaGedolim*) cites the statement of R' Yaakov Alfandari, 'To us, *Mahari ibn Lev (R' Yosef ibn Lev), *Maharashdam (R' Shmuel de Medina) and Maharshach are to be considered like *Rif, *Rambam and *Rosh.'

R' Yosef ben Yitzchak ibn Ezra

ר' יוֹסֵף בֶּן יִצְחָק אִבְּן עֶזְרָא

b. Constantinople (now Istanbul) (?), Turkey
c. 5300/1540
d. Sofia (Bulgaria), 5362/1602

R' Yosef left his native Constantinople at a young age to learn under *R' Shmuel de Medina in Salonica. He later left Salonica to assume the rabbinate of Sofia. *R' Shabsai Yonah was among his disciples.

In the prefaces of his printed works, R' Yosef hints that he authored many other works — but only two have been published: *Atzmos Yosef, chidushim* on *Maseches Kiddushin* with selected *chidushim* on other *masichtos* (Salonica, 5361/1601), and *Massa Melech* (Salonica, 5361/1601), on the laws of taxation and communal practices. His *Atzmos Yosef* is a classic and is invaluable to the student of *Maseches Kiddushin*. It is quoted extensively by the later commentators, and has been reprinted numerous times. *Massa Melech* was part of a larger work on the entire *Choshen Mishpat*. *R' Yosef Escapa's comments to this work were printed in *Avodas Massa* (Salonica, 5606/1846).

R' Aharon Zelig of Zolkiew

רַבִּי אַהֲרֹן זֶעלִיג בֶּן מֹשֶׁה מִזוֹלְקְוָוא

d. Zolkiew, Poland, 5363/1603

R' Aharon Zelig's fame rests on his work *Amudei Sheva* (Cracow, 5395/1635), containing comments and glosses on the *Zohar* which he compiled from authoritative sources.

R' Yisrael Seruk

רַבִּי יִשְׂרָאֵל סְרוּק

b. Safed (?)
d. Eretz Yisrael, before 5364/1604

Nothing is known about R' Yisrael's youth, not even his father's name. Two other persons living in his era are known to have carried the family name Seruk. One was R' Zecharyah ibn Seruk, author of a commentary on *Esther* (*Peirush al Megillas Achashveirosh*; Venice, 5320/1560). The other was R' Zecharyah's kinsman, R' Chaim ibn Seruk, a resident of Safed, who helped in the publication of the above work, and was sent by *R' Yosef Caro to supervise the printing of his *Beis Yosef* to *Tur Orach Chaim* and *Yoreh Deah* in Venice in the year 5311/1551.

R' Yisrael is said to have studied under the *Ari as soon as the latter arrived in Safed, before *R' Chaim Vital became the Ari's disciple. It is therefore not surprising that many of R' Yisrael's dissertations which were transmitted to him by the Ari do not appear in any of R' Chaim's works, as these topics were not discussed during R' Chaim's term of study.

After the death of the Ari, R' Yisrael set about disseminating the doctrines of his master throughout Europe. He lectured throughout Italy, in various places in Germany, and in Amsterdam. Among his disciples were *R' Menachem Azaryah of Fano, *R' Aharon Berechyah of Modena, and *R' Avraham Herrera in Amsterdam. He was instrumental in winning for the doctrines of the Arizal the pre-eminent place they later enjoyed among European kabbalists, forever relegating the study of *Ramak's *kabbalah* to a subordinate position. The winning over of such a distinguished personage and fervent follower of Ramak as R' Menachem Azaryah could not but have this effect, in spite of the latter's protestations that the two systems complemented each other and that the study of both were equally necessary.

Among R' Yisrael's works are a kabbalistic essay expounding his doctrine (published in *R' Yosef Shlomo Delmedigo's *Matzreif LaChachmah* [Basel, 5389/1629]); *Karah Mikreh* (Salonica, 5512/1752); and *Ne'im Zemiros Yisrael* (Lvov, 5554/1794), a kabbalistic commentary to the Ari's Shabbos liturgy.

After R' Yisrael's death, his daughter married R' Shlomo Shloiml of Dreznitz, who settled in Safed to occupy himself with *kabbalah*. R' Shlomo's biographical letters describing the Safed of his day and recording the recollections of the sages of his generation about the Arizal and his disciples are among the important historical documents dealing with this topic. They have been printed in various works, such as *Matzreif LaChachmah*, and they comprise the major part of *Shivchei HaArizal*.

R' Shmuel de Uzeda

רַבִּי שְׁמוּאֵל בֶּן יִצְחָק דִּי אוּזֵידָה

b. Safed, Eretz Yisrael, c. 5300/1540
d. c. 5365/1605

R' Shmuel was descended from a Spanish family originating in Uceda, Spain. A disciple of the *Ari and *R' Chaim Vital, R' Shmuel is best known for his popular homiletic commentary on tractate Avos, Midrash Shmuel (Venice, 5339/1579), which has gone through numerous printings, four of them in the author's lifetime. This commentary is an anthology of the many earlier commentators who wrote on Avos; many of these commentaries have been preserved only in R' Shmuel's work.

R' Shmuel headed an academy in Safed, where both Talmud and kabbalah were studied. In 5357/1597 he traveled to Constantinople to raise funds for his institution, and while there he published his commentary on Ruth, entitled Iggeres Shmuel. His commentary Lechem Dimah on Lamentations was published posthumously (Venice, 5366/1606). These commentaries follow the style set in Midrash Shmuel. It is of interest that in spite of his proficiency in kabbalah, R' Shmuel included almost no kabbalistic material in his commentaries, although the ideas underlying some of the comments are rooted in the kabbalah.

R' Moshe Mos of Premysl

רַבִּי מֹשֶׁה מָת בֶּן אַבְרָהָם מִפְּרֶמִיסְלָא

b. Premysl, Poland, c. 5300/1540
d. Apta (Opatow), Poland, 5366/1606

A disciple of *Maharshal, R' Moshe served as rabbi of Belz, Premysl, and Apta (Opatow). He is known for his halachic compendium Matteh Moshe (Cracow, 5351/1591) on the laws of prayer, benedictions, holidays, and so

on, in which he cites many customs of Maharshal.

R' Moshe also authored Ho'il Moshe (Prague, 5372/1612), which is comprised of Be'er Moshe, a commentary on *Rashi's Torah commentary, and Ba'er Heitev, sermons; in this work he mentions his chidushim on the Talmud.

He also wrote Taryag Mitzvos (Cracow, 5341/1581), enumerating the six hundred thirteen commandments, in rhyme, with a commentary; and also added an index to the Cracow edition of *R' Yaakov ibn Chaviv's Ein Yaakov (5347/1587).

R' Moshe maintained a halachic correspondence with the *Bach and with *R' Binyamin Aharon Solnik.

The surname Mos is assumed by some to be an abbreviation of Machzikei Torah or Marbitzei Torah (supporters of Torah).

R' Avraham Yagel dei Galiccho

רַבִּי אַבְרָהָם יָגֵל בֶּן חֲנַנְיָה גָּאלִיקוֹ

b. Monselice, Northern Italy, c. 5300/1540
d. after 5366/1606

R' Avraham was born into a rich Italian family which was involved in the banking business. R' Avraham himself was drawn into the family banking establishment, although he despised the practices of the business. From his literary output it is evident that he nevertheless devoted a great deal of his time to the study of Torah and secular disciplines. Because of his involvement in a bitter inheritance squabble, R' Avraham was thrown into prison. There he wrote the most intriguing of his works, Gei Chizayon. The work uses the literary device of conversations between the author and his dead father to set down the author's innermost thoughts. The son tells the father about the vicissitudes of his life and pours out before him his pain and suffering. In the second part of the work the father takes the son on a tour of *gehinom*, and shows him the people who inhabit this underworld. Not surprisingly, R' Avraham finds that in *gehinom*, as in this world, bankers hold a prominent place. Part of this work was printed in Alexandria (5640/1880) and the rest of it is still extant in manuscript.

R' Avraham also wrote *Lekach Tov* (Venice, 5355/1595), parts of which *R' Yeshayah Horowitz deemed important enough to include in his *Shnei Luchos HaBris*. This work is designated for the education of the young and is an important inspirational (*mussar*) work which explains the fundamentals of Judaism in the form of a conversation between a teacher and his student. It has been reprinted many times and translated into several languages.

His other printed works are *Moshia Chossim* (Venice, 5347/1587), prayers and instructions on how to conduct oneself during a plague, and *Eishes Chayil* (Venice, 5366/1606), a guide for married life, in the form of a commentary on *Proverbs* 31.

However, most of R' Avraham's works were never published. These include his magnum opus *Beis Yaar HaLevanon*, a religious-philosophical treatise of encyclopedic scope, and various treatises on philosophy, science, mathematics, astronomy, and astrology.

R' Yehudah Loeve (Maharal of Prague)

רַבִּי יְהוּדָה לֵיוְוָא בֶּן בְּצַלְאֵל
(מַהֲרַ"ל מִפְּרָאג)

b. Posen (?), Poland, c. 5286/1526
d. Prague, Czechoslovakia, 18 Elul 5369/1609

R' Yehudah, the youngest of four sons, was probably born in Posen, sometime between 5272/1512 and 5286/1526 (the

later date is more probable), to R' Betzalel ben Chaim of Worms. R' Chaim was a grandson of R' Loeve the Elder of Prague (died c. 5200/1440), a Torah scholar and kabbalist of legendary fame who traced his ancestry to R' Hai Gaon and King David. R' Betzalel's brothers, R' Yaakov and R' Helmann, were accomplished scholars and the progenitors of famous families (see *R' Eliezer Ashkenazi Ish Tzvi, *R' Shmuel Eliezer Eidels).

An old tradition has it that R' Betzalel's brothers traveled to Poland to study in its famous yeshivos, while he remained in Worms to take care of his aged father. R' Chaim consoled his eldest son with a blessing that because of his filial devotion he would have four sons who would 'illuminate the Diaspora.' This actually occurred. The eldest of these sons, *R' Chaim ben Betzalel, is famous in his own right. R' Sinai served as *rosh yeshivah* in Prague and rabbi of Nikolsburg, and R' Shimshon served as rabbi of Kremenitz (Poland). The fourth and most illustrious son, R' Yehudah, received his education from his father R' Betzalel, from the sages of his generation, and largely from intense study on his own. In his works he never mentions any of his teachers by name.

Maharal's life story is woven through with wondrous anecdotes from his earliest youth. About his marriage, it is related that when he was engaged to his future wife Perel, his wealthy prospective father-in-law, R' Shmuel ben Yaakov of Prague, known as 'Reich Shmelke' (the rich Shmelke), promised to support him and his family. However, before the marriage could take place, the man became impoverished and was unable to keep his promise. Being an honest man, he notified Maharal and told him he was at liberty to find another match. Maharal answered that he would still wed his betrothed, but due to their meager finances the wedding had to be postponed.

During this time Perel opened a commission bakery, and with the profits she was able to sustain herself and her elderly parents. One day, a soldier on horseback stuck a spear into a loaf of bread and carried it off. Perel ran after him and begged him not to rob her of the bread which was the only means of support for her parents and herself. Greatly moved, the soldier explained that he had not eaten for three days, as it was wartime and he had no money with him. However, he gave her a pretty shawl as security, saying that if he would not pay for the bread within twenty-four hours, she could sell the shawl. Perel agreed and after several days, seeing that the soldier did not return, she unfolded the shawl in order to determine its worth — and was stunned to discover that it was lined with pure gold! She at once wrote Maharal that good fortune had smiled upon them and the wedding could take place.

Maharal served as rabbi in several localities. His first rabbinical post was in Nikolsburg, Moravia (Czechoslovakia), to which he was elected in 5313/1553; eventually he became Chief Rabbi of all Moravia. Maharal enacted many edicts for the religious and economic improvement of the communities of Moravia during the twenty years he served as their spiritual leader.

He left Nikolsburg in 5333/1573 and settled in Prague, where he opened a yeshivah and taught numerous disciples. Maharal, who was an outspoken opponent of the widespread *pilpul* method of Talmudic study introduced by *R' Yaakov Pollak, opened his yeshivah especially for the purpose of expounding Talmud and *halachah* using a logical method without *pilpul*. He also stressed the study of *Mishnah* and established

Mishnah study groups throughout Prague. Among his disciples were *R' David Ganz and *R' Yom Tov Lipman Heller, author of the *Tosefos Yom Tov* commentary to the *Mishnah*.

Maharal took an active part in the interests of the community, as he had done in Moravia, and he was responsible for the formulation of the by-laws (*takanos*) of the newly founded communities of Bohemia as well.

In Prague, Maharal began redacting and publishing his many manuscripts. His first work was *Gur Aryeh* (Prague, 5338-39/1578-79), a super-commentary to *Rashi's Torah commentary.

In 5344/1584, Maharal temporarily left Prague and accepted the rabbinical post of Posen, only to return to Prague in 5348/1588 and continue his work there. Maharal's fame as a saint and miracle worker spread along with his reputation for wisdom, and even came to the ears of Emperor Rudolph II of Austria, who had a private audience with him at the royal palace in the winter of 5352/1592.

That same year Maharal again left Prague and reassumed the rabbinical post of Posen and its neighboring communities, remaining there until 5358/1598, when the Prague community officially installed him as their Chief Rabbi.

Maharal was a profound thinker and a prolific author. He synthesized kabbalistic concepts with aggadic and midrashic material, discarding the kabbalistic terminology and presenting his material in a style uniquely his own. His writings stress the conceptual aspect of the *aggados*, pointing out that they contain profound truths, for which one must delve beneath their exterior veneer. Maharal emphasizes repeatedly that all of the sayings of the Sages 'are profound and true' and may not be disregarded. Maharal strongly rebukes the Jewish thinkers who sometimes reject the words of the *Tannaim* and *Amoraim*. Thus, he objects to *R' Avraham ibn Ezra's interpretation of the phrase אֲרַמִּי אֹבֵד אָבִי (*Deut.* 26:5), which counters the understanding of the Sages, and after a lengthy explanation remarks, "I have elaborated on this for [the benefit of] those who attempt to be wiser than the Sages, and have demonstrated that they [i.e., the Sages] knew the inner depths of wisdom and that no secret was hidden from them . . ." (*Gevuros Hashem*, ch. 54). Maharal insists on this tenet not only in regard to broad issues. Rather, he maintains that even down to the most minute details, the words of the Sages are full of allusions to the secrets known to them from 'the depths of wisdom.' Moreover, each of seemingly conflicting opinions of the Sages contains truths and profound wisdom. Maharal wrote an entire work, *Be'er HaGolah*, to explain some *aggados* which, superficially understood, seem to contradict what is represented by science to be the truth about physical phenomena, and which seem, on the surface, to be illogical. One part of this work is dedicated to a scathing criticism of *R' Azaryah min HaAdomim's *Me'or Einayim*, which dared to state the supposition that the Sages were wrong in some of their statements.

Just as he was unique and original in his approach to the *aggados,* so was Maharal original in his outlook upon Jewish education. He objected to many solidly entrenched practices and did not hesitate to voice his reservations. Thus he was against the practice of teaching young children Talmud. Instead, he felt that the system proposed in the *Mishnah* (*Avos* 5:21) should be followed. A child should be started on the study of Scripture in his fifth year and should concentrate on this study for five years. In his tenth year the child should be intro-

duced to a five-year program of *Mishnah* study. Only in the fifteenth year should one begin to study the Talmud.

Maharal argues for this system on psychological and educational grounds, contending that the minds of children are not sufficiently mature to grasp the intricate arguments of the Talmud. Only after the foundation has been laid with a strong knowledge of Scripture and *Mishnah* can the Talmud be approached. However, his primary objection is based on his insistence that the words of the Sages not be controverted.

Maharal was also opposed to the practice of teaching children the weekly portion — *sidra*. This system has the result that the ends of the longer *sidras* are not studied at all. Rather, the Scriptures should be studied in sequence from beginning to end. He also stressed the great importance of *chazarah* — intensive and constant review of one's learning (*Derush al HaTorah*). Maharal felt that the study of the *Mishnah* was essential also for adults, and instituted *Mishnah* study groups in Prague and other towns. The author of *Tosefos Yom Tov* (R' Yom Tov Lipman Heller) relates in the preface to his work that he was inspired to write this classic commentary because of his participation in one of these groups.

Maharal's works on *hashkafah* have made a profound impression on Jewish thought to this day. According to an oral tradition transmitted by Chabad *chassidim*, the *Baal HaTanya* (*R' Shneur Zalman of Liadi) based his work on the concepts expounded by the *Arizal and Maharal; the Koznitzer *Maggid* (*R' Yisrael Hopstein) wrote commentaries to explain some of the difficult passages in Maharal's work. The study of Maharal's works was strongly stressed in the Pshis'cha branch of Polish *chassidus,* and this influence is clearly discerned in the works of the *Sfas Emes* and *Avnei Nezer*, among others. The *mussar* movement also recognized the importance of these works, and in recent times R' Eliyahu Eliezer Dessler (the *mashgiach* of Poneviez) and R' Yitzchak Hutner (the *rosh yeshivah* of Yeshivas Rabbeinu Chaim Berlin) based their profound discourses primarily on Maharal's concepts.

His other works (besides *Gur Aryeh*) are as follows: *Gevuros Hashem* on the Exodus (Cracow, 5342/1582); *Derech Chaim* (Cracow, 5349/1589), a commentary on tractate *Avos*; *Netzach Yisrael* (Prague, 5359/1599), about the rewards of the world to come and the Messianic era; *Tiferes Yisrael* (Prague, 5353/1593), on the giving of the Torah; *Nesivos Olam* (Prague, 5356/1596), on ethics; *Be'er HaGolah* (Prague, 5358/1598), a commentary on some aggadic Talmud passages; *Or Chadash* (Prague, 5360/1600), on the Book of *Esther*; *Ner Mitzvah* (Prague, 5360/1600; with *Or Chadash*), on the *Chanukah* festival; *Chidushei Aggados* (London, 5720/1960), his commentary to the *aggados* in the Talmud; a dissertation for the Sabbath preceding Passover (*Derush LeShabbos HaGadol*, Prague, 5349/1589); a dissertation on the Torah (Prague, 5353/1593); a eulogy on the death of R' Akiva Ginsburg (Prague, 5358/1598); and a sermon for the Sabbath after *Rosh Hashanah* (*Derush LeShabbos Shuvah*, Prague, 5444/1684).

A responsum by Maharal was printed under the name *Teshuvah Be'Inyan Agunah* (Prague, 5349/1589); this very rare publication has been republished in modern times (Jerusalem, 5732/1972; with *Gur Aryeh* v. 5). Some halachic essays and summaries of *halachos* are interspersed in Maharal's writings on *hashkafah*, e.g., *Gevuros Hashem* ch. 48-51, 63, and *Hilchos Pesach* (at the end

of this volume in the London edition of 5714/1954).

Maharal is also quoted as an authoritative halachist by the *Bach, the *Magen Avraham, the *Taz and others. Among his published halachic works are *Chidushei Maharal*, a commentary on *Tur Yoreh Deah* (Sulzbach, 5535/1775), and *Chidushei Gur Aryeh* (Lemberg, 5623/1863), a Talmud commentary on tractates *Shabbos*, *Eruvin* and *Pesachim*.

Among the many wondrous deeds of Maharal, it is related that in order to combat the popular blood libel that Christians used against the Jews almost every Passover, Maharal constructed the *Golem*, a man he had fashioned out of clay and, with kabbalistic incantations, endowed with life and supernatural powers in order to detect plots against the Jewish community and to protect it.

Many of Maharal's descendants attained fame themselves. *R' Chaim Yair Bacharach and *R' Naftali Katz (author of *Semichas Chachamim*) were just two of his many famous descendants.

Maharal's reputation was not restricted to Jews alone, and his fame lingered on for centuries among the gentile population of Prague. In 5677/1917 the municipal government had a statue of Maharal erected in front of the municipal building; it remains there to this day.

R' Yaakov Kopelman

רַבִּי יַעֲקֹב קוֹפֶּלְמַאן בֶּן שְׁמוּאֵל בּוּנָם

b. Poland, 5317/1557
d. Brisk Dakau, Poland, 5370/1610

At the age of twenty-eight, R' Yaakov produced his *Ohel Yaakov* (Freiburg, 5344/1584), a commentary on selected passages of *R' Yosef Albo's *Sefer Halkkarim*. After studying in Frankfurt am Main for many years, he returned to

Poland on account of the plague which had broken out in Frankfurt am Main. He composed *Omek Halachah* (Cracow, 5359/1599), expositions of mathematical passages in the Talmud, illustrated by diagrams. This book received the approval of the Council of Four Lands (see **Historical Introduction**). R' Yaakov is also the author of a Yiddish translation of the *Targum* to the five *Megillos* and of the *Targum Sheini* on *Esther*.

[Kopelman is not a family name, but a nickname for Yaakov, equivalent to the name Kopel which is still in use today.]

R' Eliyahu ibn Chaim (Ranach)

רַבִּי אֵלִיָּהוּ אִבְּן חַיִּים (רָאנַ"ח)

b. Adrianople (Edirne), Turkey, c. 5290/1530
d. Constantinople (now Istanbul), Turkey
c. 5370/1610

In his native Adrianople, R' Eliyahu studied under R' Mordechai Matalon. Upon reaching maturity he occupied himself with teaching Talmud and *halachah*. In 5335/1575 he was called on to become Chief Rabbi of Constantinople, thus filling the most prestigious rabbinical post in Turkey, the occupant of which was officially recognized by the Sultan as the supreme religious authority of the Jews in his empire. R' Eliyahu held this position until his death. His opinion on halachic matters began to be sought from far and wide, and his contemporaries estimated the number of his responsa to be in the thousands.

R' Eliyahu is best known for his responsa, *Teshuvos R' Eliyahu ibn Chaim* (Constantinople, 5370/1610). Additional responsa by him are to be found in *Mayim Amukim* (Venice, 5407/1647), which contains his and *R' Eliyahu Mizrachi's responsa and includes his *chidushim* on tractate *Kesubos*. Later Talmudists and halachists gave much

weight to his decisions and praised his erudition, among them *R' Akiva Eiger, who referred to him often.

R' Eliyahu also composed sermons on the Torah entitled *HaNosen Imrei Shefer* (Venice, 5370/1610). A disciple of his who published R' Eliyahu's responsa reports that he wrote *chidushim* to many tractates of the Talmud, as well as numerous other works.

His son R' Michael, who was already a brilliant scholar while in his teens, died at the young age of twenty, greatly saddening and breaking the spirit of his father. R' Eliyahu's daughter was married to R' Nissim Benveniste; and *R' Moshe Benveniste, author of She'eilos UTeshuvos Bnei Moshe, was his grandson from this union.

R' Moshe Galante I (Maharam Galante)

רַבִּי מֹשֶׁה בֶּן מָרְדְּכַי גַּאלַאנְטֵי
(מַהֲרַ"ם גַלַנְטִי)

b. Rome, Italy, c. 5280/1520
d. Safed, Eretz Yisrael, c. 5370/1610

The elder brother of *R' Avraham Galante, R' Moshe emigrated with his brother to *Eretz Yisrael* in about 5300/1540. R' Moshe studied under *R' Yosef Caro, who ordained him at the age of twenty-two. An accepted halachic authority, he became Chief Rabbi of the Safed community after the death of *R' Moshe Trani in 5340/1580.

R' Moshe's works include an index to Scriptural passages found in the *Zohar*, entitled *Mafte'ach HaZohar* (Venice, 5326/1566); *Kehilos Yaakov* (Safed, 5338/1578), a homiletic-kabbalistic commentary on *Ecclesiastes*; and *She'eilos UTeshuvos Maharam Galante*, a volume of responsa (Venice, 5368/1608). A second volume of responsa which was ready for publication was never printed. Two kabbalistic dissertations' by R'

Moshe, titled *Sod HaMalbush* and *Maamar LeChassan,* were printed in the commentary to *Ruth* by R' Ovadyah Hamon of Bertinoro.

R' Moshe was the father of R' Yedidyah Galante, the author of *chidushim* to some *masichtos* of the Talmud (printed together with his father's responsa), and the grandfather of *R' Moshe (ben Yehonasan) Galante II.

R' Yaakov Castro (Maharikash)

רַבִּי יַעֲקֹב בֶּן אַבְרָהָם קַשְׁטְרוֹ (מַהֲרִיקַ"ש)

b. Egypt, c. 5285/1525
d. Cairo, Egypt, 5370/1610

R' Yaakov was a disciple of *R' Levi ibn Chaviv and *Radvaz. While still in his youth, he played an important role in shaping the halachic and educational path of Egyptian Jewry. He held a rabbinical post in Cairo and also established a yeshivah there.

During a trip to *Eretz Yisrael* in 5330/1570, R' Yaakov spent his stay in Safed at the home of *R' Yosef Caro, and he recorded various customs which he observed at the home of the elderly sage.

Eventually R' Yaakov became the leader of Egyptian Jewry, his halachic decisions being accepted by them even in preference to the decisions of the *Shulchan Aruch.* His responsa entitled *Ohalei Yaakov* (Leghorn, 5543/1783) contain a wide correspondence with leading figures of the period, among them *R' Moshe Trani and R' Yosef Caro.

R' Yaakov's chief work is *Erech Lechem* (Constantinople, 5378/1618), a commentary on the *Shulchan Aruch,* which in many instances subscribes to the view of *Rama — although R' Yaakov was unaware of Rama's work.

R' Yaakov's halachic opinions are cited in the works of later authors, such as *R' Yaakov Chagiz, *R' Shmuel Garmizan,

*R' Moshe ibn Chaviv, and the *Pri Chadash.* He also composed *Toldos Yaakov* (Jerusalem, 5625/1865), *chidushim* on *Maseches Beitzah;* his *chidushim* on other tractates have not been published. Other works are *Hilchos Nezirus,* published by R' Moshe Chagiz in *Halachos Ketanos* (Venice, 5464/1704), and *Kol Yaakov,* sermons, which has not been preserved.

R' Mano'ach Hendel

רַבִּי מָנוֹחַ הָעֶנְדִיל בֶּן פְּתַחְיָה

b. Brestitzka, Poland (Volhynia), c. 5300/1540
d. Vienna, Austria, 22 Tammuz 5371/1611

R' Mano'ach Hendel authored *chidushim* and emendations to the Talmud entitled *Chachmas Mano'ach,* printed posthumously by his son R' Moshe (Prague, 5372/1612), and later in the Vilna edition of the Talmud. The son mentions that his father wrote many works on various subjects from philosophy to *kabbalah,* and on such secular disciplines as astronomy and geometry. R' Mano'ach's super-commentary to the kabbalistic matter in *R' Bachya's Torah commentary to *Genesis* was published in the same year as the *chidushim,* under the title *Mano'ach Matza Chein* (Prague, 5371 or 5372/1611 or 1612). He also authored and published *Mano'ach HaLevavos* (Lublin, 5356/1596), the first commentary written on the classic *mussar* work *Chovos HaLevavos.*

R' Manoach was considered one of the great halachic authorities of his day, and *R' Yehoshua Falk HaKohen included him in the *beis din* which presided over a *get* proceeding in Vienna. This became a *cause célèbre* in its time (see *Teshuvos Masas Binyamin* §75-76). A responsum by R' Mano'ach has recently been printed by R' Y. Lewin in *Demuyos Ve'Eruyim Historiyim* (Jerusalem, 5748/1988).

R' Mordechai Yafeh (Levush)

רַבִּי מָרְדְּכַי בֶּן אַבְרָהָם יָפֶה (לְבוּשׁ)

b. Prague, Bohemia (now Czechoslovakia)
c. 5295 /1535
d. Posen, Poland, 3 Adar II 5372/1612

In his youth R' Mordechai studied under *Maharshal and *Rama. Although he was not much younger than Rama, he held him in great reverence and was especially loyal to him throughout his life, upholding his decisions and stressing his role as the ultimate halachic authority. In 5313/1553 R' Mordechai married, and we may assume that he then returned to his home town, Prague. He occupied himself with teaching and headed a ye-shivah. It was then that he began to write his monumental Levush on the four parts of Shulchan Aruch.

Because of the persecution of Bohemian Jewry and their expulsion from Prague by King Ferdinand, R' Mordechai traveled to Italy in 5321/1561. It is related that he exploited this opportunity to study astronomy and related sciences, which enabled him to fully comprehend *Rambam's explanations of lunar and solar calculations regarding the determining of the Jewish calendar. However, R' Mordechai himself relates in his preface to Levush HaChur that his commentary to the portions of Rambam which deal with astronomy is based on knowledge acquired in his youth from his teachers. Perhaps he merely perfected his knowledge of the sciences during his sojourn in Italy.

In 5332/1572, he accepted the position of rabbi of Horodna (Grodno, in Lithuania), followed by the rabbinate of Lublin, and later that of Kremenitz. In 5358/1598, when the *Maharal of Prague left Posen to settle in Prague, R' Mordechai returned to Poland to officiate as rabbi of Posen, and he remained in this city until his death. He was active until his last days, taking part in the halachic controversy surrounding a questionable get given in Vienna. His last communication on this matter was signed three days before his death and is printed in the responsa of *Maharam Lublin.

R' Mordechai was deeply involved in communal activities and regarded as the head of the 'Council of Three Lands,' the supreme Jewish legislative board of Eastern Europe (see **Historical Introduction**).

R' Mordechai was also a kabbalist, having studied under *R' Matisyahu Delacrot. He composed a super-commentary, entitled Levush Even Yekarah (Lublin, 5355/1595), to the kabbalistic Torah commentary of *R' Menachem Recanati. Even his halachic works are interspersed with kabbalistic information.

R' Mordechai is popularly known as 'the Levush' after the ten works which he wrote, each beginning with the word Levush and called by the general name Levush Malchus, after the royal garments worn by the author's Biblical namesake Mordechai (Esther 8:15). Each individual work has the word Levush as the first word in its title, followed by a word (or words) from the two verses in Esther 8:15-16) which describe Mordechai's royal garments, and the joy which gripped the city of Shushan upon Haman's downfall. In addition to Levush Even Yekarah, these works are: Levush HaTecheiles and Levush HaChur (Lublin, 5350/1590), both on Tur Orach Chaim; Levush Ateres Zahav (Cracow, 5354/1594) on Yoreh Deah; Levush HaButz VeHaArgaman (Cracow, 5358/1598) on Even HaEzer; Levush Ir Shushan (Cracow, 5359/1599) on Choshen Mishpat; Levush HaOrah (Prague, 5364/1604), a super-commentary to *Rashi's Torah commentary (in which he disputes many interpretations appearing in *Gur Aryeh,* written by his distinguished contemporary Maharal of Prague); *Levush Pinas Yikras* (Lublin, 5355/1595), a commentary to *Moreh Nevuchim (Guide for the Perplexed)* and its commentaries; *Levush Eider HaYakar* (Lublin, 5355/1595),a commentary to Rambam's *Hilchos Kiddush HaChodesh,* containing also a short commentary — *Beurei Yafeh* — to *Tzuras HaAretz,* *R' Avraham ben Chiya HaNassi's treatise on astronomy; and *Levush Simchah VeSasson,* sermons, which was never published.

[R' Mordechai reprinted the work on Orach Chaim in Lublin thirteen years after its first printing (5363/1603) and prefaced it with the following information: An otherwise unknown (to us) scholar, R' Yosef ben Menachem Yisrael, also known as R' Yosef HaLavan, approached the author and showed him that he had composed a similar work on *Orach Chaim.* R' Mordechai agreed to incorporate R' Yosef's work into his own, and to print it in the form of marginal glosses wherever the latter's work contained material not found in R' Mordechai's *Levush*.]

R' Mordechai explains in his introduction to his monumental halachic codex that he had perceived the need for a short halachic code at a very young age, for although *R' Yosef Caro's encyclopedic *Beis Yosef* was accepted enthusiastically by scholars and satisfied their needs, it was nevertheless too lengthy to be convenient for practical use by the multitudes. During his sojourn in Italy, R' Mordechai heard that R' Yosef Caro was preparing an abridged version of his work and desisted from beginning such a monumental undertaking. He decided instead to write commentaries to three very important works: Rambam's *Moreh Nevuchim,* R' Menachem Recanati's kabbalistic commentary to the Torah,

and *Hilchos Kiddush HaChodesh* in Rambam's *Mishneh Torah.* When, however, the *Shulchan Aruch* was finally published, R' Mordechai found it to have two shortcomings: the reasons for the decisions were entirely omitted, and the views of the Ashkenazic scholars were completely disregarded. He thereupon began writing his work, but stopped short upon hearing that *Rama was in the midst of writing his notes to the *Shulchan Aruch.* However, after seeing that Rama, too, wrote with the utmost brevity, not mentioning the reasons for his decisions, he resumed composing his work. R' Mordechai wished to present a comprehensive halachic code which would avoid the lengthy style of *Beis Yosef* and the overly terse and legal style of the *Shulchan Aruch.*

Although *Levush* gained popularity during R' Mordechai's lifetime, after his death the *Shulchan Aruch* was accepted as the code of law practically universally. *Levush* is, however, a most important work for the halachic student wishing to penetrate to the depth of a subject; it is cited extensively by the major commentaries on the *Shulchan Aruch.*

Several commentaries were written on *Levush: Eliyah Rabbah,* by *R' Eliyah Shapira, itself a very important work (printed with *Shulchan Aruch Orach Chaim,* Sulzbach, 5512/1752); *Eliyah Zuta* (by the same author, printed with *Levush HaTecheiles VeHaChur,* Prague, 5461/1701); and *Chaguras Shmuel* by R' Shmuel ben Uziel of Landsberg, to part of *Levush Ateres Zahav* (Frankfurt an der Oder, 5532/1772; and with *Levush,* Berditchev, 5579/1819). A short commentary to *Levush* on *Orach Chaim* was written by *R' Yom Tov Lipman Heller (*Malbushei Yom Tov;* Warsaw, 5654/1894).

Of all Rama's disciples it is perhaps the *Levush* who most closely resembled the venerated teacher. Aside from composing a comprehensive halachic code, the disciple also emulated his mentor's outlook. Like Rama, he occupied himself with astronomy and related sciences, and shared the former's view that a synthesis between the *kabbalah* and philosophy was possible and desirable.

R' David Ganz

רַבִּי דָּוִד בֶּן שְׁלֹמֹה גַּאנְז

b. Lippstadt, Germany, 5301/1541
d. Prague, Bohemia (now Czechoslovakia)
8 Elul 5373/1613

At a young age, R' David wandered from his native Germany to Cracow and stayed at the house of Rama who, in R' David's own words, raised and taught the young boy. R' David later settled in Prague (5324/1564), where he studied secular disciplines, especially astronomy and mathematics, and wrote his works. He is best known for his *Tzemach David* (Prague, 5352/1592), a historical chronicle divided into two parts, Jewish and non-Jewish chronology; the second part draws heavily on works of Christian chronologers. R' David writes in his introduction that the knowledge of history brings one closer to G-d, to recognizing the thread of Divine Providence and realizing how G-d protects his people: although many kingdoms have arisen and fallen, the Jewish nation continues to exist.

An expert astronomer and mathematician, R' David corresponded with some of the foremost scientists of his day, such as Tycho Brahe and Johann Kepler, and was allowed access to the observatory in Prague. He also composed a work on astronomy with a heavy stress on the calculation of the Jewish calendar, and an introduction in which he traces the development of this science among Jews and non-Jews. This work is entitled *Nechmad VeNaim* (Jessnitz, 5503/1743) and also appeared in an abridged version, likewise written by R' David, entitled *Magen David* (Prague, 5372/1612). Although R' David was familiar with the Copernican, heliocentric view of the planetary system, he rejected this in favor of the old Ptolemaic geocentric system. R' David also composed other works in this field and in the field of mathematics, but they were not published.

R' Yehoshua Falk Katz

רַבִּי יְהוֹשֻׁעַ פַלק בֶּן אַלֶכְּסַנְדְרִי כּ"ץ [כֹּהֵן צֶדֶק]

d. Lemberg, Poland (now Lvov, Russia)
19 Nissan 5374/1614

In his youth R' Yehoshua learned under *Rama (to whom he was related) and later under *Maharshal. He married Beila, the learned daughter of R' Yisrael Eidels, a communal leader *(parnas)* of the Jewish community in Lemberg, and the wealthy father-in-law supported his gifted son-in-law for decades after his marriage. R' Yehoshua founded a yeshivah at the home of his father-in-law in Lemberg. Among his outstanding disciples were *R' Yehoshua ben Yosef of Cracow, *R' Avraham Rappaport Shrentzel and *R' Yissachar Ber Eilenburg.

R' Yehoshua Falk, who had sufficient means of support from his father-in-law, declined to officiate in a rabbinical post — feeling that these offices would take away too much time from his learning — and chose instead to serve the *klal* by teaching and writing his classic works.

Although acknowledging the great positive accomplishment of *R' Yosef Caro in his *Beis Yosef* commentary on *Tur* — the organization of all the information pertinent to *halachah* around the order of the *Tur* — R' Yehoshua Falk nevertheless felt there still was place for further commentary. *R' Yosef Caro in his *Beis Yosef* had not concentrated sufficiently, in R' Yehoshua's opinion, on explaining the *Tur* itself, using that work primarily as a means of organizing his material, and many times — again, in R' Yehoshua's opinion — his conclusions were sometimes based on erroneous premises which were not compatible with the sources. In addition, the *Shulchan Aruch* had shortcomings: It was too brief, needed some explanation (R' Yehoshua was not totally satisfied with R' Mordechai Yafeh's attempts in this area), and some of the decisions needed correction.

R' Yehoshua Falk decided to write a work which would correct these shortcomings. He divided his intended work into four parts: *Perishah,* a concise commentary concentrating on understanding the view of *Tur*; *Derishah,* a more elaborate commentary investigating the sources themselves and establishing the correct conclusions to be drawn from them; and notes on *Rama's *Darchei Moshe,* bringing it up to date with all decisions and opinions cited after it was written. These three parts were given the general name *Beis Yisrael* but are today known as *Derishah UPerishah* (on *Yoreh Deah:* Lublin, 5395/1635; on *Even HaEzer:* Lublin, 5398/1638; and on all four *Turim:* Wilhermsdorf, 5486-87/1726-27). The fourth part is known as *Sma* (an acronym for *Sefer Me'iras Einayim*), a short and sufficient commentary on the *Shulchan Aruch* itself. This last commentary brought him much fame in the realm of *halachah,* and was quoted frequently with much praise by all *Shulchan Aruch* commentators. R' Yehoshua Falk, however, did not live long enough to complete the *Sma* on the

entire *Shulchan Aruch,* and it seems that only the section on *Choshen Mishpat* was written (Prague, 5366/1606), and was thereafter published in most editions of the *Choshen Mishpat.* His *Tur* commentary, which he completed on all four parts of that work, is published in all editions of the *Tur* prevalent today.

Ironically, his *Sefer Meiras Einayim* started a cycle which would eventually partially negate one of the aims which the codifiers of the *Shulchan Aruch* had attempted to achieve — the simplification of the *halachah* and the providing of a short method for allowing one to become proficient in this branch of Torah. Beginning with this commentary, a multitude of commentaries and super-commentaries have been written on the *Shulchan Aruch,* making its study a difficult and time-consuming task. Nevertheless, it may be said that the original goal was partially realized, for it is difficult to even imagine the confusion and insuperable obstacles to reaching halachic conclusions which would have ensued had the *Shulchan Aruch* not been written.

R' Yehoshua Falk also wrote *Kuntres R' Yehoshua Falk HaKohen* (Sulzbach, 5452/1692), a pamphlet containing enactments which were passed at the 'Council of Three Lands' which met at Gramnitz in 5367/1607, where he presided; most of these rulings concern the laws of usury. He also wrote responsa, *chidushim* on the Talmud, commentaries on the Torah, and some kabbalistic and philosophical treatises. All were destroyed by a fire in Lemberg.

R' Yehoshua's wife, Beila, was noted for her piety, exemplary character, charity, and erudition. She outlived her illustrious husband, settled in *Eretz Yisrael* after his death, and was buried in Jerusalem near the grave of the prophet

Zecharyah. Her son R' Yosef, in his preface to *Derishah UPerishah* to *Yoreh Deah*, cites a number of halachic customs that his mother had put into practice based on her own reasoning. Interestingly, the *Magen Avraham*, the great commentator to *Orach Chaim*, refers disparagingly to one of these customs of the 'rabbanis wife of the Sma' — namely her contention that on Yom Tov the *berachah* over the candle-lighting be recited before the kindling (on the Sabbath the candles are lit first and then the *berachah* is said) — but *R' Yechezkel Landau in his glosses *(Dagul MeRevavah)* to *Shulchan Aruch* upholds her scholarship, concluding with the verse in *Exodus* (35:25) '. . . woman [lit. women] whose heart has been elevated in wisdom . . .'

A widely held misconception about R' Yehoshua's family name should be corrected here; he did not have a one. Falk (or Walk) is a popular nickname for Yehoshua (today the name is pronounced Falik), and Katz is merely an acronym for *Kohen Tzedek,* and is only another way of saying HaKohen. The modern family name Katz evolved from this acronym, as did the name Segal from *Segan Leviyah*. R' Yehoshua referred to himself as his contemporaries did — as R' Falk HaKohen.

R' Yitzchak Chayes

רַבִּי יִצְחָק בֶּן אַבְרָהָם חַיּוֹת

d. Prossnitz (now Prostejov), Czechoslovakia
c. 5376/1616

A descendant of the sages of Provence, R' Yitzchak served successively in the rabbinates of Prossnitz and Prague (5344-47/1584-87), attracting numerous disciples with his erudition and saintliness. *R' David Ganz writes of him in his *Tzemach David*, 'The great rabbi whose fame is spread throughout the Diaspora; he cultivated many disciples and furthered the knowledge of Torah . . .' It seems that R' Yitzchak was a fervent adherent of the *pilpul* method of learning so popular during that era, and is strongly taken to task for this by *R' Chaim Yair Bacharach *(Teshuvos Chavos Yair* §123).

R' Yitzchak wrote *Pnei Yitzchak* (Cracow, 5351/1591) in two parts: a) *Apei Ravrevei,* laws found in *Shulchan Aruch Yoreh Deah* set to rhyme, and b) *Apei Zuta,* a commentary on the poetic part *(Apei Ravrevei)* with additional halachic material. To this, two poetic elegies written by R' Monish Chayes, R' Yitzchak's son, were added: one elegy on the destruction of the city of Posen by fire in the year 5350/1590, and another to lament the death of R' Monish's eighteen-year-old son. R' Yitzchak also wrote *Pachad Yitzchak* (Lublin, 5333/1573), a commentary on the Talmudic passage in *Gittin* which deals with the destruction of the Temple and other aggadic matters; and *Siach Yitzchak* (Prague, 5347/1587), the laws of *Pesach* set to rhyme.

R' Yitzchak's son, R' Menachem Monish Chayes, was rabbi of Vilna and one of the prominent rabbis of his age, and his (R' Menachem's) grandson, R' Yitzchak Chayes (born to his son R' Yaakov), was the author of *Zera Yitzchak* on the *Mishnah* (Frankurt on the Oder, 5492/1732), and was one of the prominent rabbis of his generation. In later generations we find many well-known personages bearing the family name Chayes proudly, among them R' Tzvi Hirsh Chayes of Zolkiew. R' Yechiel Hillel Altschuler, the author of *Metzudas David* on *Neviim* and *Kesuvim,* proudly proclaims in his preface that he is descended from R' Yitzchak Chayes.

R' Meir ben Gedalyah
(Maharam Lublin)

רַבִּי מֵאִיר בֶּן גְּדַלְיָה (מַהַר"ם לוּבְּלִין)

*b. Lublin or Cracow, Poland
5318/1558
d. Lublin, Poland, 16 Iyar 5376/1616*

R' Meir was born into an eminent family of scholars. His grandfather, R' Asher, was one of the first rabbis of Cracow; he headed a yeshivah there, and left behind a work on *kabbalah.*

Maharam studied in Cracow under R' Yitzchak Shapira, who eventually took the gifted young man as his son-in-law. R' Meir always prided himself on his kinship to R' Yitzchak, and almost invariably signed his responsa, ''Meir . . . son-in-law of 'the king,' the *gaon* R' Yitzchak *Kohen Tzedek.*'' R' Yitzchak did not leave any published works, but his son, R' Yaakov, published a work on the Torah called *Be'er Mayim Chaim* (Lublin, 5376/1616); one of its two parts is *Even Yaakov* on *Rashi,* containing mostly commentaries the author had heard from his venerated father.

At the young age of twenty-four, Maharam already occupied the post of *rosh yeshivah* in Lublin, and before he was thirty (5347/1587), he was called to serve as rabbi and *rosh yeshivah* of the prestigious community of Cracow, in succession to his father-in-law who had passed away in 5342/1582. His next post was in Lemberg, where he spent at least fourteen years until 5373/1613.

Not much is known about R' Meir's sons. Two of them — R' Gedalyah and R' Yitzchak — published their father's responsa. One of his sons-in-law — R' Yosef Yoske ben Elyakim (d. 2 Tishrei 5412/1651) — was *rav* of Lemberg. A second son-in-law — R' Mordechai — was *rav* of Brezan and co-author (together with *R' Avraham Chaim Shor and the latter's grandson R' Chaim) of the classic work *Tzon Kodashim* on most of *Seder Kodashim.*

Due to a delicate personal conflict — in which an influential scholar claimed that Maharam had offended the honor of *R' Yehoshua Falk, the greatly respected *rosh yeshivah* and author who also resided in Lemberg — a schism formed in the community and Maharam was forced to leave the city by order of the local municipal government. He then returned to his native Lublin where the post of rabbi was vacant, and occupied that post until his death.

Maharam concentrated on improving the quality of the program offered by his yeshivah, and numerous disciples flocked to him, among them such greats as the *Shelah, *R' Nassan Shapira II, and *R' Yehoshua ben Yosef of Cracow.

Maharam strongly opposed the uncritical acceptance of the *Shulchan Aruch* as the ultimate authority on *halachah.* He considered it a closed book, written without detailing the reasons for its decisions, and gleaning conflicting decisions from various authors instead of independently analyzing each subject from the sources.

In response to *R' Yeshayah Horowitz's query about a halachic inference R' Yeshayah attempted to draw from the *Shulchan Aruch,* he writes: 'It is not my custom to occupy myself with [the study of] the authors of the *Shulchan Aruch,* and surely not to base any halachic ruling on an inference from fine points in their language' (*Teshuvos* §11).

Maharam's halachic decisions were sought far and wide, and inquiries poured in even from Italy and Turkey. Some of his responsa were published by his sons and titled *Manhir Einei Chachamim BeHalachah* or, as it is more popularly known, *She'eilos UTeshuvos Maharam Lublin* (Venice, 5378/1618).

His work *Me'ir Einei Chachamim* (Venice, 5379/1619), *chidushim* on the Talmud, is considered indispensable in the understanding of *Tosafos,* and is published in most editions of the Talmud. His unpublished works, mentioned in his son's introduction to his responsa, include: *Maor HaGadol,* a commentary on the *Tur; Maor HaKattan,* a commentary on *Shaarei Dura; Ner Mitzvah,* a commentary on *Smag; Torah Or,* sermons based on the Torah; and *Or Shivas HaYamim,* an uncompleted halachic compendium equaling the *Shulchan Aruch* in scope.

Maharam was also acquainted with *kabbalah,* as can be seen from one of his responsa (§83). However, he does express his reservations about publicizing *kabbalah* matters, and states that his grandfather R' Asher's kabbalistic work (*Emek Berachah*) was not printed for this reason (loc. cit.). Ironically, R' Meir's son, R' Gedalyah, in his preface to his father's *Teshuvos,* promises to publish this work 'if *Hashem* will grant life.'

R' Moshe Mordechai Margolies

רַבִּי מֹשֶׁה מָרְדְּכַי בֶּן שְׁמוּאֵל מַרְגָּלִיּוֹת

b. Posen (?), Poland, c. 5300/1540
d. Cracow, Poland, 10 Kislev 5377/1616

R' Moshe's father, R' Shmuel, was rabbi of Posen and was highly regarded. (He is cited in *Vikuach Mayim Chaim* 77:4.) Very little is known about R' Moshe's life except that he was a *rosh yeshivah* in Cracow after that post was left vacant by the death of *R' Yosef Katz in c. 5351/1591.

He authored *Chasdei Hashem* (Cracow, 5349/1589), kabbalistic commentaries on the thirteen attributes of G-d as enumerated in *Exodus* (34:6,7), and on *Psalms* 62:13; the commentary on *Psalms* 62:13 explains the verse in

twenty-six different ways. He also was editor of the publication of the *Zohar Chadash* with *Midrash HaNe'elam* in Cracow (5363/1603), adding many features (emendations by the Arizal, his own comments, etc.) to this work. R' Moshe Mordechai also wrote a *selichah* commemorating the martyrs' deaths of two brothers who were killed in Warsaw in the year 5356/1596 (*Selichah,* Cracow, 5357/1597), and a prayer called *Maaneh Rach* (Cracow, 5349/1589), which is cited by the *Shelah.*

R' Shabsai Sheftl Horowitz I

רַבִּי שַׁבְּתַי שֶׁעֶפְטִיל
בֶּן עֲקִיבָא הַלֵּוִי הֹורוֹוִיץ

b. 5325/1565
d. Prague, Bohemia (now Czechoslovakia)
5379/1619

A close kinsman of the *Shelah, R' Shabsai Sheftl was titled *HaRofei,* indicating that his occupation was in the field of medicine. His father, R' Akiva (probably the brother of R' Avraham Horowitz, the *Shelah's father), was killed during a wave of religious pogroms.

R' Shabsai Sheftl composed *Shefa Tal* (Hanau, 5372/1612), a popular kabbalistic work which follows the views of *Ramak. Arranged as a commentary on *Iggeres HaTaamim* (a kabbalistic work ascribed to R' Aharon of Cardena but actually authored by R' Aharon Avraham ben Baruch), it is actually a textbook about the fundamentals of *kabbalah* and is recommended for beginners. He also authored *Nishmas Shabsai HaLevi* (Prague, 5376/1616), a kabbalistic treatise on matters pertaining to the soul, and a commentary on *Moreh Nevuchim* (*Guide for the Perplexed*) which was not published. An abridged version of *Shefa Tal* by R' Avraham Ankavah, entitled *Chamar Chadas VeAtik,* was published in

Leghorn in 5604/1844 (together with *Otzros Chaim*).

R' Shlomo Ephraim Lunshitz

רַבִּי שְׁלֹמֹה אֶפְרַיִם בֶּן אַהֲרֹן לוּנְטְשִׁיץ

b. Lenshitz (Leczica) (?), Poland
d. Prague, Bohemia (now Czechoslovakia)
7 Adar II 5379/1619

A disciple of *Maharshal, R' Ephraim (the name Shlomo was added during an illness) served as *rosh yeshivah* in Lemberg and, from 5364/1604 until his death, as rabbi of Prague. R' Shlomo Ephraim excelled in the field of homiletics and he authored the following works, all classics in this field: *Ir Giborim* (Basel, 5340/1600); *Olelos Ephraim* (Lublin, 5350/1590); *Kli Yakar*, a very popular Torah commentary (Lublin, 5362/1602); *Sifsei Daas* (Prague, 5370/1610); *Orach LeChaim* (Lublin, 5355/1595), two sermons for the holidays and a liturgical poem for recitation during the meal; and *Amudei Sheish* (Prague, 5371/1611). *Rivevos Ephraim*, mentioned in the introduction to *Orach LeChaim*, was never published.

R' Ephraim also authored *selichos* to be said at a special service on 2 Adar, in remembrance of the suffering of the Jews of Prague during the pogroms perpetrated upon them in 5371/1611.

R' Binyamin Aharon Solnik of Podayetz (Podhajce, Podgaitsy)

רַבִּי בִּנְיָמִין אַהֲרֹן בֶּן אַבְרָהָם סָלְנִיק
מִפּוֹדְהַיְיץ

d. Podayetz, Poland (now Russia)
c. 5380/1620

R' Binyamin Aharon was a disciple of *R' Shlomo ben Yehudah Leib, *Rama, *Maharshal, and *R' Nassan Nata Shapira I. He lived for many years in Cracow, where he studied under Rama and where he remained for many years

after his mentor's death. After serving as rabbi in various congregations, he accepted the rabbinate of Podayetz (in Eastern Galicia) and remained in this position until his demise. He was a staunch supporter of Rama's rulings, upholding his view even when his own (R' Binyamin's) inclination differed from it. He may thus be counted among those authorities in the generation after Rama who were instrumental in bringing about the unqualified acceptance of the *Shulchan Aruch* both by the masses and by the rabbis.

R' Binyamin's responsa, *Masas Binyamin* (Cracow, 5393/1633), which contains one hundred-twelve answers to inquiries and a few pages of glosses to the *Shulchan Aruch,* is a respected halachic work which is quoted as an authority by later scholars. The author was blind and sick for at least the last ten years of his life, but this did not hinder him from writing decisions on difficult questions. Especially poignant is his responsum — occasioned by his own blindness — about the permissibility of a blind man being called up to the Torah. One is amazed by the great number of sources cited in this responsum. R' Binyamin mentions the opinions of his contemporaries, such as *R' Yehoshua Falk, *R' Mordechai Yafeh and others, with great respect.

R' Binyamin also wrote a work in Yiddish containing all of the laws pertaining to women, titled *Mitzvas HaNashim* (Cracow, 5337/1577), which enjoyed great popularity during the author's lifetime and went into many editions.

Two of R' Binyamin's sons — R' Avraham and R' Yaakov Yekl — were respected Torah scholars, cited in their father's work. R' Yaakov Yekl is the author of *Nachalas Yaakov* (Cracow, 5402/1642), a super-commentary on

*Rashi's commentary to *Chumash*, which also contains some criticism of *R' Eliyahu Mizrachi's commentary. The other son, R' Avraham, who was rabbi of Brisk, corresponded with the greats of his generation (the *Bach*, R' Meir Katz and the *Pnei Yehoshua*). R' Binyamin's son-in-law, R' Menachem Mann, was rabbi of Vienna. *R' Yechezkel Katzenel-lenbogen, rabbi of Hamburg and author of *Knesses Yechezkel,* and his contemporary, *R' Aryeh Leib, author of *Shaagas Aryeh,* were R' Binyamin's descendants.

R' Menachem Azaryah of Fano (Rama of Fano)

רַבִּי מְנַחֵם עֲזַרְיָה בֶּן יִצְחָק בְּרָכְיָה מִפַאנוֹ
(רְמַ"ע מִפַאנוֹ)

b. Fano (?), Italy, 5308/1548
d. Mantua, Italy, 4 Av 5380/1620

A most outstanding scholar since his earliest youth, Rama of Fano was also blessed with great wealth which he had inherited from his parents. Besides generously dispensing alms to the poor, R' Menachem also used his wealth to procure rare and important manuscripts and to publish others. When he was only twenty-six years old, *R' Yosef Caro sent him his work *Kessef Mishneh,* which Rama published, defraying some of the expense from his own pocket.

R' Menachem, who is also known as R' Emmanuel, studied under R' Yishmael Chanina of Vallmontone and R' Ezra of Fano, later rabbi of Mantua, who instructed him in *kabbalah.* He married the daughter of R' Yitzchak Foa, rabbi of Reggio, a noted Torah personality in his day. (Responsa by him are printed in *Pachad Yitzchak* and *Teshuvos Rama MiFano.*)

Besides his preoccupation with the study of Talmud and *halachah,* Rama was an ardent kabbalist. He struck up a close relationship with *R' Moshe Cor-dovero, to whom he sent generous sums of money. R' Moshe sent him a copy of his kabbalistic masterpiece, *Pardes Rimonim,* part of which Rama summarized and provided with a commentary entitled *Pelach HaRimon* (Venice, 5360/1600). After R' Moshe's demise in 5330/1570, Rama paid one thousand ducats to R' Moshe's widow for allowing his scribes to make him a copy of *Or Yakar,* R' Moshe's extensive commentary on the *Zohar.*

The arrival of *R' Yisrael Seruk in Italy brought about a turning point in Rama's kabbalistic knowledge. R' Yisrael, who had studied under the *Ari, introduced R' Ezra of Fano and Rama to the kabbalistic doctrines of the new master, and Rama became an ardent follower of the Ari's school. He was instrumental in disseminating these teachings throughout Italy, and no doubt the great interest in *kabbalah* shown by subsequent generations of scholars in Italy is largely due to his influence. His disciples were numerous and his reputation spread far beyond the borders of Italy. *R' Avraham Abale Gombiner cites R' Menachem's views with great reverence in his authoritative commentary, *Magen Avraham* to *Shulchan Aruch Orach Chaim,* and such luminaries as *R' Yehoshua ben Yosef, author of *She'eilos UTeshuvos Pnei Yehoshua,* wrote commentaries on Rama's *Assarah Maamaros.* (R' Yehoshua's commentary was plagiarized and published under a different scholar's name; see preface to *She'eilos UTeshuvos Pnei Yehoshua,* vol I.)

Rama had a saintly appearance and was regarded as a holy man, revered by all who came in contact with him. He was a very prolific author and composed many works, mostly of a kabbalistic nature. Most of these works do not focus on the technical side of the *kabbalah,* but concentrate more on its moral and ideological aspect — thus making the works accessible even to those scholars not fully acquainted with the intricacies of the 'secrets of the Torah.' Here are found many elucidations of obscure *aggados*, and edifying concepts to live with. Perhaps this can be attributed to R' Menachem's youthful immersion in Ramak's writings, and their lasting influence upon him.

R' Menachem's halachic works are *Teshuvos Menachem Azaryah* (Venice, 5360/1600); *Alfasi Zuta*, a short halachic treatise based on *Rif's Sefer HaHalachos* with additional *chidushim* (v. 1: Jerusalem, 5645/1885, v. 1,2: Jerusalem, 5739-40/1979-80).

Among his works on the *kabbalah*, the best known is his *Assarah Maamaros* (*Ten Essays*), a compendium of various treatises, or *maamarim*, some of which are substantial works themselves. This compendium, which the author had probably planned to print in installments, was not published in its entirety during the author's lifetime, and it is impossible today to establish which ten treatises the author had originally contemplated including in it. The first printing of *Assarah Maamaros* (Venice, 5360/1600) included *Maamar Chikur Din* on Divine justice and judgment; *Maamar Em Kol Chai*, intended as sermons for *Rosh Hashanah*, with an emphasis on the matriarch Sarah and the patriarchs; and *Maamar HaMidos*, about the thirteen rules (*midos*) for Biblical exegesis and their kabbalistic significance. His *Maamar Olam Kattan*, on the various configurations of the soul, was published in *R' Yosef Delmedigo's Matzreif LaChachmah* (Basel, 5389/1629); and *Maamar Halttim* (Cracow, 5404/1644), a kabbalistic exposition on the twenty-eight times (*ittim*) mentioned in *Ecclesiastes*, and other time-related concepts, was published separately. This *maamar* also

discusses astronomic concepts mentioned in the Talmud and *midrash*. These two *maamarim* were added to the three mentioned previously and were printed together (Frankfurt am Main, 5448/1688) under the name *Amaros Tehoros*, with a commentary, and it is these five discourses which have come to be known as *Assarah Maamaros*.

Other *maamaros* are *Maamar Tzivos Hashem* (Hamburg, 5422/1662; together with *Maamar Olam Kattan* as *Maamar HaChamishi VeHaShishi*); *Maamar Yonas Eilem* (Amsterdam, 5408/1648); *Maamar Meah Kesita* (Aleksenitz, 5527/1767) on the Tetragrammaton (four-lettered Name of G-d); *Maamar Mayan Ganim* (Munkacs, 5660/1900), on the festivals and *sefiras ha'omer*; *Maamar HaNefesh* (Piotrkow, 5663/1903); *Maamar HaRekiyim* and *Maamar HaYesodos* (Chernowitz, 5620/1860); *Maamar Shabsos Hashem* (Warsaw, 5650/1890; in *Derech Emunah*); and *Maamar HaMiluim* (Aleksenitz, 5526/1766; in *Tikunei Shabbos*).

Other works of R' Menachem are: *Kanfei Yonah* (Koretz, 5546/1786), general rules on *kabbalah* and *kavanos* for the prayers; *Sefas Emes* (Lubachov, 5659/1899), a miscellany arranged alphabetically; *Ayin-beis Yedios* (Lvov, 5627/1867), introductory rules for the study of *kabbalah*; and *Gilgulei Neshamos* (Prague, 5448/1688), on the transmigration of souls.

A dispute with R' Avraham Amigo about the procedure to be used in waving the *lulav* and circling the *bimah* with it caused Rama to write a responsum called *Yemin Hashem Romemah* (Venice, 5365/1605; also in *Toldos Adam*, Venice, 5360/1600). He also authored *Seder Avodah Rabbah VeZuta* which is printed in many old *siddurim* and separately (Venice, 5350/1590), an elaborate liturgical description of the daily and holiday Temple service, written in rhyme.

R' Vidal Tzarfati

רַבִּי וִידָאל בֶּן יִצְחָק צָרְפַתִּי

b. Fez, Morocco, c. 5300/1540
d. Fez, Morocco, c. 5380/1620

Scion of an illustrious rabbinical family which traced its origin to *Rabbeinu Tam, and was therefore called Tzarfati (French), R' Vidal was the rabbi of Fez and *R' Aharon ibn Chaim served under him in his beis din. He composed Derech HaKodesh (Husyatin, 5668/ 1908), a commentary on Sifra; and sermons on the Torah entitled Tzuf Devash, on Esther entitled Megillas Sesarim, on Psalms entitled Otzar Nechmad, and on Ruth entitled Hatza'as Rus (all in Amsterdam, 5478/1718). He also composed a short commentary on Midrash Rabbah entitled Imrei Yosher (in Midrash Rabbah, Warsaw, 5634/1874); and comments on *R' Eliyahu Mizrachi's commentary to Rashi (in his descendant R' Shmuel Tzarfati's Nimukei Shmuel; Amsterdam, 5478/1718). *Chida comments that R' Vidal's writings are very concise and deep, and that intense concentration is necessary to plumb their depths.

R' Yom Tov Tzahalon (Maharit Tzahalon)

רַבִּי יוֹם טוֹב בֶּן מֹשֶׁה צָהֲלוֹן
(מהריט"ץ – מַהֲרִי"ט צָהֲלוֹן)

b. Safed, Eretz Yisrael, c. 5319/1559
d. Safed (?), Eretz Yisrael, c. 5380/1620

R' Yom Tov was born into a family of Spanish exiles residing in Safed. A certain R' Moshe Tzahalon, who is mentioned with the title Chacham in the responsa of *Mabit (v. 3, §29), and is a correspondent of *R' Yosef Caro (Avkas Rochel, §76), is probably R' Yom Tov's father.

A disciple of the otherwise unknown R' Moshe Besodo, R' Yom Tov may also have studied under R' Yosef Caro for a short period. Although he spent most of his life in Safed, R' Yom Tov left Eretz Yisrael on a few occasions and is known to have visited Lebanon, Syria and Turkey. While in Safed in the years 5356-59/1596-99, R' Yom Tov received the coveted semichah ordination at the hands of R' Yaakov bei Rav II (grandson of the re-establisher of the semichah; see Historical Introduction).

R' Yom Tov began his halachic career while yet a young man, already taking part in the halachic controversy occasioned by a questionable chalitzah act performed by a daughter-in-law of the famed R' Yosef Caro.

This was a turbulent era in the history of Safed. In 5344/1584 the Druze revolted against the Turks and a period of unrest began which lasted until 5351/ 1591. In the year 5351/1591 itself, there was a crop failure which resulted in famine. R' Yom Tov left Safed and eventually Eretz Yisrael at this time, not to return until c. 5355/1595.

R' Yom Tov wrote numerous responsa, of which one volume was printed in Venice (5454/1694), and two additional volumes (Teshuvos Maharit Tzahalon HeChadashos) have recently been published (Jerusalem, v. #1, 5740/ 1980; v. #2, 5741/1981). In addition to this, he wrote an extensive commentary to Avos D'Rabbi Nassan, entitled Magen Avos. R' Yom Tov completed this work at the young age of seventeen; it remains unpublished. He also wrote an extensive commentary to the five Megillos and published the part on Megillas Esther in Safed (5337/1577) under the name Lekach Tov. This extremely rare sefer was republished recently in a limited edition (Jerusalem, 5737/1977). On the title page of this work the publisher states that the author wrote it as a *Purim* gift for his father. R' Yom Tov mentions *chidushim* to *mesechtos* and sermons, but these are not extant. Some of his *chidushim* to *Bava Metzia* were printed with his responsa in Venice. *Chida writes about R' Yom Tov that in his generation it was said that the *kushyos* (Talmudic difficulties) raised by him were impossible to resolve.

R' Chaim Vital

רַבִּי חַיִּים בֶּן יוֹסֵף וִיטַאל

b. Safed, Eretz Yisrael, 5303/1543
d. Damascus, Syria, 1 Iyar 5380/1620

R' Chaim's father, R' Yosef Vital, was an expert scribe whose meticulousness and saintly character caused his *tefillin* and *mezuzos* to be much sought after. In 5301/1541 R' Yosef left his native Calabria (Southern Italy) — he was also nicknamed 'Calabres' — and settled in Safed where, soon thereafter, his son R' Chaim was born.

From his earliest youth, a glorious future was predicted for R' Chaim by great sages such as *R' Yosef Caro and R' Shabsai Lapidos, a kabbalist in Safed. The latter indicated to R' Chaim that if he would occupy himself with the study of *kabbalah* and neglect worldly pursuits, he would rise to an unheard-of degree in this field.

R' Chaim became a disciple of *R' Moshe Alsheich, and studied Talmud and *halachah* under him. R' Chaim was highly regarded by R' Moshe, and the latter ordained him with the *semichah* ordination (see **Historical Introduction**), which he had previously received from R' Yosef Caro. R' Chaim, who was ordained in 5350/1590, was one of the last to receive the *semichah*.

R' Chaim began his kabbalistic studies under *R' Moshe Cordovero. He attained a thorough knowledge in this field, and in 5329/1569, at the young age of twenty-six, he began composing a commentary on the *Zohar*, the principal book of *kabbalah*, according to the teachings and views of his master. This commentary was later incorporated by *R' Avraham Azulai in his *Zaharei Chamah* (Venice, 5415/1655).

The year 5330/1570 was a turning point in R' Chaim's life. It was in this year that the *Ari established his home in Safed with the primary purpose of transmitting his extensive and sacred kabbalistic secrets to R' Chaim. Indeed, R' Chaim became the Ari's foremost disciple and expounder of his school of thought.

At first R' Chaim had difficulty in comprehending the intricate secrets which the Ari revealed to him. Once, while both were in Tiberias, the Ari took R' Chaim for a ride in a small boat. At a precise spot the Ari filled a cup with water and commanded R' Chaim to drink. After R' Chaim drank, the Ari assured him that he would thenceforth be able to absorb the sublime wisdom, as the water he had given him to drink was from the Biblical well of Miriam. From then on, reports R' Chaim, he truly began to understand the master's discourses.

The Ari, who committed almost nothing of his vast teachings to writing, relied solely upon R' Chaim to accurately transcribe his kabbalistic system and works for future generations, and disregarded attempts by other disciples in this field, as their writings had shortcomings due to a lack of proper comprehension. When the Ari died, in the summer of 5332/1572, R' Chaim was recognized as his successor, for only he was trusted by the master to accurately transmit his thoughts to writing. A group of the Arizal's disciples signed a formal declaration whereby they bound themselves to be subordinate to R' Chaim and not to divulge the secrets of the *kabbalah* to others without the master's permission. Like his teacher the Ari, R' Chaim was known as a saintly man with the power to perform miracles.

R' Chaim remained in Safed for only a few years after the Arizal's demise. By 5338/1578 he had already moved to Jerusalem, and in 5344/1584 was appointed *dayan* there through the recommendation of his teacher, R' Moshe Alsheich. R' Chaim later settled in Damascus (c. 5353/1593), where he resided until his death.

R' Chaim devoted his energies to arranging the many kabbalistic dissertations he had heard from the Ari in the proper sequence, in order to represent a complete doctrine and school of thought. This work was called *Eitz Chaim* and was divided by R' Chaim into eight parts (*Shemonah She'arim*). This is, however, not identical with the classic published *kabbalah* work *Eitz Chaim* (see below). R' Chaim kept his manuscripts tightly locked away, not allowing anyone to see them, as he feared that he would be punished — his life span shortened — for disseminating these 'secrets of the Torah'. Once, when he fell seriously ill, his brother R' Moshe accepted five hundred gold coins in return for the key to R' Chaim's locked closet. Within three days, about one hundred scribes copied most of the manuscripts, which were subsequently returned to their original place. It was thus that the kabbalistic doctrine of the Ari began to circulate among the kabbalists of *Eretz Yisrael*. Even after he had put down the Arizal's *kabbalah* in writing, R' Chaim Vital still devoted considerable time and energy to elucidating his master's teachings. He wrote explanations of difficult points, clarified concepts, and resolved contradictions in

the Arizal's system. These writings are known as the *mahadurah basra* (lit. second edition) of the *Eitz Chaim*. R' Chaim did not want these writings to be published, and had them buried in the cemetery. However, a generation later, *R' Yaakov Tzemach and *R' Avraham Azulai, in a dream, received permission from R' Chaim to exhume the manuscripts, and they did so. These manuscripts, along with the ones which were not ordered by R' Chaim to be buried, but rather were left in the possession of his son, *R' Shmuel Vital, formed the nucleus of the many books of the Ari's *kabbalah* which were later published.

R' Chaim's best-known and monumental work on the Ari's *kabbalah* is *Eitz Chaim*. There are two arrangements of this work. The first is *Shemonah She'arim*, by R' Shmuel Vital (R' Chaim's son), in which all the material is divided into eight parts. The various parts were published separately over a long period of time in various arrangements. Long after R' Shmuel's demise an edition containing all of the sections was printed in Jerusalem (5723/1963). The second and better-known arrangement by *R' Meir Popperos divides the *Eitz Chaim* into *Pri Eitz Chaim*, *Derech Eitz Chaim*, and *Nof Eitz Chaim*. The part named *Derech Eitz Chaim*, containing the fundamentals of the Arizal's *kabbalah*, was later printed (Koretz, 5542/1782) under the name *Eitz Chaim* and is now referred to by this name, and the part called *Pri Eitz Chaim*, containing kabbalistic *kavanos* for the prayers, performance of the *mitzvos* and observance of the festivals, was printed in two differing versions (Koretz, 5542/1782; there, 5545/1785; see *R' Meir Popperos). Other partial arrangements of R' Chaim's writings are: *Otzros Chaim* (Koretz, 5543/1783); *Likutei Shas* (5543/1783); *Arba*

Meios Shekel Kessef (Koretz, 5564/1804); Likutei Torah (Zolkiew, 5535/1775); Mevo She'arim (Koretz, 5542/1782), an introduction to the Arizal's kabbalah; Olas Tamid (Salonica, 5614/1854), kabbalistic commentaries to the prayers; and glosses on the Zohar (printed in many editions of the Zohar).

A collection of hitherto unpublished treatises on kabbalah by R' Chaim has recently been published under the title Kesavim Chadashim L'Rabbi Chaim Vital (Jerusalem, 5748/1988), including (among others) a commentary to Sefer Yetzirah, and an additional part of Shaarei Kedushah. R' Chaim also composed Eitz HaDaas Tov, sermons on the Torah (Zolkiew, 5626/1866) and on Nach (Jerusalem, 5666/1906) which, interestingly, are almost devoid of kabbalistic overtones and rather resemble the style of R' Chaim's other mentor — R' Moshe Alsheich. R' Chaim mentions in his preface that he was twenty years old when he wrote this work. In the field of mussar (ethics and inspiration) he authored Derech Chaim (Jerusalem, 5698/1938); the first six chapters of Chida's Lev David were actually copied verbatim from a treatise authored by R' Chaim Vital; and Shaarei Kedushah (Amsterdam, 5475/1715), an inspirational work containing instruction and exhortations for a life of utmost holiness, which will ultimately elevate the person to the point where he will be worthy of Divine inspiration (ruach hakodesh). R' Chaim is the author of Sefer HaGoralos (Jerusalem, 5623/1863), a small treatise about astrology and related matters; HaTechunah (Jerusalem, 5626/1866), on astronomy; and Shivchei R' Chaim Vital (Ostroh, 5586/1826), autobiographical material and visions. An improved and more complete edition of the last work was printed in Jerusalem (5714/1954) as Sefer HaChezyonos. Although R' Chaim is known mainly for his proficiency in the kabbalah, he was also great in the field of Talmud and halachah. Some of his responsa survive in Be'er Mayim Chaim (Bnei Brak, 5726/1966), the responsa of his son, R' Shmuel Vital. A lengthy halachic essay by R' Chaim appears in She'eilos UTeshuvos Maharit (v. 1, §72) in the form of a halachic query addressed to *R' Yosef Trani. R' Chaim's chidushim to many tractates of the Talmud were printed in the El HaMekoros edition of the Talmud (Jerusalem, 5719/1959) as Chaim Shnayim Yeshaleim.

R' Yitzchak Uziel

רַבִּי יִצְחָק בֶּן אַבְרָהָם עֻזִּיאֵל

b. Fez, Morocco, c. 5310/1550
d. Amsterdam, Holland, c. 5382/1622

R' Yitzchak's family traced its genealogy back to a distinguished Spanish family, many members of which had fled Spain in 5252/1492. One of these, R' Yosef ben Avraham Tzarfati, a distinguished Talmud scholar and disciple of R' Shmuel of Valencia, settled in Fez, where he was greatly respected. R' Avraham Uziel (probably a grandson of R' Yosef) was a prominent scholar and poet in Fez. Among his disciples was *R' Vidal Tzarfati, and he is mentioned in the responsa (Chut HaMeshulash) of R' Shlomo ben Tzemach Duran.

R' Yitzchak Uziel left Fez in about 5365/1605 because of a famine, and became rabbi of Oran, Algeria. Shortly thereafter (5366/1606) he traveled to Amsterdam, where he taught and also occupied himself with business; *R' Menasheh ben Yisrael was one of his pupils. R' Yitzchak was instrumental in the formation of one of the first Portuguese congregations, Neveh Shalom (5368/1608), and when the first rabbi of the congregation resigned in 5370/1610, R' Yitzchak was chosen to be his successor. He had a profound influence on the community of newly professed Jews, most of whom had been born and raised as Christians, and whose outlook had not yet divested itself of many subtle Christian influences. R' Yitzchak was steadfast and outspoken in his criticism of the negative tendencies he saw in his congregation, and this made him unpopular in some circles. In 5378/1618 some of the congregants broke off from *Neveh Shalom* and formed another congregation.

R' Yitzchak wrote a Hebrew grammar work, *Maaneh Lashon* (Amsterdam, 5387/1627), and was considered an able poet.

R' Yissachar Ber Eilenburg

יִשָּׂשכָר בֶּער בֶּן יִשְׂרָאֵל אֱלִיעֶזֶר אַיְילֶנְבּוּרְג

b. Posen, Poland, c. 5330/1570
d. Austerlitz, Moravia (Czechoslovakia)
5383/1623

R' Yissachar was a disciple of *Maharal and *R' Mordechai Yafeh, and learned *kabbalah* from *R' Yisrael Seruk. He became rabbi of Gorizia (Italy) and the surrounding province of Friuli in 5360/1600, and some years later of Austerlitz (Czechoslovakia). R' Yissachar Ber is famous for his Talmud commentary *Be'er Sheva* (Venice, 5374/1614), which is a substitute for the *Tosafos* commentary on some tractates upon which no *Tosafos* exist. A small collection of responsa and halachic rulings, *Be'er Mayim Chaim*, is appended to this work. He is also the author of a super-commentary on *Rashi's Torah commentary, entitled *Tzeidah LaDerech* (Prague, 5383-84/1623-24). *R' Azaryah Figo was one of his disciples.

R' Yaakov Rabino

רַבִּי יַעֲקֹב בֶּן יִצְחָק רַבִּינוֹ

b. Yanov, Poland (?), c. 5310/1550
d. Prague, Bohemia (now Czechoslovakia)
c. 5383/1623

Next to nothing is known about this master teacher of generations. Although he is known to have been from Yanov, it is not known which of the three towns by this name in Eastern Europe can claim him as their son, but it is speculated that he was from the Yanov in the vicinity of Lublin.

An expert in aggadic and midrashic literature, R' Yaakov dedicated his life to the compilation of midrashic material in the Yiddish vernacular in order to make it accessible to the masses, and especially to women. *Tzenah URe'enah*, his most popular work, is a translation of the Torah into the vernacular, greatly expanded with the addition of much material from the *midrashim* and the medieval commentators, from *Rashi and *R' Bachya to R' Yitzchak Caro, and arranged according to the portions of the week. For centuries, *Tzenah URe'enah* has served as a textbook for women, going through countless editions, including translations into Hebrew, Hungarian, and other languages. An English translation in three volumes was published by Mesorah Publications (Brooklyn, 5743-44/1983-84).

R' Yaakov is also credited with the authorship of *Sefer HaMaggid* (Lublin, 5383/1623), a Yiddish translation of the *Neviim* and *Kesuvim*, based on *Rashi* and some midrashic material. This translation, which bears R' Yaakov's name on the title page of the early editions, became very popular; it made the previous attempts by *R' Eliyahu Bachur and others at Bible translation obsolete, and it survived subsequent attempts to supplant it. However, a noted bibliographer has demonstrated that the popular *HaMaggid* was not composed by R' Yaakov. He had prepared a work similar to *Tzenah URe'enah* on *Neviim* and *Kesuvim,* but this was probably never printed. The *HaMaggid* translation, prepared by an anonymous scholar, retained only the title of R' Yaakov's work (R' Chaim Lieberman, *Ohel Rachel,* v. #2).

R' Yaakov's *Meilitz Yosher* (Lublin, 5382/1622), additions to the *Tzenah URe'enah,* is an anthology of insights on the Torah culled from such works as *Akeidah, Abarbanel, Maaseh Hashem* and others. This work, probably because of the nature of the anthologized material and its lengthier style, never achieved the popularity of the *Tzenah URe'enah* and was printed only three times.

In the realm of *halachah,* R' Yaakov composed *Shoresh Yaakov* (Cracow, 5345/1585) on *Shulchan Aruch Yoreh Deah.*

Recently a scholarly edition of the *Tzenah URe'enah* in Hebrew was begun by R' Moshe M. Kozak (Vol. I, Jerusalem, 5735/1975). The translation demonstrates that in the course of the numerous editions of this work, many deletions and variations have crept into the text.

R' Aharon Sasson

רַבִּי אַהֲרוֹן בֶּן יוֹסֵף שָׁשׁוֹן

b. Salonica, Turkey (now Greece), c. 5310/1550
d. Constantinople (now Istanbul), Turkey 5385/1625

R' Aharon was a disciple of R' Mordechai Matalon, and son-in-law of R' Shlomo HaLevi the Elder (*HaZakein*), author of *Lev Shlomo* on *Pirkei Avos* (Salonica, 5325/1565) and one of the prominent *rabbanim* of Salonica. R' Aharon headed an academy and at-

tracted prominent disciples, among them *R' Chaim Shabsai and *R' Shabsai Yonah. He also maintained a lively correspondence with his colleagues, and his responsa, *Toras Emes* (Venice, 5386/1626), contains two hundred thirty-two Talmudic and halachic articles. In the introduction, we are told of his *chidushim* on *Mishneh Torah, Tur,* the Talmud, and his kabbalistic writings, which were all destroyed by fire.

His son R' Yosef, who lived in Venice, was a considerable Torah scholar, and his grandson R' Chaim Aharon (son of R' Yosef) was a colleague of *R' Yehudah Rozanes, and is mentioned in the latter's *Mishneh LaMelech* (*Issurei Biah,* ch. 18) as the author of the (unknown) work *Hein Yishlach* .

R' Shlomo Adeni

רַבִּי שְׁלֹמֹה בֶּן יְשׁוּעָה עֲדֶנִי

b. Sana, Yemen, 5327/1567
d. Hebron, Eretz Yisrael, c. 5385/1625

R' Shlomo experienced a most turbulent childhood. When he was four years old, his father, who was the *rav* of Sana, decided to emigrate with his family to *Eretz Yisrael* . His mother died during the journey, and a short time after arriving in Safed all of his brothers and sisters died in an epidemic.

Although suffering emotionally and also physically, often being hungry or sick, R' Shlomo nevertheless pursued his Torah studies. After several years his father moved to Jerusalem, where R' Shlomo was able to study under *R' Betzalel Ashkenazi. In 5342/1582 his father died, and his plight worsened to the point of not even having any garments to wear. Eventually a kindhearted person undertook his support, and even married him off.

After his marriage R' Shlomo moved to

Hebron, and there, at the age of twenty-two, he began to compose his monumental *Mishnah* commentary *Meleches Shlomo*, which he finished thirty-three years later.

R' Shlomo began his work by arranging a compilation of commentaries in an abridged fashion and writing them as marginal glosses on his *Mishnah*. Later, someone who appreciated the value of R' Shlomo's work urged him to write his commentary in a more elaborate and readable manner, and even donated paper, ink, and other necessary writing materials. Nonetheless, this valuable work remained unpublished until 5646/1886, when it was published in its entirety in the Vilna edition of the *Mishnah*.

R' Shlomo studied *kabbalah* under *R' Chaim Vital. *Chida (a native Hebronite) lauds R' Shlomo's great piety and diligence in his studies and adds that he had heard (a century after R' Shlomo's demise) many wonderful things about him. He authored (according to Chida's testimony) a work establishing the correct spellings of words in the Bible (similar to *Or HaTorah* by *R' Menachem de Lonzano), based on many manuscripts and oral traditions. R' Shlomo is also alleged to have made a copy of his mentor R' Betzalel Ashkenazi's notes to *Seder Kodashim*; R' Betzalel's *Shittah Mekubetzes*, which is printed in the Vilna edition of the Talmud, is partly based on a manuscript said to have come from the pen of R' Shlomo.

R' Yisrael Najarah

רַבִּי יִשְׂרָאֵל בֶּן מֹשֶׁה נַאגַ׳אְרָה

d. Gaza, Eretz Yisrael, 5389/1629

R' Yisrael studied under his father, R' Moshe ben Levi, a scholar of repute. [R' Moshe was a disciple of the *Arizal and the author of *Lekach Tov* (Constantinople, 5335/1575), comments on the Torah with reasons for the *mitzvos*.] From earliest youth R' Yisrael was captivated by the art of poetry, being extremely talented in this field. He authored many diverse types of song, including the *Kah Ribon Olam* hymn recited on Friday nights in many Jewish homes. He, however, met with strong opposition from the kabbalists of Damascus and Safed for his composition of secular poetry. *R' Menachem de Lonzano was especially critical of R' Yisrael.

R' Yisrael later settled in Safed, where he published his *Zemiros Yisrael* (5346/1586), a collection of poetic compositions set to well-known Arabic and Turkish tunes. R' Yisrael explained that the people were accustomed to singing these songs together with some of their indecent lyrics, and felt that if his compositions were to replace these lyrics he would have performed a great service to the public.

R' Yisrael's other works include *Mesachekes BeTeivel* (Safed, 5347/1587), a poetic composition dramatizing the insignificance of this world; *Shochatei HaYeladim*, on the laws of *shechitah* and *bedikah*, in rhyme (published with *Zemiros Yisrael*); *Meimei Yisrael,* various poetic compositions (published with *Zemiros Yisrael*); *Kli Machazik Berachah* (Venice, 5375/1615), on the laws of *Birkas HaMazon* and the various *berachos*; *Pitzei Ohev* (Constantinople, 5358/1598), a commentary on the book of *Job*; and *Pizmonim* (Vienna, 5618/1858).

Due to an outbreak of pestilence, R' Yisrael was forced to flee to Gaza, where he became Chief Rabbi and remained until his death.

R' Chaim Algazi

רַבִּי חַיִּים בֶּן אַבְרָהָם אַלְגַּאזִי

d. Constantinople (now Istanbul), Turkey
c. 5389/1629

A disciple of *R' Yosef Trani, R' Chaim authored *Nesivos Mishpat* (Constantinople, 5429/1669), a commentary on *R' Yerucham's halachic work, *Meisharim*, which deals with monetary law.

R' Avraham Monson

רַבִּי אַבְרָהָם מוֹנְסוֹן

d. Constantinople (now Istanbul), Turkey
c. 5390/1630

A disciple of *R' Betzalel Ashkenazi, R' Avraham was appointed *dayan* in Cairo in 5353/1593, a post he held for ten years. He then moved to Constantinople, where he held the post of *rosh yeshivah* until his death.

Although his works have not been preserved, some of his wide halachic correspondence is contained in the works of *R' Shmuel de Medina, *R' Shlomo HaKohen, and *R' Yom Tov Tzahalon.

R' Yeshayah Horowitz
(the *Shelah*)

רַבִּי יְשַׁעְיָה בֶּן אַבְרָהָם הַלֵּוִי הוֹרוֹוִיץ
(של"ה)

b. Prague (?), Bohemia (now Czechoslovakia)
c. 5320/1560
d. Tiberias, Eretz Yisrael, 11 Nissan 5390/1630

R' Yeshayah Horowitz was descended from a line of scholars. The inscription on the tombstone of his grandfather, R' Shabsai Sheftl, read, 'He left nothing unlearned. The whole Torah was virtually on his lips.'

R' Yeshayah's father, R' Avraham, a disciple of *Rama, was also a scholar of note and the author of the following

works: *Emek Berachah* on the laws of benedictions (Cracow, 5357/1597); *Chessed L'Avraham,* a commentary on *Rambam's philosophical preface — *Shemonah Perakim* — to his *Mishnah* commentary on *Avos* (printed in most editions of the Talmud); *Bris Avraham* (Lublin, 5337/1577), an inspirational work; and *Yesh Nochalin* (Prague, 5375/1615), his ethical will.

It is known that in the year 5350/1590 R' Avraham was residing in Lemberg, Poland; it was there that he wrote his work *Emek Berachah*, and it is possible that it was in that country that R' Yeshayah was born.

R' Yeshayah and his brother studied under their father during their youth, and also under some of the great rabbis of Poland. R' Yeshayah journeyed to Cracow where he became a pupil of *R' Shlomo R' Leibush of Lublin. This great and saintly scholar made a very deep impression on the young R' Yeshayah, who considered him his primary mentor. He also studied under *Maharam Lublin and *R' Yehoshua Falk Katz. His talents were recognized at an early age, and his signature appears as early as 5350/1590 on an enactment of the Council of Four Lands. It was then that his rabbinical career began, his posts taking him throughout Poland and Russia, to important Torah centers such as Dubno, Ostroh, Posen and Cracow.

R' Yeshayah's reputation spread far beyond the confines of Poland and Russia, and he was called to serve the rich and flourishing community of Frankfurt am Main about 5366/1606. R' Yeshayah remained there until 5374/1614, when the calm of the community was disturbed by the anti-Semitic Fettmilch uprising. [On 27 Elul 5374/1614, Vincent Fettmilch, a popular leader, together with a rabble of townspeople, attacked the Jewish ghetto in Frankfurt. Although the Jews resisted the attack, they were overpowered. They were, however, permitted to leave the ghetto, but their property and belongings were plundered and burned. They did not return to their homes until 19 Adar of the next year (5376/1616). The day of 20 Adar was designated a joyous day and called *Purim Vinzenz.*]

Returning to Prague, R' Yeshayah served as rabbi together with *R' Ephraim Lunshitz, and in 5379/1619, after the latter's death, R' Yeshayah was named his successor.

R' Yeshayah at this time was a renowned halachist and kabbalist and an experienced spiritual leader, but his soul yearned for the pure air of *Eretz Yisrael.* When his wife died in 5380/1620, he began to think seriously of departing for the Holy Land, which he did in 5381/1621, leaving his friends and family and resigning his post as rabbi of Prague. The time of his departure was revealed only to one or two of his most intimate friends, but not to the public or even to his children — R' Yeshayah knowing full well that they would do everything possible to dissuade him from leaving. When his son *R' Sheftl accidentally learned of his father's intended departure, he implored him not to leave, but R' Yeshayah told him that he had already made up his mind to emigrate to the Holy Land.

As a consolation to his children and numerous disciples, R' Yeshayah set out to write an ethical will in which he would outline the ideal way of life, customs and laws for the whole year, elaborations on the fundamental tenets of Judaism, basic instruction in *kabbalah,* a commentary to the Torah, and many miscellaneous matters. This monumental work, one of the gems of Jewish ethical literature, was called *Shnei Luchos HaBris* (Amsterdam, 5409/1649), or, in short, *Shelah.* It won

its saintly author everlasting fame, and both the work and its author are reverently called the *Shelah HaKadosh* (the holy *Shelah*). This work, which the author had envisioned as a mere testament, grew in size and scope as it was being written, and R' Yeshayah could not finish it while yet in Prague. He completed it only after spending a number of years in *Eretz Yisrael,* and sent it to his children in Europe.

R' Yeshayah's journey took him through Germany and Italy, and from there on to Syria, where he was received in the old Jewish communities of Aleppo and Chamah with the greatest respect. In Damascus he was asked by the scholars of the city to become their spiritual leader. There also, a delegation from Safed appeared before him, offering him the rabbinate of that city. However, R' Yeshayah, who had his heart set on living in Jerusalem, accepted the offer to be rabbi and *rosh yeshivah* of the Ashkenazim in Jerusalem, without a salary.

In *Eretz Yisrael,* R' Yeshayah was given the opportunity to acquaint himself with the kabbalistic writings of *R' Chaim Vital — thus becoming familiar with the system of the *Ari, which was practically unknown in Europe at that time — and with other kabbalistic manuscripts.

But in 5385/1625, life in Jerusalem was made intolerable for Jews by the tyrannical rule of ibn Farukh and his brother-in-law, Othman Aga, who extracted large sums of money by pillage and torture. During the *Shabbos* morning service on the eleventh day in the month of *Elul,* fifteen rabbis and leaders of both the Sephardic and Ashkenazic communities were arrested without warning or cause. R' Yeshayah headed the list of those who were arrested, and he was not released until fifteen days — spent in constant terror — had elapsed.

Some of the captives were not released until *Rosh Hashanah*. The community was forced to pay an exorbitant ransom to free its leaders. Fearing for his life, R' Yeshayah decided to flee Jerusalem, first stopping in Safed and then continuing to Tiberias where he finally settled and spent his last days. He was buried near the tomb of Rambam.

R' Yeshayah's other outstanding work which was written in the Holy Land is *Shaar HaShamayim* (Amsterdam, 5477/1717), a kabbalistic commentary on the *siddur*. R' Yeshayah conceived the plan to write this commentary in 5382/1621, when he entered Jerusalem — the Biblical 'Gate of the Heavens' *(Shaar HaShamayim)* — auspiciously on the Friday of *Parashas VaYetzei,* the Biblical portion which contains the reference to Jerusalem as the heavenly gate for prayer. The author's motivation for composing a *siddur* commentary is illuminating. Since it is the nature of *siddurim* to have extensive circulation, the author felt that in this way he could share in the prayers of all of Israel. The approbations to this *siddur* show the awe and reverence with which the *Shelah* was regarded even by his contemporaries. The *Bach* writes, 'When we saw and read them (R' Yeshayah's works) we felt an effusion of holiness ... There is no question that regarding anyone who prays in it [i.e. the *Shelah's siddur*], his prayer will not be unanswered!' *Tosefos Yom Tov* writes, 'For he [R' Yeshayah] is a holy and awesome man ... no doubt additional Divine inspiration was visited upon him from Heaven [in the Holy Land] ...'

His other works are *Bigdei Yesha,* a commentary on the halachic work *Mordechai*. The part on *Seder Moed* was published (Amsterdam, 5517/1757 and in the Vilna edition of the *Rif*) together with *chidushim* by his son R' Sheftl; and that on *Berachos* (Amsterdam, 5489/1729) together with *Emek Berachah*; the rest of the work was not published. He also wrote notes on the *Zohar* (in the *Zohar* edition of Vilna, 5642/1882); notes on his father's treatise *Emek HaBerachah* (Cracow, 5357/1597) concerning the laws of benedictions; and notes on his father's testament *Yesh Nochalin* (Prague, 5357/1597). Recently his *Mitzvas Tefillin* (Jerusalem, 5740/1980) has been published. Various extracts from *Shnei Luchos HaBris* have been published. Responsa by R' Yeshayah are found in *Chut HaShani* by R' Shmuel Bacharach.

R' Shimon Zev Auerbach

רַבִּי שִׁמְעוֹן זְאֵב וָואלְף
בֶּן דָוִד טָעבֶל אוֹיעֶרְבַּאךּ

b. Posen, Poland, c. 5310/1550
d. Prague, Bohemia (now Czechoslovakia)
17 Cheshvan 5392/1631

The son-in-law of *Maharshal,* R' Shimon Zev served as rabbi of Turbin and Luboml (Poland). After his father-in-law's death in 5334/1573, R' Shimon Zev served as rabbi and *rosh yeshivah* in Lublin (5338-44/1578-84), where numerous disciples flocked to his lectures. During the same period, *Maharam Lublin directed a neighboring yeshivah in the same city.

Because of a quarrel with Maharam Lublin, R' Shimon Zev left Lublin to serve as rabbi of Premysl, from where he returned to his home town Posen, where he was rabbi for many years (c. 5380-89/1620-29). Later he served in the Vienna rabbinate for a short while, and from there he went to Prague to officiate as rabbi of that prestigious community and as Chief Rabbi of Bohemia.

Nothing remains in writing from R' Shimon Zev, but his importance can be gauged by the positions he held, among which were the most important rabbinates in Europe.

A kabbalistic comment by R' Shimon Zev is cited in *Kav HaYashar* (ch. 65), and a custom he instituted in Vienna is cited in *Ateres Zekeinim* to *Shulchan Aruch Orach Chaim,* §585.

R' Shmuel Eliezer Eidels (Maharsha)

רַבִּי שְׁמוּאֵל אֱלִיעֶזֶר
בֶּן יְהוּדָה הַלֵּוִי אִידְלְשׁ (מַהַרְשָׁ"א)

b. Posen (?), Poland, c. 5315/1555
d. Ostroh, Poland (now Ostrog, Russia)
5 Kislev 5392/1632

In his youth Maharsha studied in Posen, where he became the son-in-law of R' Moshe (Ashkenazi) Heilprin, author of *Zichron Moshe* (Lublin, 5371/1611). He continued his studies in the home of his parents-in-law, and founded a large yeshivah there, supported by his mother-in-law, Eidel; therefore he was called after her name, R' Shmuel Eidels.

Maharsha spent twenty years at his yeshivah in Posen, but upon the death of his mother-in-law (c. 5365/1605) he was forced to seek a rabbinical post in order to support his family. He successively served the communities of Chelm, Lublin (after the death of *R' Meir of Lublin in 5376/1616), and Ostroh (c. 5385/1625). In Ostroh, he again was able to establish a large yeshivah and train many disciples.

Maharsha produced two very important and comprehensive Talmud commentaries, *Chidushei Halachos* (Lublin, 5372-81/1612-21), and *Chidushei Aggados* (Lublin-Cracow, 5387-92/1627-32), which are included in most modern editions of the Talmud; later editions combined these two works and merged them into one commentary. In *Chidushei Halachos* he carefully analyzes the Talmud text and the commentaries of *Rashi and Tosafos in order to properly comprehend their true meaning in depth. Indeed, it is a foregone conclusion among scholars that one has not fully comprehended these texts if he has not touched upon the difficulties raised by Maharsha. Every serious student of the Talmud must resort to his commentary. The *aggadah* is carefully examined in *Chidushei Aggados* and an interpretation offered so as to present a clearer comprehension of its secrets.

Maharsha and his commentary were hallowed by successive generations. The great scholar and kabbalist, *R' Yonah Landsofer, in his ethical testament to his children, exhorts them to study the commentary of Maharsha: "His words are remarkably concise and very profound, and they fathom the true meaning of Torah. He definitely possessed *ruach hakodesh* (Divine inspiration), for without it, it would be impossible for a man to author such a work." The *Baal Shem Tov said of Maharsha, "If the world knew his true holiness they would lick the earth which is upon his grave" (*She'eiris Yis-rael,* ch. 6). In later times, the *Chazon Ish* emphasized the study of Maharsha and proclaimed that from the day the study of Maharsha was neglected, the knowledge of basic Talmudic comprehension was lost *(Kovetz Iggaros,* Vol. 1, p.25).

R' Avraham Chaim Shor

רַבִּי אַבְרָהָם חַיִּים בֶּן נַפְתָּלִי הִירְשׁ שׁוֹר

d. Lemberg, Poland, 9 Teves 5392/1632

R' Avraham Chaim's father, R' Naftali Hirsh ben Moshe Ephraim Zalman Shor, known as R' Hirsh Elsasser (implying his origin from Alsace in Northern France), was a well-known and respected disciple of *Rama (appearing in his responsa) and is mentioned as the revered mentor of *R' Yoel Sirkis in his *Bayis Chadash*

(*Bach*). There is a tradition that R' Hirsh married Rivkah, the daughter of R' Yisrael, son of *R' Shalom Shachna of Lublin. The *Mordechai* in the Talmud edition of Lemberg (5620-25/1860-65) was corrected according to the emendations of R' Yisrael and R' Hirsh.

R' Avraham Chaim served as rabbi of Belz, Kremenitz and Satanov, and ended his life in Lemberg. However, R' Avraham Chaim's legacy is not his halachic decisions, nor the sermons he may have delivered to his community, but the *chidushim* he presented to his disciples. His most popular works are his *chidushim* on the Talmud entitled *Toras Chaim* (Vol. 1, Lublin, 5368/1608; Vol. 2, Cracow, 5394/1634), which are often quoted by later commentators.

In this often-reprinted work, the author is revealed to us as a very independent thinker, who does not shrink from criticizing the interpretations of *Rashi and Tosafos, repudiating them and giving his own original commentaries. His comments are noted for their incisiveness and clarity. The work also contains many often-quoted explanations on the aggadic material of the Talmud. It is, after *Maharsha and *Maharam Lublin, one of the more important works on the Talmud.

He also authored *Tzon Kodashim* (Wandsbeck, 5689/1829), *chidushim* on the Talmud order *Kodashim*. This is probably the first comprehensive collection of *chidushim*, after the generation of the Tosafos, to be written on this difficult section of the Talmud. R' Avraham Chaim relates that he authored this work together with R' Mordechai, rabbi of Berzan (d. Lemberg, 21 Tishrei 5391/1631). However, close to a century passed before R' Chaim ben Ozer, R' Avraham Chaim Shor's grandson, published this work with his own substantial additions. Another of R' Avraham Chaim's works is *Bedek HaBayis* (Amsterdam, 5493/1733, with *Gur Aryeh* by R' Yehudah Aryeh ben David) on the *Tur* and *Beis Yosef* in *Hilchos Gittin* and *Chalitzah*.

R' Hirsh Shor was, according to the family tradition, descended from the French Tosafist and Torah commentator *R' Yosef Bechor Shor, a line that boasted of many illustrious persons in its ranks. R' Avraham Chaim's brother, *R' Ephraim Zalman Shor, was the author of *Tevuos Shor* (Lublin, 5376/1616), and another brother, R' Shmuel Shor, was the great-grandfather of R' Alexander Sender Shor, author of the well-known halachic work also called *Tevuos Shor* on *Hilchos Shechitah*. The famous halachic authority *R' Ephraim Zalman Margulies of Brodi was descended from this branch of the family.

R' Aharon ibn Chaim

רַבִּי אַהֲרֹן בֶּן אַבְרָהָם אִבְּן חַיִּים

b. Fez, Morocco, c. 5320/1560
d. Jerusalem, Eretz Yisrael, c. 5392/1632

A disciple of his father, R' Avraham — a *dayan* of Fez — and of R' Yosef Almosnino, R' Aharon served on *R' Vidal Tzarfati's *beis din* in Fez, and was rabbi in Cairo, Smyrna, and Venice.

R' Aharon is famous for his comprehensive commentary on *Sifra* entitled *Korban Aharon* (Venice, 5369/1609). It is considered to be one of the best commentaries to this halachic *midrash* which has been commented upon by numerous scholars. R' Aharon traveled to Italy with the intention of printing the short, concise commentary he had compiled on the *Sifra,* which concentrated on the translation of difficult words and the simple meaning of the passages. However, upon arriving in Venice he acquainted himself with the writings of the contemporary Italian and German rabbis and saw the meticulous and intricate method (pilpul) they used as the basis for their decisions, and he realized that his commentary was too simple and would be ignored. Immediately he began to rewrite the commentary, taking into consideration the implications of the Sifra in regard to parallel discussions in the Talmud and its commentaries. This feat attests to the author's acumen and his complete mastery over his sources.

He prefaced his work with a smaller work — Midos Aharon — basically a commentary on the baraisa of R' Yishmael, which lists the thirteen fundamental rules (midos) the Sages employed to derive their teachings from the Scriptures, discussing the manifold and complicated rules and definitions which concern these midos. This masterful work won the author the admiration of the greatest scholars of later generations. *R' Yeshayah Horowitz borrowed generously from it in his Shelah, acknowledging his debt, and *R' Shlomo of Chelm, author of Mirkeves HaMishneh, declared (in the preface to that work) that no scholar could attain perfection without having read Midos Aharon. Indeed, all subsequent commentators on the Sifra made use of this monumental work. R' Aharon also published Lev Aharon (Venice, 5369/1609), a commentary on Joshua and Judges, stressing the unity between the plain meaning of the verses and the exegesis of the Sages. R' Aharon mentions several other unpublished works, among them commentaries on Mechilta, Sifra, Chumash, and the Prophets.

At the end of his life R' Aharon settled in Jerusalem, and his grave is reported to be on the Mount of Olives near that of *R' Shalom Sharabi.

R' Nassan Nata Shapira II

רַבִּי נָתָן נָטָע בֶּן שְׁלֹמֹה שַׁפִּירָא (הַשֵּׁנִי)

b. Poland, 5345/1585
d. Cracow, Poland, 13 Av 5393/1633

A grandson and namesake of *R' Nassan Nata ben Shimshon, R' Nassan Nata served as rabbi and rosh yeshivah of Cracow from 5377/1617 until his death. The *Shach was one of his prominent disciples.

A scholar of extraordinary stature, besides delivering Talmudic discourses he strove to disseminate the kabbalistic teachings of the *Ari in Poland through his dissertations. He wrote Megaleh Amukos (Lemberg, 5555/1795) — a Torah commentary — and a second work bearing the same name which contains 252 different explanations on the first verse of Parashas VaEschanan, published in Cracow in 5397/1637.

Among his Talmudic works are his glosses on Sefer HaHalachos of *Rif, contained in Chidushei Anshei Shem (together with glosses of other greats) and published in all prevalent editions of the Rif.

Many of his other works remain in manuscript; of these one Torah commentary, Megaleh Amukos Tinyana, has recently been published (New York, 5742/1982).

His epitaph reports that Elijah the Prophet was wont to appear before him.

R' Ephraim Zalman Shor

רַבִּי אֶפְרַיִם זַלְמָן בֶּן נַפְתָּלִי הִירְשׁ שׁוֹר

d. Lublin, Poland, 28 Tishrei
5394/1633

R' Ephraim Zalman was a younger brother of *R' Avraham Chaim Shor. According to the family tradition, R' Ephraim Zalman was the son-in-law of R' Shaul Wahl (see *R' Shmuel Yehudah Katzenellenbogen). He served successively as rabbi of Shebreshin, Horodna (Grodno), Brisk, and Lublin.

R' Ephraim Zalman composed *Tevuos Shor* (Lublin, 5376/1616), a summary of the *Beis Yosef* commentary on the *Tur* with many new additions and insights. This is not identical with the much more famous work, having the same name, on *Hilchos Shechitah* by R' Alexander Sender Shor, a kinsman of R' Ephraim Zalman who lived more than a century later.

R' Yaakov Yekl Shor, R' Ephraim Zalman's son, who was also rabbi of Brisk (5412-15/1652-55), and prior to that in Lutzk, is the author of a work on tractate Sanhedrin — *Pilpala Charifta*, or *Beis Yaakov* (Amsterdam, 5453/1693). A responsum by R' Yaakov is found in *Teshuvos Geonei Basrai* (§ 45,46), and he is cited in *Chelkas Mechokeik* on *Shulchan Aruch Even HaEzer* (17:78).

R' Avraham Herrera

רַבִּי אַבְרָהָם בֶּן דָוִד אֵירֵירָה

b. Spain (?), c. 5330/1570
d. Amsterdam, Holland, 5395/1635

R' Avraham was born into an influential family of Marranos who retained high government positions in Spain. The family was able to emigrate from Spain and settle in Italy. R' Avraham was a successful businessman, but he also devoted time to the study of religious philosophy and the *kabbalah*. R' Avraham's far-flung business activities brought him to Raguza (Dubrovnik, now Yugoslavia), where he met *R' Yisrael Seruk, one of the foremost disciples of the *Ari. The young Avraham was completly won over by this veteran kabbalist. He became R' Yisrael's avid disciple, and eventually came to be considered an adept kabbalist himself. He continued his business career and was sent to Cadiz, Spain, as a mercantile emissary of

the Sultan of Morocco. While he was in Cadiz, the city was taken by the English (5357/1596). R' Avraham was captured and held as a hostage (in or near London); since his captors insisted that he was a Spanish subject. The negotiations to free him dragged on and R' Avraham was not freed before the summer of 5359/1599. Sometime after this he moved to Amsterdam, where Marranos were then beginning to settle in significant numbers, as the liberal government of Holland permitted them to practice their Jewish religion openly. R' Avraham presumably remained there for the rest of his life.

R' Avraham wrote two kabbalistic works in Spanish, and set aside a sum of money for their translation into Hebrew after his death. *R' Yitzchak Abohab III translated the works, entitled *Shaar HaShamayim* and *Beis Elokim*, into Hebrew, and had them published (Amsterdam, 5415/1655). Segments of these *sefarim* were also translated into Latin by Christian intellectuals interested in the *kabbalah*.

R' Avraham was held in high regard by the Sephardic community of Amsterdam, and *R' Menasheh ben Yisrael sought his approbation to one of his works.

R' Eliyahu Loanz

רַבִּי אֵלִיָהוּ בֶּן מֹשֶׁה לוֹאַנְץ

b. Frankfurt am Main, Germany, 5324/1564
d. Worms, Germany, 21 Tammuz 5396/1636

Popularly known as R' Eliyahu *Baal Shem,* he was a descendant of *Rashi and R' Yochanan Luria (antecedent of *Rama, *Maharshal, and *Maharam Padua) and a grandson of *R' Yoselman of Rosheim. He was a disciple of R' Akiva Frankfurt, R' Yaakov Ginsburg, and *Maharal of Prague. R' Eliyahu served successively in the rabbinates of Fulda,

Hanau, Friedburg and Worms, where he also officiated as *rosh yeshivah*. Some assert that he also spent some time in Poland, where he served as rabbi of Chelm. According to this view he is identical with the R' Eliyahu, rabbi of Chelm and antecedent of *R' Tzvi Ashkenazi, of whom the latter relates in his responsa *(Teshuvos Chacham Tzvi §93)* that he is reputed to have created a *golem* through a kabbalistic formula. However, it has been shown conclusively that Chacham Tzvi's antecedent is not identical with R' Eliyahu Loanz.

A very gifted and talented writer, R' Eliyahu prepared many books of previous sages, which had remained in manuscript, for print. Among these are *Darchei Moshe* on *Tur* by Rama, gathered from the latter's marginal glosses. As a reward for this work, R' Eliyahu was presented by Rama's brother with Rama's *Zohar* commentary. He also edited Maharshal's commentaries to *Smag* and *Shaarei Dura,* and wrote a preface to *Shefa Tal*.

R' Eliyahu authored *Rinas Dodim* (Basel, 5360/1600), a homiletic commentary on *Song of Songs* containing some kabbalistic matter; and *Michlal Yofi* (Amsterdam, 5455/1695), on *Ecclesiastes,* in the same style. Both commentaries contain much ethical matter and exhortations to live a life of piety and good deeds. R' Eliyahu also wrote poetry and published a poem titled *Vikuach HaYayin im HaMayim* (printed together with *Zemiros VeTishbachos,* liturgy for the Sabbath table by his mentor R' Akiva Frankfurt, Basel, 5359/1599) in which, as suggested by the name, wine and water take part in a debate in which each one holds forth on its own merits, proving its point with Biblical verses. He wrote a long commentary on the *Zohar (Aderes Eliyahu),* in which he cites commentaries on the *Zohar* from Rama's

manuscript which belonged to him; *Tzafnas Paane'ach* on the *Tikunei Zohar; Maaglei Tzedek,* a super-commentary on *R' Bachya's Torah commentary; and a lengthy commentary on *Bereishis Rabbah* up to *Parashas VaYeishev;* all of these were not published. A halachic responsum from his pen is printed in *Teshuvos Chut HaShani* (§22).

A saintly personality, R' Eliyahu was known as a performer of miracles, having the power to cure the sick with his prayers and amulets, and was therefore surnamed *Baal Shem,* master of the holy names of G-d by which he performed his acts of mercy.

R' Yaakov HaLevi Patras (Patrai)

רַבִּי יַעֲקֹב בֶּן יִשְׂרָאֵל לְבֵית הַלֵּוִי

b.Greece, c. 5320/1560
d. Zante, Greece, 5396/1636

As indicated by his name, R' Yaakov was born or derived from Patras (in the Peloponnesus, Greece).

R' Yaakov is known for his responsa *She'eilos UTeshuvos R' Yaakov (Mahari) LeVeis HaLevi* (Venice, 5374/1614). *Chida reports that he was a successful merchant and had connections in high government circles, but that this did not deter him from his studies. He served as rabbi of Zante (the island of Zakynthos in the Ionian Sea). Toward the end of his life R' Yaakov revised and added to his work of responsa and reprinted it (Venice 5392-94/1632-34). A funeral oration on R' Yaakov delivered by *R' Azaryah Figo is found in *Binah LaIttim* (no. 73).

R' Gedalyah Lipshitz

רַבִּי גְּדַלְיָה בֶּן שְׁלֹמֹה זַלְמָן לִיפְּשִׁיץ

Lublin, Poland, late 16th — early 17th century

A disciple and relation of *Maharam Lublin, R' Gedalyah oversaw the publication of his master's responsa in Venice, where he published his own work at the same time. The table of contents printed in that edition was written by him.

In his youth, at the age of twenty-six, R' Gedalyah composed a running commentary to *R' Yosef Albo's Sefer HaIkkarim, but due to his strained financial condition he was unable to publish it until the latter part of his life. The commentary, Eitz Shasul (Venice, 5378/1618), is divided into a running commentary called Shorashim, with Anafim — longer comments and criticisms of R' Yosef Albo's views, with some tangential matter. His mentor, *R' Meir Lublin, is cited in this work (Anafim, Maamar 1, ch. 11).

R' Yosef Yospa Han Norlingen

רַבִּי יוֹסֵף יוֹזְפָּא הַאן נוֹירְלִינְגֶן בֶּן פִּנְחָס

b. Frankfurt am Main, Germany, c. 5330/1570
d. Frankfurt am Main, Germany
9 Nissan 5397/1637

One of the pillars of the old Frankfurt am Main community, R' Yosef served as head dayan of the city, and was greatly revered by all. Except for the two years 5374-76/1614-16, when the Jews were expelled from Frankfurt (see *R' Yeshayah Horowitz), R' Yosef spent his entire life there. He was very active in the life of the community, founding burial societies, societies for ethical improvement, and charitable organizations.

R' Yosef's fame is based on his Yosef Ometz (Frankfurt, 5483/1723), the first part of which deals with the laws and regulations covering all aspects of Jewish life, with a strong accent on customs in general, and the customs of Frankfurt in particular. The work has a certain charm about it, and the spiritual purity and saintliness of the author shine out from each page. There is a definite tendency towards stringency and a strong resem-blance to the type of piety exemplified by the Chassidei Ashkenaz of yore, of the school of *R' Yehudah HaChassid. The second part deals mainly with ethics and exhortation to leading a pious and exemplary life. Another work, containing glosses to Shulchan Aruch, is unpublished.

The name Han is derived from the family house called 'Zum rothen Hahn', presumably because it had on it a shield with a red rooster.

R' Yosef's grandson, R' Yosef Yospa Koshman, wrote a work similar in content to, and based upon, Yosef Ometz — called Noheg KaTzon Yosef (Hanau, 5478/1718).

R' Yosef Trani (Maharit)

רַבִּי יוֹסֵף בֶּן מֹשֶׁה מִטְרָאנִי (מַהֲרִי"ט)

b. Safed, Eretz Yisrael, Tishrei or Cheshvan
5329/1568
d. Constantinople (now Istanbul), Turkey
14 Tammuz 5399/1639

R' Yosef was the son of *R' Moshe Trani, then one of the rabbis of Safed, and an outstanding Torah personality in a glorious generation. From his very birth great hopes were placed on R' Yosef. He relates in a short pamphlet containing terse biographical and historical notes (see Teshuvos UPiskei Maharit HaChadashos, pp. 19-27) that the venerable *R' Moshe Alsheich had seen a great [spiritual] light over the house on the night of his birth; that his name had been chosen prior to his birth by *R' Moshe Cordovero (died 5330/1570); and that his father had remarked that the year of his birth — (5)329 — had the numerical value of Ish Chai (a valiant man), the laudatory title given Benayahu ben Yehoyada's father (II Samuel 23:20). R' Yosef had the good fortune to be blessed by *R' Yosef Caro before the latter's death (Nissan 5335/1575).

R' Moshe Trani died in the year 5340/1580, when his son was in his twelfth year. While still a young boy, R' Yosef studied with R' Moshe ibn Makir, author of *Seder HaYom*, and at the age of fourteen he began to study under R' Shlomo Sages, whom he considered his main mentor. At the early age of seventeen he was already considered an accomplished scholar and began to put his thoughts in writing. That same year (5346/1586) he married a descendant of R' Yosef Caro. His marriage ushered in an unsettled period; he was forced to flee Safed because of an outbreak of the plague. At first he went to Gaza and later to Egypt, but in 5348/1588 he went to Damascus, and studied there for one and a half years with an unidentified colleague whom he refers to as a scholar of great and keen acumen. The year 5349/1589 found him in Jerusalem and Hebron; he returned to Safed only at the end of the year. Four years later, in 5354/1594, he was appointed to head one of the yeshivos of Safed, and in 5360/1600 he became rabbi of the Beis Yaakov congregation, filling the post held by his father for many years.

Meanwhile, Safed had declined considerably. Outbreaks of the plague struck it periodically, and periods of hunger were not uncommon. In addition, the attitude of the local authorities was now one of oppression and exploitation, and the population gradually dwindled because of the excessive taxation. On one occasion R' Yosef was imprisoned because the community had fallen behind in its payments. R' Yosef was forced to travel abroad twice to raise money for the impoverished community. He reached Constantinople and was widely acclaimed in the local scholarly community, and when he traveled to this city a second time (5364/1604) he was importuned by the wealthy ibn Ya'ish brothers to stay on and head a yeshivah founded and funded by them.
*R' Yaakov Emden (*Eitz Avos, Avos* 5:10) relates that he heard from his father (who studied in Constantinople not long after R' Yosef's death) that the Ya'ish brothers gave R' Yosef an equal share in the profits of their considerable business ventures, and treated him as a full partner. Eventually R' Yosef was recognized as Chief Rabbi of Constantinople and the leader of Turkish Jewry. Numerous scholars studied under him, among them the brothers *R' Chaim and *R' Yehoshua Benveniste, *R' Chaim Algazi and R' Shlomo HaLevi.

One of his outstanding enactments in Constantinople was the establishment of a board which supervised the *kashrus* of the city, and answered all questions which arose concerning dietary laws in the community.

An expert halachist, his decisions were sought far and wide. His responsa are considered among the classics, and are valued both for their halachic value and for the theoretical points raised in them as they apply to the study of the Talmud. He wrote *chidushim* on most of the Talmud, on the *halachos* of *Rif and on other Talmudic commentaries as well as *Rambam, but most of this was lost. His responsa were collected by his sons and printed in three parts (*Teshuvos Maharit*, Vol. 1, Constantinople, 5401/1641; Vol. 2-3, Venice, 5405/1645); these include his *chidushim* to the Talmud and *Rif* of tractate *Kidushin,* and to the Talmud of *Kesubos* and the first two *perakim* of *Shabbos*. A volume of additional works by R' Yosef was published recently (5738/1978) in Jerusalem. It includes the following: (a) additional responsa — *Teshuvos Maharit HaChadashos*; (b) excerpts from a work on the laws of *get,* cited in *Sefer Shemos* by R' Simchah HaKohen of Belgrade (Venice,

5417/1657), (c) excerpts from *Tzuras HaBayis*, a treatise about the description of the Second Temple in tractate *Midos*, which are cited in R' Chaim Alfandari's *Derech HaKodesh* (in *Maggid MeReishis*, Constantinople, 5470/1710). His sermons were published as *Tzafnas Paane'ach* (Venice, 5407/1647).

A super-commentary to *R' Eliyahu Mizrachi's super-commentary on *Rashi*, and a Talmudic lexicon similar to *R' Nassan ben Yechiel's *Aruch*, have not been preserved.

R' Aharon Berechyah of Modena

רַבִּי אַהֲרֹן בְּרֶכְיָה בֶּן מֹשֶׁה מִמּוֹדֵינָא

d. Italy, 26 Tammuz 5399/1639

A disciple of the 'Chassid R' Hillel of Modena' and of *R' Menachem Azaryah of Fano, R' Aharon Berechyah is best known as the author of *Maavar Yabok* (Mantua, 5386/1626), a compilation of laws, customs, prayers and rites concerning preparation for death and interment regulations for the burial society, interspersed with kabbalistic information. It became a very popular work and was republished numerous times. R' Aharon was revered for his great piety, and *Chida reports that he was alleged to have had a *maggid,* a heavenly angel who instructed him. *R' Yehudah Aryeh de Modena was a close relative of his (R' Aharon's mother was a cousin of R' Yehudah).

R' Aharon Berechyah also wrote *Ashmores HaBoker* or *Me'irei Shachar* (Mantua, 5384/1624), a guide for the *Me'irei HaShachar* society, a group which rose before dawn to invoke the Almighty through prayers and supplications. His other works are *Me'il Tzedakah* (Mantua, 5507/1747), and *Bigdei Kodesh* (Venice, 5503/1743), prayers and selected texts for devotional purposes.

Most of R' Aharon's major works remain unpublished. Chida reports that he saw a comprehensive commentary by R' Aharon Berechyah on *Tikunei Zohar*, as well as a kabbalistic digest according to the system of the *Ari, arranged in four parts.

R' Yoel Sirkis (the *Bach*)

רַבִּי יוֹאֵל בֶּן שְׁמוּאֵל סִירְקִיס (בַּ"ח)

b. Lublin, Poland, c. 5321/1561
d. Cracow, Poland, 20 Adar 5400/1640

The *Bach's* father, R' Shmuel, was a respected member of the Lublin community. In his youth, the *Bach* had the privilege of being in the presence of *Maharshal, and he mentions that he had occasion to observe his actions, deriving several halachic conclusions from these observations.

In his early years the *Bach* studied under the rabbi of Lublin, *R' Shlomo R' Leibush, and R' Hirsh Shor (Elsasser); later he learned with R' Meshulam Feivush, in Brisk. While still a youth he was invited to fill the rabbinate of the Lithuanian town Pruszany, and thereafter officiated in numerous rabbinical positions throughout Poland, Galicia, and Podolia (Poland/Russia); among them Lukov, Luboml, Medziboz, Belz, Shidlow, Brisk, and finally Cracow (from 5379/1619).

Being a man of means, R' Yoel maintained a large yeshivah and supported some of the students with his own funds. Among his disciples were such luminaries as his son-in-law, *R' David HaLevi (author of *Turei Zahav*), *R' Menachem Mendel Krochmal, *R' Gershon Ashkenazi, and *R' Menachem Mendel Auerbach.

R' Yoel composed an extensive commentary on the entire *Tur* titled *Bayis Chadash*, and abbreviated *Bach*, after which he is called. This commentary carefully analyzes the text of the *Tur*, the sources of each passage, and the *Beis Yosef* commentary, bringing about new insights and sometimes different decisions. It is printed in most prevalent editions of *Tur*.

The *Bach* also wrote emendations to the entire printed Talmud text and the commentaries of *Rashi, Tosafos, *Rosh, and *Rif. These emendations appear in the margin of most prevalent Talmud editions and are almost indispensable. He also authored *Meishiv Nefesh*, a commentary on *Ruth* (Lublin, 5377/1617; together with his *Be'er Mayim* on *Rashi* to *Ruth*); and responsa in two parts: *She'eilos UTeshuvos Bayis Chadash* (Frankfurt, 5457/1697), and *She'eilos UTeshuvos Bayis Chadash HaChadashos* (Koretz, 5545/1785). He also wrote a kabbalistic commentary on the prayers, a commentary on *Ramak's *Pardes Rimonim*, and *chidushim* on the Talmud and *Shulchan Aruch*, which were not published.

The *Bach* was outspoken and uncompromising in his opinions and did not fear to voice them even when his decisions countered those of his contemporaries. He ruled that *chadash* (grain which had taken root after Passover) could be eaten in the Diaspora, contrary to the ruling of *Rama and to what seems to have been the accepted view in his day (see *Bach* to *Yoreh Deah* ch. 293, and *Teshuvos Bach HaChadashos* §42). Legend has it that his outspokenness caused him to be dismissed from several rabbinates.

R' Avraham Azulai

רַבִּי אַבְרָהָם בֶּן מָרְדְּכַי אֲזוּלָאִי

b. Fez, Morocco, c. 5330/1570
d. Hebron, Eretz Yisrael, 24 Cheshvan
5404/1643

R' Avraham was born in Fez to a family descended from Castillian refugees who had fled Spain in 5252/1492 and settled in Morocco.

Since his earliest youth he longed to journey to *Eretz Yisrael* in order to study *kabbalah* under the disciples of the *Ari and *R' Chaim Vital. His plan, however, was not realized until about 5370/1610, when he and his entire family, along with their fortune, set out for the Holy Land. After a stormy journey, the shaky ship finally docked at the port of Damietta (Egypt). The passengers went ashore, leaving all their belongings aboard. While they were on land a strong storm wind blew the ship, anchor and all, out to sea where it sank with all of R' Avraham's possessions on board. In recognition of the miracle of having escaped death, R' Avraham's signature from that time on was in the form of a ship.

R' Avraham first settled in Hebron, but due to pestilence he was forced to move to Jerusalem in 5379/1619. Upon the further spreading of the plague, he moved to Gaza. There he wrote (or at least completed) two of his works, *Chessed L'Avraham* and *Baalei Bris Avraham*. After the plague ceased, he returned to Hebron.

R' Avraham composed a compendium of four works called *Kiryas Arba*, including *Or HaChamah, Zoharei Chamah, Or HaLevanah*, and *Or HaGanuz*. Of these, only *Or HaGanuz* remains unpublished. His published works are: *Or HaChamah*, which incorporates segments of the *Zohar* commentary *Or Yakar* of *Ramak and commentaries by his disciple R' Chaim Vital, which R' Chaim wrote before he studied under the Arizal (v. 1 and 2, Jerusalem, 5636/1876 and, with extensive additions, Premysl, 5656-57/1896-97; v. 3, Salonica, 5602/1842; v. 4, Premysl, 5658/1898); *Zoharei Chamah*, a digest of *R' Avraham Galante's voluminous (unpublished) commentary *Yare'ach Yakar* on the *Zohar* (v. 1, Venice, 5410/1650; v. 2, Premysl, 5643/1883; v. 3 and 4, Lvov, 5642, 5654/1882,1894); *Or HaLevanah*, emendations and variant readings in the *Zohar* (on *Genesis*, Premysl, 5659/1899); and his comments to *Kilaim* 3:5 and 5:5 (*Peirush al . . .*, Amsterdam, 5616/1856). His kabbalistic treatise *Chessed LeAvraham* (Amsterdam, 5445/1685) is very popular. He also authored *Baalei Bris Avram* (Vilna, 5632-34/1872-74), a commentary on *Tanach*. Unpublished are his comments on *Levush* and several other works. R' Avraham also wrote an extensive commentary to the entire *Mishnah*, titled *Ahavah BeTaanugim*. The part on *Seder Nezikim* has recently been published (Jerusalem, 5746/1986), and the commentary on *Avos* was printed separately a few years earlier (Jerusalem, 5740/1980).

R' Avraham was the progenitor of many distinguished scholars, rabbis, and kabbalists. His two sons-in-law were distinguished rabbis: R' Binyamin Zevi, a scholar in Hebron (died 5450/1690), whose son was R' Avraham Chaim Yisrael Zevi, author of *Orim Gedolim* and rabbi of Hebron for thirty years; and R' David Yitzchaki, rabbi of Jerusalem from 5449/1689 to his death in 5454/1694, whose son was R' Avraham Yitzchaki, head of a yeshivah in Jerusalem and author of *She'eilos UTeshuvos Zera Avraham* (Constantinople, 5492/1732). However, his most famous descendant is his great-great-grandson (son of R' Yitzchak Zerachyah, son of R' Yeshayah, son of R' Yitzchak, son of R' Avraham, all of them prominent scholars) — *R' Chaim Yosef David Azulai (Chida), halachic scholar and kabbalist par excellence, father of Hebrew bibliography, and a legendary figure in his own time.

R' Meir Schif (Maharam Schif)

רַבִּי מֵאִיר בֶּן יַעֲקֹב הַכֹּהֵן שִׁיף
(מַהֲרַ"ם שִׁי"ף)

b. Frankfurt am Main, Germany
5368/1608
d. Prague, Bohemia (now Czechoslovakia)
5404/1644

R' Meir's father was a respected scholar and *rosh yeshivah* in Frankfurt, the scion of an ancient family which counted its antecedents among the oldest settlers in this most prestigious town in the Rhine valley.

R' Meir's fame as a brilliant scholar manifested itself very early, and at the young age of seventeen he was already rabbi of nearby Fulda, where he headed a prominent yeshivah.

R' Meir's lectures, as recorded in his published *chidushim*, give us a glimpse into this intellectual giant's world. His comments are terse, incisive, and pertinent to the proper understanding of the subject matter, and his conclusions are profound and far-reaching. They are truly among the gems of Talmud commentary and perhaps may be ranked together with the comments of his predecessor *Maharsha. However, the shortness of his remarks makes them very difficult to understand; perhaps they were written as notes and not intended for publication in the form in which the author left them. They were published almost a century after the author's death as *Chidushei Halachos* (v. 1 on *Gittin*, Homburg vor der Hoehe, 5496/1736; v. 2 on *Beitzah, Bava Metzia, Kesubos, Chullin, Gittin, Bava Kamma, Sanhedrin, Shabbos, Zevachim*, with some sermons, Homburg vor der Hoehe, 5497/1737). The greater part of the *chidushim* are printed in most big Talmud editions prevalent today. R' Mordechai Mardush of Poritzk wrote a commentary (*Beur*) to the *chidushim*, which is printed in all modern editions of the *chidushim*.

In addition to his great erudition, R' Meir was also known for his saintliness, and a contemporary (in the additions to *Tzemach David*) writes of him, 'The prophet Elijah of blessed memory revealed himself to him.'

According to his grandson, R' Meir's *chidushim* covered the entire Talmud and *Tur*, and he also composed a commentary on the Torah and kabbalistic works, which were not preserved.

In 5404/1644, he was appointed rabbi of the prestigious community of Prague, but died at the age of thirty-six, soon after his arrival in that city.

R' Chaim Shabsai (Maharchash)

רַבִּי חַיִּים שַׁבְּתַי (מַהַרְחָ"ש)

b. Turkey, c. 5317/1557
d. Salonica, Turkey (now Greece)
13 Nissan 5407/1647

One of the outstanding Talmudic scholars in an age rich in scholarship, and a disciple of *R' Aharon Sasson, R' Chaim is known to have been a *dayan* in R' Aharon's *beis din* in 5363/1603, and to have headed the prominent yeshivah of the congregation Shalom in Salonica. There many rabbis studied under him, the best-known being *R' Chisdai Perachia, author of *Toras Chessed*.

In 5367/1607 R' Chaim was retained as Chief Rabbi of Salonica, and his halachic decisions were sought from far and near. In one instance, his opinion on a halachic question was sought from as far away as South America, this being probably the first recorded responsum addressed to the New World. His collection of responsa, entitled *Toras Chaim*, in three volumes (Salonica, 5473-82/1713-22), contains numerous responses. The second volume of this work contains a section titled *Kuntres Moda'a VeOness* (a pamphlet on the laws of protest and duress), which is a fundamental work in this complicated and important topic in *halachah*. A commentary on this section by two later scholars — R' Yirmiyahu, rabbi of Mattersdorf, and his son, R' Yo'av of Tzelim — entitled *Moda'a Rabba UModa'a Zuta*, was published in Lemberg (5558/1798). Additional responsa, mainly on the laws of *Even HaEzer* — including an extensive section on the laws of *agunah*, highly prized by later scholars — are known as *She'eilos UTeshuvos Maharchash* (Salonica, 5411/1651). R' Chaim's *chidushim* to the tractates *Yoma* and *Taanis* were printed in his son R' Moshe's *Toras Moshe* (Salonica, 5537/1777). *R' David Conforte, who knew him personally, reports that R' Chaim wrote *chidushim* on almost the entire Talmud and wrote a large volume of sermons.

R' Azaryah Figo

רַבִּי עֲזַרְיָה בֶּן אֶפְרַיִם פִיגוֹ

b. Venice, Italy, 5339/1579
d. Rovigo, Italy, 5407/1647

Although his childhood was spent mainly concentrating on secular studies, when he reached his late teens R' Azaryah realized how he had wasted his time, and zealously betook himself to the study of Talmud and *halachah*. In his preface to *Gidulei Terumah*, R' Azaryah laments the 'foolishness' of his youth, and thanks *Hashem* for having opened his eyes to the true calling of a person in his temporal life.

In 5367/1607 he was elected rabbi of Pisa, where he remained for twenty years, thereafter becoming a *dayan* and preacher to the Sephardic community in Venice. He delivered Talmúdic lectures in Venice and had numerous pupils, among them, *R' Moshe Zacut (Ramaz).

R' Azaryah authored *Gidulei Terumah* (Venice, 5403/1643), a commentary to *Sefer HaTerumos* of *R' Shmuel HaSardi. The *Gidulei Terumah* is a monumental halachic accomplishment. R' Azaryah did not have the *sefarim* necessary for researching the complex topics which are the subject of this *sefer,* due to the burning of the Talmud in Italy by papal order in 5314/1554 (see *R' Eliyahu Bachur*), and the consequent interdict against possessing most *sefarim*. He relates (in his preface) that he had only the *masichtos Bava Kamma, Shevuos* and *Nazir* while writing this work, and that most of the important works of the *Rishonim* were not at his disposal. Nevertheless he succeeded in finding the correct source of each ruling in the *Sefer HaTerumos* in the Talmud and *poskim* — relying no doubt in large measure on his memory — and in interpreting the various views of the halachists correctly. The *Shach frequently quotes *Gidulei Terumah*.

R' Azaryah was one of the celebrated *darshanim* of his generation, and is perhaps even better known for his contribution to the field of *derush*. He authored *Binah LaIttim* (Venice, 5408/1648), sermons on various topics, arranged according to the 'times' (*ittim*) enumerated in *Ecclesiastes* 3:1-8. Its inspiring contents caused this to become a very popular work, and it was reprinted many times.

R' Yoshiyahu Pinto (Riaf)

רַבִּי יֹאשִׁיָהוּ בֶּן יוֹסֵף פִּינְטוֹ (רִיא"ף)

b. Damascus, Syria, c. 5325/1565
d. Damascus, Syria, Adar 5408/1648

R' Yoshiyahu was a disciple of *R' Yaakov Abulafia, who ordained him with the *semichah* ordination he had received from his grandfather, *R' Yaakov bei Rav.

After the death of *R' Chaim Vital in 5380/1620, R' Yoshiyahu was appointed Chief Rabbi of Damascus and Aleppo. He wished to settle in Safed, and journeyed there in 5385/1625, but due to family pressures was forced to return to Damascus.

R' Yoshiyahu is best known for his commentary on *Ein Yaakov*, entitled *Meor Einayim* (v. 1 Amsterdam, 5403/1643, v. 2 Mantua, 5503/1743; later in some editions of *Ein Yaakov*) or simply *Riaf,* after his acronym. He also authored *Kessef Nivchar* (Damascus, 5365/1605), a Torah commentary; *Kessef Mezukak* (Venice, 5388/1628), fifteen essays explaining difficult passages (*aggados*) of the Talmud and verses of the Torah; *Kessef Tzaruf* (Amsterdam, 5388/1628) on *Proverbs*; *Kessef Nimas* on *Lamentations*, which remains unpublished; and *Nivchar MiKessef* (Aleppo, 5629/1869), responsa, printed together with a biography of the author by R' Eliyahu Chiya Sasson.

R' Shmuel Vital (*R' Chaim Vital's son) was his son-in-law.

R' Shimshon of Ostropolle

רַבִּי שִׁמְשׁוֹן בֶּן פֶּסַח מֵאוֹסְטְרוֹפּוֹלִי

d. Polnoe, Poland (now Russia)
3 Av 5408/1648

R' Shimshon was a grandson (daughter's son) of R' Shimshon ben Betzalel, rabbi of Kremenitz, a brother of *Maharal of Prague. Very little is known about his personal life. Since his grandfather after whom he was named was still alive in the year 5357/1597, it can be assumed that he was born about 5360/1600. During his short lifetime he gained great renown, and was considered a legendary figure while still alive. Wondrous stories about him have been preserved in oral traditions handed down from generation to generation, and these are a true reflection of the esteem and reverential awe in which he was held.

A scholar of outstanding stature, and a most saintly personality, R' Shimshon was regarded as a holy man, and hidden secrets of the Torah were revealed to him by *ruach hakodesh* (Divine Inspiration). He himself mentions 'secrets of the Torah' revealed to him in dreams and by deceased Torah greats, and *R' Moshe Chaim Luzzato ascribes a wondrous spiritual dialogue to him in his *Derech Eitz Chaim*.

R' Shimshon applied the method of *remmez* (finding hidden allusions by various ingenious methods) to *kabbalah*, and his excellence and brilliance in this field was legendary in his day. His sharp and masterful explanations for seemingly unintelligible texts were famous and were spread by word of mouth for generations; many authors cite his words.

He authored *Dan Yadin* (Amsterdam, 5427/1767), a commentary on the kabbalistic work *Karnayim*; *Machneh Dan*, an extensive commentary on the *Zohar*, quoted in *Dan Yadin*; and a host of other works which were never published.

Shortly after his death, various collections *(likutim)* of his sayings were printed; the most popular of these is named *Likutei Shoshanim* (Dyhernfurth, 5454/1694; printed with *Maamar Halttim*). R' Shmuel Shamama wrote a commentary, *Perach Shoshan* (Leghorn, 5585/1825; printed with *Karnayim*), to this treatise. Recently an improved edition of this collection, with many additional entries, has been published by R' Avraham Y. Bombach as *Nitzutzei Shimshon* (Bnei Brak, 5740/1980), together with a comprehensive biography of R' Shimshon and a reprint of a rare

kabbalistic treatise, *Tzitz Sadai* (Lublin, 5394/1634), by R' Yehudah Leib ben Moshe Aharon Shmuel from Kremenitz. A kabbalistic responsum by R' Shimshon (printed in *Likutei Shoshanim*), dealing with a difficult text related to the Passover *Haggadah*, is printed in many *Haggados*; a commentary, *Shemesh UMagen* (Jerusalem, 5651/1891), was written on it.

R', Shimshon met a tragic martyr's death in Polnoe (Poland/Ukraine), together with ten thousand Jews, on 3 Av 5408/1648. A contemporary close to the events (*R' Nassan Nata Hanover, *Yevein HaMetzulah*), reports that R' Shimshon gathered around him three hundred sages, all dressed in their burial shrouds and *taleisim*, and they engaged in intensive prayer until their gruesome deaths at the hand of the Cossack mob in the synagogue of the town. Another contemporary relates that R' Shimshon was aware of the impending catastrophe and had warned the Jewish communities to repent or to face Divine punishment — but that his call had not been heeded.

R' Yehoshua ben Yosef of Cracow

רַבִּי יְהוֹשֻׁעַ בֶּן יוֹסֵף מִקְּרַקָא

b. Vilna, Lithuania
d. Cracow, Poland, 27 Av 5408/1648

R' Yehoshua was born in Vilna into a family of scholars. His brother, R' Mordechai (*dayan* in Lemberg and *rav* of Tomashov; d. 5409/1649), and brother-in-law, R' Avraham, filled rabbinic posts, and his father, R' Yosef, was a *talmid chacham*. In Vilna, R' Yehoshua learned together with another brilliant youth, R' Meir HaKohen (father of the *Shach*). At a young age he left his home town and traveled to study in the famous yeshivos of Poland. He was a disciple of R' Shmuel of Premysl, son of the rabbi of Cracow, R' Feivush; and of *Maharam

Lublin and *R' Yehoshua Falk Katz. R' Yehoshua ben Yosef successively held the rabbinical posts of Horodna (Grodno; c. 5393-98/1634-38), Tiktin, Premysl and Lemberg, and was finally called upon to be *rosh yeshivah* in Cracow. Among his pupils were such greats as the *Shach,* *R' Gershon Ashkenazi, and *R' Menachem Mendel Auerbach.

A noted halachist, R' Yehoshua carried on an active correspondence with the foremost sages of his time: the *Bach, the *Taz, *R' Nassan Shapira II, *R' Menachem Mendel Krochmal, *R' Moshe (the author of *Chelkas Mechokeik*), and the two sons of *R' Binyamin Aharon Solnik of Podayetz — R' Yaakov Yekl and R' Avraham. R' Yehoshua was also an expert kabbalist and corresponded with *R' Shimshon of Ostropolle on aspects of 'the secrets of the Torah'. According to the testimony of his grandson (in the preface to *Teshuvos Pnei Yehoshua*), he wrote a commentary on *Rama of Fano's *Assarah Maamaros,* which was stolen and published in Amsterdam under a different name.

R' Yehoshua was truly one of the great luminaries of his generation, and even his older contemporaries addressed him in terms of the greatest reverence. The *gaon,* R' Nassan Shapira II of Cracow, marveled at his powerful memory and his incisiveness. His grandson (in the aforementioned preface) relates that he had total recall of the entire Talmud with the *Rosh, together with the halachic codices and responsa literature. Indeed, this is evident from his writings. He was very outspoken, and in a response to the *Chelkas Mechokeik's* objection to an interpretation because it contradicted *Maggid Mishneh* and *Tur (Teshuvos Pnei Yehoshua,* Part 2, §5), he remarked, 'And what of it! We too have human understanding!'

This spirit of independence led him to reject the blind acceptance of the *Shulchan Aruch* as the last word in *halachah,* and to protest against the assertion of one of his colleagues that one was obliged to accept the ruling of *Shulchan Aruch* even when it contradicted one's own view. He cites the Talmudic dictum, 'A judge may rule only according to what his eyes [i.e., his intelligence] see,' and adds, 'I have, with G-d's help, already begun to compose [a work] of criticism on the *Rishonim* and *Acharonim,* for there is no place for deference in the words of the Living G-d [i.e., the Torah], and am confident that the *gaon* and *chassid,* our teacher, the *Beis Yosef* of blessed memory, will not be offended . . .'

R' Yehoshua authored *Meginei Shlomo* (Amsterdam, 5475/1715), designed to answer all difficulties *Tosafos* raises against *Rashi. It is related that he told his disciples that Rashi had once appeared before him and declared, 'Happy is your lot in the World to Come, and it will be good for you in this world, for you rescue me from the mouths of the lions and their cubs [i.e., the Tosafists].' On the day of his death he suddenly exclaimed, 'Make place for our teacher; the light of our eyes, Rashi, has come to escort me, as I always took his part in answering the refutations of the Tosafists.'

R' Yehoshua's other work is a collection of responsa, *She'eilos UTeshuvos Pnei Yehoshua* (v. 1, Amsterdam, 5475/1715; v. 1 and 2, Lemberg, 5620/1860). Additional responsa are found in the works of his contemporaries: *Teshuvos Bach (Yeshanos* and *Chadashos), Teshuvos Geonei Basrai,* and in the responsa of R' Meir HaKohen (at the end of *Gevuras Anashim*).

The famed *gaon* *R' Yaakov Yehoshua, author of *Chidushei Pnei Yehoshua,* was a grandson of R' Yehoshua ben Yosef's daughter.

R' Yehudah Aryeh (Leon) de Modena

ר' יְהוּדָה אַרְיֵה בֶּן יִצְחָק דֵּי מוֹדֵינָא

b. Venice, Italy, 5331/1571
d. Venice, Italy, 5408/1648

A disciple of R' Chizkiyah Fintzi, R' Yehudah Aryeh displayed extraordinary talent and ability in his early youth, both in Talmudic learning and secular studies. He had an astoundingly versatile mind, and became expert in such diverse subjects as music, mathematics, philosophy, science, etc. He spoke and wrote Italian and Latin fluently, wrote good poetry, and was an expert orator. Above all, he was a master of Jewish learning, and was considered to be one of the foremost *rabbanim* in Italy. After his marriage, he encountered great difficulty in earning a livelihood, despite his great versatility and capability. At various times he was a teacher, a cantor, an editor of manuscripts; he dabbled in a host of other occupations (twenty-six by his own count), yet barely managed to eke out a livelihood. At various periods of his life he worked for Hebrew publishing houses. In 5354/1594 he was appointed to the Venice rabbinate and seems to have served as a rabbi and preacher in this city until the end of his life. His family life was also not serene: his wife often ailed, several of his children died at a very young age, and his only surviving son was a ne'er-do-well who traveled to Brazil and was never heard from again.

A very distinctive facet of R' Yehudah's personality is his lifelong opposition to the *kabbalah*. In this he was perhaps unique among Italian rabbis of his day. He wrote *Ari Nohem* (Leipzig, 5600/1840), a scathing polemic against the *kabbalah* and its supporters. He admits,

however, that Rama of Fano, who had been his *sandek*, was a great man, and grants admiration to his kinsman, the well-known kabbalist *R' Aharon Berechyah Modena. Although *Ari Nohem* was first published two centuries after R' Yehudah's demise, the work and its arguments were known and many replies were written to it, notably *R' Moshe Chaim Luzzato's *Choker UMekubbal*, R' Yitzchak Isaac Chover of Suvalk's *Magen VeTzinah*, R' David Luria's *Kadmus Sefer HaZohar*, and others. In spite of R' Yehudah's strident tone, he himself seems to have been somewhat ambivalent in his attitude toward the *kabbalah*. *Chida (*Shem HaGedolim*) reports that he read R' Yehudah's autobiography (*Chayei Yehudah*) in manuscript, and that in it R' Yehudah relented in his opposition to the kabbalistic belief in the transmigration of souls (*gilgul neshamos*). An incident which R' Yehudah had witnessed caused him to change his previously held denial of this concept. (The printed editions of *Chayei Yehudah* do not contain this passage.)

R' Yehudah was a prolific writer and wrote many works — many of which were never published. He was a superb polemicist and, in addition to the above-mentioned *Ari Nohem*, he wrote *Magen VeTzinah* (Breslau, 5616/1856), a defense of the Talmud; *Ben David*, against the belief in the transmigration of souls (in the anthology *Taam Zekeinim*, Frankfurt am Main, 5615/1855); and *Magen VeCherev* (unpublished), an anti-Christian polemic. In 5612/1852 Y.S. Reggio published (at Gorizia) a work called *Bechinas HaKabbalah*, comprised of *Kol Sachal*, an attack upon Judaism allegedly written by an anonymous Jew, and *Shaagas Aryeh*, attributed to R' Yehudah Modena, a refutation of the arguments advanced in *Kol Sachal*. The weak presentation of the traditional position lead many to doubt R' Yehudah's authorship of this work. It is suspected that this work is a fabrication concocted by Y. S. Reggio himself.

In the field of *aggadah* and *mussar* R' Yehudah published *Beis Yehudah* (Venice, 5395/1635), a collection of *aggados* from the Talmud which were not included in *R' Yaakov ibn Chaviv's *Ein Yaakov* (incorporated in later editions of *Ein Yaakov*); *Beis Lechem Yehudah* (Venice, 5385/1625), an index of the passages in *Ein Yaakov* arranged according to subjects; *Midbar Yehudah* (Venice, 5362/1602), sermons and eulogies; *Sur MeRa* (Venice, 5356/1596), about the vice of gambling (R' Yehudah discusses the halachic aspects of card-playing at length in his responsa); *Tzemach Tzaddik* (Venice, 5360/1600), *mussar*; and *Tzli Eish* (Venice, 5369/1609), a popular condensation of *R' Yitzchak Abarbanel's commentary on the *Haggadah*.

R' Yehudah also wrote *Lev HaAryeh* (Venice, 5372/1612), advice on how to improve one's memory, and many small (published) works. His poetry has been collected in *Divan of R' Yehudah Aryeh of Modena* (Philadelphia, 5692/1932), and a collection of epitaphs written by R' Yehudah for gravestones in Venice was published as *Luchos Avanim* (Berlin, 5641/1881). A moving prayer composed by R' Yehudah (*Yom Zeh Mishkal Kol Chatosai*) prefaces the *Yom Kippur Kattan* service.

R' Yehudah also wrote an autobiography, *Chayei Yehudah* (Kiev, 5671/1911), in which he relates many of the episodes in his life. Especially moving is his narrative of his daughter's death. This is probably the first Jewish autobiography. His only contribution to the field of *halachah* is his volume of responsa, *Ziknei Yehudah* (Jerusalem, 5716/1956).

R' Shabsai Yonah

רַבִּי שַׁבְּתַי יוֹנָה

d. Salonica, Turkey (now Greece), c. 5410/1650

A disciple of *R' Avraham de Boton, *R' Aharon Sasson and *R' Yosef ibn Ezra (author of *Atzmos Yosef*), R' Shabsai authored *Shai LaMora* (Salonica, 5413/1653), responsa and *chidushim* on *Shulchan Aruch Choshen Mishpat*. He also wrote a commentary on *Toldos Adam VeChavah* of *R' Yerucham, which has not been preserved. His son, R' David Yonah, was one of the recognized halachists of Salonica; some of his *chidushim* are printed in his father's *Shai LaMora*.

R' Avraham Rappaport Shrentzel

רַבִּי אַבְרָהָם בֶּן יִשְׂרָאֵל יְחִיאֵל הַכֹּהֵן רַפּוֹפוֹרט שְׁרֶנְצִיל

b. Vienna (?), Austria, 4 Teves 5345/1584
d. Lemberg, Poland, 18 Sivan 5411/1651

R' Avraham's father was a communal leader and recognized Torah scholar in Cracow, and his grandfather, R' Aryeh Leib, was a rabbi in Prague. (A responsum by R' Yisrael Yechiel is found in his son's responsa §1.) One of R' Yisrael's daughters, Breindl, was married to the celebrated magnate R' Isaac R' Yekls who built the famous 'R' Isaac R' Yekels *Shul*' in Cracow. Indeed, Breindl is credited with influencing her husband to build this synagogue.

R' Avraham was a child prodigy, and at his *bar-mitzvah* he gave a *drashah* in the Cracow synagogue. This *drashah* was published (Cracow, 5358/1598) — probably the first such publication of its kind in history — as *Neki Chapayim UVar Mitzvah* (a pun on the verse in *Psalms* 24:4). This extremely rare volume was reprinted (Frankfurt am Main, 5685/1925) by R' A. Freiman on the occasion of his son's *bar-mitzvah*. In his youth, R'

Avraham studied under his father and R' Meshulam Feivush, the *rav* of Cracow.

R' Avraham married the daughter of R' Mordechai Shrentzel of Lemberg, a noted scholar and successful merchant, and he studied under *R' Yehoshua Falk HaKohen in that town. Being a man of means, R' Avraham declined a rabbinical position, but chose instead to found a yeshivah in his home. He headed the yeshivah for over forty-two years and taught many disciples. R' Avraham was also an important member of the Council of Four Lands (see **Historical Introduction**), and the caretaker of all funds for the needy in the Holy Land — due to which he received the honorary title *Mara DeAra DeYisrael* (Master of the Land of Israel) — and was noted for his charity.

R' Avraham authored a collection of responsa entitled *She'eilos UTeshuvos Eissan HaEzrachi* (Ostroh, 5456/1696), the second part of this work contains sermons, eulogies and commentaries to aggadic passages in the Talmud. Interspersed among the responsa are the writings of the rabbis and scholars who communicated with R' Avraham, e.g., *R' Yom Tov Lipman Heller (*Tosefos Yom Tov*), *R' Yehoshua ben Yosef, and others. R' Avraham also wrote a *Seder Gittin* (manual for writing and giving a *get*) which is cited extensively by *R' Ephraim Zalman Margulies in his *Tiv Gittin,* but remains unpublished.

R' Eliezer ben Yitzchak ibn Archa

ר' אֱלִיעֶזֶר בֶּן יִצְחָק אִבְּן אַרְחָא

b. Safed (?), Eretz Yisrael
d. Hebron, Eretz Yisrael, 15 Cheshvan
5412/1651

R' Eliezer's father — R' Yitzchak ibn Archa — was a *talmid chacham* of standing in Safed, and is considered to have been a disciple of the *Ari. R'

Eliezer left Safed and lived most of his life in Hebron, where he served as *rav* and mainstay of the small Jewish community in the City of the Patriarchs. He also lived in Gaza for short periods of time, probably when conditions in Hebron made it virtually impossible for him to stay there.

*Chida testifies that R' Eliezer wrote many works, among them commentaries on *Ein Yaakov* (*R' Yaakov ibn Chaviv's compendium of the *aggados* in the Talmud), and on the *Midrash Rabbah*. His responsa, *She'eilos UTeshuvos R' Eliezer ibn Archa,* have recently been printed by Mechon Yerushalayim (Jerusalem, 5738/1978).

R' Avraham Alegri

רַבִּי אַבְרְהָם בֶּן שְׁלֹמֹה אַלֵּיגְרִי

d. Constantinople (now Istanbul), Turkey,
5412/1652

R' Avraham authored *Lev Same'ach* (Constantinople, 5412/1652), a commentary on *Rambam's *Sefer HaMitzvos,* and responsa with the same title (Salonica, 5414/1654).

R' Daniel Esterosah

רַבִּי דָּנִיֵּאל אִיסְטְרוֹסָה

d. Salonica, Turkey (now Greece)
5413/1653

A disciple of R' Mordechai Kalai, R' Daniel is most famous for his responsa *Magen Giborim* (Vol. 1, Salonica, 5414/1654; Vol. 2, Salonica, 5604/1844). He also composed *chidushim* on tractate *Avodah Zarah* (printed in *Ben Avraham* by R' Chaim Avraham Esterosah, Salonica, 5586/1826), and regulations on the correct spelling of names with regard to *gittin* (printed in *Yerech Avraham* by R' Chaim Avraham Esterosah, Salonica, 5575/1815).

R' Daniel stood at the head of the

famous Portugal community in Salonica, and among his disciples was *R' David Conforte.

R' Yom Tov Lipman Heller

רַבִּי יוֹם טוֹב לִיפְּמַאן בֶּן נָתָן הַלֵּוִי הֶעלָּער

b. Wallerstein (Bavaria), Germany, 5339/1579
d. Cracow, Poland, 6 Elul 5414/1654

R' Yom Tov's father died, a young man of eighteen, before his illustrious son was born. The gifted youngster was raised by his paternal grandfather, R' Moshe Wallerstein, "whose name was well known throughout Yehudah and Yisrael" (preface to Maadanei Yom Tov); according to his epitaph he was rabbi of the communities of Germany.

The young R' Yom Tov was sent to learn under R' Akiva Gunzburg in Friedburg, and later he studied under *R' Yehudah Loeve (Maharal) and *R' Ephraim Lunshitz in Prague. There he married the daughter of a respected businessman, and at the young age of eighteen (5357/1597), he was appointed to the position of dayan in Prague. After many years (in Cheshvan 5385/1624) he accepted the rabbinate of Nikolsburg (Moravia/Czechoslovakia), where he remained for only several months before being called upon (in Adar 5385/1625) to serve the community of Vienna. He is reputed to have secured for the Jews the section called Leopoldstadt as a permanent Jewish quarter. In 5387/1627 he returned to Prague, where he was appointed rabbi of the community.

Because of the Thirty Years' War, the government imposed heavy taxes on the Jewish communities of Bohemia, including that of Prague, which was forced to pay an annual tax of forty thousand thalers — an exorbitant sum in those days. As R' Yom Tov was the Chief Rabbi, he was compelled against his will to preside over the commission which had the task of dividing that sum among the members of the community for payment. Although he acted with the greatest circumspection, some members complained of unfair treatment. They accused R' Yom Tov before the civil authorities of having been bribed to spare the rich and put the burden of the tax upon the poorer class. Emperor Ferdinand II addressed a severe warning to R' Yom Tov not to repeat such proceedings. However, R' Yom Tov's enemies, not satisfied, slandered him again to the emperor, claiming that his work Maadanei Melech (Prague, 5388/ 1628) contained negative statements about the emperor and Christianity. An immediate order was issued for his arrest and, on the fifth day of Tammuz, 5389/1629, R' Yom Tov set out for Vienna, arriving there a week later. He later commemorated the day of his arrest (5 Tammuz) as a fast day for himself and all succeeding generations of his family.

In Vienna, R' Yom Tov was imprisoned and, following a trial before a court of Christian clergymen, he was sentenced to death and his writings were ordered burnt. However, through the intervention of some distinguished members of the Jewish community, the death sentence was commuted to a monetary fine and the incriminated writings were ordered to be rectified by the elimination of all traces of negative attitudes towards Christianity and government. R' Yom Tov was also prohibited from holding any rabbinical post in the entire Austrian Empire; however, his friends succeeded in having the prohibition restricted to Prague only.

R' Yom Tov was released after a confinement of forty days, and on the eve of Yom Kippur he returned home, where he remained bedridden for three months, recovering from the ordeal he had undergone.

In 5391/1631, R' Yom Tov left Prague and journeyed to Lublin, Poland, for the marriage of his son. There he was received with great honor and his erudition was appreciated. In 5392/1632 he was called to the rabbinate in Nemirov, in the Ukraine, and in 5403/1643 he was appointed rabbi of Ludmir (Vladimir), Poland (Volhynia/Russia). While rabbi of Ludmir, R' Yom Tov obtained renewal at the Council of Four Lands (see **Historical Introduction**) of the decrees against purchasing the rabbinate, thereby gaining for himself additional enemies. In 5403/1643, he was slandered before the governor of the provinces of Volhynia, and ordered by him to leave Ludmir. This sentence, however, was repealed due to the intervention of some influential Jews in Warsaw. A few months thereafter he received an invitation from the community of Cracow to serve as its spiritual leader and successor to the *Bach. He gladly accepted, and arrived in Cracow on 28 Cheshvan 5404/1643. When *R' Yehoshua ben Yosef (Pnei Yehoshua), the rosh yeshivah of Cracow, passed on a few years later, R' Yom Tov succeeded him as head of that advanced Talmudic center.

During the Cossack uprising of 5408-09/1648-49 (see **Historical Introduction**), R' Yom Tov composed selichos (supplications) and a memorial prayer dedicated to those who had perished in the massacre. He also did much to alleviate the plight of the numerous agunos [women whose husbands had been reported killed, but the validity of the evidence attesting to their deaths was questionable on a halachic basis]. In keeping with the traditional approach of great halachic authorities, R' Yom Tov used all of his erudition to find a way out of the dilemma in which these women found themselves.

R' Yom Tov composed many outstanding works, the best-known being his Mishnah commentary, Tosefos Yom Tov (Prague, 5357/1597; with many additions by the author, Cracow, 5404/1644), published in almost all big Mishnah editions. It is a clarification, through recourse to the Talmud and codes, of many complex and difficult problems arising in the Mishnah. It is indispensable to the serious student and is discussed by virtually all later Mishnah commentators as well as by Talmud commentators. The author was inspired to write this work because of the renewed interest in Mishnah study which was stimulated by Maharal of Prague. The author felt that the commentary of Rav left many questions unanswered because of its brevity. R' Yom Tov's lengthy commentary was abridged by R' Meshulam Katz and titled Ikkar Tosefos Yom Tov (Lemberg, 5550/1790).

One of R' Yom Tov's other works is a comprehensive commentary on *Rosh's halachic commentary to the Talmud. Of this he published: Maadanei Melech and Lechem Chamudos, a double commentary on the Rosh to Berachos, Chullin, Nidah, Bechoros, Halachos Ketanos, Hilchos Nidah and Mikvaos (Prague, 5388/1628; in subsequent editions the names were changed to Maadanei Yom Tov and Divrei Chamudos); and Pilpula Charifta (Prague, 5386/1626), to the Rosh on Seder Nezikin. These two works are now printed in the prevalent editions of the Talmud on the margin of the Rosh. Other works include Bris Melach (Prague; publication date unknown), in Yiddish, on the laws of salting meat; Tzuras HaBayis (Prague, 5362/1602), on the description of the Third Temple in the book of Ezekiel, and related topics; Derush Chidushei HaLevanah (Vilna, 5626/1866), a treatise on the passages in the Talmud and midrash pertaining to the waxing and waning of the moon; *Malbushei Yom Tov* (Warsaw, 5655-57/ 1895-97), glosses on *Levush* to section *Orach Chaim; Toras HaAsham,* on *Rama's *Toras Chatas* (Jerusalem, 5737/ 1977); *Megillas Eivah* (Breslau, 5596/ 1836), an autobiography; notes on *Tur Even HaEzer* (Metz, 5525/1765, together with *Chidushei HaRashba,* and later in the prevalent editions of *Tur*); notes on R' Yosef ben Yitzchak HaLevi's *Givas HaMoreh* (Prague, 5372/1612), a critique of *Moreh Nevuchim;* and a commentary on *R' Yedayah Bedersi's (HaPenini) *Bechinas Olam* (Prague, 5358/1598). He left many unpublished works, of which the following are known: *Tuv Taam,* a commentary on the kabbalistic material contained in the Torah commentary of *R' Bachya; *Leket Shoshanim,* a grammatical treatise; *Darchei Horaah,* a guide to decisions in ritual laws when the authorities disagree; *Seder Shemos Gittin,* on the laws of divorce; a super-commentary on ibn Ezra's Torah commentary; *Parashas HaChodesh,* a commentary on *Hilchos Kiddush HaChodesh* in Rambam's *Mishneh Torah;* and responsa, most of which are unpublished (some are printed in *Teshuvos Geonei Basrai* and *Teshuvos Tzemach Tzedek*).

R' Yom Tov also popularized the ethical treatise of Rosh — *Orchos Chaim* — by dividing it into seven parts and having a portion recited each day in his Vienna congregation, and he also translated the work into Yiddish (Prague, 5386/1626). During his rabbinate in Vienna, he instituted a special *Mi SheBeirach* for those who refrained from speaking idle talk in the synagogue.

According to the testimony of R' Zelig Margolies (*Chiburei Likutim,* Amsterdam, 5475/1715), R' Yom Tov died penniless, without even leaving sufficient money to purchase shrouds, for he never accepted gifts and was most careful never to have any monetary dealings with the community, for fear of coming into contact with money not earned honestly. R' Yom Tov had many distinguished descendants, among them *R' Aryeh Leib HaKohen Heller, famed author of *Ketzos HaChoshen.*

R' Yosef Shlomo Delmedigo (Yashar of Candia)

רַבִּי יוֹסֵף שְׁלֹמֹה בֶּן אֵלִיָהוּ דֶּילְמֶדִיגוֹ
(יָשָׁ"ר מִקַּנְדִיָא)

b. Candia, Crete, 25 Sivan 5351/1591
d. Prague, Bohemia (now Czechoslovakia)
15 Tishrei, 5416/1655

R' Yosef (also known as Yashar, an acronym for Yosef Shlomo *Rofei* [physician]) was born in Candia into the prestigious Delmedigo family, one of the foremost on the island of Crete. His antecedents had emigrated there from Germany in the beginning of the fifteenth century, and had been among the founders and leaders of the Ashkenazic community.

R' Yosef exhibited amazing mental brilliance in his early youth. His parents gave him a thorough Torah education, and also saw to it that the young genius fulfilled himself in the secular disciplines as well. He studied philosophy, the sciences, mathematics and medicine. He excelled in astronomy and spoke several languages.

At the age of fifteen he traveled to Italy and enrolled in the University of Padua, where he studied under Galileo. He also took advantage of the opportunity to make the acquaintance of the leading rabbis of nearby Venice. Upon the completion of his studies at the age of eighteen, R' Yosef returned to his native Candia, where he got married and practiced medicine.

At this time he began to put his thoughts to paper; he wrote an encyclopedic treatise — *Bais Yaar HaLevanon* — a summary of all the branches of knowledge studied in his days; this treatise was never published. He also began to amass an amazing library consisting of 7,000 volumes. He possessed an unfailing memory and an amazing faculty for learning, and virtually 'swallowed' the thousands of *sefarim* he acquired.

R' Yosef soon left his native Candia, and spent the rest of his life wandering, living in a place for a few years and then moving on. We do not know the reason for this restlessness, and R' Yosef himself does not provide any hint in his writings. A disciple (R' Moshe Metz, in a letter printed in *Sefer Eilim*) writes that it was his love of knowledge and the enmity of unspecified people which caused his mentor to wander throughout the world.

His first stop was in Cairo, where he was challenged to debate a prominent Moslem scholar in public on problems of mathematics. The youthful scholar easily bested his eminent opponent; however, he made sure to assuage the hurt feelings of his opponent and parted with him in friendship. From there he traveled to Constantinople where he studied *kabbalah* with R' Yaakov ibn Nachmias. Then he went to Wallachia (now Rumania) and further pursued his study of the *kabbalah* with R' Shlomo Aravi in Yassi. In the year 5389/1629 he went to Poland, where his fame as a doctor was widespread. He finally settled in Vilna, where he served as a personal physician to Prince Radzivil of Lithuania.

There an otherwise unknown scholar — R' Zerach ben Yitzchak of Troki (a town near Vilna) — entreated R' Yosef to answer a number of questions which were bothering him. The questions were wide ranging, from problems of mathematics and astronomy, to philosophy and *kabbalah* — a sum of 82 queries. The questions are presented in his *Sefer Eilim*, while Yashar's replies are expounded in the treatise *Mayan Ganim*, which itself was comprised of thirteen subdivisions, each with a different name, according to the topics discussed. The *Sefer Eilim*, together with four subdivisions of the *Mayan Ganim*, was published by the author in Amsterdam (5391/1631).

From Poland Yashar went to northern Germany and officiated as *rav* of the nascent Jewish community of Hamburg. Here he began to write his work *Matzreif LaChachmah* (Basel, 5389/1629), a spirited defense of the *kabbalah* against the attack upon it by Yashar's maternal great-grandfather, R' Eliyahu Delmedigo. Several small treatises were attached to the *Matzreif LaChachmah,* among them R' Shlomo Meinsterl's biography of the *Arizal, *Maamar Olam Kattan* by *Rama of Fano, and other kabbalistic pamphlets.

Yashar himself admitted to one of his disciples that in his youth, when he was a student at Padua, he had been enthralled by Aristotelian philosophy, and had repudiated the *kabbalah* as irrational. He had a change of heart at the age of twenty-seven when he met two great intellectuals — R' Yaakov ibn Nachmias and R' Shlomo Aravi — who were also firm adheren*s of the *kabbalah*. It was at this point of his life that he began to immerse himself in the *kabbalah* and felt a renewal of spirit within himself (preface to *Novlos Chachmah*).

In the year 5388/1628 Yashar was appointed *rav* of the new Sephardic community of Amsterdam. There his colleague in the rabbinate, *R' Menashe ben Yisrael, prevailed upon R' Yosef to publish (part of) his *Sefer Eilim* and *Mayan Ganim* in R' Menashe's printing house. A disciple of R' Yosef published another one of his master's *sefarim* on *kabbalah* — *Novlos Chachmah* — in Basel (5391/1631), together with various small writings on *kabbalah* (by others) which he found at R' Yosef's home. At first R' Yosef was greatly upset when he heard of this unauthorized publication, but later he relented and gave his permission to release this work. He expresses his wish that G-d grant him the privilege to live in *Eretz Yisrael* so that he should be able to study the Arizals' *Eitz Chaim*. (This classic of *kabbalah* was not available in the Diaspora in Yashar's days; the kabbalists of the Holy Land did not permit this holy work to be studied outside of the Holy Land.)

Very little is known about the last 25 years of R' Yosef's life. He settled in Frankfurt am Main where he was the community's physician. Later yet he resided in Prague, where he died. The epitaph inscribed on his tombstone attests to the great regard in which he was held during his generation.

Besides the above-mentioned works, Yashar wrote numerous works which he refers to in his printed *sefarim*. According to one count he wrote twenty-six treatises (preface to *Eilim*, ed. Odessa, 5631/1871), on topics ranging from algebra to philosophy.

R' Naftali Hirtz Bacharach

רַבִּי נַפְתָּלִי הִירְץ בֶּן יַעֲקֹב אֶלְחָנָן

Frankfurt am Main, Germany
17th century

R' Naftali Hirtz was the author of *Emek HaMelech* (Amsterdam, 5408/1648), a profound kabbalistic treatise expounding the kabbalistic system of the *Ari. The book has approbations from the leading scholars of the time, including *R' Yom Tov Lipman Heller and *R' Yehoshua ben Yosef of Cracow. However, it was met with disapproval from some kabbalistic masters (see *Shem HaGedolim*) who claimed that R' Naftali Hirtz's work included distorted information on the Arizal's *kabbalah,* from writings originating from unreliable writers. They felt that the only reliable writings were the authentic ones of *R' Chaim Vital, who alone was to be relied upon in the transmission of the Ari's teachings. *R' Chaim HaKohen severely criticizes *Emek HaMelech* in his introduction to *Mekor Chaim.* However, some later masters, notably the *Baal HaTanya,* founder of *Chabad* chassidism, make extensive use of *Emek HaMelech,* and R' Tzadok Rabinowitz HaKohen of Lublin dismisses the objections to *Emek HaMelech (Sefer HaZichronos* at the end of *Divrei Soferim,* p. 24).

R' Menashe ben Yisrael

רַבִּי מְנַשֶּׁה בֶּן יוֹסֵף בֶּן יִשְׂרָאֵל

b. Island of Madeira, Portugal, 5364/1604
d. Middelburg, Holland, Kislev 5418/1657

Born a Marrano in Portugal, R' Menashe was taken while yet an infant to Amsterdam, which had become a haven for the unfortunate Marranos. R' Menashe's father had been accused of 'Judaizing' by the Inquisition, but had managed to escape being burnt at the stake in an auto-da-fé. After a short stay in France he finally settled in Amsterdam, where the family openly returned to its faith and took the family name 'ben Yisrael'.

In Amsterdam R' Menashe received a thorough Talmudic education, and had the good fortune to study under *R' Yitzchak Uziel. Two years after the latter's death in 5380/1620, the eighteen-year-old Menashe was proclaimed his successor as rabbi of the Sephardic community Neveh Shalom in Amsterdam. In addition to his Jewish education, R' Menashe received a comprehensive secular education. He was fluent in ten languages; he had great knowledge in many disciplines, especially medicine, mathematics and astronomy; and he was well read in classical literature and in the writings of early Christian theologians. Of course, his wide-ranging interests also encompassed the spectrum of Jewish learning and thinking, giving him an understanding of the Jewish trends of thought, from the rationalistic school of *Rambam (see the Rishonim) to the writings of the later kabbalists, as well as a proficiency in the Hebrew language and grammar.

R' Menashe's fame as a scholar spread beyond the confines of the Jewish community, and he communicated with many Christian theologians and scholars. Indeed it is said that Cromwell's interest in the official readmission of Jews to England was kindled by the attention shown in Puritan circles to R' Menashe's work, Esperanca de Israel. Among his Gentile friends was the famous artist Rembrandt van Rijn, who made an etching of R' Menashe, and prepared the copper plates illustrating some copies of R' Menashe's Piedra Gloriosa o de la Estatua de Nebuchadnesar (Amsterdam, 5417/1657), a Spanish work on the meaning of Nebuchadnezzar's statue (Daniel 3).

In Amsterdam, in 5387/1627, R' Menashe founded the first Jewish printing establishment in Holland, and he used it to print all the Jewish literature needed by the community. This press employed a new typeface which was later copied by many European printing houses.

In 5399/1639 the three Sephardic communities in Amsterdam united to form the congregation Neveh Shalom and designated *R' Shaul Mortera as rav, with R' Yitzchak Abohab de Fonseca as assistant rav. R' Menashe received a minor appointment in the newly formed kahal and he now found himself without an adequate means of livelihood. He decided to settle in the New World where business prospects were promising.

In 5400/1640 R' Menashe was already prepared to make the long journey over the Atlantic in order to settle at Pernambuco (now Recife), Brazil, which had been taken by the Dutch in 5391/1631 and was heavily populated by Jews. However, just then this young, budding New World community engaged R' Yitzchak Abohab de Fonseca as their rabbi, and the Amsterdam kahal designated R' Menashe his successor. Now as assistant to Chief Rabbi R' Shaul Mortera, his financial problems were solved and he decided to stay in Amsterdam. Later, in 5404/1644, the wealthy Pereira brothers founded a yeshivah and appointed R' Menashe its head.

R' Menashe was very anxious to have Jews settle in England, from where they had been expelled in 5050/1290. In addition to the obvious practical considerations, R' Menashe saw in the Jews' readmission to England a preparatory step toward the ultimate redemption, basing this on the belief that only after the Jews had been dispersed in every country of the four corners of the earth could the Messiah be expected. Toward this aim he published his Spes de Israelis (Hope of Israel; Amsterdam, 5410/1650) in Latin, setting forth his view that the American Indians were the descen dants of the ten lost tribes, therefore the 'New World' was already inhabited by Jews; and that the immediate barrier to the coming of the Messiah was the fact that some areas on the European continent were barred to the Jews. This work raised much interest among Christian Protestant theologians, especially among the Puritans in England, and a second edition was prepared shortly thereafter, with an English preface containing an address to the Parliament exhorting its members to consider readmission of the Jews to the country. R' Menashe stressed his belief that England was the *ketzeh haaretz* (lit., end of the earth) referred to as the extent of the Jewish Diaspora. This work was immediately translated into English and went into three editions in the years 5410-12/1650-52. The many translations and editions this work underwent are an eloquent tribute to its author. In addition to the Latin and English editions already mentioned, Spanish (*Esperanca de Israel*), Dutch, Yiddish, and Hebrew (*Mikveh Yisrael*, Amsterdam, 5458/1698) translations were made, some of them going into multiple editions. Several replies to R' Menashe were published, one by a member of Parliament.

In 5415/1655 R' Menashe traveled to England, bringing with him a pamphlet addressed to Cromwell titled *Humble Addresses to the Lord Protector.*, outlining his arguments for allowing Jews to settle in England. He was received very cordially by many members of the English Parliament, and Oliver Cromwell granted him an audience, but stopped short of granting R' Menashe's plea on an official level. Public opinion was against admission of Jews, and Cromwell wished to avoid defeat on this issue in Parliament. However, the following year England declared war against Spain, and the status of the rich and important Marranos residing in the country could be resolved only with their declaration that they were Jews rather than Spaniards. Cromwell granted them leave to stay on an informal basis, and the status quo was preserved later upon the restoration of the monarchy. Thus the seed planted by R' Menashe bore fruit immediately. While he was in England he composed *Vindiciae Judeaorum* (London, 5416/1656) in English to refute some of the anti-Semitic libels which the anti-Jewish party had circulated during the debate about readmission of the Jews.

Although he had succeeded in arousing sympathy for Jews in England, R' Menashe did not accomplish his goal — official legalization of the Jewish status quo in England; only in 5513/1753 were Jews granted English citizenship. However, Oliver Cromwell seems to have agreed to let Jews live in England and practice their religion on an informal basis. R' Menashe left England a broken and penniless man, feeling that he had not accomplished his purpose. This was intensified by personal tragedy, for his son Shmuel, who had accompanied him, passed away on the second day of *Rosh Hashanah* (5418/1657) at a young age. R' Menashe sailed with the coffin of his beloved son to Middelburg, Holland, where his brother lived. Soon after his arrival he himself died, at the young age of fifty-three.

R' Menashe authored many works, mostly on the matters of faith which perturbed Amsterdam's Portuguese community which consisted of erstwhile Marranos who had been instilled with Christian theology during their youth. In keeping with his purpose, almost all of his works were written in Portuguese, Spanish or Latin. One of his

Hebrew works is *Nishmas Chaim* (Amsterdam, 5412/1652; with a copper-engraved portrait of the author) about the nature of the soul, transmigration of souls *(gilgul)* and related matters. This work, although it embraces the views of the kabbalists on this topic, is also replete with citations from the thinkers of antiquity and testimonies both by Jews and Gentiles. Other Hebrew works are: *Mikveh Yisrael* (Amsterdam, 5418/1658), a Hebrew translation of his *Spes de Israelis; Pnei Rabbah* (Amsterdam, 5388/1628), an index to *Midrash Rabbah,* arranged topically and according to the verses of the Bible; *Teshuas Yisrael* (Vienna, 5574/1814), a Hebrew translation of his *Vindiciae Judeaorum*; and glosses to the *Mishnah* (Amsterdam, 5391-92/1631-32). One of the better known of his Spanish and Latin works is *Conciliador*, in four parts, an attempt to explain difficult passages of the Bible. The first part was published in Spanish and Latin (Amsterdam or Frankfurt am Main, 5392/1632), while the next three parts appeared only in Latin (Amsterdam, 5401/1641, 5410/1650, 5411/1651). An English translation has been published (London, 5602/1842). Of his foreign language works which have not been translated into Hebrew or English we shall mention only his two Portuguese *halachah* summaries, *Thesauro dos Dinim,* a sort of short *Shulchan Aruch* in five parts (parts 1-4, Amsterdam, 5405/1645; part 5, 5407/1647), and *Dinim de Sehita y Bedica* (Amsterdam, 5396/1636). Interestingly, part of the *Thesauro* was reprinted in Portugal between the two World Wars (Oporto, 5691-92/1931-32).

R' Menashe was greatly appreciated as a preacher in his generation, and *R' Yosef Shlomo Delmedigo, who knew R' Menashe personally, lauds his great knowledge and his fame as a scholar in the Christian world.

R' Moshe ben Yitzchak Yehudah Lema

רַבִּי מֹשֶׁה בֶּן יִצְחָק יְהוּדָה לֵימָא

b. c. 5365/1605
d. Brisk, Lithuania, c. 5418/1658

Very little is known about the life of this outstanding sage; Lema is not his family name, but an unusual and obscure nickname for Yehudah.

A disciple of *R' Yehoshua ben Yosef of Cracow, in about 5397/1637 R' Moshe was appointed to the rabbinate of Slonim (Lithuania), and in about 5410/1650 to that of Vilna, a most prestigious community, known as the 'Jerusalem of Lithuania.'

In Vilna R' Moshe also instructed students, and among the most famous of these were *R' Ephraim HaKohen, author of *Shaar Ephraim;* *R' Hillel, author of *Beis Hillel;* and *R' Aharon Shmuel Kaidanover. The *Shach* was a member of his Vilna *beis din.*

R' Moshe left Vilna in 5415/1655 to assume the rabbinate of Brisk, where he spent the last three years of his life.

R' Moshe composed *Chelkas Mechokeik* (Cracow, 5430/1670), a running commentary on *Shulchan Aruch Even HaEzer,* later published in almost all editions. His authority as a halachist was immediately recognized in his generation and *Beis Shmuel,* the almost contemporary commentary to *Even HaEzer,* quotes him extensively with great reverence. *Chacham Tzvi relates that he heard from his forebears about the greatness of R' Moshe and that one should not deviate from his rulings.

R' Shabsai Sheftl Horowitz II

רַבִּי שַׁבְּתַי שֶׁעֶפְטִיל
בֶּן יְשַׁעְיָה הַלֵּוִי הוֹרוֹוִיץ

b. Ostroh (Ostrog), Poland (now Russia)
c. 5350/1590
d. Vienna, Austria, 28 Nissan 5420/1660

The son of the *Shelah, R' Shabsai Sheftl studied under his father and under *R' Shlomo Ephraim Lunshitz, whom he revered greatly. After the Shelah left for Eretz Yisrael, R' Shabsai Sheftl was appointed preacher and dayan in Prague, serving in this capacity for six years. He later became rabbi of Fuerth, then Frankfurt am Main, and in 5402/1642 he was elected rabbi of Posen, where he founded a yeshivah. In 5414/1654, he became rabbi of Vienna, where he remained until his death.

In 5409/1649 R' Shabsai Sheftl published his father's work, Shnei Luchos HaBris, which he prefaced with an extensive introduction entitled Vavei HaAmudim. Actually this introduction is a treatise in itself, not connected directly to Shelah. Rather, it is a collection of ethical sermons, centered around six central themes (peace, justice, truth, Torah study, service [of G-d], and kind deeds), which are mentioned in Avos (1:2,18) as being the 'pillars' which hold up the world.

R' Shabsai Sheftl mentions in Vavei HaAmudim that he wrote a commentary on many tractates of the Talmud, and a commentary on Issur VeHeter, but they have never been published.

R' Sheftl's son, R' Yeshayah, was also a prominent rabbi, officiating as the rabbi of Frankfurt am Main. R' Yeshayah's son, R' Avraham, published (Amsterdam, 5489/1729) the first edition of Chidushei HaRitva to five tractates (Eruvin, Taanis, Moed Kattan, Kesubos, Bava Metzia) with glosses by his father and grandfather.

R' Eliezer Ashkenazi Ish Tzvi

רַבִּי אֱלִיעֶזֶר בֶּן שְׁמוּאֵל אַשְׁכְּנַזִי אִישׁ צְבִי

b. Poland, c. 5330/1570
d. Jerusalem, Eretz Yisrael, c. 5420/1660

R' Eliezer was called Ish Tzvi after his paternal grandfather, R' Tzvi Hellman (a first name) of Worms, who was also an uncle of *Maharal of Prague. R' Eliezer's father, R' Shmuel Ish Tzvi, was known in his generation as R' Shmuel Chassid because of his extraordinary piety and excellence of character. In their old age, he and his wife left Europe and settled in Eretz Yisrael, and there R' Shmuel died. R' Shmuel's four sons were all prominent rabbis and scholars. The one who is best known today is R' Eliezer, who left behind a published work. R' Eliezer studied under R' Meshulam Feivush of Cracow, and was a colleague of the *Bach.

R' Eliezer is known for his Talmudic work, Damessek Eliezer (Lublin, 5406/1646), a comprehensive commentary on tractate Chulin which has been likened in scope to Maharshal's Yam shel Shlomo. He also wrote Siach Yitzchak (Lublin, 5405/1645), a commentary on the prayers, and Tikun Soferim (Prague, 5418/1658), a guide for scribes. His Damessek Eliezer, highly valued by Talmudic scholars, is very rare. Until modern times it underwent only one printing, and the greater part of this printing was burned before publication. The renowned gaon, R' Shalom Mordechai Schwadron of Brezan, relates in the preface to his Daas Torah on Yoreh Deah how he went to considerable lengths to obtain a copy of this prized work, and that many of his rulings which departed from the hitherto accepted way were based on the views of R' Eliezer Ish Tzvi. *R' Chaim Benveniste also cites Damessek Eliezer often in his Knesses HaGedolah. The approbations to this work show that R' Eliezer was held in great reverence by his contemporaries and was regarded as one of the greatest Talmudic scholars of his time. These approbations indicate that the work *Damessek Eliezer* was written on the entire Talmud. Indeed, the *gaon* R' Meir Auerbach of Jerusalem possessed a manuscript copy of the work to tractate *Pesachim*.

R' Eliezer served as rabbi of Apta (Opatow), Poland. However, upon the commencement of the Cossack uprisings in 5408/1648 (see **Historical Introduction**) he left Poland. He eventually traveled to Jerusalem in 5411/1651, and there he spent the last years of his life.

R' Chaim HaKohen

רַבִּי חַיִּים בֶּן אַבְרָהָם הַכֹּהֵן

b. Egypt, c. 5345/1585
d. Leghorn, Italy, c. 5420/1660

A disciple of *R' Chaim Vital, R' Chaim HaKohen resided in Aleppo, Syria. He conceived the novel idea of composing a kabbalistic commentary on the entire *Shulchan Aruch*. Of this work, only the sections to *Orach Chaim* and part of *Yoreh Deah* have been preserved. However, the author indicates that he completed the work to all four parts of the *Shulchan Aruch*. The entire work is entitled *Mekor Chaim,* and is divided into separate sections, each named for one of the twelve stones of the *choshen* (see *Exodus* 28:17-20). The printed sections are *Tur Odem* (Amsterdam, 5415/1655), dealing with the daily laws; *Tur Pitdah* (Leghorn, 5415/1655) on *Hilchos Shabbos* and *Eruvin*; *Tur Barekes* (Amsterdam, 5414/1654) on the laws of the various *Yamim Tovim*; and *Tur Yahalom* (Leghorn, 5415/1655) on the laws of mourning.

R' Chaim authored *Toras Chacham*

(Venice, 5414/1654), sermons arranged according to the portions of the Torah. *Chida (Shem HaGedolim)* reports that he saw a manuscript, probably written by R' Chaim himself, containing *Ateres Zahav* on the Book of *Esther*, and *Menoras Zahav* on *Ecclesiastes*. Chida also claims that *Toras Chessed,* R' Chaim's commentary on *Ruth*, was published by *R' David Lida (under his own name) as *Migdal David* (Amsterdam, 5440/1680). For reasons unclear to us, R' David did not disclose the name of the true author, and merely alluded to him in the preface with a veiled hint.

R' Chaim composed a lamentation over the destruction of the Temple, entitled *Kol BeRamah,* which is incorporated in the *Tikun Chatzos* (midnight service) and found in most prayer books. When already in his advanced old age, R' Chaim traveled to Europe for the purpose of publishing his works, took sick while in Leghorn, and died there.

R' Shaul Mortera

רַבִּי שָׁאוּל הַלֵּוִי מוֹרְטֵירָא

b. Venice, Italy, 5356/1596
d. Amsterdam, Holland, 5420/1660

A figure who stood at the head of the Portuguese community of Amsterdam, R' Shaul was one of the founders and directors of *Kesser Torah,* an important Sephardic Talmud Torah (i.e., yeshivah) in that city. The renowned kabbalist and Talmudic scholar, *R' Moshe Zacut, was his disciple. R' Shaul was the head of the *beis din* which excommunicated the philosopher Baruch Spinoza, a member of the Portuguese community in Amsterdam, for spreading his heretical ideas.

He authored *Givas Shaul* (Amsterdam, 5405/1645), sermons on the Torah — his only published work — and many other works, which remained unpublished. *R' Moshe Rivkah's, author of *Be'er HaGolah*, makes note of R' Shaul in his work (*Even HaEzer* 16:1), mentioning a lengthy halachic decision written by the latter, and greatly praising his halachic acumen and expressing the wish that R' Shaul publish his many works.

R' Menachem Mendel Krochmal

רַבִּי מְנַחֵם מֶעְנְדֶל בֶּן אַבְרָהָם קרוֹכְמַל

b. Cracow, Poland, c. 5360/1600
d. Nikolsburg (Mikolav), Moravia (now Czechoslovakia), 2 Shevat 5421/1661

A disciple of the *Bach, when yet a young man R' Menachem Mendel was appointed *dayan* in Cracow, and given special permission by his teacher to establish his own yeshivah. There he taught some very prominent scholars, among them *R' Menachem Mendel Auerbach and *R' Gershon Ashkenazi, who later became his son-in-law.

In 5396/1636 he accepted the rabbinate of Kremsir, in Moravia. Several years later he moved on to the rabbinate of Prossnitz, and finally became Chief Rabbi of Nikolsburg and all of Moravia, a post he held until his death.

R' Menachem Mendel was greatly influential in the life of Moravian Jewry. He presided over the meeting held in Dresnitz in 5419/1659 by the Moravian Jewish communities, in which a constitution having no less than three hundred eleven paragraphs was adopted. He strongly protected the rights of the poor against the rich, who in various ways wished to take advantage of the latter in their unfortunate situation.

He also was watchful in protecting the economy. Gentile fishermen, realizing that the Jews were willing to pay any amount of money in order to secure fish for the Shabbos meal, began to dramatically raise their prices. Observing this, R'

Menachem Mendel decreed that no Jew in Nikolsburg was to purchase fish for a number of weeks, until the reasonable market price was restored. This boycott was called in order to safeguard the economy of the community and to assure the poor also of access to this delicacy in honor of the Sabbath (see *Teshuvos Tzemach Tzedek* §28).

R' Menachem Mendel applied himself to the difficult task of solving the plight of the many women whose husbands were reported missing during the Cossack massacres of 5408-09/1648-49, and helped many of the Polish refugees to obtain positions in the rabbinates of Moravia.

R' Menachem Mendel is most famous for his volume of responsa, *Teshuvos Tzemach Tzedek* (Amsterdam, 5435/1675), which is a classic in the field of *halachah* and is cited by most halachists after his time, among them the *Magen Avraham*. It is called so because 'Tzemach Tzedek' numerically equals 'Menachem Mendel'.

R' Menachem's son, R' Yehudah Leib, succeeded his father in the Nikolsburg rabbinate. He published his father's responsa, to which he added glosses, and a responsum of his own appears at the end of the volume.

R' Yosef ben Shaul Escapa

ר' יוֹסֵף בֶּן שָׁאוּל אֶסְקַפָּא

b. Salonica, Turkey (now Greece), c. 5331/1571
d. Smyrna (now Izmir), Turkey,
26 Teves 5422/1662

One of his generation's foremost halachic authorities in Turkey, R' Yosef was a colleague of R' Chaim Shabsai and seems to have served in a rabbinic capacity during the latter's tenure in the rabbinate of Salonica. *R' David Conforte (*Korei HaDoros*) reports that R' Yosef taught many students there. He also lived for a while in Constantinople. *R' Chaim Benveniste mentions in a responsum (Bo'ei Chayei, Choshen Mishpat, v.1, §5) that he and R' Yosef studied at the same yeshivah in Constantinople. R' Chaim studied under *R' Yosef Trani in Constantinople, so it is surmised by some writers that R' Yosef Escapa was also a disciple of this gadol; however, this is not corroborated by any other source. This is also unlikely because of their comparative ages; these two gedolim — R' Yosef Escapa and R' Yosef Trani — were approximately equal in age.

In c. 5390/1630 R' Yosef was appointed to serve in the rabbinate of Smyrna. He was soon joined by R' Azaryah Yehoshua Ashkenazi (a disciple of R' Chaim Shabsai) and shared the rabbinate with him until R' Azaryah's demise (14 Cheshvan 5408/1647). Thereafter, until his death, R' Yosef was the undisputed leader of Smyrna's Jewish community. He founded a yeshivah and taught a great number of students.

The ill-fated false Messiah Shabsai Tzvi, a native of Smyrna, was a student of his, and R' Yosef was the pseudo-Messiah's first opponent. When R' Yosef was apprised (c. 5309/1649) that his disciple claimed to be the Messiah and had uttered the ineffable four-letter Name of G-d, R' Yosef immediately sensed the danger, excommunicated his disciple and declared his blood to be forfeit. Shabsai Tzvi had to flee Turkey and spent the next decade and a half in Eretz Yisrael before again declaring himself to be the Messiah. By then R' Yosef was no longer alive, and it was left to one of his successors in the Smyrnian rabbinate — *R' Aharon Lapapa — to be in the forefront of the opposition to the would-be Messiah and his cohorts.

R' Yosef's mind remained sharp and alert to the end despite his advanced age. R' David Conforte relates, "Once when I went to Izmir I had the privilege to meet with him [R' Yosef] and to learn from him . . . He was at that time greatly advanced in age — close to a hundred years old" (Korei HaDoros).

R' Yosef wrote an extensive commentary named Rosh Yosef on the Tur and its major commentary — Beis Yosef — but only a small portion was published. R' Yosef himself printed portions of this work on Orach Chaim (from Hil. Pesach and further; Smyrna, 5418/1658) and Choshen Mishpat (on the first 96 chapters; Smyrna, 5419/1659). A volume of his responsa, also named Rosh Yosef, was printed after his death, together with miscellaneous chidushim (Frankfurt an der Oder, 5469/1709). His comments to the laws of taxes and communal ordinances (perhaps this is a section of Rosh Yosef) were published as Avodas Massa (Salonica, 5606/1846).

R' Meir Popperos

רַבִּי מֵאִיר בֶּן יְהוּדָה לֵיב הַכֹּהֵן פָּאפֵּירוֹש

b. Prague, Bohemia (now Czechoslovakia)
c. 5384/1624
d. Jerusalem, Eretz Yisrael, Adar 5422/1662

R' Meir was born into a prominent Bohemian family which boasted many distinguished rabbis among its ranks. (R' Yaakov HaKohen Poppers, author of Teshuvos Shev Yaakov and rabbi of Frankfurt am Main, was from this family.)

R' Meir began his kabbalistic studies at the tender age of thirteen, and at a young age settled in Eretz Yisrael, where he studied kabbalah under R' Yisrael Ashkenazi and *R' Yaakov Tzemach. He had access to the writings of R' Chaim Vital as preserved by his son *R' Shmuel Vital in Damascus. He also studied the later writings of R' Chaim Vital (mahadurah basra) which had earlier been buried, and the collections of the Ari's *kabbalah* edited and written by R' Yaakov Tzemach and by other followers of the Ari. R' Meir dedicated his entire life to the arranging, editing, and dissemination of the kabbalistic system of the *Ari, as expounded in the writings of *R' Chaim Vital.

R' Meir writes, in his introduction to his arrangement of R' Chaim Vital's *Eitz Chaim,* that the manuscripts of R' Chaim Vital were without any systematic order, since he had written them following each discourse which the Ari delivered, and that the Ari did not wish to lecture following a pattern, so that those unworthy of the holy teachings would be unable to synthesize and comprehend them. However, observing that the discourses now became a closed book for all, R' Meir sorted the manuscripts under various subject headings, determined a proper sequence to the discourses involving each individual subject, and called the entire work *Eitz Chaim.* He divided it into three major parts: *Derech Eitz Chaim,* containing the fundamentals of *kabbalah*; *Pri Eitz Chaim,* containing the ritualistic information pertaining to prayers, holidays and the purposes of the *mitzvos*; and *Nof Eitz Chaim,* containing the treatises dealing with souls, reincarnation, comments on the Bible, and *Zohar* commentary.

These works served as basic textbooks for the Ari's *kabbalah* for generations to come and, with some variations, were reprinted several times. R' Meir's compilation of R' Chaim Vital's writings differs from the *Shemonah She'arim* arranged by *R' Shmuel Vital (R' Chaim's son) in arrangement and in content, for he had at his disposal, in addition to the manuscripts used by R' Shmuel, a later version of R' Chaim's writings *(mahadurah basra),* and he also included the writings of his mentor R' Yaakov

Tzemach (the work called *Otzros Chaim*).

The tripartite work *Eitz Chaim* was not at first printed, and probably was not meant to be. The Ari's *kabbalah* was initially considered by its adherents to be designated merely for the elite, and were disseminated among them in manuscript form. Part of the work *Derech Eitz Chaim* was first published more than a century after the compiler's demise as *Eitz Chaim* (Koretz, 5542/1782); this part of the compilation (and not R' Chaim Vital's compilation by the same name) is now commonly known as *Eitz Chaim.* The part called *Pri Eitz Chaim* was published (partially) in two different editions: Koretz, 5542/1782 and there, 5545/1785. Later a composite edition merging both versions was printed (Dubrovna, 5564/1804). It has been demonstrated that the first edition is really the work *Meoros Nassan* by *R' Nassan Nata Shapira III, in which he assembled basically the same material as that which was compiled by R' Meir in *Pri Eitz Chaim.* The part of the work called *Nof Eitz Chaim* was not printed. However, the *sefer Likutei Torah* (Zolkiew, 5535/1775) is considered to be a part of this work (R' Yosef Avivai in *Moriah,* Sivan 5741/1981).

R' Meir also wrote many original works — according to one opinion, as many as thirty-nine. Among these are *Meorei Or* (in *Meoros Nassan*; Warsaw, 5627/1867), a kabbalistic encyclopedia; and *Mesilos Chachmah* (Shklov, 5545/1785), a short introduction to the *kabbalah* together with a commentary to a kabbalistic diagram (tree) by *Maharshal portraying the interrelationship between the upper spiritual worlds. Another of his works is *Or Tzadikim* (Hamburg, 5450/1690), kabbalistic customs and ethics. This work was rearranged by R' Tzvi Hirsh Chazzan of Posen and published with additions as *Or HaYashar.* This was later adapted to the *siddur* and enjoyed considerable popularity. R' Meir also wrote *Or Rav,* a *Zohar* commentary; *Massuk HaOr,* a commentary on *Ein Yaakov*; *Or HaAvukah*; and other kabbalistic treatises which were never published.

Recently a number of R' Meir's works have been published by Chevras Ahavas Shalom: *Or Zarua* (Jerusalem, 5746/1986), a commentary on the above-mentioned compilation *Eitz Chaim,* printed together with *Or Shabbos* (a commentary to the Ari's *zemiros* for Shabbos), and a reprint of R' Meir's glosses to *Pri Eitz Chaim* and of his glosses to the Ari's work *Taamei HaMitzvos*; *Or Tzach* (Jerusalem, 5744/1984), a summary of R' Chaim Vital's introduction to the Ari's *kabbalah*, printed together with a reprint of R' Meir's *Mesilos Chachmah,* and *Maftechos Mevo She'arim* (an index to R' Chaim Vital's *Mevo She'arim*) with annotations by *R' Yaakov Tzemach; *Or Ner* (Jerusalem, c. 5745/1985), about the transmigrations (*gilgulim*) of souls; and *Torah Or* (Jerusalem, 5749/1989) on the kabbalistic portions of Ramban's commentary to the Torah.

R' Shabsai HaKohen (the *Shach*)

רַבִּי שַׁבְּתַי בֶּן מֵאִיר הַכֹּהֵן (שַׁ"ךְ)

b. Amstibovi (?), Lithuania, 5382/1622
d. Holleschau, Moravia (now Czechoslovakia)
1 Adar Rishon 5423/1663

R' Shabsai's father, known as R' Meir Ashkenazi because of his German origin, was a respected scholar, rabbi of Amstibovi (Lithuania) and later of Mohilev (Mogilev, now Russia). He was the author of responsa which are printed with his son's *Gevuras Anashim,* and is mentioned many times in his son's works. The *Shach* also mentions a custom, regarding the separation of *challah,*

which was practiced by his mother (*Yoreh Deah* 326:4). R' Meir's father, R' Moshe, was rabbi of Donhausen (near Ansbach, Germany) and *dayan* in Frankfurt am Main.

R' Shabsai was a child prodigy, and at the age of twelve was accepted at the yeshivah of *R' Yehoshua ben Yosef; he also studied under *R' Yehoshua Heshel of Cracow. He married the daughter of R' Shimon Wolf of Vilna, great-grandson of *Rama (and brother of *R' Moshe, author of *Mahadurah Basra*). His father-in-law provided for all his needs, so that the *Shach* was able to concentrate, undisturbed, upon his studies.

Soon after his marriage, R' Shabsai was appointed to the post of *dayan* in the Vilna *beis din,* headed by *R' Moshe, the author of *Chelkas Mechokeik.* In 5405/1645 he went to Cracow, and in the following year published his work on *Shulchan Aruch Yoreh Deah* entitled *Sifsei Kohen,* and abbreviated *Shach,* after which he is called. He began this monumental work at the age of eighteen, and the greatest scholars of the generation wrote their approbations to it.

However, the *Shach's* serene Torah study was disturbed by the Cossack massacres of 5408-09/1648-49 (see **Historical Introduction**). It was at this time that he composed his *Megillas Eifah* (Lodz, 5684/1924), depicting the trials and tribulations of his generation, and *Selichos VeKinos* (Amsterdam, 5411/1651), liturgical compositions for recitation on 20 Sivan, the day chosen to commemorate the massacres. One of these pieces, a moving composition titled *Kel Maleh Rachamim* — which also contains a eulogy for one of the martyrs, the aged sage, R' Yechiel of Nemirov — is printed in many *siddurim.*

When the combined forces of the Russian Czar and the Cossack hordes reached Vilna in the summer (23 Tammuz) of 5415/1655, the *Shach* fled to Lublin, only to flee that city three months later when the Cossacks massacred 10,000 Jews there on 14 Tishrei 5617/1656. The *Shach* now sought refuge in Bohemia, first spending a short time in Prague, then in Dresnitz, until he became rabbi of Holleschau in Moravia, where he remained until his death at the young age of forty-one.

The *Shach*, in his short lifetime, became known as a superior Talmudist and halachist of the highest authority. His decisions were accepted in most cases as the final word of the law.

The *Shach* was an independent thinker, and he did not hesitate to disagree with his predecessors or contemporaries, and render decisions according to Talmudic logic and deduction. He wrote *Nekudos HaKessef* (Frankfurt an der Oder, 5437/1677) — critical comments on *Turei Zahav,* the work of his contemporary *R' David HaLevi — which was first published only after both sages were no longer alive. These criticisms were quite extensive. *Turei Zahav's* preface, and a page of additions (*daf haacharon*) which was printed by R' David immediately after the first publication of his work (and appended to copies of the work), were also unsparingly analyzed and criticized. R' Shabsai felt that the main thrust of *Turei Zahav's* additions was directed at refuting his *Sifsei Kohen,* although R' David did not mention it by name; R' David had seen *Sifsei Kohen* only after *Turei Zahav* had been published. The *Turei Zahav's* grandson, R' Yoel ben Gad, wrote *Maginei Zahav* (Prague, 5480/1720), a defense of his grandfather's views.

The *Shach* emphasized in his introduction that he had no personal feud with the *Taz*, who was thirty-five years his senior and an accepted authority; to the contrary, he was a friend and admirer of his older contemporary. He stated that his refutations were inspired only by his love of the truth.

The *Shach* also composed the *Sifsei Kohen* commentary on *Shulchan Aruch Choshen Mishpat,* published together with the text in Amsterdam, 5413/1653. This work differs slightly from the commentary on *Yoreh Deah.* Unlike the *Yoreh Deah* commentary, it does not comment on the *Shulchan Aruch* in a continuous manner, nor does it attempt to explain the text; R' Shabsai no doubt felt that for this purpose the *Sefer Meiras Einayim* (by *R' Yehoshua Falk HaKohen) was sufficient. In many instances he contented himself with merely adding some references to the responsa literature. It is only where he wants to elaborate on a novel view of his, or where he felt that the *Shulchan Aruch* or some other authority had erred, does he go into elaborate and extensive discussion. One is also led to the impression that in this work the *Shach* was more assertive and independent in refuting the views of his predecessors, and is tempted to attribute this to his maturation in years and his growing acceptance in the scholarly community as an authority par excellence.

Many commentaries were written on the *Shach*, the most prominent being the *Pri Megadim's Sifsei Daas* (by *R' Yosef Tumim) and there is not a later work on *Yoreh De'ah* and *Choshen Mishpat* which does not deal with his views extensively. Indeed it is — together with *Turei Zahav* (on *Yoreh Deah*) and *Sefer Meiras Einayim* (on *Choshen Mishpat*), — required learning for any student of the Codes, and it is inconceivable today to be considered an expert in these areas of *halachah* without a thorough knowledge of R' Shabsai's works.

Other works of the *Shach* are *HaAruch* (Berlin, 5527/1767), a commentary on *Tur Yoreh Deah* (only part of it was published); and *Tekafo Kohen* (Frankfurt an der Oder, 5427/1667), on the rules of appropriation (*tefisah*), without prior consent of a *beis din*, of articles whose ownership is disputed, and the rules for deciding cases in which ownership cannot be established with surety. (R' Shabsai wrote the latter work in one month when he was a mere youth of nineteen years. *R' Yonasan Eibeschutz summarized this work and wrote a commentary on it which is included in his *Urim VeTumim*.) R' Shabsai's other works are *Gevuras Anashim* (together with responsa by his father, R' Meir; Dessau, 5457/1697) on chapter 154 of *Shulchan Aruch Even HaEzer; Po'el Tzedek* (Jessnitz, 5480/1720), a poetical arrangement of the 613 commandments; and a homiletic, pilpulistic discourse on the part of the *Haggadah* liturgy starting with *Kamah Maalos* (together with R' Shlomo Haas' *Kerem Shlomo;* Pressburg, 5600/1840; and separately many times).

The *Magen Avraham* cites glosses by the *Shach* on *Shulchan Aruch Orach Chaim* in his comments to *Hilchos Pesach,* but these were never published. A lengthy responsum by the *Shach* is printed in *Or Tzvi* by R' Tzvi Hirsh Galler. *Chida reports that the proofreader in an unspecified edition of the *Shach* remarked that R' Shabsai had written a large volume commenting on the Talmud. This work, however, is unknown.

On studying the *Shach,* one is often overwhelmed by the veritable mountain of quotations from earlier authorities, and Chida, himself endowed with an extraordinary memory, attributes the *Shach's* overpowering mental abilities to supernatural powers. Chida also points out R' Shabsai's surprisingly prolific output. When the *Shach* on *Yoreh Deah* was

published, this in itself a monumental task for even a much older scholar, R' Shabsai was merely twenty-four years old and had already written a lengthy commentary on the *Tur* to which he refers in *Sifsei Kohen.* In his preface to the work he prays that he be able to publish other works which he had already written.

R' (Avraham) Yehoshua Heshel of Cracow

רַבִּי [אַבְרָהָם] יְהוֹשֻׁעַ הֶעֶשִׁיל
בֶּן יַעֲקֹב מִקְרַאקָא

b. Brisk, Poland
d. Cracow, Poland, 20 Tishrei 5424/1663

R' Yehoshua Heshel [the name Avraham was added at the end of his life, probably because of an illness] studied under his father, R' Yaakov, who was rabbi of Brisk and later of Lublin. At an early age he displayed an extremely sharp wit and a keen mind, which caused him to be considered a child prodigy. Many humorous anecdotes attesting to the extraordinary brightness and wit of his youth have become part of Jewish folklore. His father took him as an assistant at his yeshivah in Brisk, and later, when R' Yaakov assumed the rabbinate of Lublin, R' Yehoshua Heshel became his father's right hand man. Upon R' Yaakov's death in 5404/1644, R' Yehoshua Heshel became *rosh yeshivah* and thereafter Chief Rabbi of Lublin.

R' Yehoshua Heshel remained in Lublin until 5414/1654, when he was called to Cracow to succeed *R' Yom Tov Lipman Heller. There he remained until his last day. Because of the great reverence in which he was held, he was called 'The *Rebbe,* Reb Heshel'.

Beside being acknowledged as an outstanding scholar, R' Yehoshua Heshel was regarded as a saint and was known to be extremely charitable and kind. Due to the Cossack pogroms of 5408-09/ 1648-49 and the later Swedish invasion in 5416/1656 (see **Historical Introduction**), R' Yehoshua Heshel spent almost two years in Vienna in order to induce the rich and influential Jews of the Viennese community to extend a helping hand to their unfortunate brethren in Eastern Europe. He also traveled to many communities which had not been affected by the pogroms in order to raise funds for the victims. While R' Yehoshua Heshel was in Nikolsburg, the noted rabbi of the community, *R' Menachem Mendel Krochmal, treated him with the utmost awe and respect. On one occasion R' Menachem Mendel refused to rule on a halachic question which had been brought to the attention of both rabbis as they were having a Sabbath meal together, because his own opinion differed from that of R' Yehoshua Heshel (see *Teshuvos Tzemach Tzedek* §107).

R' Yehoshua Heshel's yeshivah was always filled to capacity and many of the greatest scholars of the age were his disciples. In spite of R' Heshel's reputation for sharp-wittedness and intricate *pilpul*, it seems that he restricted his ability in this aspect to the field of *drush*, homiletics, as can be seen by the brilliant gems attributed to him in various works and in oral tradition. In contrast, a disciple of his reports (preface to *Chidushei Halachos*) that he would forbid his disciples to draw parallels and comparisons from extraneous passages and to concentrate instead on the nuances of the text being studied. Indeed, his *chidushim* on the Talmud which have come down to us exhibit this tendency.

Among his most famous pupils were the *Shach, *R' Aharon Shmuel Kaidanover, *R' Hillel ben Naftali Hertz, *R' Shmuel ben Uri Shraga Feivush, and *R' Gershon Ashkenazi.

R' Yehoshua Heshel composed many works, but due to his modesty he refused to publish them and only fragments of his vast legacy have been preserved in the works of his disciples. One of these works is *Toldos Aharon* (Lublin, 5442/1682), selected notes taken by R' Aharon Klinker of his master's discourses on tractates *Bava Kamma, Bava Metzia,* and *Bava Basra.* This work was later reprinted as *Chidushei Halachos* (Frankfurt am Main, 5483/1723). Other works are *Amudei Shittim LeVeis Levi,* or *Beis Levi* (Prague, 5551/1791), similar notes by R' Levi Pollak on the same tractates with additional material on tractates *Shevuos, Avodah Zarah* and others, with some responsa by R' Yehoshua Heshel; notes on the *Smag* (in the *Smag* edition of Kopust, 5567/1807); and *Chanukas HaTorah* (Piotrkov, 5660/1900), an anthology of homiletic gems on the Torah, selected passages of Talmudic *Aggadah* and scattered verses of *Tanach,* attributed to R' Heshel in the works of his disciples and later works, and collected by R' Chanoch Ehrsohn.

Many of his halachic decisions are quoted in the works of his contemporary sages and those of later generations, e.g. *Shach, Chacham Tzvi, Chelkas Mechokeik, Teshuvos Tzemach Tzedek, Nachalas Shivah,* and others. Some responsa by him are printed in *Teshuvos Geonei Basrai, Teshuvos Geon Tzvi, Asifas Zekeinim,* and in the previously mentioned *Amudei Shittim.*

Many of R' Heshel's descendants were famous scholars. R' Moshe ben Avraham MiGeza Tzvi, rabbi of Horodna and author of *Tiferes Moshe,* was his grandson and disciple; and *R' Yechezkel Landau, author of *Noda BiYehudah;* R' Yosef Babad, author of *Minchas Chinuch;* and *R' Avraham Yehoshua Heshel, the famous chassidic rabbi of Apta and author of *Ohev Yisrael,* are just a few among the many illustrious descendants of R' Heshel.

R' Berechyah Beirech ben Yitzchak Isaac Shapira

ר' בְּרֶכְיָה בֵּירֶךְ בֶּן יִצְחָק אֵיזִיק שַׁפִּירָא

d. Constantinople (now Istanbul), Turkey
28 Teves 5424/1664

R' Berechyah was a disciple of *R' Nassan Nata Shapira II. He filled the post of *dayan* in Cracow during the rabbinates of *R' Yehoshua ben Yosef and the *Tosefos Yom Tov*. In his later years he attempted to travel to *Eretz Yisrael* in order to settle there, but died in Constantinople, in the middle of his journey.

He authored *Zera Beirech* (v. I, Cracow, 5406/1646; v. II, Amsterdam, 5422/1662), explanations of difficult passages in the *midrashim* on the Torah. The explanations are based on concepts culled from the Talmud and *midrashim* and seek to find the *pshat*. In his preface, R' Berechyah decries the tendency in vogue to disregard the *pshat* and to explain difficulties with the method of *pilpul* — with far-fetched and intricate constructions. He also opposed the dissemination of the *kabbalah* in print, asserting that 'the secret teaching' was designated to be taught orally in a limited setting. Nevertheless, here and there in his work one finds allusions to kabbalistic themes. R' Beirech's work was very popular in its day; it was reprinted a number of times, and was used extensively by *darshanim*.

The first volume of *Zera Beirech* also contains a small treatise — *Ateres Tzvi* — by the author's brother-in-law, R' Tzvi ben Shalom Melish, a son-in-law of the *Tosefos Yom Tov*.

R' Berechyah's grandson, R' Berechyah ben Elyakim Getzl, rav of Klimentov and *darshan* in Yavrov (both in Poland), was also a famed *darshan*. He authored *Zera Beirech Shelishi, pilpulim* on the Torah, printed (partially) in Halle, 5474/1714, and *Zera Beirech Shelishi*, on the beginning of *Maseches Berachos* (Frankfurt an der Oder, 5496/1736).

R' Yaakov Tzemach

רַבִּי יַעֲקֹב בֶּן חַיִּים צֶמַח

b. Portugal, c. 5330/1570
d. Jerusalem, Eretz Yisrael, c. 5425/1665

R' Yaakov was brought up as a Marrano in his native Portugal, and earned his living as a physician. In about 5375/1615, when already in his thirties, he fled to Turkey and settled in Salonica, where he learned the rudiments of Judaism and returned to the faith of his forefathers. In approximately the year 5379/1619 he settled in Safed, where he devoted six years to intense study of the Talmud and *halachah*, becoming a master in these fields. This stupendous feat is eloquent testimony to R' Yaakov's extraordinary intellectual abilities.

In 5385/1625, R' Yaakov journeyed to Damascus in order to study *kabbalah* under *R' Shmuel Vital, son and spiritual heir of *R' Chaim Vital. It was there that R' Yaakov was privileged to make use of R' Chaim's manuscripts, which had been compiled and arranged by R' Shmuel.

In Damascus, R' Yaakov compiled his first kabbalistic work, *Naggid UMetzaveh* (Amsterdam, 5472/1712), about the customs and rituals of the *Ari. This is his most popular work; it went through numerous editions. For eighteen years R' Yaakov concentrated on his kabbalistic studies. He not only had access to R' Shmuel Vital's library, but also to a second version of R' Chaim Vital's works. R' Chaim had ordered that these manuscripts be buried with him, and they had been; but later, in a dream, he gave permission to R' Yaakov and to *R' Avraham Azulai to exhume them.

R' Yaakov was a prolific author and he arranged many works of the Ari's *kabbalah*: *Kol BeRamah* (Koretz, 5445/1685) and *Zohar HaRakia* (Koretz, 5545/1785) — both commentaries on portions of the *Zohar; Otzros Chaim* (Jerusalem, 5667/1907); *Olas Tamid, kavanos* on the prayers by R' Chaim Vital with R' Yaakov's arrangement and additions (Salonica, 5414/1654); *Adam Yashar* (Cracow, 5645/1885); and *Tzemach Tzaddik* (Koretz, 5545/1785). Most of the works attributed to him are his arrangements of R' Chaim Vital's writings. R' Yaakov also composed *Zer Zahav,* a kabbalistic commentary on *Shulchan Aruch Orach Chaim,* and *Zivchei Shelamim* on the laws of slaughtering; both of these works were not published.

R' Avraham ibn Chananyah

רַבִּי אַבְרָהָם אִבְּן חֲנַנְיָה

b. Salonica, Turkey (now Greece)
c. 5365/1605
d. Jerusalem, Eretz Yisrael, c. 5425/1665

R' Avraham was a disciple of R' Mordechai Kalai and *R' Yosef Trani. According to some writers, R' Avraham served as rabbi of Belgrade, Yugoslavia — but there is no concrete evidence of this. He later settled in *Eretz Yisrael*, and was regarded as one of the pre-eminent Torah scholars of Safed. Circa 5411/1651 the community of Safed dispatched R' Avraham to the Diaspora on a fund-raising mission [as it was customary to send a prominent scholar to act as a fund raiser]. In this capacity he stayed for a while in the Yugoslavian city of Belgrade, where a close friendship developed between R' Avraham and the *rav* of the city, R' Simchah HaKohen. The latter relates in his *Sefer HaShemos* (Venice, 5417/1657), that R' Avraham gave him a copy of R' Yosef Trani's treatise on the spelling of personal names in *gittin*; R' Simchah

incorporated this treatise in his work. After his return to *Eretz Yisrael,* R' Avraham settled in Jerusalem, where he became a member of *Yeshivah Beis Yaakov*. (see *R' Yaakov Chagiz*). He seems also to have lived in Hebron for a while.

In 5423/1663 much pressure was put upon the Jewish inhabitants of Jerusalem by the Arab governors, who demanded exorbitant and unjust taxes. Unable to pay, most of the populace fled to Ramalah, including R' Avraham. There he served as spiritual leader of the refugees until the situation improved in Jerusalem and all returned.

R' Avraham wrote *chidushim* on the Talmud and an extensive work on the *Shulchan Aruch,* and many other works which were not published.

Recently, Mechon Yerushalayim has published *Beis Avraham* (Jerusalem, 5744/1984), a collection of writings by R' Avraham which have withstood the ravages of time. This collection contains the part of his commentary to *Shulchan Aruch Even HaEzer* ch. 17; this fragment is in itself a substantial work. Also included are a number of responsa and his *chidushim* to the *aggados* in *Maseches Berachos.*

An interesting episode reported by R' Yaakov Chagiz (in R' Yaakov Emden's *Toras HaKanaos*) demonstrates that R' Avraham also had an interest in the study of *kabbalah*, and was no doubt proficient in it. He relates that Nassan Ashkenazi of Gaza, Shabsai Tzvi's major prophet and propagandist, was a brilliant student of R' Yaakov's father, R' Moshe Chagiz. The latter forced his erratic pupil to divulge to him the source of his knowledge of certain kabbalistic practices (*kabbalah maasis*). Nassan admitted that he had stolen a manuscript dealing with these secrets from R' Avraham, when the latter had left his dwelling place because of a plague.

R' Avraham's son-in-law, R' Moshe Nazir, was a prominent Torah scholar who resided in Hebron and Jerusalem. None of R' Moshe's writings were published, but his son, R' Yosef Nazir, *rav* of Cairo (d. 5474/1713), incorporated some of his father's writings in his collection of responsa, *Matteh Yosef* (Constantinople, 5477/1717).

R' Nassan Nata Shapira III

רַבִּי נָתָן נָטַע בֶּן רְאוּבֵן דָּוִד טֶעבֶל שַׁפִּירָא

b. Cracow, Poland
d. Reggio nell' Emilia, Italy, I Iyar 5426/1666

R' Nassan Nata was the son of R' Reuven David, who served as *dayan* in Cracow (R' Nassan's birthplace), and the grandson of *R' Nassan Shapira II. After serving as rabbi in various Polish cities, R' Nassan emigrated to *Eretz Yisrael*, where he assumed the position of rabbi of the Ashkenazic community of Jerusalem. R' Nassan was renowned for his profound knowledge of *kabbalah*, and indeed all of his works which have come down to us are in this field.

After the Cossack massacres of 5408-09/1648-49 (see **Historical Introduction**), the financial support of the Ashkenazic community of Jerusalem, which had partly been provided by the Polish and Russian Jews, was severely reduced due to the plight of the contributors. It was due to this that R' Nassan was forced to journey to Europe in order to raise funds. R' Nassan arrived in Italy in 5415/1655 and was warmly received in Venice by *R' Moshe Zacut. The latter induced him to publish a short kabbalistic treatise, *Tuv HaAretz* (Venice, 5415/1655), on the holiness of *Eretz Yisrael*, in which he also took to task those who criticized the current inhabitants of the Holy Land and thereby discouraged the giving of donations to alleviate their plight. R' Moshe Zacut graced this *sefer* with an enthusiastic preface, and exhorted the public to be of help to R' Nassan. From Italy he traveled to Germany and finally to Amsterdam, where he made the acquaintance of *R' Menashe ben Yisrael. It was from R' Nassan that R' Menashe learned about the deplorable condition of the Jews in Poland, and he used this information when, in the winter of 5415/1655, he implored Oliver Cromwell and the English public to allow Jews to emigrate to England. R' Menashe reported that a letter had been received from Jerusalem (presumably by R' Nassan) relating that, of seven hundred widows and other poor people of Ashkenazic ancestry who had settled in Jerusalem, four hundred had recently died of hunger. Although R' Menashe did not succeed fully in his mission, nevertheless, the publicity it engendered deeply impressed some of the Christians of England and Holland, and a significant sum was raised for the Jerusalem community. A responsum in *R' Yaakov Chagiz' Halachos Ketanos (1:92) probably refers to this incident.

R' Nassan then returned to Jerusalem, but shortly thereafter, in the summer of 5417/1657, he was again sent to raise funds in Europe. In 5420/1660 he was again in Venice, where he published his *Matzas Shimurim*, a kabbalistic treatise on the precepts of *tefillin, tzitzis,* and *mezuzah*. In the same year he published there *Yayin HaMeshumar*, to demonstrate on kabbalistic grounds the importance of the prohibition against drinking wine prepared by gentiles and the shaving of the beard, two observances in which Italian Jewry was notoriously lax. After accomplishing his mission, R' Nassan settled in Italy (Reggio nell' Emilia), where he died.

In addition to the above-mentioned

works, he left several large works in manuscript: *Toras Nassan,* explanations of selected passages of the *Zohar* (published in Lemberg, 5645/1885); and *Meoros Nassan,* a large, comprehensive work detailing the kabbalistic meditations (*kavanos*) which should accompany the prayers according to the *Arizal's system (unpublished; but see *R' Chaim Vital). R' Moshe Zacut and R' Binyamin HaKohen, the foremost kabbalists in Italy, wrote notes on this work.

Two of R' Nassan's sons-in-law (R' Yechiel and R' Nesanel, both from the prominent Foa family) were rabbis in Reggio.

R' David HaLevi (the *Taz*)

רַבִּי דָּוִד בֶּן שְׁמוּאֵל הַלֵּוִי (טַ"ז)

b. Ludmir (Vladimir), Poland (now Russia)
5346/1586
d. Lemberg (Lvov), Poland (now Russia)
26 Shevat, 5427/1667

R' David's maternal grandfather was R' Yitzchak ben Betzalel (R' Yitzchak Betzalel's), rabbi of Ludmir in the province of Volhynia and a scholar much venerated by *Rama and *Maharshal (see their responsa). R' David's older brother, R' Yitzchak HaLevi, was a greatly respected scholar, and a few of his responsa are cited in his more famous younger brother's works. He was rabbi of Ludmir and Chelm, author of *She'eilos UTeshuvos Mahari HaLevi* and *Chidushei Mahari HaLevi* (both printed in Neuwied, 5496/1736), and the teacher of many well-known sages.

In his youth, R' David studied under his older brother, R' Yitzchak HaLevi, and later under the *Bach,* who took him as his son-in-law. Afterwards he moved to Cracow where, in great poverty, he pursued his studies. From there R' David was called to serve as rabbi of Potolitsh, a small town in Eastern Galicia (Poland),

but with the small salary he received, he was reduced to dire straits.

In 5379/1619, the *Bach* was appointed Chief Rabbi of Cracow, and on his way to that city he passed through Potolitsh. Observing R' David's mode of living he was aghast, and upon his arrival in Cracow he addressed a letter to R' David expressing his sorrow over his beloved son-in-law's financial condition and expressed his hope that salvation would soon be at hand. Soon after this, R' David moved to the prestigious community of Posen, served as unofficial rabbi while the rabbinate post of that town was vacant, and remained there for more than twenty years.

In about 5403/1643 R' David returned to his native Volhynia, and was appointed to the rabbinate of the old and prominent town of Ostroh, where *Maharsha had served as rabbi some years earlier. There R' David headed the famous yeshivah, and was soon recognized as one of the greatest rabbis of his time. His disciples and associates implored him to publish his *chidushim* on the *Tur* and *Shulchan Aruch,* and his rulings on matters of *halachah.* He published his *Turei Zahav* on *Yoreh Deah* in Lublin in the year 5406/1646, while at the same time his younger contemporary, *R' Shabsai HaKohen (the *Shach*), was publishing his competing commentary *Sifsei Kohen* in Cracow.

R' David's peace was again disturbed by the Cossack uprising of 5408-09/1648-49 (see **Historical Introduction**), and he was forced to flee, first to Lublin and then to Moravia. Finally he was called upon to serve in one of the rabbinates of Lemberg, where he remained until the end of his life.

R' David's last days were saddened by the violent deaths of his two sons, Mordechai and Shlomo, who were martyred in the great riots which occurred in

Lemberg in the spring (8-20 Sivan) of 5424/1664. R' David's last days coincided with the era of messianic fervor which held Jewry in its grip with the advent of the false Messiah Shabsai Tzvi. When conflicting reports about the impending coming of the Messiah reached Poland in 5426/1666, R' David, already at the advanced age of eighty, decided to send his son R' Yeshayah and his nephew (and stepson) *R' Aryeh Leib (later rabbi of Cracow and author of Teshuvos Shaagas Aryeh) to investigate these reports. The two arrived in Turkey in Tammuz, and were warmly received by Shabsai Tzvi, who gave them a letter addressed to R' David, accompanied by a present. We do not know the outcome of this incident nor do we know what impression they formed of Shabsai Tzvi. Two months later the false Messiah apostatized and rejected Judaism for Islam. It is safe to assume that when the messengers arrived in Poland the news of the "Messiah's" apostasy had preceded them, thus making their mission irrelevant.

R' David is famous for his extensive Shulchan Aruch commentary, Turei Zahav, abbreviated Taz, after which he is called, and which is published in almost all editions of the Shulchan Aruch, especially Orach Chaim and Yoreh Deah where it is printed directly next to the text. Only the work on Yoreh Deah was published during his lifetime (Lublin, 5406/1646) and gained him a reputation as a foremost halachist. Commentaries were written on Turei Zahav, most notable among them Mishbetzos Zahav (in Pri Megadim), and all later commentators delve into its decisions. R' David's contemporary and rival, R' Shabsai HaKohen, wrote critical glosses (Nekudos HaKessef) to Turei Zahav on Yoreh Deah, but R' David never saw these criticisms since R' Shabsai's work was published after his death. His daughter's son, R' Yoel ben Gad, wrote a point-by-point refutation of the *Shach's treatise called Maginei Zahav (Prague, 5480/1720). The Turei Zahav never alludes directly to Shach in his work, for both commentaries were published at approximately the same time. However, R' David added an additional page after publication which the Shach took to be an indirect attack on his Sifsei Kohen (although the work is not mentioned there explicitly) and he responded to R' David's criticism in a short treatise called Kuntres Acharon which is appended to the Sifsei Kohen.

These two commentaries are indispensable to any student of Yoreh Deah, and rabbinical ordination is based on the applicant's knowledge of them. The work on Yoreh Deah and the one on Orach Chaim are the most important of R' David's works and they (with Shach and Magen Avraham) form the backbone of halachah in these parts of Shulchan Aruch. The commentaries on Even HaEzer and Choshen Mishpat were published when those parts of Shulchan Aruch had already been provided with adequate commentaries, thus relegating Turei Zahav to a secondary position. The first part of the commentary on Choshen Mishpat (until ch. 246) was published (Hamburg, 5452/1692) by the famous gaon *R' Tzvi Ashkenazi (Chacham Tzvi) with accompanying notes. The second part was published many years later (Berlin, 5521/1761). The work on Even HaEzer was printed even later by the Taz's descendant, R' Gad ben Yoel (a great-grandson of the author of Maginei Zahav), with notes by his father, R' Yoel. The Turei Zahav had written an updated version (mahadurah basrah) of this work, but the manuscript was stolen and only the first draft was printed. Thus the citations from Taz in Beis Shmuel (its author saw the updated draft of *Turei Zahav* in manuscript) are not always found in the printed work.

A distinguishing feature of *Turei Zahav* is that it goes into lengthy explanation of *Tur's* views, analyzing the most subtle nuances of that Code's language, and it is therefore that this work is to be regarded as a commentary to *Tur* as well as to the *Shulchan Aruch*. Indeed, R' David named his work *Turei Zahav* to highlight its aspect as a *Tur* commentary. In the preface to *Yoreh Deah* he stresses the obligation we have to defend and interpret the views of the earlier sages, but adds that when the object is to arrive at a ruling on a *halachah*, this must be tempered with a genuine regard for the truth, so that sometimes their views have to be disregarded in the final *halachah*. However, with typical modesty, he laments the fact that he has, by necessity, been forced into such a situation. When R' David printed his work he was already regarded as one of the greatest sages of his age, and his rulings were readily accepted with great reverence by most of the contemporary rabbis. By contrast his rival, R' Shabsai HaKohen, was yet a relatively unknown young man, and it took time for him to be recognized. Nevertheless, a scant twenty years after they were first published, it was found necessary to print both works side by side alongside the text of the *Shulchan Aruch* (Wilhermsdorf, 5437/1677), and they remain in this cherished place up to this day.

R' David also wrote *Divrei David* (Dyhernfurth, 5449/1689), a super-commentary to *Rashi's Torah commentary, and a volume of responsa (see preface to *Divrei David*; *Magen Avraham* and *Chok Yaakov* to *Orach Chaim* §461) which was never published. Responsa by him appear in *Teshuvos Geonei Basrai, Teshuvos*

Bach HaChadashos, and *Teshuvos Pnei Yehoshua*.

R' Yosef Shaul Nathanson (5568-5635/1808-1875), Chief Rabbi of Lemberg, reported that during his tenure in the rabbinate at Lemberg, the grave of the *Taz* was accidentally opened. His body was found intact and his shrouds had not disintegrated, even though two hundred years had elapsed since the time of his death.

R' Aharon Lapapa

רַבִּי אַהֲרֹן בֶּן יִצְחָק לַפַּפָּא

b. Magnesia (Manisa), Turkey, c. 5350/1590
d. Smyrna (now Izmir), Turkey
26 Iyar 5427/1667

A disciple of R' Avraham Motal and *R' Yosef Trani, R' Aharon learned in the yeshivos of Salonica and Constantinople. He began his rabbinic career in Magnesia prior to 5392/1632, serving in this poor community without pay while heading a yeshivah in which many prominent Turkish rabbis received their schooling. In his old age he accepted the post of *dayan* (judge of civil cases), which had been left vacant by the demise of *R' Yosef Escapa, rabbi of Izmir (Smyrna). The functions of the rabbinate were split between R' Aharon as *dayan*, and *R' Chaim Benveniste as *moreh tzedek*, who ruled on matters of daily and festival law (*Orach Chaim*) and the *kashrus* of food, *nidah*, etc. (*Yoreh Deah*). R' Aharon was installed in his new post on *Rosh Chodesh* Iyar 5425/1665. On 6 Teves 5426/1665, the false Messiah Shabsai Tzvi was in Smyrna — and proclaimed R' Chaim Benveniste, R' Aharon's colleague in the rabbinate, the supreme rabbi of Smyrna, effectively dismissing R' Aharon from his post. The false Messiah had, no doubt, learned of R' Aharon's disbelief in his messianic identity, and took advantage of the multitude's loyalty to disarm a dangerous foe. R' Aharon was compelled to stay in his house for a protracted period, for he feared to venture onto the streets. When the Sabbatean frenzy died down after Shabsai Tzvi's conversion to Islam, the question of R' Aharon's rabbinate was again revived. He died shortly thereafter, and it is not known whether or not he ever returned to his post.

R' Aharon's fame as a halachist was widespread, and he wrote many responsa. Some of his responsa and *chidushim* to *Tur Choshen Mishpat* were published in *Bnei Aharon* (Izmir, 5434/1674). *Chida reports that he also wrote a commentary on *Rabbeinu Yerucham's *Toldos Adam VeChavah* and anthologized *chidushim* on the Talmud (*Shittos Mekubatzos*) in the style of *R' Betzalel Ashkenazi, but these were not published.

R' Yaakov Temerlis

רַבִּי יַעֲקֹב [אַשְׁכְּנַזִי] בֶּן אֶלְעָזָר תְּמֶרְלִישׁ

b. Worms, Germany
d. Vienna, Austria, 6 Nissan 5428/1668

One of his generation's most outstanding figures of learning and piety, R' Yaakov was greatly revered as a holy man and kabbalist of the first rank. He came to Poland from his native Worms (Germany) in his young years, settled at first in Lublin and later in Kremenitz, where he stayed for a long time. From there his fame, both as a Talmudic scholar and as a kabbalist, spread far and wide, and his yeshivah was very well attended. He had numerous disciples, among them *R' Aharon Shmuel Kaidanover. Toward the end of his life R' Yaakov settled in Vienna.

R' Yaakov composed *Sifra DiTzniyusa DeYaakov* (Amsterdam, 5429/1669), a profound kabbalistic commentary on the Torah. The glowing approbations given

this work by the greatest scholars of the age attest to the great renown of the author and the reverence in which he was held. *R' Yitzchak, rabbi of Posen and one of the foremost scholars of his day, declared that the author was worthy of having 'the *Shechinah* rest upon him.' Although R' Yitzchak voiced his reservations about publishing 'secrets of the Torah,' he waived these objections before the author's expressed will in his last testament. R' Aharon Shmuel Kaidanover calls him 'The Teacher of the entire Diaspora . . . not a mortal being but rather similar to an angel . . .' Another disciple, a fellow townsman, writes that R' Yaakov was known to have fasted every day for forty years.

Besides *Sifra DiTzniyusa DeYaakov*, R' Yaakov authored a volume of halachic responsa, a comprehensive commentary on Torah and the five *megillos,* and various treatises on kabbalistic themes, all unpublished.

R' Yehoshua (Rephael) Benveniste

רַבִּי יְהוֹשֻׁעַ (רְפָאֵל) בֶּן יִשְׂרָאֵל בֶּנְבְנִשְׁתְּ

b. Constantinople (now Istanbul), Turkey
c. 5350/1590
d. Constantinople (now Istanbul), Turkey
c. 5428/1668

The Benveniste family was one of the most prestigious among Sephardic Jewry, tracing its origin to Castille, where Don Avraham Benveniste had been a Minister of Finances to King John II (early 15th century) and official Chief Rabbi of the realm. A great-grandson, R' Yehudah, was among the exiles who founded the Spanish community in Salonica; he served as its rabbi for a time. He spent considerable amounts of money to stock his private library, which he made available to the scholars of the city. R' Yehudah's son, R' Moshe, a doctor by profession, was a confidant of the Sultan and used his influence and wealth to help his brethren and to further Torah study. R' Moshe's son, R' Yisrael, was greatly revered for his piety; his sons cite his customs in their works and even quote him in connection with a ruling regarding a civil case. All of R' Yisrael's sons and sons-in-law were scholars of stature, but the names of his sons R' Yehoshua and *R' Chaim outshine the rest. Another famous member of the Benveniste clan is *R' Moshe Benveniste, author of the collection of responsa *Pnei Moshe* and son of R' Yisrael's brother, R' Nissim. The maternal grandfather of the Benveniste brothers was *R' Yehoshua Soncin.

In his youth R' Yehoshua Benveniste studied under *R' Yosef Trani. He turned his attention also to auxiliary Torah studies, becoming very proficient in Hebrew grammar and poetry. R' Yehoshua also studied medicine, although it appears he never practiced this profession. He served as a *dayan* in one of the communities of Constantinople.

R' Yehoshua is best known for his extensive commentary on the halachic parts of thirty tractates in *Talmud Yerushalmi*, entitled *Sedeh Yehoshua*, of which the commentaries to seventeen tractates were published (*Seder Zeraim*: Constantinople, 5421/1661; *Sedarim Moed, Nashim, Nezikin*: Constantinople, 5509/1749).

R' Yehoshua also wrote many responsa, of which only a small portion survived a great fire in Constantinople. Of these, the part on *Choshen Mishpat* was published as *She'eilos UTeshuvos Shaar Yehoshua* (Vol. 1, Jerusalem, 5742/1982; Vol. 2 is in preparation). His other works are: *Oznei Yehoshua* (Constantinople, 5437/1677), sermons; *Avodah Tamah* (Constantinople, 5480/1720), a commentary on the Yom Kippur

service ; *Seder HaGet* (Constantinople, 5474/1714), on the procedures to be followed in writing and giving a bill of divorce; *Seder Chalitzah* (in *Get Pashut* by *R' Moshe ibn Chaviv, together with *Seder HaGet*; Ortakoi, Constantinople, 5479/1719).

R' Moshe of Lublin

רַבִּי מֹשֶׁה בֶּן יִצְחָק בּוּנְמָשׁ מְלוּבְּלִין

d. Lublin, Poland, 21 Kislev 5429/1668

R' Moshe was the scion of a very distinguished family: he was a great-great-grandson of *Rama. His mother was the daughter of R' Bunom, whose father — R' Avraham Meisels — was Rama's son-in-law. R' Avraham Meisels was a wealthy scholar, author of a commentary on the *Tur*. R' Yitzchak (R' Moshe's father), who was entrusted with the privilege of editing this work (never published), was also a scholar of note. R' Moshe's younger brother, R' Shimon Wolf, was a lay leader of the Vilna community and the *Shach's* father-in-law, and R' Moshe himself became the son-in-law of the illustrious Talmud commentator *Maharsha. In his youth R' Moshe was rabbi of Luboml (Poland), and later of the prestigious community of Lublin.

He wrote *Mahadurah Basra* on the Talmud (Lublin, 5430/1670), containing additional *chidushim* by his father-in-law together with his own writings. The *chidushim* on the *aggados* are all by R' Moshe, but those on the halachic parts of the Talmud are by him and his father-in-law. Presumably in the early editions the printers differentiated between the *chidushim* of Maharsha and his son-in-law, but this distinction has been lost in the editions prevalent today. R' Moshe relates that his *chidushim* had been much more substantial but that much material had been lost during his wanderings, presumably during the Cossack uprising (see **Historical Introduction**). Some of Maharsha's writings had also been lost.

R' Yonah Tumim

רַבִּי יוֹנָה בֶּן יְשַׁעְיָה תְּאומִים

b. Prague, Bohemia (now Czechoslovakia)
5356/1596
d. Metz, France, 15 Nissan 5429/1669

R' Yonah was born into a family prominent for its scholars. His great-grandfather R' Nassan Veidel (Feitel) was rabbi of Frankfurt am Main, and was reputed to eclipse even the great *R' Shalom Shachna with his erudition. R' Yonah married Beila, the daughter of R' Meir Wahl, rabbi of Brisk, the son of the fabled R' Shaul Wahl.

R' Yonah served successively as rabbi of many communities of Poland (Nemirov, Luboml, Belz, Horodna, Pinsk), heading large yeshivos in all his rabbinical posts and teaching many disciples. The Cossack revolts in 5408-09/1648-49 and 5415/1655 and the attendant havoc it wreaked upon the Jewish communities of Poland forced R' Yonah to leave Pinsk and the country. He stayed for a short time in Vienna, thereafter accepting the rabbinate of Metz, where he remained until his death. He was offered the prestigious rabbinate of Posen, but decided not to return to Poland because of the continuing state of unrest in that country.

R' Yonah composed *Kikayon DeYonah* (Amsterdam, 5390/1630), *chidushim* on many tractates of the Talmud. This is a truly remarkable work, perhaps to be ranked only after such classics as *Maharsha and *Maharam. The questions and comments are short and clear, to-the-point and pertinent, and the solutions innovative and far-reaching. An upgraded edition was published in Vienna (5694/1934), with corrections and references to parallel passages in other commentaries, compiled by the late *gaon* R' Michael Dov Weissmandl of Neitra. *Chidushim* on ch. 17 of *Shulchan Aruch Even HaEzer* by R' Yonah, taken from a defective manuscript which was probably part of a much more comprehensive work, were added to this edition.

R' Yonah served as a *rosh yeshivah* for fifty-three years of his life. *R' Yitzchak of Posen, one of the most prestigious scholars of his age, who accepted the rabbinate of Posen after it had been declined by R' Yonah, and R' Nissan ben Yehudah, author of *Beis Yehudah Chidushei Mahariran*, were among his disciples.

Many of R' Yonah's descendants were famous people. His sons were prominent rabbis. R' Yitzchak Meir authored *Kosnos Or* on *Ein Yaakov* (Amsterdam, 5444/1684), a collection of commentaries on the *aggados,* and he served as rabbi in many communities. His brother, R' Yehoshua Feivl, was rabbi of Premysl and author of *Panim Masbiros* (printed with *Taamei HaMesorah*; Zolkiew, 5491/1731), a rebuttal to a responsum in *She'eilos UTeshuvos Panim Meiros*. R' Chaim Yonah Tumim, author of the rare and often-cited treatise, *Aleh D' Rabbi Chaim Yonah* or *Kuntres D'Rabbi Chaim Yonah*; *R' Baruch Frankl-Tumim, author of *Baruch Taam,* and many other luminaries were descendants of R' Yonah.

R' Moshe Rivkah's

רַבִּי מֹשֶׁה בֶּן נַפְתָּלִי הִירְשׁ רבְקֵשׁ

b. Prague, Bohemia (now Czechoslovakia)
c. 5355/1595
d. Vilna, Lithuania, 4 Elul 5431/1671

R' Moshe's father, R' Naftali Hirsh ben Pesachyah, as his father before him, had been a scribe in Prague, and was a student of *R' Yehoshua Falk HaKohen. As a proofreader for the Jewish printing establishment in Lublin, R' Naftali Hirsh added many rulings found in the margin of his mentor's copy of the *Shulchan Aruch* to the edition of the Code which appeared in Lublin in the year 5356-57/ 1596-97. (No copies of this edition are known of today; its existence is inferred from R' Moshe Rivkah's preface to *Be'er HaGolah*.) R' Moshe's sister was the mother of *R' David Lida, rabbi of many communities in Poland and Lithuania and later in Amsterdam, and the author of many published works.

One of the pillars of the ancient learned Vilna community, R' Moshe serenely devoted himself to his studies in his extensive library for many years. However, in 5415/1655, when the Cossacks entered Vilna (see **Historical Introduction**), he was forced to flee his beloved Vilna along with the other inhabitants.

R' Moshe arrived in Amsterdam, where he was favorably received by the community. The Sephardic rabbis of Amsterdam, *R' Shaul Mortera and R' Yitzchak Abohab de Fonseca, greatly respected him.

It was in Amsterdam that R' Moshe was induced to write his important work, *Be'er HaGolah* (Amsterdam, 5422-26/1662-66). Desiring to publish a new edition of the *Shulchan Aruch,* R' Ephraim Boeno and R' Yaakov Castilo turned to R' Moshe to assist them in their work by correcting the text and indicating the sources for every ruling. R' Moshe at first refused, but later involved himself in the work. This resulted in his *Be'er HaGolah,* a very accurate reference work for the sources of the *Shulchan Aruch* with some glosses, published with almost every edition of the *Shulchan Aruch* since.

R' Moshe also wrote a treatise, *Klalei HaHoraah,* on the rules to be followed in arriving at halachic decisions; a commentary to the entire *Mishnah;* and

revisions and additions to his *Be'er HaGolah.* None of these were published.

In spite of the great respect R' Moshe enjoyed in Amsterdam, he longed to return to Vilna, and succeeded in doing so before his death.

The *Vilna Gaon was a descendant of R' Moshe: his paternal grandfather, R' Eliyah Chassid (son of the Vilna rabbi R' Moshe Kremer), was the son-in-law of R' Pesachyah, son of R' Moshe. In his *Beur* to *Shulchan Aruch,* the Vilna Gaon refers to his antecedent's work in almost every entry.

R' David Conforte

רַבִּי דָּוִד קוֹנְפוֹרְטִי

b. Salonica, Turkey (now Greece), c. 5378/1618
d. Cairo (?), Egypt, after 5431/1671

Although R' David was an eminent scholar and the author of Talmudic and halachic works (which were not preserved), he is best known for his *Korei HaDoros* (Venice, 5506/1746). This is a historical work, arranged chronologically, which begins with the *Rabbanan Sevurai* (the Torah scholars in the period immediately after the *Amoraim*) and extends to the author's own day. This work is very important for the first-hand information it imparts about R' David's generation.

In his native Salonica, R' David studied Talmud and *halachah* under his grandfather, R' David Conforte, and under R' Mordechai Kalai, R' Baruch Angel and *R' Daniel Esterosah. He also learned *kabbalah* under one of *R' Chaim Vital's disciples, and studied Hebrew grammar and Jewish philosophy. In general, R' David distinguished himself in fulfilling the dictum of the *Mishnah* (*Avos* 4:1): 'Who is a wise man? He who learns from every person', and made it a point to learn from all the scholars he met on his extensive travels.

In 5404/1644 R' David traveled to Egypt, where he studied under R' Avraham Iscandari. One year later, in 5405/1645, he left Egypt for Jerusalem. On the way to Jerusalem he stopped at Gaza where he met R' Moshe Najarahh (*R' Yisrael Najarahh's son) and studied with him for a short time. He stayed in Jerusalem for a while, returning to his native Salonica before 5408/1648. In 5412/1652 he settled in Jerusalem with his family. During his stays in Jerusalem he studied the Zohar with *R' Yaakov Tzemach. At one point R' David had occasion to sojourn in Smyrna, where he took advantage of the opportunity to study under *R' Yosef Escapa, author of Rosh Yosef on Tur Orach Chaim and Choshen Mishpat, when that venerable sage was already close to one hundred years old. He later moved to Egypt and became a dayan in Cairo.

R' David was a prominent halachic scholar and maintained a halachic correspondence with *R' Chaim Benveniste. He refers to a collection of his responsa (unpublished), and excerpts from his responsa are cited in She'eilos UTeshuvos Darchei No'am (by his contemporary, R' Mordechai HaLevi, rav of Cairo) §43 and 59.

R' David married a granddaughter of *R' Menachem de Lonzano, a daughter of the latter's son, R' Adonikam.

R' Moshe Benveniste

רַבִּי מֹשֶׁה בֶּן נִסִּים בֶּנְבְנִשְׁתְּ

b. Constantinople (now Istanbul), Turkey
c. 5369/1609
d. Constantinople (now Istanbul), Turkey
after 5431/1671

R' Moshe studied under his father, R' Nissim (a brother of R' Yisrael, who was the father of *R' Chaim and *R' Yehoshua Benveniste, both very prominent rabbis), who was a prominent scholar in

Constantinople. His mother was the daughter of *R' Eliyahu ibn Chaim. An authoritative halachist, his decisions were sought on all sorts of halachic problems and appear in his extensive responsa, Pnei Moshe (Part 1, Constantinople, 5429/1669; Part 2, Constantinople, 5431/1671; Part 3, Constantinople, 5479/1719). He also authored Riv Leshonos, which has not been preserved.

R' Avraham Gediliyah

רַבִּי אַבְרָהָם בֶּן שְׁמוּאֵל גְּדִילְיָא

b. Jerusalem (?), Eretz Yisrael, c. 5350/1590
d. Jerusalem, Eretz Yisrael, 5432/1672

R' Avraham was born in Eretz Yisrael, probably in Jerusalem. Later he settled in Hebron and was one of its prominent scholars. He is best known for his commentary Bris Avraham on Yalkut Shimoni, which he published together with a new edition of Yalkut Shimoni in Leghorn (5410-5417/1650-57). During his sojourn in Leghorn, R' Avraham served as a proofreader in the printing firm of R' Yedidyah Gabbai.

R' Avraham returned to Eretz Yisrael in 5410/1650, after printing the first volume of his sefer, and remained there until 5412/1652. At that point he again returned to Leghorn, took up permanent residence there, and worked as an editor and proofreader. However, he returned to Jerusalem in 5420/1660, and remained there until his death.

R' Avraham Reuven Katz

רַבִּי אַבְרָהָם רְאוּבֵן
בֶּן [יְהוֹשֻׁעַ] הָאשְׁקִי כַּ"ץ

b. Prague, Bohemia (now Czechoslovakia)
d. Prague, Bohemia (now Czechoslovakia)
17 Nissan 5433/1673

R' Reuven's father, R' Hashki HaKohen, a noted scholar, was a son-in-law of the noted *darshan* *R' Ephraim Lunshitz, and served as an official of the Prague community. His son, R' Reuven HaKohen, was a noted kabbalist.

R' Reuven collected and categorized all the available kabbalistic material which is pertinent to the interpretation of the Torah, and arranged it according to the verses of the Torah. He called this very interesting work *Yalkut HaReuveni* (Wilhermsdorf, 5441/1681). This work earned its author everlasting fame. Generations of *darshanim* since have used the material in this anthology as building blocks for their sermons. He also wrote a second work called *Yalkut HaReuveni* (Prague, 5420/1660), a much shorter treatise in which kabbalistic information was gathered on many subjects and arranged in alphabetical order; only half of this work (till the letter *kaf*) was published.

R' Reuven also wrote an original commentary on the *vidui* (confession), entitled *Davar ShebiKedushah* (Sulzbach, 5444/1683); and *Oneg Shabbos* (Sulzbach, 5444/1684), kabbalistic *kavanos* (meditations), customs, laws, and liturgy relating to the Sabbath. This work was very popular, going through at least thirteen printings. It was published three times in one year (5460/1700), in three different places.

R' Chaim Benveniste

רַבִּי חַיִּים בֶּן יִשְׂרָאֵל בֶּנְבָנִשְׁתִּ

b. Constantinople (now Istanbul), Turkey
5363/1603
d. Izmir [Smyrna], Turkey, 17 Elul 5433/1673

The younger of the two famous Benveniste brothers (the other was *R' Yehoshua), R' Chaim was a disciple of *R' Yosef Trani, who highly respected him for his acute intellect and erudition. At the age of twenty-one he was appointed supervisor of the *kashrus* requirements of the community, a position usually reserved for one of the elder scholars.

In 5404/1644, R' Chaim accepted the rabbinate of Tire, near Izmir, where he remained for nearly fifteen years until he was instated as one of the rabbis of Izmir in 5418/1658. During the period of messianic fervor surrounding Shabsai Tzvi (5425-27/1665-67), R' Chaim became an adherent of the movement, but subsequently repented of his attachment to the false Messiah when the latter became a Moslem.

R' Chaim compiled his monumental work *Knesses HaGedolah* (Leghorn, 5418/1658; Constantinople, 5476-78/1716-18; Izmir, 5420/1660, 5491/1731, 5494/1734, a digest of halachic material gathered from all available sources from the time of *R' Yosef Caro until his own day, and arranged in order of the *Shulchan Aruch*. A most important and authoritative work, it is cited by all the later halachists. *Chida declared that no decision should be rendered without first consulting *Knesses HaGedolah*. R' Chaim later added new material to the work and called the extensive additions *Sheyarei Knesses HaGedolah* (Izmir, 5431/1671; Constantinople, 5477/1717).

R' Chaim also composed *Dina DeChaye* (Constantinople, 5502/1742), a commentary on *Smag;* three volumes of responsa entitled *Ba'ei Chaye* (Salonica, v. 1-2, 5548-51/1788-91; v. 3, 5548/1788); *Chamra VeChaye* (Leghorn, 5562/1802), *chidushim* on tractate *Sanhedrin,* containing much material from the *Rishonim; Pesach MeUvin* (Venice, 5452/1692), on the laws of the *Pesach Seder,* and *She'eilos UTeshuvos R' Chaim Benveniste* (Constantinople, 5503/1743), a small collection of responsa pertaining to the laws of *Orach Chaim*.

R' (Yisrael) Yaakov Chagiz

רַבִּי (יִשְׂרָאֵל) יַעֲקֹב בֶּן שְׁמוּאֵל חַאגִּיז

b. 5380/1620
d. Constantinople (now Istanbul), Turkey
5434/1674

R' Yaakov's birthplace is unknown. Some contend that it was Jerusalem, while others maintain that he was born in Fez (Morocco) or Leghorn (Italy). He seems to have spent a considerable portion of his young adulthood in Italy, and is reported to have served as a *rav* in Pisa. His given name was Yaakov; the name Yisrael was added during one of the many serious illnesses which he suffered. His father, R' Shmuel, is the author of *Mevakesh Hashem* (Venice, 5357/1597) on the Torah, and *D'var Shmuel* (Venice, 5356/1596) on *Midrash Devarim Rabbah*.

R' Yaakov's erudition became manifest at a young age; before he was thirty he had already composed a comprehensive commentary on the *Mishnah* entitled *Eitz HaChaim* (Leghorn, 5413-15/1653-55). This commentary introduces all the passages of *Rashi's commentary to the Talmud which are pertinent to the *Mishnah*, thus enabling the student to study the *Mishnah* with *Rashi*. Upon his arrival in Leghorn for the purpose of having this work published, he was approached by the rich and influential Vega brothers, who desired to establish a yeshivah in Jerusalem, and having observed R' Yaakov and knowing his reputation, wished to have him head it.

Conditions in Jerusalem were quite poor during this period. This was largely due to the great pestilence which had struck Jerusalem in 5408/1648 and caused most of the inhabitants to flee to other locations, leaving the community disorganized.

R' Yaakov accepted the offer and settled in *Eretz Yisrael* (c. 5418/1658).

There he established the famous Yeshivah Beis Yaakov, which not only supplied the needs of the scholars who studied there, but also served as a governing body for the entire city, as the most prominent scholars belonged to its faculty or membership.

As he was a very gifted organizer and educator, R' Yaakov's endeavors did much for the resettlement of Jerusalem, whose population increased due to his efforts. *R' Moshe Galante II reports that the students of Yeshivah Beis Yaakov knew much of the Talmud and *Shulchan Aruch* virtually by heart, a prodigious feat even in those days. Yeshivah Beis Yaakov was one of the leading academies of higher Jewish learning for many generations, and many prominent scholars obtained their learning in this *beis hamidrash*.

After the death of his first wife, R' Yaakov became the son-in-law of R' Moshe (ben Yonasan) Galante, the most prominent rabbi in Jerusalem at that time. His son, *R' Moshe Chagiz, was also a very prominent rabbi and author who was well known for his uncompromising fight against the Sabbatean heresy, and his son-in-law was *R' Moshe ibn Chaviv. Both were among his outstanding students.

Another one of R' Yaakov's disciples at the very inception of the yeshivah was the brilliant but erratic Nassan ben Binyamin Ashkenazi of Gaza, infamous for the role he played as Shabsai Tzvi's major prophet. Nassan came to Jerusalem at the young age of nine and studied under R' Yaakov for seven years. As reported by R' Yaakov Emden (*Toras HaKanaos*), R' Yaakov Chagiz was among the first rabbis to recognize the danger posed by Shabsai Tzvi and Nassan even before the former's public conversion to Islam.

Besides his *Mishnah* commentary, R'

Yaakov wrote *Korban Minchah* (Izmir, 5435/1675), miscellaneous *dinim* and commentaries to *Tanach*; a small treatise entitled *Dinei Birkas HaShachar* (Verona, 5408/1648); *Pesil Techeiles* (Venice, 5412/1652), *R' Shlomo ibn Gabirol's poetic listing of the *mitzvos* (*azharos*) with a summary of *R' Shimon Duran's commentary (*Zohar HaRakia*) to this poem, with R' Yaakov's additions; *Techilas Chachmah*, rules fundamental to the Talmud, and *Orach Mishor*, *mussar*, both printed together with *Sefer HaKerisus* by *R' Shimshon of Chinon (Verona, 5407/1647); and *Halachos Ketanos* (Venice, 5464/1704), two volumes of short responsa to the various questions which would be asked of the author by the students of the yeshivah every Friday. Because of the brevity of these responses, *Halachah Ravachas* (Jerusalem, 5655/1895), a lengthy commentary by R' Bentzion Alkalai, was written upon it. R' Yaakov also authored a Spanish translation of *Menoras HaMaor* (*Menora de la Luz*, Leghorn, 5417/1657). Some of his other works were never published.

In 5434/1674 R' Yaakov set out for Constantinople to publish his *Lechem HaPanim*, a commentary on *Shulchan Aruch*, but he died there at the young age of fifty-four, before achieving his goal; this work was never printed.

R' David de Lara

רַבִּי דָּוִד בֶּן יִצְחָק הַכֹּהֵן דִּי לַארַא

b. Amsterdam (?), Holland, 5362/1602
d. Hamburg, Germany, 5434/1674

R' David's birthplace is not known with certainty. According to some he was born in Amsterdam, while others argue for Lisbon or Hamburg. He certainly lived for some time in Amsterdam, where he studied under *R' Yitzchak Uziel. As an adult he settled in Hamburg,

where he served as *rav* to the Portuguese community.

R' David, who was a great linguist, devoted himself to providing comprehensive lexicons defining the Talmud's loan words from Latin and Greek. Among his works are *Ir David* (Amsterdam, 5398/1638), a dictionary of the Greek and Latin words appearing in the Talmud and *midrash*; *Kesser Kehunah* (Hamburg, 5429/1669), a supplement to the *Aruch* of *R' Nassan ben Yechiel; and *Divrei David* (Leiden, 5418/1658), a small treatise which explains a poetic riddle by *R' Avraham ibn Ezra. R' David also published a number of works in Portuguese: a partial translation of *Reishis Chachmah*, parts of Rambam's philosophical works, and a treatise on *mussar*. Additionally, R' David wrote *Beis David*, a talmudical dictionary; *Pirchei Kehunah*, a collection of ethical sayings culled from the Talmud and *midrashim*; *Ohel David* on synonyms; and *Ozar Rav*, a glossary of Arabic terms used by Jewish writers. These last four works were never published.

R' Shmuel Garmizan

רַבִּי שְׁמוּאֵל גַּרְמִיזָאן

b. Salonica, Turkey (now Greece)
c. 5365/1605
d. Jerusalem, Eretz Yisrael, c. 5435/1675

A leading rabbinic figure in Turkey, R' Shmuel emigrated to *Eretz Yisrael* before 5406/1646, in which year his signature appeared on a document exempting Torah scholars from taxation.

In 5407/1647 R' Shmuel traveled abroad, probably in order to raise funds for the Jerusalem community. Stopping in Malta and observing the spiritual decline of the community, he felt it his duty to remedy the situation, and spent some years there answering halachic questions and organizing the community's religious institutions. On his way back to *Eretz Yisrael* he was captured by pirates, and *R' Shmuel Abohab, the venerable rabbi of Venice, saw to it that he was ransomed.

Upon his return to Jerusalem (5420/1660) R' Shmuel Garmizan joined the Yeshivah *Beis Yaakov*, founded by *R' Yaakov Chagiz. One of the scholars who studied with him was *R' Moshe ibn Chaviv.

R' Shmuel was a prolific author. He wrote extensive commentaries on many *masichtos* of the Talmud, some of which are still extant in manuscript; *chidushim* on the *Tur*; *chidushim* on the *sedarim* of *Zeraim* and *Taharos*; *chidushim* on the *Yerushalmi*; sermons, and many other miscellaneous works. *R' Chizkiyah de Silva and other authors quote R' Shmuel in their writings. In spite of his tremendous literary output, almost all of R' Shmuel's works remain unpublished. In recent times some of his works have been printed: *Mishpetei Tzedek* (Jerusalem, 5705/1945), responsa; *Imrei Binah* (Jerusalem, 5748/1988), *chidushim* on *Maseches Chullin*; *Imrei Binah* on *Maseches Sanhedrin* (Jerusalem, 5749/1989); and *Imrei Binah* on *Maseches Bava Metzia* (Jerusalem, 5749/1989). A multi-volume edition of *Imrei Binah* on *Maseches Kidushin* is being prepared for publication. R' Chizkiyah de Silva cites a commentary by him in *Pri Chadash (Or HaChaim* §606). *Chida saw some of R' Shmuel's works and expressed his amazement at the author's greatness and prolific output.

R' Binyamin HaLevi Ashkenazi

רַבִּי בִּנְיָמִין בֶּן מֵאִיר הַלֵּוִי אַשְׁכְּנַזִי

d. near Aleppo, Syria, c. 5435/1675

Educated in his native Safed, R' Binyamin studied *kabbalah* under R' Chiya Rofei, one of the disciples of *R' Chaim

Vital. As conditions in Safed deteriorated, R' Binyamin moved to Jerusalem. During the hardships the Jerusalem community endured under the tyrannical rule of ibn Farukh, R' Binyamin was part of a delegation which toured the Diaspora to raise funds. R' Binyamin left Safed again in 5417/1657 to raise money for the ransom of his son Shlomo. R' Binyamin spent considerable time in Italy, where he instructed some of the greatest kabbalists of that country — R' Eliezer Nachman Foa and *R' Moshe Zakut. R' Binyamin had a special influence upon R' Moshe Zakut, who considered himself his disciple and corresponded with R' Binyamin on kabbalistic subjects, even after the latter had left Italy and returned to Safed.

R' Binyamin was greatly revered by the Italian scholars, who lauded him as a saintly and most knowledgeable person. In his old age, in the year 5428/1668, R' Binyamin was again sent to raise money for the community of Safed, but died before he could return to *Eretz Yisrael*, in a village near Aleppo.

His son R' Shlomo was also a prominent scholar, who authored *Lev Shlomo* (Salonica, 5568/1808). In this work, several extensive halachic dissertations by R' Binyamin are cited.

R' Aharon Shmuel Kaidanover (Maharshak)

רַבִּי אַהֲרֹן שְׁמוּאֵל בֶּן יִשְׂרָאֵל קֵידַנוֹבֶּר (מַהַרְשַׁ"ק)

b. Vilna, Lithuania/Russia, c. 5374/1614
d. Chmelnik, Poland, 19 Tammuz 5436/1676

R' Aharon Shmuel was probably a native of Vilna. (Kaidanover, which implies origin from the Lithuanian town Kaidan, was his family name and was borne also by his son.) He married a daughter of one of the local *dayanim* (R' Avraham R' Lazar's). He studied under R' Yaakov of Lublin and his son, *R' Yehoshua Heshel of Cracow, and served in the *beis din* of Vilna under *R' Moshe (the *Chelkas Mechokeik*), together with the *Shach and *R' Eph-raim HaKohen. During the Cossack invasion of Vilna in 5415/1655 (see **Historical Introduction**), he fled to Lublin (Poland), where he had the misfortune to be overtaken by the Cossack invasion of that city and the ensuing massacre. His two daughters were killed, his son R' Hirsh narrowly escaped death, and R' Aharon Shmuel himself was wounded. The family fled to Austria, where R' Aharon Shmuel served as rabbi of a small town. Afterwards he served successively in the rabbinates of Fuerth (Germany), Nikolsburg (Moravia; now Czechoslovakia), Glogau (Ger-many/Poland) and Reisha (Rzeszow, in Poland). He then returned to Germany to serve as rabbi of Frankfurt am Main, but soon answered the call of Brisk in his homeland, Lithuania. After the year 5431/1671 he was elected to Poland's most prestigious rabbinate of those days, that of the capital, Cracow. There he remained until the end of his life.

R' Aharon Shmuel had a strong, independent character, and looked with dismay at the prevailing trend to accept without reservation the opinions of such contemporary *Shulchan Aruch* commentators as the *Shach and the *Taz. In a responsum to *R' Shmuel ben David HaLevi (*Teshuvos Nachalas Shivah* §50), he chides the latter for not having Beis Yosef's *Tur* commentary and relying instead on *Shach* and *Taz*. He declares rather frankly, 'Your Honor has concentrated on the works of the *Acharonim* — the work[s] of the *Shach* and the *Taz*. As for me, I am opposed to this and occupy myself with the study of the early *poskim* and the Talmud . . . for the *Acharonim* confuse one's logic and memory . . .

Your Honor should sell their works [i.e., the *Acharonim*] and buy [instead] the four *Turim* with *Beis Yosef.*' In another responsum he tells his correspondent, 'First I must inform Your Honor that it is not my custom to study the works of the *Acharonim*, especially those written in our generation . . . I have no regard for their conclusions, except where they have arrived at the truth.'

R' Aharon Shmuel wrote and published *Birkas HaZevach* (Amsterdam, 5429/1669), *chidushim* and emendations to the difficult and little-studied *Seder Kodashim*, together with *chidushim* on the related sections in *Rambam*. This work remains one of the most important works in this field, is often quoted by the *Magen Avraham* and other authors, and was reprinted by the *Chafetz Chaim* (with the deletion of the *chidushim* on *Rambam*) in his drive to revive interest in the study of *Kodashim*. His collection of responsa, *She'eilos UTeshuvos Emunas Shmuel* (Frankfurt am Main, 5443/1663); *Birkas Shmuel* (Frankfurt am Main, 5442/1682), pilpulistic comments on the Torah, based, in part, on the *kabbalah*, with additions by the author's son; and *Tiferes Shmuel* (Frankfurt am Main, 5456/1696), short notes on a few tractates of the Talmud, on the *Rosh* and *Chidushei Maharsha, Tur Yoreh Deah* and *Choshen Mishpat* — were all published posthumously by his son, R' Hirsh. These notes have been incorporated into the prevalent editions of these works.

R' Aharon Shmuel's son, R' Tzvi Hirsh, was the author of the popular devotional and ethical (*mussar*) classic, *Kav Ha-Yashar* (Frankfurt am Main, 5465/1705). The *Shach's* brother, R' Nachum HaKohen, rabbi of Sochatshov (Poland), was Maharshak's son-in-law, and R' Gedalyah Moshe, author of *Chemed Moshe* on *Shulchan Aruch Orach Chaim* (Fuerth 5529/1769), was his descendant.

R' Shmuel Vital

רַבִּי שְׁמוּאֵל בֶּן חַיִּים וִויטַאל

b. Damascus (?), Syria
d. Cairo, Egypt, c. 5437/1677

The son of *R' Chaim Vital and son-in-law of *R' Yoshiyahu Pinto, R' Shmuel was probably born in Damascus, where he officiated as a *dayan* for most of his life. He also succeeded his father as the principal disseminator of the kabbalistic doctrine of the *Ari. Among those who studied with R' Shmuel were such outstanding kabbalists as *R' Yaakov Tzemach and *R' Meir Popperos.

R' Shmuel inherited the vast collection of kabbalistic manuscripts — *Eitz Chaim* — written by his father. He rearranged these works into the compendium of the Arizal's *kabbalah* known as *Shemonah She'arim*. He retained his father's system of arranging the material under eight gates (*Shemonah She'arim*), but changed the original arrangment somewhat.

In 5423/1663, R' Shmuel left Damascus and settled in Cairo, where he remained until his death. Among his writings were a kabbalistic commentary on the *siddur* according to the system of the Ari, containing *kavanos* (kabbalistic meditations for the prayers), called *Chemdas Yisrael* (Munkacs, 5661/1901); *Mekor Chaim*, sermons (Leghorn, 5552/ 1792); and *Be'er Mayim Chaim*, responsa by him, his father, his father-in-law, and other *gedolim* (Bnei Brak, 5726/1966). He also wrote *Chachmas Nashim* on *Shulchan Aruch Even HaEzer*, which is cited in R' Aharon Alfandari's *Yad Aharon* and in R' Michl R' Yosep's *Michal HaMayim*; *Totzaos Chaim*, sermons on the Torah; and *Shaar HaShamayim* on astronomy and astrology — none of which were published.

R' Shmuel also collected his father's and his own *chidushim* on the Talmud, the entire *Shulchan Aruch* and the *Levush*, in a work called *Chaim Shnayim Yeshaleim*. The part of this work pertaining to the Talmud was printed in the *El HaMekoros* edition of the Talmud (Jerusalem, 5719/1959).

R' Ephraim HaKohen

רַבִּי אֶפְרַיִם בֶּן יַעֲקֹב הַכֹּהֵן

b. Vilna, Lithuania, 5376/1616
d. Ofen [Budapest], Hungary
13 Sivan 5438/1678

R' Ephraim HaKohen was a descendant of R' Ephraim Fishl ben Moshe Yehudah, the first rabbi of the Ashkenazic community in Jerusalem. Some say that this R' Ephraim Fishl is the same as the scholar having the same name who was rabbi of Brisk and other European communities and a son-in-law of Maharshal. R' Ephraim married Rachel, the daughter of R' Eliyahu, a grandson of the fabled R' Eliyahu Baal Shem of Chelm.

A disciple of *R' Moshe (the *Chelkas Mechokeik*), he was appointed *dayan* in Vilna in 5396/1636 and served in that capacity for almost twenty years. During the Cossack invasion of Vilna in 5415/ 1655 (see **Historical Introduction**), R' Ephraim fled to Moravia (now part of Czechoslovakia), where he served as rabbi of Trebitsch and then Braude. After six years of tranquility, R' Ephraim again had to take up the wanderer's staff because of military strife in the region. He settled first in Prague and then in Vienna, and finally, in 5426/1666, he was appointed rabbi of Ofen (Budapest), one of the most prominent communities of Hungary, which was then under Turkish rule.

R' Ephraim engaged in widespread halachic correspondence which reached as far as Turkey and Jerusalem, from where *R' Moshe Galante II and *R' Moshe ibn Chaviv, respectively, sought his opinion on halachic matters. At the end of his life he was offered the Chief Rabbinate of the Ashkenazic community of Jerusalem, which his grandfather R' Ephraim Fishl had previously held. He accepted the offer, but unfortunately died before being able to make the trip.

R' Ephraim authored the responsa work She'eilos UTeshuvos Shaar Ephraim (Sulzbach, 5489/1729). Among his pupils was his grandson, *R' Tzvi Ashkenazi, the Chacham Tzvi; and his son R' Aryeh Yehudah Leib, who published his father's work.

A poignant story is told by R' Aryeh Yehudah Leib in his preface, regarding the publication of Shaar Ephraim. In the year 5438/1678 a plague raged in Ofen and claimed the life of his older brother, R' Chizkiyahu. During the seven days of mourning, the younger son, R' Leib, was also infected with the plague. Upon hearing of this, R' Ephraim enveloped himself in his tallis and prayed that his own life be taken instead of his young son's. Immediately the great sage's prayer was answered; the son became well and the father took sick and died shortly thereafter. Just before his death R' Ephraim called his son and enjoined him to edit and publish his (R' Eph-raim's) two works, She'eilos UTeshuvos Shaar Ephraim, and Machaneh Ephraim, sermons on the Torah. R' Yehudah Leib eventually settled in Jerusalem in 5445/1685. There he compiled and edited Shaar Ephraim, which he printed, along with his notes and some of his own responsa, while on a trip to Europe. Machaneh Ephraim was never published.

R' Chisdai ben Shmuel HaKohen Perachia

ר' חִסְדַאי בֶּן שְׁמוּאֵל הַכֹּהֵן פְּרַחְיָא

d. Salonica, Turkey (now Greece)
8 Elul 5438/1678

A leading Torah authority in Turkey, R' Chisdai was a disciple of *R' Chaim Shabsai. *R' Aharon Perachia and R' Yaakov de Boton (a great-grandson of *R' Avraham de Boton and author of She'eilos UTeshuvos Eidus BeYaakov, d. 5447/1687) were his disciples.

He authored a volume of responsa titled Toras Chessed (Salonica, 5483/1723). Among the more distinguished of his correspondents we find the illustrious *R' Chaim Benveniste.

He also wrote an extensive work on Tur Choshen Mishpat, and chidushim on various mesichtos. None of these were published.

R' Shalom Shabazi Mashta

רַבִּי שָׁלוֹם בֶּן יוֹסֵף שַׁבְּזִי מַשְׁתָּא

Yemen, 17th century

Like all of the scholars of Yemen, R' Shalom adhered to the code of *Rambam in every detail. Since Rambam prohibited the rabbinate to be used as a profession, R' Shalom earned his livelihood as a weaver of talleisos (prayer shawls).

For a time R' Shalom resided in Sana, but due to government persecution he was forced to move to Ta'iz. R' Shalom is greatly revered by Yemenite Jewry as a tzaddik, and pilgrimages to Mari Shalom's tomb in Ta'iz took place on a regular basis. Prayer at his tomb was considered to be especially effective, and many wondrous tales are told about this.

Most of the piyutim recited by the Yemenite communities were composed by R' Shalom, and some estimate the number of his compositions to be as high as one thousand five hundred. He wrote in Hebrew and Arabic, many of his hymns having half of each verse in one language and the remaining half in the other.

Concerning the surname Mashta, it is related that the king of Yemen once wished R' Shalom to convert to Islam and sent his soldiers to R' Shalom's home. Becoming aware of this, R' Shalom hid in a great trough full of dough, called *mashta* by the Yemenites. Thus he eluded the soldiers, and derived this name. This event may have actually involved one of R' Shalom's forebears, because, as Yemenite scholars have pointed out, the name Mashta was already used by R' Shalom's father.

R' Moshe ben Avraham MiGeza Tzvi

רַבִּי מֹשֶׁה בֶּן אַבְרָהָם מִגֶּזַע צְבִי

d. Horodno (Grodno), Lithuania (Russia), c. 5441/1681

A maternal grandson and disciple of *R' Yehoshua Heshel of Cracow, R' Moshe was raised in his grandfather's house. His father, R' Avraham (a nephew of *R' Eliezer Ish Tzvi), seems to have been martyred as a result of religious persecution; R' Moshe constantly refers to him as *HaKadosh* (the holy one), a formula reserved for martyrs. In his youth R' Moshe lived in Brisk, where he instructed young men in Torah learning; he later became rabbi of Horodno. In 5441/1681 he was invited to become rabbi of the prominent city of Cracow, but he declined the post.

R' Moshe composed *Tiferes LeMoshe,* an important work on *Shulchan Aruch Yoreh Deah* (Berlin, 5536/1776). The sages of later generations cite this work extensively, especially *R' Akiva Eiger. The noted *gaon* *R' Yechezkel Landau of Prague, in his approbation to this work, calls R' Moshe 'a *gaon* among *geonim*', and states that he was 'unique in his generation'. R' Moshe also wrote a work on *Shulchan Aruch Even HaEzer,* which was not published. His notes on the Talmud are found in the Vilna edition (5640/1880).

R' Shmuel HaLevi

רַבִּי שְׁמוּאֵל בֶּן דָּוִד הַלֵּוִי

b. Mezeritch (Miedzyrzecz, near Poznan), Poland, 5384/1624
d. Kleinsteinbach, Germany, 5441/1681

R' Shmuel was exiled from his native Poland, probably during the Swedish invasion in 5415-18/1655-58. He stayed- for a few years at Halberstadt (East Germany), where he suffered great privation. Later he became rabbi at Bamberg (Bavaria, Germany), but he had to leave this rabbinate because of an unspecified controversy. He settled in the small community of Kleinsteinbach, where he served as rabbi until his death.

A disciple of the *Taz, R' Shmuel composed *Nachalas Shivah* (Amsterdam, 5427/1667), containing the correct texts for various halachic documents (e.g. bills of divorce, etc.). A popular work, it is used by officiating rabbis to this day, and a number of shortened versions have been made. R' Shmuel, drawing on his knowledge of the different customs practiced in the various communities of Poland and Germany, produced in his work all the different variations of these texts, and added an extensive commentary elaborating on the significance of each detail. The work also contains chapters on the general laws of documents and on the spelling of names in *gittin.*

R' Shmuel later wrote many additions and corrections to his work. These were printed in *Mahadurah Basra LeSefer*

Nachalas Shivah (Frankfurt am Main, 5441/1681), in which he also responded to thirteen criticisms *R' Chaim Yair Bacharach had raised (in *Teshuvos Chut HaShani*) against the author's opinion on the value of the *kesubah* payments. (R' Chaim Yair wrote a rebuttal in his *Teshuvos Chavos Yair* §1.) Most of R' Shmuel's corrections (but not the additions) were incorporated into subsequent editions of *Nachalas Shivah*.

After R' Shmuel's death, his son, R' Avraham, collected his responsa and published them as a second volume of *Nachalas Shivah* (Fuerth, 5452/1692). The two works are printed together with the prevalent editions of *Nachalas Shivah*.

R' Avraham (Abale) Gombiner (the *Magen Avraham*)

רַבִּי אַבְרָהָם (אַבָּלִי)
בֶּן חַיִּים הַלֵּוִי גּוֹמְבִּינֶר (מָגֵן אַבְרָהָם)

b. Gombin, Poland, c. 5394/1634
d. Kalish, Poland, Tishrei 5443/1682

Turbulent times marked R' Avraham's youth, during which his father was martyred by the Cossack mobs in 5415/1655 (see **Historical Introduction**). He thereupon left Gombin and settled in Lissa, where he studied under his relative, R' Yaakov Yitzchak Gombiner. (However, in the one place where the *Magen Avraham* cites this *gadol* — *Orach Chaim* 453:8 — he does not refer to him as his mentor.)

After completing his studies, R' Avraham moved to the city of Kalish, becoming a teacher of young children. An oral tradition preserved by the natives of Kalish relates that in 5420/1660 the *Shach, who was visiting Kalish on the occasion of the marriage of his son to the daughter of one of the lay leaders of the community, held a Talmudic discourse, during which he raised a prob-

lem which none of the great scholars of Kalish could answer. One of R' Avraham's young students, being present at the lecture, related the problem to R' Avraham, who immediately advanced a satisfactory reply. The student reported this to the *Shach*, who was greatly impressed with the clarity of R' Avraham's logic. The two met and discussed Talmudic problems for many hours. This incident revealed R' Avraham as a Torah scholar of stature to the community in which he had lived for several years, and where his greatness had gone unnoticed. After further examination, the rabbi of Kalish, R' Yisrael Shapira, son of *R' Nassan Nata Shapira II, appointed R' Avraham *moreh tzedek*, responsible for rendering halachic rulings on matters pertaining to daily life, i.e. all matters pertaining to the *Shulchan Aruch* parts *Orach Chaim* and *Yoreh Deah*. Later he filled the post of *dayan*.

The famous *Shulchan Aruch* commentator *R' Eliyah Shapira, whose two classic works *Eliyah Zuta* and *Eliyah Rabbah* on the *Levush* to *Orach Chaim* are second in importance only to *Magen Avraham*, relates that R' Avraham taught him in his youth (see his *Eliyah Zuta* to *Levush HaTecheiles* 242:4).

R' Avraham is known to all Torah scholars through his monumental *Shulchan Aruch* commentary, *Magen Avraham* (Dyhernfurth, 5452/1692), on the entire *Orach Chaim* section. Completed in 5431/1671, and originally titled *Ner Yisrael*, R' Avraham decided to publish it as early as 5433/1673, and sent it with his brother to Amsterdam. However, due to his brother's untimely passing before being able to make the journey, the manuscript was returned to R' Avraham, who further redacted it. Consequently, when R' Shmuel ben Yosef, a *dayan* in Cracow, published a comprehensive two-part commentary to

Orach Chaim named Olas Tamid (to the first part of Orach Chaim) and Olas Shabbos (from Hilchos Shabbos and further; Amsterdam, 5441/1681), R' Avraham subjected the treatise to a close scrutiny. Upon finding that the work did not measure up to his own standards of Torah scholarship, he set down his objections to Olas Tamid's rulings. Notwithstanding Olas Tamid's initial popularity, it could not stand up to the critical analysis of Magen Avraham, nor compete with the popularity and acceptance of the latter work once it was published. As a result, Olas Tamid was completely superseded and almost forgotten; it was never reprinted until modern times. Ironically, some of the latent interest in Olas Tamid in modern days lies in its importance in understanding Magen Avraham's terse objections to the former's rulings.

With its publication, Magen Avraham joined Turei Zahav, which was subtitled Magen David, to become the standard Orach Chaim commentaries. The two commentaries were printed together under the joint title Maginei Eretz.

The famous gaon *R' Chaim Yair Bacharach had completed a commentary on Orach Chaim, but reports in the preface to his Teshuvos Chavos Yair that he refrained from publishing it because of the excellence of the joint commentary of Turei Zahav and Magen Avraham. In the biography of R' Zalman of Volozhin (Toldos Adam, Part 1) it is reported that this famous disciple of the Vilna Gaon valued the Magen Avraham's opinion as much as that of one of the early masters (Rishonim), and the Vilna Gaon himself refers to Turei Zahav and Magen Avraham in virtually every paragraph of his Shulchan Aruch commentary.

An eminent kabbalist, R' Avraham also stresses the views of the kabbalists, especially the *Ari, in his halachic decisions. In most cases, the rulings in Magen Avraham are considered authoritative against the opinions of other commentators, and he is revered by all segments of Jewry. Because of its terse language and great profoundness many commentaries were written upon Magen Avraham, the most famous among them being Machatzis HaShekel and Pri Megadim.

R' Avraham also composed Zayis Raanan (Dessau, 5464/1704), a short commentary on Yalkut Shimoni. Excerpts from it were printed in the margin of the Yalkut edition of Warsaw, 5638/1878, which is today the standard edition. He also wrote Shemen Sasson (Dessau, 5464/1704), a series of pilpulistic discourses on the Torah until section Toldos; and a short commentary on Tosefta order Nezikin (Amsterdam, 5452/1692, and in today's standard editions). A commentary on Shulchan Aruch Even HaEzer and chidushim on tractates Zevachim and Menachos were not published.

R' Avraham's son-in-law, R' Moshe Yekusiel Koifman (a first name), is the author of Lechem HaPanim on Yoreh Deah (Hanau, 5476/1716), Chukei Daas on Yoreh Deah and Chukei Chaim on Orach Chaim (both in Berlin, 5459-60/ 1699-1700), Chukei Derech on Even HaEzer (Amsterdam, 5453/1693), and Chukei Mishpat on Choshen Mishpat (Dyhernfurth, 5461/1701). This group of works with the word Chukei in their names is a series of commentaries on the short summary of the Shulchan Aruch, under the name Yismach Yisrael (Cracow, 5386/1626) by R' Yisrael Shmuel Califari of Cracow. In Chukei Derech R' Moshe quotes from his father-in-law's unpublished commentary, and he published a halachic responsum by him in the second part of Lechem HaPanim.

R' (Nissim) Shlomo ben Avraham Algazi I

רַבִּי (נִסִּים) שְׁלֹמֹה בֶּן אַבְרָהָם אַלְגַּאזִי

b. Bursa (Brusa), Turkey, c. 5370/1610
d. Jerusalem, Eretz Yisrael, c. 5443/1683

R' Shlomo was born into a prominent Sephardic family. His maternal grandfather was R' Yosef Benveniste de Segovia, son of R' Meir, both authors and scholars. R' Meir's descendants published *Doveiv Sifsei Yeshanim* (Smyrna, 5431/1671), containing R' Meir's observations on the rules of *kal vachomer* and *dayo*, assorted comments by R' Yosef, *chidushim* by R' Shlomo Algazi, and *Sefas Emes* by R' Shlomo's brother, R' Moshe. R' Avraham Algazi (R' Shlomo's father) corresponded with *R' Yosef Trani.

R' Shlomo began his studies under his father and the poet and scholar R' Yosef Gansu. Later he went to neighboring Gallipoli, where he became a disciple of R' Yosef Sasson and R' Meir de Boton (son of *R' Avraham de Boton and author of *She'eilos UTeshuvos R' Meir de Boton*, Izmir, 5440/1680). Some scholars contend that R' Shlomo emigrated to Jerusalem in c. 5395/1635, returned to his native Turkey in 5406/1646 for the purpose of publishing his works, and then returned again to Jerusalem c. 5430/1670. Others assert that the first time R' Shlomo was in Jerusalem was in the year 5430/1670.

R' Shlomo lived in Smyrna for a considerable period of time, and established a Talmud academy there. Many distinguished scholars studied in this yeshivah, among them *R' Aharon Lapapa, author of *Bnei Aharon* (Izmir, 5434/1674), who later married R' Shlomo's daughter and officiated as rabbi of Smyrna; R' Chaim Algazi, author of *Banei Chayei* (Ortakoi, Constantinople, 5472/1712), rabbi of Rhodes;

and *R' David Conforte. When the false Messiah, Shabsai Tzvi, began his ill-fated adventure (5425/1665), R' Shlomo, who was at this time rabbi of Izmir, and his son-in-law, R' Aharon Lapapa, were among the first and strongest opponents of the new Messianic movement, and almost single-handedly defended traditional Judaism against Shabsai Tzvi and his powerful and numerous followers. However, he was forced to flee Smyrna due to the influence of the false Messiah's followers in the community. When Shabsai Tzvi converted to Islam (in the fall of 5426/1666), the community called upon R' Shlomo to return to his post. He refused, leaving the post to his son-in-law, and returned (or went) to Jerusalem in about 5430/1670. Sometime during the period after 5426/1666 he began to use the additional name Nissim. Probably he was seriously ill during that time and was given an additional name, as is customary.

In Jerusalem he joined the Yeshivah Beis Yaakov, founded by *R' Yisrael Yaakov Chagiz. There he wrote his work *Gufei Halachos*. He returned to Turkey in 5435/1675 to print this work, but later returned to *Eretz Yisrael*, where he died.

R' Shlomo was a prolific author and, as can be seen from his literary legacy, a masterful preacher. R' Shlomo was extremely gifted and innovative and, as he himself mentions in one of his works, his *chidushim* on the Talmud were so numerous that it would be impossible for him to set them down in writing. Because of his extreme sharpness his contemporaries dubbed him הָרַב הַמְפֻלְפָּל, 'the sharp-witted *rav*.' However, he later realized that using sharpness was not the best way to reach the truth and to serve the public. Instead, he now concentrated on finding the 'straight paths' to the truth, and endeavored to write works setting down the methodology of the Talmud (i.e., the general rules followed in the presentation of the Talmudic debates, and the rules for deriving and deciding *halachah*, which are clarified in the Talmud), thereby helping the scholars to find 'a path through the oceans of the Talmud.'

He published the following: *Yavin Shemuah* (Venice, 5399/1639), a commentary on R' Yeshuah HaLevi's *Halichos Olam*, dealing with Talmudic rules and related topics; *Ahavas Olam* (Constantinople, 5403/1643), sermons; *Halichos Keili* (Smyrna, 5423/1663), rules pertaining to the Talmud and Tosafos; *Gufei Halachos* (Smyrna, 5435/1675), a sequel to *Halichos Keili*, containing rules and *chidushim* to the Talmud and *Rambam*; *Lechem Sesarim* (Venice, 5424/1664), *chidushim* on tractate *Avodah Zarah*, with some responsa; assorted *chidushim* in *Doveiv Sifsei Yeshanim* (see above); *Hamon Rabbah* (Constantinople, 5404/1644), an index to *Midrash Rabbah* arranged according to the *Tanach*; *Zehav Shivah* (Constantinople, 5443/1683), on the *aggadah* of the Talmud and one dissertation on a Talmudic passage; *Me'ulefes Sapirim*, an anthology of inspirational passages from the *Zohar*, together with *Kiloris LaAyin*, commentaries on the *aggadah* of the Talmud (Constantinople, 5420/1660); *Ratzuf Ahavah* (Verona, 5409/1649), aggadic commentaries; *Taavah LaEinayim* (Salonica, 5415/1655), on the *aggadah* and *Maseches Avos*; and *Sheima Shlomo* (Smyrna, 5419/1659), comments on the Torah. R' Shlomo also composed a comprehensive work on the *Baal Halttur* and *Tur Choshen Mishpat*, called *Ziknas Shlomo*, which he worked on, with interruptions, for most of his life. This work was seen by *R' David Conforte but was subsequently lost.

*Chida is effusive in his praise of R' Shlomo, saying he had heard wondrous reports about his profundity and concentration and that he was 'accustomed to miracles.' This was attributed to the fact that he learned Torah 'for its own sake,' i.e., without ulterior motives, and never derived pleasure from the honor he was accorded for his knowledge of Torah.

Many of R' Shlomo's descendants were famous Torah scholars. His grandson, R' Shlomo Algazi II, a prize pupil of *R' Chizkiyah de Silva, was first a *dayan* in Jerusalem and later the distinguished *rav* of Cairo for forty-five years. Chida (who met him) writes about him with great enthusiasm and reports that 'his piousness and diligence in learning was legendary,' and that 'he would distribute his substantial salary to the poor.' None of his writings (which were seen by Chida) have been published. The greatgrandson of R' Shlomo Algazi I, *R' Yisrael Yaakov ben Yom Tov Algazi, was the rabbi of Jerusalem and the author of *Sheima Yaakov, She'eiris Yaakov,* and other works, and his (R' Yisrael Yaakov's) famous son was *R' Yom Tov Algazi, known as Rit Algazi, Chief Rabbi in Jerusalem and author of the well-known commentary on *Ramban's *Hilchos Bechoros,* and many other works.

R' Avraham Amigo

רַבִּי אַבְרָהָם הַלֵוִי אֲמִיגוֹ

b. Adrianople (Edirne) or Constantinople (now Istanbul), Turkey, c. 5370/1610
d. Jerusalem, Eretz Yisrael, c. 5443/1683

In his younger years R' Avraham was rabbi of Adrianople. He did not stay there very long, but settled in Jerusalem, where he joined the Yeshivah Baalei HaBatim. This yeshivah had been founded by the Vega brothers who lived in Leghorn, and was under the supervision of *R' Yisrael Yaakov Chagiz as a branch of the *Beis Yaakov* academy. There he struck up an acquaintance with

*R' Shlomo Algazi, *R' Moshe ibn Chaviv and *R' Shmuel Garmizan, who quote him with reverence in their works. R' Shlomo HaLevi, one of the rabbis of Smyrna (She'eilos UTeshuvos Lev Shlomo), refers to him in ecstatic terms, using such phrases as, 'The great luminary, unique in the generation' — and refuses to debate about a ruling rendered by R' Avraham. R' Avraham also made use of the opportunity to study kabbalah under *R' Yaakov Tzemach. Among his disciples were R' David HaKohen (author of Daas Kedoshim on Shulchan Aruch Orach Chaim) and *R' Chaim Abulafia (author of Eitz Chaim, and other works).

R' Avraham's halachic correspondence was very extensive, his decisions being sought not only in Eretz Yisrael, but throughout Turkey and Egypt. *Chida reports that 'This gaon was very highly regarded by the Turkish rabbis . . . I have seen their writings in which they address him with the greatest reverence.' Unfortunately his responsa and Talmudic and halachic chidushim, seen by Chida, have not been preserved in full, but some of his responsa have survived in a manuscript collection of responsa by many rabbis of the era. He is cited by *R' Chizkiyah de Silva in Pri Chadash, and by *R' Moshe ibn Chaviv in Ezras Nashim.

R' Avraham was one of the strongest opponents of the false Messiah Shabsai Tzvi, and a major power in forcing the latter to leave Jerusalem.

R' Nassan Nata Hanover

רַבִּי נָתָן נָטַע בֶּן מֹשֶׁה הַנוֹבֶּר

b. Ostroh, Poland (now Ostrog Russia),
c. 5360/1600
d. Ungarisch-Brod (Uherski Brod), Moravia
(now Czechoslovakia), 20 Tammuz 5443/1683

A disciple of *Maharsha, R' Nassan Nata was an eyewitness to the horrible persecutions of the Cossack uprising (see **Historical Introduction**), as he himself wandered from city to city, narrowly escaping death and torture. He went first to Prague, and then to Venice, where he wrote a historical account of the entire Cossack devastation. His Yevein Ha-Metzulah (Venice, 5413/1653) gives a brief description of the Polish government of the time and its relationship to the Cossacks, the origin of the uprising, and all its gruesome details. He also paints a very vivid picture of Jewish life in Poland, and of the yeshivos. The work was so popular that it was later translated into Yiddish, German, and English.

R' Nassan Nata studied kabbalah in Venice, and became rabbi of Leghorn. He remained there only a short time, next taking up the rabbinate of Yassi (Iasi) and Pakshan (Pascani; both in Rumania). He thereafter accepted the rabbinate of Ungarisch-Brod, Moravia, where he was killed by a stray bullet while at his prayers.

R' Nassan Nata composed Taamei Succah (Amsterdam, 5412/1652), a homiletic explanation of the Succos festival; Safah Berurah (Prague, 5420/1660), a dictionary of Hebrew words translated into German, Italian and Latin; and Shaarei Tzion (Prague, 5422/1662), a collection of prayers and customs gleaned from kabbalistic works, which to this day has enjoyed great popularity.

In his works, R' Nassan Nata also refers to a commentary he composed on the midrash Ossios de Rabbi Akiva, a kabbalistic treatise entitled Neta Ne'eman; and to Neta Shaashuim, a Torah commentary.

R' Chaim Bochner

רַבִּי חַיִּים בֶּן בִּנְיָמִין זְאֵב בּוֹכְנֶר

b. Cracow, Poland, c. 5370/1610
d. Fuerth, Germany, 17 Shevat 5444/1684

R' Chaim's father, R' Wolf Bochner,

was one of the richest men in Cracow, and his son's financial situation was secure. R' Chaim devoted himself to the study of Torah. He studied Talmud and *halachah* under R' Yisrael Zeligman Ganz, *kabbalah* under *R' Yaakov Temerlis, and Hebrew grammar under R' Shabsai Sofer of Premysl. In his adult years he was considered one of the foremost Torah scholars in Cracow, where he conducted a yeshivah in his own house. Later in his life R' Chaim left his native Poland and served as rabbi of the Austrian communities of Ebenfurth and Lakenbach. Upon the expulsion of the Jews from Austria in 5430/1670 (see **Historical Introduction**), he was forced to wander through Poland and Germany, finally settling in Fuerth, where he remained until his death.

R' Chaim authored *Or Chadash* (Amsterdam, 5431/1671), on the laws of benedictions; *Totzaos Chaim* (Hamburg, 5470/1710), a digest in Yiddish of *R' Eliyahu Bachur's *Pirkei Eliyahu* (grammatical rules set to rhyme) — also called *Perek Shirah* — with additional related grammatical material. He also wrote *Beis Tefillah*, a commentary to the *Siddur*; *Mayim Chaim*, dissertations; and *Psora Dedahavah*, an abridged version of the *Shulchan Aruch*, all of which remain unpublished.

R' Avraham Yosef Shlomo Graziano

רַבִּי אַבְרָהָם יוֹסֵף שְׁלֹמֹה בֶּן מָרְדְּכַי גְּרַאצְיָאנוֹ

b. Pesaro, Italy, c. 5380/1620
d. Modena, Italy, Cheshvan 5445/1684

Elected Chief Rabbi of the important city of Modena in 5426/1666, R' Avraham Yosef Shlomo wrote extensive responsa, which remain unpublished. He also composed notes (unpublished) on the *Shulchan Aruch*, mentioned in works of later Italian halachists, and commen-

taries on *Psalms, Proverbs* and *Job*, all unpublished. One of the most avid bibliophiles of his age, R' Yosef amassed an extensive library. He would affix his acronym *Ish Ger* to his acquisitions, and many of his *sefarim* were graced with his marginal notes. His notes to *Teshuvos Rama MiFano* have been published in the Jerusalem edition of this work (5723/1963).

R' Yitzchak of Posen

רַבִּי יִצְחָק בֶּן אַבְרָהָם מִפּוֹזֶן

d. Posen (Poznan), Poland, 15 Sivan 5445/1685

One of the outstanding Talmudic scholars and rabbis of his age, R' Yitzchak studied under *R' Yonah Tumim, R' Tzvi Hirsh HaLevi of Vilna (virtually unknown), R' Avraham (the rabbi of Bar [Poland/Russia]), and R' Yaakov Shor (son of *R' Ephraim Zalman Shor, the author of *Tevuos Shor*), rabbi of Brisk. He served successively in the rabbinates of Lutzk, Horodno, Vilna (5424/1664), and Posen (5427/1667), where he remained until his death. R' Yitzchak gained great renown for his Talmudic scholarship, erudition in the *kabbalah*, pure character, and outstanding piousness. His contemporaries were unstinting in their admiration for him, as evinced by their salutations to him and by the titles given him in the numerous approbations he bestowed upon published works. He appears to have been considered the foremost rabbinic personage of his generation.

Many of the most illustrious scholars of his day, among them *R' Avraham Abale Gombiner and *R' Menachem Mendel Auerbach, sought his views on halachic matters (the former reproduced excerpts of R' Yitzchak's responsum in his classic commentary *Ateres Zekeinim* to *Shulchan Aruch*, ch. 1); and the famous Italian kabbalist *R' Moshe Zacut corresponded with him about fine points of the *kabbalah*. *Chida reports that R' Moshe had made R' Yitzchak's acquaintance when he traveled to Poland in his youth, and that the two had studied together.

R' Yitzchak refrained from publishing any of his work, hence his name is virtually unknown today. However, his literary legacy remained in manuscript for centuries after his death. In 5601/1841 a small pamphlet called *Eil Yitzchak*, containing a kabbalistic commentary on the liturgical poem *Chad Gadya* which is recited in Ashkenazic communities at the end of the Passover *seder*, was printed in Lemberg. Ironically, R' Yitzchak himself intimated in his approbation to *R' Yaakov Temerlis' *Sifra DiTzniyusa D'Yaakov* that he was opposed to the dissemination of *kabbalah* in print. Half a century later a small portion of his responsa *Be'er Yitzchak* was printed in Vienna (5656/1896), and an additional handful of responsa was published together with *Tosefos HaRosh* to *Succah* (Jerusalem, 5663/1903). A substantial volume of responsa *(Teshuvos R' Yitzchak MiPosna)* has recently been published by *Mechon Yerushalayim* (Jerusalem, 5742/1982).

R' Eliyahu ben Yehudah Kovo

ר' אֵלִיָּהוּ בֶּן יְהוּדָה קוֹבוֹ

b. Salonica, Turkey (now Greece)
c. 5390/1630
d. Salonica, Turkey (now Greece)
8 Kislev 5449/1688

Son-in-law of R' Moshe Chaim (son of *R' Chaim Shabsai), and the Chief Rabbi of Salonica, R' Eliyahu was one of the distinguished Torah authorities in the Ottoman Empire. R' Eliyahu filled various rabbinic posts in Salonica, and after the death of his father-in-law (14 Elul 5445/1685) he was appointed to suc-

ceed him as Chief Rabbi. R' Eliyahu's views on halachic matters were greatly respected and sought; *R' Aharon HaKohen Perachia speaks of him with great reverence. R' Eliyahu died at a young age during a plague which ravaged Salonica and also caused the death of his two sons. *R' Tzvi Ashkenazi, famous as the *Chacham Tzvi*, spent part of his youth in Salonica and studied under R' Eliyahu.

R' Eliyahu compiled *Tana D'bei Eliyahu*, a collection of 451 responsa (תנא has a numerical equivalent of 451), but most of this work was lost. His grandsons managed to collect 26 of their grandfather's responsa, and printed them as *She'eilos UTeshuvos Aderes Eliyahu*, in the collection *Shnei HaMeoros HaGedolim* (Constantinople, 5499/1739), which also contains *She'eilos UTeshuvos Pnei Yehoshua* by R' Eliyahu's son-in-law, R' Yehoshua Chandali, and *chidushim* by R' Yehudah Almoda.

R' Moshe Galante II (HaRav HaMagen)

רַבִּי מֹשֶׁה בֶּן יְהוֹנָתָן גַּלאנְטֵי
(הָרַב הַמָּגֵ"ן)

b. Safed, Eretz Yisrael, 5380/1620
d. Jerusalem, Eretz Yisrael, 21 Shevat 5449/1689

A grandson of *R' Moshe Galante I, R' Moshe studied under R' Baruch Barzilai, an outstanding *rosh yeshivah* and halachist of Safed in the early seventeenth century. R' Moshe later settled in Jerusalem, which had become a prominent Torah center in his day, and lectured before numerous disciples, among them *R' Chizkiyah de Silva, *R' Avraham Yitzchaki, *R' Yisrael Yaakov Chagiz — who later became his son-in-law — and R' Yehudah Leib HaKohen, son of *R' Ephraim HaKohen who was the author of *Teshuvos Shaar Ephraim*.

R' Moshe was appointed Chief Rabbi

of Jerusalem and was particularly instrumental in the development of the city into the great Torah center it became during the latter half of the seventeenth century. He especially endeavored to increase the enrollment and elevate the scholarly level of the newly founded Yeshivah Beis Yaakov, which became the most prestigious Torah institution in the Jerusalem of his day. After the premature death of his son-in-law *R' Yaakov Chagiz — the founder and *rosh yeshivah* of *Beis Yaakov* — R' Moshe Galante took over the leadership of this prestigious and important Torah institution.

Although R' Moshe's authority in Jerusalem was undisputed, he and the Torah sages of his day promulgated a rule that thenceforth no one be authorized to use the title 'Rav of Jerusalem.' In his endeavors to better the lot of the community, R' Moshe made many trips to Turkey and Europe in order to raise funds, and was most honorably received in every locality.

R' Moshe authored *Magen HaElef*, responsa and *chidushim* on the Talmud, which was never published; *Zevach HaShelamim* (Amsterdam, 5458/1698), a Torah commentary; *Korban Chagigah* (Venice, 5469/1709), sermons for the festivals and *chidushim* on tractate *Chagigah;* and notes on *Rambam's *Mishneh Torah,* which were never published.

R' Menachem Mendel Auerbach

רַבִּי מְנַחֵם מֶעָנְדִיל בֶּן מְשׁוּלָם זַלְמָן אוֹיעֶרְבַּאךְ

b. Vienna, Austria, c. 5380/1620
d. Krotoshin, Poland, 20 Tammuz 5449/1689

R' Menachem Mendel was born into the wealthy and prominent Auerbach-Fischhof family in Vienna (which was related to *Rama). His maternal grandfather, R' Aryeh Leib Rofei, was a prominent physician, rabbi of Vienna, and author of many (unpublished) works. His brothers R' Chaim and R' Wolf (whose testament was published together with *Mekor Chachmah* by R' Yissachar Ber ben Moshe Pesachyah, Berlin, 5471/1711) were also prominent scholars. R' Menachem Mendel married the daughter of the prominent Cracow merchant Yehudah Leib ben Moshe HaKohen. He studied under the *Bach, *R' Yehoshua ben Yosef of Cracow, and *R' Menachem Mendel Krochmal. In Cracow he occupied himself with banking and was considered wealthy. He also served as one of the *dayanim* of the community. After 5410/1650 R' Menachem Mendel returned to his native Vienna, and it is assumed he stayed there until the expulsion of the Jews from Vienna in 5430/1670. He accepted the rabbinates of Rausnitz (Moravia), and (in 5433/1673) of Krotoshin, where he remained until his death.

R' Menachem Mendel authored *Ateres Zekeinim*, a commentary on *Shulchan Aruch Orach Chaim* (Dyhernfurth, 5480/1720, and in many later editions of the *Shulchan Aruch*). It consists of short comments, explanations, and references to parallel sources. Some scholars have argued that the printed work merely contains selections from R' Menachem Mendel's work. His *Akeres HaBayis*, a commentary on *Shulchan Aruch Choshen Mishpat*, remains unpublished.

R' Hillel ben Naftali Hertz

רַבִּי הִלֵּל בֶּן נַפְתָּלִי הִירְץ

b. Brisk, Lithuania, 5375/1615
d. Zolkiew, Poland, 22 Teves 5450/1690

A disciple of R' Tzvi Hirsh Darshan of Brisk, *R' Yehoshua Heshel of Cracow (to whom he was related by marriage), and of *R' Moshe (the author of *Chelkas Mechokeik*), R' Hillel served for a time as dayan under R' Moshe in the *beis din* in Vilna. There his reputation grew as a competent halachist, and he successively retained various rabbinates in Lithuania until 5430/1670, when he was called upon to serve the 'Three Communities' — Altona, Hamburg, and Wandsbeck. After staying in Germany for ten years, he accepted the rabbinate of Zolkiew (Poland), where he remained until his death.

R' Hillel is best known for his halachic commentary on the *Shulchan Aruch,* entitled *Beis Hillel,* of which the parts pertaining to *Yoreh Deah* and *Even HaEzer* were published (Dyhernfurth, 5451/1691). The part on *Orach Chaim* and *Choshen Mishpat,* and a Torah commentary, remain unpublished. A responsum by him appears in *She'eilos UTeshuvos Emunas Shmuel* (§52) by *R' Aharon Shmuel Kaidanover.

R' Aharon Tumim

רַבִּי אַהֲרֹן בֶּן מֹשֶׁה תְּאוֹמִים

b. Prague, Bohemia (now Czechoslovakia)
c. 5390/1630
d. Chmielnik, Poland, 2 Av 5450/1690

R' Aharon began his career as a preacher in Prague, a position he held from 5419/1659 until 5432/1672, when he was elected rabbi and *rosh yeshivah* of Worms, as successor to R' Shimshon Bacharach. He was a very popular preacher and wherever he went the people would throng to hear his discourses. He had a strong leaning towards the ingenious and far-fetched *pilpul* method so popular in his day, and this no doubt added to his appeal. *R' Chaim Yair Bacharach — who, in his *Teshuvos Chavos Yair* (§124), strongly criticized R' Aharon and other Torah greats for their excessive (in R' Chaim Yair's view) use of the *pilpul* — wrote an entire treatise, *Yair Nesiv,* outlining his

views on the *pilpul* method, with a detailed critique of one of R' Aharon's works. (However, he later wrote a note in the margin of this treatise requesting that it never be published.) In spite of this, R' Chaim Yair's respect for R' Aharon is beyond question; he sought his opinion on a halachic problem and published R' Aharon's responsum in his *Teshuvos Chavos Yair* (§121).

In the throes of a serious illness which overcame him on Passover evening, 5435/1675, he vowed that should he recover, he would write a commentary on the *Haggadah.* Having regained his health, he published this commentary under the title *Mateh Aharon* (Frankfurt am Main, 5438/1678).

In 5437/1677 R' Aharon received a call to the rabbinate of Lissa (Poland), which he declined, but in 5447/1687 he accepted the rabbinate of Cracow. However, due to unspecified circumstances (probably the unstable political climate of Germany at this time due to the state of war with France), R' Aharon did not officially assume his post in Cracow until before Pesach of 5450/1690. No sooner had he left Worms than the city was taken by the troops of Louis XIV of France, and destroyed (Sivan 5449/1689).

R' Aharon had served in Cracow for only four months when he took part in a meeting of the Council of Four Lands (see **Historical Introduction**), in Chmielnik. There, a Polish nobleman, for reasons unknown, had him arrested and flogged on Shabbos, placed on horseback and rushed to prison. R' Aharon fell off the horse several times, and was as often remounted. Before reaching the jail he died of the torturous treatment. [There are grounds to believe that the community of Cracow owed the nobleman back-taxes.] The Jews feared to bury him in Chmielnik and brought him on Sunday to Pintshov, where he was buried (see *Kelilas Yofi*, Part 2, page 129).

R' Aharon composed, besides his *Haggadah* commentary, *Bigdei Aharon*, homilies on the Torah (Frankfurt am Main, 5470/1710), also written in an extremely pilpulistic vein; and *Choshen Aharon*, responsa and notes on *Shulchan Aruch Choshen Mishpat*, which were not published.

R' Gershon ben Yitzchak Ashkenazi (Ulif)

רַבִּי גֵּרְשׁוֹן בֶּן יִצְחָק אַשְׁכְּנַזִי (אוּלִיף)

b. Germany (?)

d. Metz, France, 11 Adar II 5453/1693

R' Gershon may have studied under *R' Meir Schif (Maharam Schif) in Frankfurt during his early youth; he cites an interpretation of a *midrash* which he heard from Maharam Schif (*Tiferes HaGershuni Parashas Shemini*). However, he left Germany, presumably while yet in his teens, to study in Cracow, which was at that time the residence of some of the greatest Talmudic scholars and rabbis in Europe. There he studied under the *Bach, *R' Yehoshua ben Yosef of Cracow, *R' Yehoshua Heshel of Cracow, and *R' Menachem Mendel Krochmal.

R' Gershon first married the daughter of R' Leib Poss, a great-granddaughter of the *Bach*, but she died at a very young age and he remarried, becoming the son-in-law of his mentor R' Menachem Mendel Krochmal. R' Gershon served for a time as a *dayan* in Cracow, but around the year 5409/1649 he left Poland to accept the rabbinate of Prossnitz (Prostejov) in Moravia, and later (after 5417/1657) that of Hanau (Germany). After the death of his father-in-law in 5421/1661, R' Gershon succeeded him as Chief Rabbi of Nikolsburg and all of Moravia. However, he left this post

shortly thereafter (c. 5424/1664) to become Chief Rabbi of Vienna. In 5430/1670 the Jews were expelled from Vienna (see **Historical Introduction**) and R' Gershon was forced into exile. Later that year he was called on to serve the community of Metz, where he remained until his death.

Having excelled in the spreading of Talmudic knowledge in all his previous rabbinical positions, R' Gershon continued his work in Metz with great zeal and success. Hundreds of disciples attended his discourses, which were considered extremely ingenious and penetrating. In addition, he was known as an expert halachist and his decisions were sought on all sorts of halachic problems.

R' Gershon's works are *Avodas HaGershuni* (Frankfurt am Main, 5459/1699), responsa; *Tiferes HaGershuni* (Frankfurt am Main, 5459/1699), discourses on the portions of the week, mostly pilpulistic in nature, in which kabbalistic material is also presented; and *Chidushei HaGershuni* (Frankfurt am Main, 5470/1710), *chidushim* on *Shulchan Aruch* and the Torah. His *chidushim* on tractate *Yevamos, Sefer HaHalachos* of *Rif (this work seems to have been his magnum opus, as stated in *R' David Oppenheim's preface to *Tiferes HaGershuni*), and *Turim*, these remain unpublished.

Among his pupils was the renowned R' David Oppenheim, rabbi of Prague. R' David was one of the wealthiest Jews of his generation, the possessor of one of the most extensive libraries ever amassed, and one of the foremost scholars of the time. R' David wrote, concerning his master, that if — G-d forbid — the Torah were forgotten, R' Gershon could restore it with his sharp memory and intellect.

When R' Gershon died, not only the community at Metz mourned his passing, but many other communities decreed a one-year ban on music and singing as a sign of mourning for the sage they considered to be the halachic giant of the generation, a sign of respect given very few spiritual leaders.

R' David Lida

רַבִּי דָּוִד בֶּן אַרְיֵה לֵיב לִידָא

b. Zwolen, Poland, c. 5385/1625
d. Lemberg (Lvov), Poland (now Russia)
27 Cheshvan 5455/1694 or 5459/1698

R' David was a disciple of *R' Yehoshua Heshel of Cracow, and a nephew of *R' Moshe Rivkah's. After his marriage he settled in Lemberg (Poland); there his son R' Pesachyah was born. R' David served in various rabbinical posts in Poland and Lithuania, among them one in the town of Lida, before being called to Mainz, Germany. From there he was elected to the prestigious post of rabbi of the Ashkenazic community of Amsterdam.

Soon after his arrival in Amsterdam in 5441/1681, he was opposed by some members of the congregation, who accused him of being a follower of the false Messianic movement of Shabsai Tzvi. Because of this he was deprived of his position. However, upon his return to Poland, he appealed his case to the Council of Four Lands (see **Historical Introduction**), who exonerated him of all suspicion and reinstated him as rabbi of Amsterdam. He printed a pamphlet called Be'er Eisek (Lublin, 5448/1688) in which he explained his side of this controversy. However, his stay in Amsterdam was not a happy one, and after his contract expired the community refused to renew it. In 5444/1684, R' David returned to Poland and settled in Lemberg, where he lived out his years.

Among his works are Ir Miklat (Dyhernfurth, 5450/1690), a listing of the six hundred thirteen commandments with references to various works; Ir David (Amsterdam, 5479/1719), sermons; Shomer Shabbos (Amsterdam, 5443/1683, in the collection Yad Kol Bo), on the laws of the Sabbath; Sod Hashem VeSharvit HaZahav (Amsterdam, 5440/1680), on the laws of circumcision, together with prayers for the mohel and sandek; and Chalukei Avanim (Fuerth, 5453/1693) on *Rashi's chumash commentary. His commentary on Shulchan Aruch Orach Chaim, entitled Be'er Mayim Chaim, was never published. Other works are attributed to him in error. For example, *Chida claims that the kabbalistic commentary Migdal David, which R' David published (Amsterdam, 5440/1680), was really authored by *R' Chaim HaKohen. Other scholars have shown that R' David himself hints at R' Chaim's authorship in his preface.

R' David's son, R' Pesachyah, was rabbi of Yassi (Iasi), Rumania, and later served in various towns in Poland.

R' Yosef HaDarshan

רַבִּי יוֹסֵף (בֶּן שְׁלֹמֹה) הַדַּרְשָׁן

b. Posen, Poland, 5361/1601
d. Posen, Poland, 5456/1696

After studying in eastern Poland, R' Yosef settled there for a time, thereby becoming a witness to the Cossack uprisings of 5408-09/1648-49 (see **Historical Introduction**). He succeeded in escaping to his native town, Posen, where he held the position of preacher for twenty years, from 5436/1676 until his death.

R' Yosef authored Yesod Yosef (Frankfurt an der Oder, 5439/1679), a very popular work on mussar; Sedeh Bochim (Frankfurt an der Oder, 5439/1679), containing a commentary on Perek Shirah, and on the liturgy for Tikkun Chatzos. VaYakhel, sermons arranged according to the weekly portions of the Torah, and VaYelaket Yosef, a kabbalistic treatise, were never published. R' Rephael Uchana wrote a commentary, Yesod Maaravi (Jerusalem, 5656/1896), to Yesod Yosef, and R' Chananyah Y.T. Lipa Deutsch composed a fourteen-volume anthology, Taharas Yom Tov, around Yesod Yosef. However, the greatest part of the material collected in these fourteen volumes have only a very tenuous connection to the subject of the text of Yesod Yosef, and the work is merely used as a literary device around which to group the assembled material.

R' Aharon ben Chaim Avraham HaKohen Perachia

ר' אַהֲרֹן בֶּן חַיִּים אַבְרָהָם הַכֹּהֵן פְּרַחְיָא

b. Salonica (?), Turkey, c. 5387/1627
d. Salonica, Turkey (now Greece)
23 Shevat 5457/1697

R' Aharon was born into a distinguished family of Turkish Jews. His father, himself a talmid chacham, was a son-in-law of R' Aharon ibn Chasson (a great rav and rosh yeshivah in Turkey, and a colleague of *R' Aharon Sasson; none of his writings were printed; see Korei HaDoros). He studied under R' Asher HaKohen ibn Ardut, about whom R' Aharon wrote, 'I have absorbed of his learning [a portion which is comparable to] what a dog slurps from the sea.' He also studied under his kinsman *R' Chisdai HaKohen Perachia, author of Toras Chessed, and under *R' Chaim Shabsai.

R' Aharon was a wealthy man and did not need to officiate as a rav for his livelihood. Nevertheless, he began to fulfill the functions of a rav at a very young age. In his Bigdei Kehunah we find a drashah which R' Aharon delivered in the year 5406/1646 — when he was only

nineteen years old. Towards the end of his life, after the death of *R' Eliyahu Kovo in 5449/1688, R' Aharon was appointed to be the Chief Rabbi of Salonica.

R' Aharon is chiefly known for his volume of responsa, Parach Mateh Aharon (Amsterdam, 5463/1703). Among his correspondents we find some of the most illustrious names of Turkish Jewry — *R' Moshe Benveniste, R' Chisdai Perachia, R' Shmuel Gaon and others. R' Chaim Alfandari writes about R' Aharon (Mutzal MeEish §62): '. . . he is (one of) the greatest of the Acharonim in (his) time.' R' Aharon also authored Pirchei Kehunah, chidushim on various mesichtos (Amsterdam, 5469/1709); Bigdei Kehunah (Salonica, 5513/1753), drashos based mainly on concepts expounded by medieval Jewish philosophers; and Zichron Devarim (Salonica, 5518/1758), miscellaneous guidelines for making halachic rulings (kelalim for the dinim of migo, kim li, et al.), rulings, and responsa. In his writings, R' Aharon refers to his chidushim on the Rif and the Tur; both of these works were not published.

R' Shmuel ben Uri Shraga Feivush

רַבִּי שְׁמוּאֵל בֶּן אוּרִי שְׁרָגָא פֵייבוּשׁ

b. Woidislaw (Wodzislaw), Poland
c. 5400/1640
d. Shidlow (?), Poland, c. 5460/1700

R' Shmuel was a disciple of *R' Yehoshua Heshel of Cracow. After the latter's death, R' Shmuel continued his studies under R' Aryeh Leib Fischel's (also known as der hoicher R' Leib, i.e. the tall R' Leib), who succeeded R' Heshel as rabbi of Cracow, and who later gave R' Shmuel his daughter in marriage.

R' Shmuel's first rabbinate was at Shidlow. There he wrote Beis Shmuel, his classic commentary to *Shulchan Aruch Even HaEzer*. In his preface he underlines that in this community he was not afforded the opportunity to be able to discuss the intricate laws dealt with in his work with fellow scholars and disciples. He published this work in Dyhernfurth (5449/1689). In 5451/1691, he became rabbi of Fuerth, Germany, where he was given the chance to review the laws of *Even HaEzer* with disciples. He then prepared an upgraded edition (*Mahadurah Basra*) of *Beis Shmuel*, with additional material from *Turei Zahav* (which had as yet not been published) and other works which had not been available to him during the initial composition of his work. He published the improved edition at Fuerth in 5454/1694 together with *Chelkas Mechokeik* by *R' Moshe of Vilna. These two works are the two most important commentaries on this part of the *Shulchan Aruch,* and have been studied by scholars since their publication.

In an approbation to a work printed in 5458/1698 he is titled 'rabbi of Shidlow.' It is assumed that he returned to his native Poland and his old rabbinate and he may have spent the rest of his years there.

Appendices and Index

TURKEY-GREECE	ERETZ YISRAEL	POLAND-LITHUANIA
	15TH CENTURY	
R' Yaakov ibn Chaviv	R' Ovadyah Yarei of Bertinoro	
	16TH CENTURY	
R' Eliyahu Mizrachi (Ra'am)	R' Yaakov Pollak	
R' David HaKohen (Radach)		
	R' Moshe Alashkar	
R' Yosef Taitatzak	R' Yaakov bei Rav	
	R' Levi ibn Chaviv	
		R' Shalom Shachna of Lublin
	R' Moshe Cordovero(Ramak)	R' Moshe Isserles (Rama)
	R' Yitzchak Luria *(Ari)*	
	R' David ibn Zimra (Radvaz)	
	R' Yosef Caro	R' Shlomo Luria (Maharshal)
R' Yosef ibn Lev	R' Moshe Trani (Mabit)	
R' Avraham de Boton	R' Shlomo Alkabetz	R' Eliezer Ashkenazi
R' Shmuel de Medina	R' Betzalel Ashkenazi	R' Shlomo ben Yehuda Leib
	R' Moshe Alsheich	
	R' Eliyahu de Vidas	
	R' Elazar Azkari	
	R' Shmuel de Uzeda	R' Moshe Mos of Premysl
		R' Mordechai Yafeh *(Levush)*
	R' Yehoshua Falk Katz	
	17TH CENTURY	
		R' Meir (Maharam) Lublin
	R' Chaim Vital	R' Yaakov Rabino
	R' Yisrael Najarah	
		R' Shmuel Eliezer Eidels (Maharsha)
		R' Avraham Chaim Shor
		R' Nassan Nata Shapira
R' Yosef Trani (Maharit)		R' Yoel Sirkis *(Bach)*
		R' Shimshon of Ostropolle
		R' Yehoshua ben Yosef of Cracow
		R' Yom Tov Lipman Heller
		R' Moshe ben Yehudah Lema
	R' Meir Popperos	R' Shabsai HaKohen *(Shach)*
		R' Yehoshua Heshel of Cracow
	R' Yaakov Tzemach	R' David HaLevi *(Taz)*
R' Chaim Benveniste		R' Moshe Rivkah's
	R' (Yisrael) Yaakov Chagiz	R' Aharon Shmuel Kaidanover (Maharshak)
		R' Avraham (Abale) Gombiner
	R' Moshe Galante II	*(Magen Avraham)*
		R' Shmuel ben Uri Shraga Feivush

AUSTRIA-GERMANY	BOHEMIA-MORAVIA	ITALY
	15TH CENTURY	
R' Yaakov Margolies		R' Yitzchak Aramah R' Yosef Yaavetz R' Yehudah Mintz R' (Don) Yitzchak Abarbanel
	16TH CENTURY	
		R' Ovadyah Sforno R' Meir (Maharam) Padua
	R' Yehudah Loeve (Maharal of Prague)	
	17TH CENTURY	
	R' Shlomo Ephraim Lunshitz R' Yeshayah Horowitz *(Shelah)*	R' Menachem Azaryah of Fano
R' Naftali Hirtz Bacharach		R' Azaryah Figo
R' Menashe ben Yisrael — Holland		
	R' Menachem Mendel Krochmal	
R' Ephraim HaKohen — Hungary		
R' Gershon ben Yitzchak Ashkenazi — France		

~§ Sefarim Composed by the Early Acharonim

This index lists all the works mentioned in this book, published and unpublished, followed by the author's name. An asterisk before the author's name means that there is a main entry in this book (or in The Later Acharonim) about this author. Otherwise the reference will indicate, after the author's name, the entry in which the work appears, and the page on which the entry begins.

Page	Name of Author	Name of Work
73	*R' Moshe Cordovero (Ramak)	אור נערב
165	*R' Meir Popperos	אור נר
66	*R' Ovadyah Sforno	אור עמים
165	*R' Meir Popperos	אור צדיקים
84	*R' Yosef Caro	אור צדיקים
165	*R' Meir Popperos	אור צח
165	*R' Meir Popperos	אור רב
122	*R' Meir ben Gedalyah (Maharam Lublin)	אור שבעת הימים
165	*R' Meir Popperos	אור שבת
107	*R' Menachem de Lonzano	אור תורה
124	*R' Shlomo Ephraim Lunshitz	אורח לחיים
183	*R' (Yisrael) Yaakov Chagiz	אורח מישור
75	R' Yochanan Kremenitzer, see *R' Moshe Isserles	אורח מישור
145	*R' Avraham Chaim Yisrael Ze'evi, see *R' Avraham Azulai	אורים גדולים
35	R' Meir Aramah, see *R' Yitzchak Aramah	אורים ותומים
177	*R' Yehoshua (Rephael) Benveniste	אזני יהושע
195	*R' Yitzchak of Posen	איל יצחק
92	*R' Shlomo Alkabetz	אילת אהבים
117	*R' Eliyah Shapira, see *R' Mordechai Yafeh, see also L.A.	אליה זוטא
117	*R' Eliyah Shapira, see *R' Mordechai Yafeh, see also L.A.	אליה רבה
73	*R' Moshe Cordovero (Ramak)	אלימה רבתי
125	*R' Menachem Azaryah of Fano	אלפסי זוטא
156	*R' Yosef Shlomo Delmedigo	אלים
46	*R' Avraham Chayon	אמרות טהורות
125	*R' Menachem Azaryah of Fano	אמרות טהורות
127	*R' Vidal Tzarfati	אמרי יושר
87	*R' Nassan Nata Shapira I	אמרי שפר
57	*R' Avraham of Prague	אנא אלקי אברהם (סליחה)
99	*R' Betzalel Ashkenazi	אספת זקנים
121	*R' Yitzchak Chayes	אפי זוטא
121	*R' Yitzchak Chayes	אפי רברבי
128	*R' Chaim Vital	ארבע מאות שקל כסף
151	*R' Yehudah Aryeh (Leon) de Modena	ארי נוהם
45	*R' Avraham Saba	אשכל הכפר
144	*R' Aharon Berechyah of Modena	אשמורת הבקר
110	*R' Avraham Yagel dei Galiccho	אשת חיל

Page	Name of Author	Name of Work
		ז
41	*R' (Don) Yitzchak Abarbanel	זבח פסח
196	*R' Moshe Galante II	זבח שלמים
73	*R' Moshe Cordovero (Ramak)	זבחי שלמים
171	*R' Yaakov Tzemach	זבחי שלמים
192	*R' (Nissim) Shlomo ben Avraham Algazi I	זהב שיבה
171	*R' Yaakov Tzemach	זהר הרקיע
145	*R' Avraham Azulai	זהרי חמה
190	*R' Avraham Abale Gombiner	זית רענן
97	*R' Avraham Galante	זכות אבות
201	*R' Aharon ben Chaim Avraham HaKohen Perachia	זכרון דברים
137	R' Moshe (Ashkenazi) Heilprin,	זכרון משה
	see *R' Shmuel Eliezer Eidels	
133	*R' Yisrael Najarah	זמירות ישראל
37,50	R' Eliyahu HaLevi,	זקן אהרן
	see *R' Moshe Capsali, see also *R' Eliyahu Mizrachi	
151	*R' Yehudah Aryeh (Leon) de Modena	זקני יהודה
192	*R' (Nissim) Shlomo ben Avraham Algazi I	זקנת שלמה
171	*R' Yaakov Tzemach	זר זהב
171	R' Berechyah ben Elyakim Getzl,	זרע ברך שלישי
	see *R' Berechyah Beirech ben Yitzchak Isaac Shapira	
171	*R' Berechiah Beirech ben Yitzchak Isaac Shapira	זרע ברך
121	R' Yitzchak (ben Yaakov) Chayes, see *R' Yitzchak Chayes	זרע יצחק
		ח
101	*R' Moshe Alsheich	חבצלת השרון
117	R' Shmuel ben Uziel of Landsberg,	חגורת שמואל
	see *R' Mordechai Yafeh	
	see חידושי	חדושי
198	see *R' Aharon Tumim	חושן אהרן
35	*R' Yitzchak Aramah	חזות קשה
40	*R' Yochanan Aleiman	חי העולמים
154	R' Zelig Margolies see *R' Yom Tov Lipman Heller	חיבורי ליקוטים
137	*R' Shmuel Eliezer Eidels	חידושי אגדות
111	*R' Yehudah Loeve (Maharal of Prague)	חידושי אגדות
35	*R' Yitzchak Abohab II	חידושי גלאנטי
199	*R' Gershon ben Yitzchak Ashkenazi (Ulif)	חידושי הגרשוני
169	R' Aharon Klinker, see *R' Yehoshua Heshel of Cracow	חידושי הלכות
146	*R' Meir Schif	חידושי הלכות
137	*R' Shmuel Eliezer Eidels	חידושי הלכות

THE EARLY ACHARONIM / *Sefarim Composed by the Rishonim*

❧ Index of Personalities

Entries in this index are arranged according to first names. In many instances surnames are also listed, giving cross references to the main entry which appears under the person's first name.

A bold face entry means that an article on the person appears in either *The Rishonim* or *The Early Acharonim*, or that one is planned for *The Later Acharonim*.

Bold face entries for persons with articles in *The Early Acharonim*, will be followed by the page number on which the article begins.

Bold face entries for persons with articles in *The Rishonim*, are followed by references to where the name occurs in *this* volume, and conclude with 'see also *R.* [= *The Rishonim*] p. 75.' If the name occurs very often in *this* volume, no references to this volume will be given.

Bold face entries with projected articles in *The Later Acharonim* are followed by references to where the name occurs in *this* volume, and conclude with 'see also *L.A.* [= *The Later Acharonim*].'

An asterisks preceding a name, within an index entry or in the text, signifies that an article on the person appears in either this volume, *The Rishonim*, or *The Later Acharonim*.

R' Akiva Horowitz, father of *R' Shabsai Sheftl Horowitz I

al-Nakavah, see *R' Yisrael al-Nakavah

Al-Sevili, see R' Avraham Al-Sevili

Alashkar, see *R' Moshe Alashkar

Albo, see *R' Yosef Albo

Alegri, see *R' Avraham Alegri

Aleiman, see *R' Yochanan Aleiman

R' Alexander Sender Shor, great-grandson of *R' Avraham Chaim Shor

*R' Alexander Zusslein HaKohen, see *R' Yosef Katz; see also *R*., p. 146

Alfandari, see R' Aharon Alfandari; R' Chaim Alfandari; R' Yaakov Alfandari

Algazi, see R' Avraham Algazi; *R' Chaim Algazi; R' Chaim Algazi; R' Moshe ben Avraham Algazi; R' (Nissim) Shlomo ben Avraham Algazi I; *R' Shlomo ben Avraham Algazi I; R' Shlomo Algazi II; *R' Yisrael Yaakov Algazi; *R' Yom Tov (Rit) Algazi

Alkabetz, see *R' Shlomo Alkabetz

Alkalai, see R' Bentzion Alkalai

Almoda, see R' Yehudah Almoda

Almosino, see *R' Moshe Almosino; R' Yosef Almosnino

Alpandari, see Alfandari

Alravi, see R' Shlomo Aravi

Alsheich, see R' Chaim Alsheich; *R' Moshe Alsheich

Altschuler, see R' Yechiel Hillel Altschuler

Amigo, see *R' Avraham Amigo; R' Avraham Amigo

Angel, see R' Avraham Galante; R' Baruch Angel

Ankavah, see R' Avraham Ankavah

Aramah, see R' David ben Avraham Aramah; R' Meir Aramah; R' Yaakov Aramah; *R' Yitzchak Aramah

Aravi, see R' Shlomo Aravi

Ari, see *R' Yitzchak Luria Ashkenazi

*R' Aryeh Leib, descendant of *R' Binyamin Aharon Solnik of Podayetz; nephew and stepson of *R' David HaLevi; see also *L.A.*

R' Aryeh Leib Fischel's, teacher and father-in-law of *R' Shmuel ben Uri Shraga Feivush

*R' Aryeh Leib HaKohen Heller, descendant of *R' Yom Tov Lipman Heller; see *L.A.*

R' Aryeh Leib Rappaport, grandfather of *R' Avraham Rappaport Shrentzel

R' Aryeh Leib Rofei, grandfather of *R' Menachem Mendel Auerbach

R' Aryeh Yehudah Leib HaKohen, son of *R' Ephraim HaKohen

Asevilli, see R' Avraham Asevilli

R' Asher, grandfather of *R' Meir ben Gedalyah (Maharam Lublin)

*R' Asher Enshkin, teacher and relative of *R' Yehudah Mintz, see also *R*., p. 152

R' Asher HaKohen ibn Ardut, descendant of *R' Yitzchak Aramah; teacher of *R' Aharon ben Chaim Avraham HaKohen Perachia

Ashkenazi, see R' Azaryah Yehoshua Ashkenazi; *R' Berman Ashkenazi; *R' Betzalel Ashkenazi; *R' Binyamin HaLevi Ashkenazi; *R' Eliezer Ashkenazi; *R' Eliezer Ashkenazi Ish Tzvi; R' Eliyahu Ashkenazi; *R' Gershon ben Yitzchak Ashkenazi (Ulif); R' Meir Ashkenazi; R' Moshe (Ashkenazi) Heilprin; Nassan Askenazi of Gaza; R' Shlomo HaLevi Ashkenazi; R' Shmuel Yafeh Ashkenazi; *R' Tzvi Ashkenazi; R' Yisrael Ashkenazi; *R' Yitzchak Luria Ashkenazi; R' Yitzchak Yafeh Ashkenazi

Auerbach, see R' Chaim Auerbach; R' Meir Auerbach; *R' Menachem Mendel Auerbach; R' Moshe Auerbach; *R' Shimon Zev Auerbach; R' Wolf Auerbach

*R' Avigdor Kara, see *R' Avraham of Prague, see also *R*., p. 151

*R' Avraham Abale Gombiner (the *Magen Avraham*) (190)

*R' Avraham Alegri (153)

R' Avraham Algazi, father of *R' Shlomo ben Avraham Algazi I

*R' Avraham Amigo (193)

R' Avraham Amigo, see *R' Menachem Azaryah of Fano

R' Avraham Ankavah, see *R' Shabsai Sheftl Horowitz I

*R' Eliyah Shapira, student of *R' Avraham Abale Gombiner; see *R' Mordechai Yafeh; see also L.A.

R' Eliyahu, father-in-law of *R' Ephraim HaKohen

R' Eliyahu Ashkenazi, see *R' Eliyahu Bachur

R' Eliyahu Baal Shem, see *R' Eliyahu Loanz

R' Eliyahu Baal Shem of Chelm, see *R' Ephraim HaKohen

*R' Eliyahu Bachur (60)

R' Eliyahu ben Elkanah Capsali, great-nephew of *R' Moshe Capsali; see also *R' Meir Katzenellenbogen

*R' Eliyahu ben Yehudah Kovo (196)

R' Eliyahu Capsali, father and teacher of *R' Moshe Capsali

R' Eliyahu Chiya Sasson, see *R' Yoshiyahu Pinto

*R' Eliyahu de Vidas (104)

R' Eliyahu Delmedigo, grandfather of *R' Yosef Shlomo Delmedigo

R' Eliyahu HaLevi (HaZakein), teacher of *R' Eliyahu Mizrachi

R' Eliyahu HaLevi, pupil, colleague and successor to *R' Eliyahu Mizrachi; pupil of *R' Moshe Capsali

*R' Eliyahu ibn Chaim (Ranach) (115)

*R' Eliyahu Loanz (140)

*R' Eliyahu Mizrachi (Ra'am)
(the Mizrachi) (50)

R' Eliyahu of Pesaro, see *R' Eliezer Ashkenazi

Emden, see *R' Yaakov Emden

R' Emmanuel, see *R' Menachem Azaryah of Fano

R' Enshkin, see *R' Asher Enshkin

R' Ephraim Boeno, see *R' Moshe Rivkah's

R' Ephraim Caro, father of *R' Yosef Caro

R' Ephraim Fishl ben Moshe Yehudah, antecedent of *R' Ephraim HaKohen

R' Ephraim Garbus, see *R' Shlomo Sirilio

*R' Ephraim HaKohen (187)

*R' Ephraim Zalman Margulies, descendant of R' Avraham Chaim Shor; see also *R' Avraham Rappaport Shrentzel; *R' Moshe Isserles; see also L.A.

*R' Ephraim Zalman Shor (139)

Escapa, see *R' Yosef ben Shaul Escapa

Esterosah, see R' Chaim Avraham Esterosah; *R' Daniel Esterosah

R' Ezra of Fano, teacher of *R' Menachem Azaryah of Fano

R' Falk HaKohen, see *R' Yehoshua Falk Katz

Fano, see R' Menachem Azaryah of Fano

R' Feitel, see R' Nassan Veidel

Figo, see *R' Azaryah Figo

Fintzi, see R' Chizkiyah Fintzi

Finzi, see R' Yaakov Finzi; R' Yitzchak Finzi of Pesaro

Firman, see R' Yosef Firman

Foa, see R' Eliezer Nachman Foa; R' Nesanel Foa; R' Yechiel Foa; R' Yitzchak Foa

Frankfurt, see R' Akiva Frankfurt

Frankl-Tumim, see *R' Baruch Frankl-Tumim

Gabbai, see R' Yedidyah Gabbai

R' Gad ben Yoel, descendant of *R' David HaLevi

Gakon, see R' Yitzchak Gakon

Galante, see *R' Avraham Galante; *R' Moshe Galante I; *R' Moshe Galante II; R' Yedidyah Galante

Galiko, see *R' Elisha Galiko; *R' Shmuel Galiko

Galler, see R' Tzvi Hirsh Galler

Gansu, see R' Yosef Gansu

R' Ganz, see *R' David Ganz; R' Yisrael Zeligman Ganz

Gaon, see R' Shmuel Gaon

Garbus, see R' Ephraim Garbus

Garmizan, see *R' Shmuel Garmizan

*R' Gedalyah ibn Yachya (95)

*R' Gedalyah Lipshitz (141)

R' Gedalyah Moshe, descendant of *R' Aharon Shmuel Kaidanover

ibn Shuiv, see R' Shmuel ibn Shuiv; R' Yehoshua ibn Shuiv; *R' Yoel ibn Shuiv

ibn Tzur, see R' Eliezer ben Shlomo ibn Tzur; *R' Yitzchak Leon ibn Tzur

ibn Verga, see *R' Shlomo ibn Verga; R' Yehudah ibn Verga; *R' Yosef ibn Verga

ibn Yachya, see R' David ben Yosef ibn Yachya; *R' Gedalyah ibn Yachya; R' Tam ibn Yachya; R' Yosef ben David ibn Yachya

ibn Yaish, see *R' Avraham ibn Yaish

ibn Zaiach, see *R' Yosef ibn Zaiat

ibn Zaiat see *R' Yosef ibn Zaiat

ibn Zimra, see *R' David ibn Zimra

R' Isaac Margolies, son of *R' Yaakov Margolies; colleague of *R' Yaakov Pollak

Iscandari, see R' Avraham Iscandari

Ish Ger, see *R' Avraham Yosef Shlomo Graziano

Ish Tzvi, see *R' Eliezer Ashkenazi Ish Tzvi; R' Shmuel Ish Tzvi

R' Issac R' Yekels, brother-in-law of *R' Avraham Rappaport Shrentzel

Isserles, see R' Elazar ben Yisrael Isserles; *R' Moshe Isserles; R' Moshe ben Elazar Isserles

R' Joselman, see *R' Yoselman Loanz of Rosheim

Kaidanover, see *R' Aharon Shmuel Kaidanover; R' Tzvi Hirsh Kaidanover

Kalai, see R' Mordechai Kalai; R' Shmuel Kalai

R' Kalman Haberkasten, father-in-law of *R' Shlomo Luria (Maharshal)

*R' Kalman Vermaisa (71)

Kanpanton, see *R'Yitzchak Kanpanton

Kara, see *R' Avigdor Kara; R' Avraham Kara

Katz, see *R' Avraham Reuven Katz; R' Meshulam Katz; *R' Naftali Katz; *R' Yehoshua Falk Katz; *R' Yosef Katz; R' Yosef ben Yehoshua Falk Katz

Katzenellenbogen, see *R' Meir Katzenellenbogen; R' Shaul Katzenellenbogen; *R' Shmuel Yehudah Katznellenbogen; *R' Yechezkel Katzenellenbogen

Kimchi, see *R' Moshe Kimchi

Klinker, see R' Aharon Klinker

Kloiber, see R' Yitzchak Kloiber

Korkos, see *R' Yosef Korkos

Koshman, see *R' Yosef Yospa Koshman

Kovo, see *R' Eliyahu ben Yehudah Kovo

Kremenitzer, see R' Yochanan Kremenitzer

Kremer, see R' Moshe Kremer

Krochmal, see *R' Menachem Mendel Krochmal; R' Yehudah Leib ben Menachem Mendel Krochmal

Labia, see *R' Shimon Labia

Landau, see R' Moshe Landau; *R' Yaakov Landau; *R' Yechezkel Landau

Landsofer, see *R' Yonah Landsofer

Landsofer, see *R' Yonah Landsofer

Lapapa, see *R' Aharon Lapapa

Lapidos, see R' Shabsai Lapidos

Lavaut, see R' Avraham David Lavaut

Lehman, see R' Meir Lehman

R' Leib Poss, first father-in-law of *R' Gershon ben Yitzchak Ashkenazi (Ulif)

R' Leib, "der hoicher", see R' Aryeh Leib Fischel's

R' Leon de Modena, see *R' Yehudah Aryeh (Leon) de Modena

*R' Levi ben Yaakov ibn Chaviv (Ralbach) (63)

R' Levi Pollak, see *R' Yehoshua Heshel of Cracow

Levush, see *R' Mordechai Yafeh

Lida, see *R' David Lida; R' Pesachyah ben David Lida

Lipshitz, see *R' Gedalyah Lipshitz

Loanz, see *R' Eliyahu Loanz

R' Loeve, see *R' Yehudah Loeve

Loeve the Elder of Prague, ancestor of *R' Yehudah Loeve

Lunshitz, see *R' Shlomo Ephraim Lunshitz

Luria, see R' David Luria; *R' Shlomo Luria; R' Yechiel Luria; *R' Yitzchak Luria Ashkenazi; R' Yochanan Luria

Luzzato, see *R' Moshe Chaim Luzzato

Mabit, see *R' Moshe Trani

Magen Avraham, see *R' Avraham Abale Gombiner

Maharal of Prague, see *R' Yehudah Loewe

Maharam Alashkar, see *R' Moshe Alashkar

Maharam Galante, see *R' Moshe Galante I

Maharam Lublin, see *R' Meir ben Gedalyah

Maharam Padua, see *R' Meir Katzenellenbogen

Maharam Schif, see *R' Meir Schif

Maharam [of] Tiktin, see *R' Menachem [of] Tiktin

Maharashdam, see *R' Shmuel de Medina

Maharchash, see *R' Chaim Shabsai

Mahari ibn Lev, see *R' Yosef ibn Lev

*Maharik, see *R' Yosef Colon, *R.*, p. 191

Maharikash, see *R' Yaakov Castro

Maharit, see R' Yosef Trani

Maharsha, see *R' Shmuel Eliezer Eidels

Maharshach, see *R' Shlomo HaKohen

Maharshak, see *R' Aharon Shmuel Kaidanover

Maharshal, see *R' Shlomo Luria

*R' Mano'ach Hendel (116)

R' Mardush, see R' Mordechai Mardush of Poritsk

Margolies, see R' Isaac Margolies; *R' Moshe Mordechai Margolies; R' Shmuel Margolies; *R' Yaakov Margolies; R' Yaakov Margolies of Regensburg; R' Zelig Margolies; see also Margulies

Margulies, see *R' Ephraim Zalman Margulies; see also Margolies

Matalon, see R' Mordechai Matalon

*R' Matisyahu Delacrot (103)

Meinsterl, see R' Shlomo Meinsterl

R' Meir Aramah, son of *R' Yitzchak Aramah

R' Meir Ashkenazi, father of *R' Shabsai HaKohen

R' Meir Auerbach, see *R' Eliezer Ashkenazi Ish Tzvi

*R' Meir ben Gedalyah (Maharam Lublin) (122)

R' Meir Benveniste de Segovia, great-grandfather of *R' Shlomo ben Avraham Algazi I

R' Meir de Boton, son of *R' Avraham de Boton, teacher of *R' Shlomo ben Avraham Algazi I

R' Meir HaKohen, father of the *Shach*, see *R' Yehoshua ben Yosef of Cracow

R' Meir HaLevi Horowitz of Tiktin, see *R' Menachem [of] Tiktin

*R' Meir ibn Gabbai (63)

*R' Meir Katzenellenbogen (Maharam Padua) (72)

R' Meir (Marcus) Lehmann, see *R' Shlomo Sirilio; R' Yoselman Loanz of Rosheim

R' Meir Perles, biographer of *Maharal of Prague; see *R' Shlomo Luria

*R' Meir Popperos (165)

*R' Meir Schif (Maharam Schif) (146)

R' Meir Wahl, father-in-law of *R' Yonah Tumim, son of R' Shaul Wahl

Meisels, see R' Avraham Meisels; R' Yitzchak Bunom's

Melish, see R' Tzvi ben Shalom Melish

*R' Menachem Azaryah of Fano (Rama of Fano) (125)

R' Menachem ben Zerach, see *R' (Don) Yitzchak Abarbanel, see also *R.*, p. 106

*R' Menachem de Lonzano (107)

*R' Menachem HaBavli (74)

R' Menachem Mann, son-in-law of *R' Binyamin Aharon Solnik of Podayetz

*R' Menachem Mendel Auerbach (197)

*R' Menachem Mendel Krochmal (164)

R' Menachem Monish Chayes, son of *R' Yitzchak Chayes

R' Menachem of Merseburg, see *R' Yaakov Pollak; see also *R.*, p. 150

*R' Menachem [of] Tiktin (*Maharam Tiktin*) (106)

*R' Menachem Reccanati, see *R' Mordechai Yafeh, *R' Menachem HaBavli; see also *R.*, p. 190

*R' Menashe ben Yisrael   (158)

Mendes, see Dona Gracia Mendes

R' Meshulam Feivush of Cracow, teacher of *R' Eliezer Ashkenazi Ish Tzvi; *R' Yoel Sirkis, *R' Avraham Rappaport Shrentzel

R' Meshulam Katz, see *R' Yom Tov Lipman Heller

Metz, see R' Moshe Metz

MiGeza Tzvi, see R' Moshe ben Avraham MiGeza Tzvi

R' Michael ben Eliyahu ibn Chaim, son of *R' Eliyahu ibn Chaim

R' Michael Dov Weissmandl of Neitra, see *R' Yonah Tumim

Michel, see R' Chaim Michel

R' Michl R' Yosep's, see *R' Shmuel Vital

Mille, see R' Yechiel Mille

Mintz, see *R' Avraham Mintz; *R' Moshe Mintz; *R' Yehudah Mintz

Mizrachi, see *R' Eliyahu Mizrachi; R' Gershon Mizrachi

Molcho, see *R' Shlomo Molcho

Monson, see *R' Avraham Monson

Mordechai, see *R' Mordechai ben Hillel

R' Mordechai, rabbi of Berzan, see *R' Avraham Chaim Shor

R' Mordechai Angel, see *R' Avraham Galante

*R' Mordechai ben Hillel, see *R' Moshe Isserles, see also R., p. 141

R' Mordechai ben Yosef, brother of *R' Yehoshua ben Yosef of Cracow

R' Mordechai HaLevi, son of *R' David HaLevi; see *R' David Conforte

R' Mordechai Kalai, mentor of *R' Daniel Esterosah, *R' David Conforte, and *R' Avraham ibn Chananyah

R' Mordechai Katz, second father-in-law of *R' Moshe Isserles

R' Mordechai Mardush of Poritzk, see *R' Meir Schif

R' Mordechai Matalon, see *R' Eliyahu ibn Chaim

R' Mordechai Matalon, see *R' Aharon Sasson

R' Mordechai Oshminer, see *R' Yosef ibn Lev

R' Mordechai Shrentzel of Lemberg, father-in-law of *R' Avraham Rappaport Shrentzel

*R' Mordechai Yafeh (The Levush)   (117)

Mortera, see *R' Shaul Mortera

Mos, see *R' Moshe Mos of Premysl

R' Moshe (Ashkenazi) Heilprin, father-in-law of *R' Shmuel Eliezer Eidels

*R' Moshe Alashkar (Maharam Alashkar)
                                        (56)

*R' Moshe Almosnino   (92)

*R' Moshe Alsheich   (101)

R' Moshe Auerbach, great-grandfather of *R' Moshe Isserles (Rama)

*R' Moshe ben Avraham MiGeza Tzvi
                                        (189)

R' Moshe ben Avraham Algazi, brother of *R' Shlomo ben Avraham Algazi I

R' Moshe ben Chaim Shabsai, son of *R' Chaim Shabsai

R' Moshe ben Elazar Isserles, see *R' Kalman Vermaisa

R' Moshe ben Levi Najarah, father of *R' Yisrael Najarah

R' Moshe ben Mano'ach Hendel, see *R' Mano'ach Hendel

R' Moshe ben Nesanel ibn Shlomo, see *R' Menachem de Lonzano

R' Moshe ben Yehudah Benveniste, grandfather of *R' Yehoshua (Rephael) Benveniste

R' Moshe ben Yitzchak Bunoms, see *R' Moshe of Lublin

*R' Moshe ben Yitzchak Yehudah Lema   (161)

*R' Moshe Benveniste   (181)

R' Moshe Besodo, teacher of *R' Yom Tov Tzahalon

*R' Moshe Capsali   (37)

R' Moshe Chagiz, father of *R' Yaakov Chagiz, see *R' Avraham ibn Chananyah

*R' Moshe Chagiz, son of *R' (Yisrael) Yaakov Chagiz, see L.A.

R' Moshe Chaim, father-in-law of *R' Eliyahu ben Yehudah Kovo, son of *R' Chaim Shabsai; see *R' Moshe Chaim Luzzato

R' Nissan ben Yehudah, disciple of R' Yonah Tumim

R' Nissim Benveniste, son-in-law of *R' Eliyahu ibn Chaim; father of *R' Moshe Benveniste; uncle of *R' Yehoshua and *R' Chaim Benveniste; see *R' Yitzchak Abohab II

R' Nissim Gerondi, see *R' Betzalel Ashkenazi; see also *R. p. 105

R' (Nissim) Shlomo ben Avraham Algazi I, see *R' Shlomo ben Avraham Algazi I

Norlingen, see *R' Yosef Yospa Han Norlingen

Oppenheim, see *R' David Oppenheim

Oshminer, see *R' Mordechai Oshminer

R' Ovadyah ben Zecharyah Hamon of Bertinoro, nephew of *R' Ovadyah Yarei of Bertinoro

*R' Ovadyah Sforno (66)

*R' Ovadyah Yarei of Bertinoro (46)

Patras, see *R' Yaakov HaLevi Patras (Patrai)

Perachia, see *R' Aharon ben Chaim HaKohen Perachia; *R' Chisdai ben Shmuel HaKohen Perachia

R' Peretz Colon, son of *Maharik, see *R' Moshe Capsali

R' Peretz HaKohen, see *R' Matisyahu Delacrot; *R' Yehudah Chayat; see also *R., p. 104

Perles, see R' Meir Perles

R' Pesachyah, son of *R' Moshe Rivkah's

R' Pesachyah ben David Lida, son of *R' David Lida

R' Pinchas Horowitz, see *R' Moshe Isserles

R' Pinchas of Antipole, see *R' Yosef ibn Lev

Pinto, see *R' Yoshiyahu Pinto

Pollak, see R' Levi Pollak; *R' Yaakov Pollak

Popperos, see *R' Meir Popperos

Poppers, see R' Yaakov HaKohen Poppers

Poss, see R' Leib Poss

Poyeto, see R' Yaakov Poyeto

Pri Chadash, see *R' Chizkiyah de Silva; *R' Yaakov Castro; see also L.A.

Pri Megadim, see *R' Yosef Tumim

Provencal, see R' David Provencal; R' Moshe Provencal of Mantua

Ra'am, see *R' Eliyahu Mizrachi

*Rabbeinu Tam, ancestor of *R' Vidal Tzarfati; see *R' Yaakov ben Meir; see also R., p. 127

Rabino, see *R' Yaakov Rabino

Rabinowitz, see R' Tzadok Rabinowitz HaKohen of Lublin

Radach, see *R' David HaKohen

Radak, see *R' Eliyahu Bachur, see also R., p. 171

Radvaz, see *R' David ibn Zimra

Ralbach, see *R' Levi ibn Chaviv

Ralbag, see *R' (Don) Yitzchak Abarbanel, see also R., p. 179

Rama, see *R' Moshe Isserles

Rama of Fano, see *R' Menachem Azaryah of Fano

Ramak, see *R' Moshe Cordovero

Rambam, see R., p. 79

Ramban, see R., p. 90

Ranach, see *R' Eliyahu ibn Chaim

Rappaport, see R' Aryeh Leib Rappaport; *R' Avraham Rappaport Shrentzel; R' Yisrael Yechiel Rappaport

Rappo, see *R' Avraham Menachem Rappo of Porto

Rashba, see R., p. 96

Rashbatz, see R., p. 110

Rashi, see R., p. 122

Reccanati, see *R' Menachem Reccanati

Rephael Uchana, see *R' Yosef HaDarshan

Reisher, see *R' Yaakov Reisher

R' Reuven David Shapira, son of R' Nassan Nata Shapira II; father of *R' Nassan Nata Shapira III

Riaf, see *R' Yoshiyahu Pinto

Rit Algazi, see *R' Yom Tov Algazi

Ritva, see R., p. 99

Rofei, see R' Aryeh Leib Rofei; R' Chiya Rofei; R' Yosef Shlomo Rofei

R' Shlomo ibn Chason, see *R' Yosef ibn Lev

*R' Shlomo ibn Gabirol, see *R' (Yisrael) Yaakov Chagiz; see also R., p. 61

*R' Shlomo ibn Verga (38)

*R' Shlomo Luria (Maharshal) (81)

R' Shlomo Meinsterl, see *R' Yosef Shlomo Delmedigo

*R' Shlomo Molcho (55)

*R' Shlomo of Chelm, see *R' Aharon ibn Chaim, see also L.A.

R' Shlomo R' Leibush, see *R' Shlomo ben Yehudah Leib

R' Shlomo Sages, mentor of *R' Yosef Trani

R' Shlomo Shloiml of Dreznitz, see *R' Yisrael Seruk

*R' Shlomo Sirilio (70)

R' Shlomo Taitatzak, father of *R' Yosef Taitatzak

R' Shmuel, father of *R' Yoel Sirkis (the Bach)

R' Shmuel Abarbanel, grandfather of *R' (Don) Yitzchak Abarbanel

*R' Shmuel Abohab, see *R' Shmuel Garmizan; see also L.A.

*R' Shmuel ben Uri Shraga Feivush (201)

R' Shmuel ben Uziel of Landsberg, see *R' Mordechai Yafeh

R' Shmuel ben Yaakov of Prague, father-in-law of *R' Yehudah Loewe

R' Shmuel ben Yisrael, son of *R' Menashe ben Yisrael

R' Shmuel ben Yosef, see *R' Avraham Abale Gombiner

R' Shmuel Chagiz, father of *R' (Yisrael) Yaakov Chagiz

R' Shmuel Chassid, see *R' Shmuel Ish Tzvi

*R' Shmuel de Medina (Maharashdam) (97)

*R' Shmuel de Uzeda (110)

*R' Shmuel Eliezer Eidels (Maharsha) (137)

*R' Shmuel Galiko (104)

R' Shmuel Gaon, see *R' Aharon ben Chaim Avraham HaKohen Perachia

*R' Shmuel Garmizan (184)

*R' Shmuel HaLevi (189)

*R' Shmuel HaSardi, see *R' Azaryah Figo; see also R., p. 90

R' Shmuel ibn Shuiv, son of *R' Yoel ibn Shuiv

R' Shmuel Ish Tzvi, father of *R' Eliezer Ashkenazi Ish Tzvi

R' Shmuel Kalai, son-in-law of *R' Binyamin Zev; disciple of *R' David HaKohen

R' Shmuel Margolies, father of *R' Moshe Mordechai Margolies

R' Shmuel of Premysl, teacher of *R' Yehoshua ben Yosef of Cracow

R' Shmuel of Valencia, relative of *R' Avraham Zacut; disciple of *R' Yitzchak Kanpanton (R., p. 113); teacher of *R' Yaakov ibn Chaviv

R' Shmuel Shamama, see *R' Shimshon of Ostropolle

R' Shmuel Shor, brother of *R' Avraham Chaim Shor and *R' Ephraim Zalman Shor

R' Shmuel Shulam, see *R' Avraham Zacut

R' Shmuel Taitatzak, brother of *R' Yosef Taitatzak; great-nephew of *R' Yosef Taitatzak

R' Shmuel Tzarfati, descendant of *R' Vidal Tzarfati

*R' Shmuel Vital (187)

*R' Shmuel Yafeh Ashkenazi (102)

*R' Shmuel Yehudah Katzenellenbogen (105)

R' Shmuel Zacut, father and teacher of *R' Avraham Zacut

Sholal, see R' Yitzchak HaKohen Sholal

Shor, see R' Alexander Sender Shor; *R' Avraham Chaim Shor; *R' Ephraim Zalman Shor; R' Hirsh Shor; R' Naftali Hirsh Shor; R' Shmuel Shor; R' Yaakov Shor; R' Yaakov Yekl Shor

Shrentzel, see *R' Avraham Rappaport Shrentzel; R' Elazar Shrentzel; R' Mordechai Shrentzel of Lemberg

Shulam, see R' Shmuel Shulam

R' Simchah HaKohen, see *R' Avraham ibn Chananyah; *R' Yosef Trani

R' Yaakov Alfandari, see *R' Shlomo HaKohen

R' Yaakov Aramah, grandson of *R' Yitzchak Aramah

*R' Yaakov bei Rav (57)

R' Yaakov bei Rav II, grandson of *R' Yaakov bei Rav

R' Yaakov ben Asher, see *R' Yosef Caro, see also *R.*, p. 144

R' Yaakov ben Chaim, uncle of *R' Yehudah Loeve (Maharal of Prague), see *R' Chaim ben Betzalel

R' Yaakov ben Yitzchak Shapiro, see *R' Meir ben Gedalyah

R' Yaakov Castilo, see *R' Moshe Rivkah's

*R' Yaakov Castro (Maharikash) (116)

R' Yaakov Chagiz, see *R' (Yisrael) Yaakov Chagiz

R' Yaakov de Boton, great-grandson of R' Avraham de Boton, see *R' Chisdai ben Shmuel HaKohen Perachia

*R' Yaakov Emden, see *R' Avraham ibn Chananyah; *R' Avraham Zacut; *R' Yosef Trani, see also *L.A.*

R' Yaakov Finzi of Reccanata, teacher of *R' Gedalyah ibn Yachya

R' Yaakov Ginsburg, mentor of *R' Eliyahu Loanz

R' Yaakov HaKohen Poppers, see *R' Meir Popperos; see also *L.A.*

*R' Yaakov HaLevi Patras (Patrai) (141)

*R' Yaakov ibn Chaviv (48)

R' Yaakov ibn Nachmias, see *R' Yosef Shlomo Delmedigo

*R' Yaakov Kopelman (114)

*R' Yaakov Landau, see *R' Moshe Capsali; see also *R.*, p. 153

R' Yaakov of Lublin, teacher of *R' Aharon Shmuel Kaidanover; father of *R' Yehoshua Heshel of Cracow

*R' Yaakov Margolies (39)

R' Yaakov Margolies of Regensburg (Ratisbon), see *R Yaakov Margolies

*R' Yaakov Pollak (52)

R' Yaakov Poyeto, see *R' Eliyahu de Vidas

*R' Yaakov Rabino (131)

*R' Yaakov Reisher, see *R' Moshe Isserles; see also *L.A.*

R' Yaakov Sasportas, see *R' Aharon of Pesaro

R' Yaakov Shor, teacher of *R' Yitzchak of Posen; son of *R' Ephraim Zalman Shor

R' Yaakov Taitatzak, nephew of *R' Yosef Taitatzak

*R' Yaakov Temerls (177)

*R' Yaakov Tzemach (171)

R' Yaakov Weil, see *R' Moshe Isserles; see also *R.*, p. 151

*R' Yaakov Yehoshua (the *Pnei Yehoshua*), great-grandson of *R' Yehoshua ben Yosef; see also *L.A.*

R' Yaakov Yekl ben Binyamin Aharon Solnik, son of *R' Binyamin Aharon Solnik of Podayetz

R' Yaakov Yekl Shor, son of *R' Ephraim Zalman Shor

R' Yaakov Yitzchak Gombiner, see *R' Avraham Abale Gombiner

Yaavetz, see R' Yitzchak Yaavetz; R' Yitzchak ben Shlomo Yaavetz; *R' Yosef Yaavetz

Yafeh, see *R' Mordechai Yafeh; *R' Shmuel Yafeh Ashkenazi; R' Yitzchak Yafeh Ashkenazi

Yarei, see *R' Ovadyah Yarei of Bertinoro

Yashar of Candia, see *R' Yosef Shlomo Delmedigo

*R' Yechezkel Katzenellenbogen, descendant of *R' Binyamin Aharon Solnik of Podayetz; see also *L.A.*

*R' Yechezkel Landau, descendant of *R' Yehoshua Heshel of Cracow; see *R' Moshe ben Avraham MiGeza Tzvi; *R' Yehoshua Falk Katz; see also *L.A.*

R' Yechiel Foa, son-in-law of *R' Nassan Nata Shapira III

*R' Yechiel Halperin, see *R' Avraham Zacuta; see also *L.A.*

R' Yechiel Hillel Altschuler, see *R' Yitzchak Chayes

R' Yechiel Luria, father of *R' Shlomo Luria

R' Yechiel Mille, see *R' Eliyahu de Vidas

R' Yechiel of Nemirov, see *R' Shabsai HaKohen

•R' Yedayah Bedersi, see *R' Yom Tov Lipman Heller; see also R., p. 177

R' Yedayah HaPenini, see *R' Yedayah Bedersi

R' Yedidyah Gabbai, see *R' Avraham Gediliyah

R' Yedidyah Galante, son of *R' Moshe Galante I

•R' Yehoshua ben Yosef of Cracow   (149)

•R' Yehoshua Boaz Baruch   (69)

R' Yehoshua Chandali, son-in-law of *R' Eliyahu ben Yehudah Kovo

R' Yehoshua Falk HaKohen, see R' *Yehoshua Falk Katz

•R' Yehoshua Falk Katz   (119)

R' Yehoshua Feivl Tumim, son of *R' Yonah Tumim

R' Yehoshua HaKohen, father of *R' Yosef ben Yehoshua HaKohen

•R' Yehoshua Heshel of Cracow   (169)

R' Yehoshua ibn Shuiv, see *R' Yoel ibn Shuiv; see also R., p. 101

•R' Yehoshua (Rephael) Benveniste   (177)

•R' Yehoshua Soncin   (73)

R' Yehudah Abarbanel, father of *R' (Don) Yitzchak Abarbanel

R' Yehudah Almoda, see *R' Eliyahu ben Yehudah Kovo

•R' Yehudah Aryeh (Leon) de Modena   (151)

R' Yehudah ben Asher, descendant of *Rosh, see *R' Avraham Zacut

R' Yehudah Benveniste, great-grandfather of *R' Yehoshua (Rephael) Benveniste; see also *R' Yaakov ibn Chaviv

•R' Yehudah Chayat   (39)

•R' Yehudah HaChassid, see *R' Yosef Yospa Han Norlingen; see also R., p.134

R' Yehudah ibn Verga, see *R' Shlomo ibn Verga

R' Yehudah Leib ben Moshe Aharon Shmuel of Kremenitz, see *R' Shimshon of Ostropolle

R' Yehudah Leib ben Moshe HaKohen, father-in-law of *R' Menachem Mendel Auerbach

R' Yehudah Leib HaKohen, see *R' Moshe Galante II

R' Yehudah Leib Krochmal, son of *R' Menachem Mendel Krochmal

•R' Yehudah Loeve (Maharal of Prague)   (111)

•R' Yehudah Mintz   (40)

•R' Yehudah Muscato   (98)

•R' Yehudah Rozanes, see *R' Aharon Sasson; see also L.A.

R' Yehudah Taitatzak, great-nephew of *R' Yosef Taitatzak

•R' Yerucham, see *R' Chaim Algazi; *R' Shabsai Yonah, see also R., p.103

R' Yeshayah Azulai, grandson of *R' Avraham Azulai

R' Yeshayah HaLevi, son of *R' David HaLevi

•R' Yeshayah Horowitz (the Shelah)   (134)

R' Yeshayah Horowitz, son of *R' Shabsai Sheftl Horowitz II

R' Yeshayah of Trani I, ancestor of *R' Moshe Trani, see R., p.187

R' Yeshayah of Trani II, ancestor of *R' Moshe Trani, see R., p. 189

R' Yeshuah HaLevi, see *R' Shlomo ben Avraham Algazi I

R' Yirmiyahu of Mattersdorf, see *R' Chaim Shabsai

R' Yishmael Chanina of Vallmontone, teacher of *R' Menachem Azaryah of Fano

R' Yisrael, son of *R' Shalom Shachna

•R' Yisrael al-Nakavah, see *R' Eliyahu de Vidas; see also R., p. 107

R' Yisrael Ashkenazi, teacher of *R' Meir Popperos

R' Yisrael Benveniste, father of *R' Yehoshua (Rephael) Benveniste and *R' Chaim Benveniste

R' Yisrael de Corial, teacher of *R' Betzalel Ashkenazi; see *R' Yaakov bei Rav; see also *Historical Introduction*

R' Yisrael Eidels, father-in-law of *R' Yehoshua Falk Katz

R' Yisrael Isser ben Yosef, father of *R' Moshe Isserles

*R' Yisrael Najarah (133)

R' Yisrael of Ravigo, teacher of *R' Gedalyah ibn Yachya

*R' Yisrael Seruk (109)

R' Yisrael Shapira, son of *R' Nassan Nata Shapira II; see *R' Avraham Abale Gombiner

R' Yisrael Shmuel Califari of Cracow, see *R' Avraham Abale Gombiner

*R' Yisrael Yaakov ben Yom Tov Algazi, great-grandson of *R' Shlomo ben Avraham Algazi; see also *L.A.*

*R' (Yisrael) Yaakov Chagiz (183)

R' Yisrael Yechiel Rappaport, father of *R' Avraham Rappaport Shrentzel

R' Yisrael Zeligman Ganz, teacher of *R' Chaim Bochner

R' Yissachar Ber ben Moshe Pesachyah, see *R' Menachem Mendel Auerbach

*R' Yissachar Ber Eilenburg (131)

*R' Yissachar Ber HaKohen (98)

*R' Yissachar Susan (94)

*R' Yitzchak Abarbanel (41)

*R' Yitzchak Abohab II (35)

R' Yitzchak Abohab III, see *R' Avraham Herrera

R' Yitzchak Abohab de Fonseca, see *R' Menashe ben Yisrael, *R' Moshe Rivkah's

*R' Yitzchak Aramah (35)

R' Yitzchak Azulai, son of *R' Avraham Azulai

R' Yitzchak ben Betzalel, grandfather of *R' David HaLevi; uncle of *R' Betzalel Ashkenaz

*R' Yitzchak ben Shmuel Adribi (91)

R' Yitzchak ben Tzaddik ibn Lev, see *R' Yosef ibn Lev; *R' Shmuel Yafeh

R' Yitzchak ben Yaakov Chayes, descendant of *R' Yitzchak Chayes

R' Yitzchak Betzalel's, see *R' Yitzchak ben Betzalel

R' Yitzchak Bunom's, grandson of *Rama; father of *R' Moshe of Lublin

R' Yitzchak Caro, uncle of *R' Yosef Caro

*R' Yitzchak Chayes (121)

*R' Yitzchak de Leon (35)

R' Yitzchak Finzi of Pesaro, see *R' Azaryah min HaAdomim (de Rossi)

R' Yitzchak Foa, father-in-law of *R' Menachem Azaryah of Fano

R' Yitzchak Gakon, student of *R' Yitzchak de Leon, teacher of *R' Avraham ben Eliezer HaLevi

R' Yitzchak HaKohen Sholal, see *R' Avraham ben Eliezer HaLevi

R' Yitzchak HaLevi, brother of *R' David HaLevi

R' Yitzchak ibn Archa, father of *R' Eliezer ben Yitzchak ib Archa

R' Yitzchak Isaac Chover of Suvalk, see *R' Yehudah Aryeh (Leon) de Modena

*R' Yitzchak Kanpanton (the *Gaon* of Castille), teacher of *R' Yitzchak de Leon and *R' Yitzchak Abohab II; see *R.*, p. 113

R' Yitzchak Kloiber, grandfather of *R' Shlomo Luria (Maharshal)

*R' Yitzchak Leon ibn Tzur (68)

*R' Yitzchak Luria Ashkenazi (the *Ari*) (78)

R' Yitzchak Meir Tumim, son of R' Yonah Tumim

*R' Yitzchak of Duren, see *R.*, p. 141

*R' Yitzchak of Posen (195)

R' Yitzchak Saba, assumed to be *R' Avraham Saba's son; father-in-law of *R' Yosef Caro

R' Yitzchak Shapiro, father-in-law and teacher of *R' Meir ben Gedalyah (Maharam Lublin)

*R' Yitzchak Uziel (130)

R' Yitzchak Yaavetz, son of *R' Yosef Yaavetz

R' Yitzchak Yafeh Ashkenazi, father of *R' Shmuel Yafeh

R' Yitzchak Yafeh, father of *R' Shmuel Yafeh

R' Yitzchak Zerachyah Azulai, great-grandson of *R' Avraham Azulai

Yitzchaki, see R' Avraham Yitzchaki; R' David Yitzchaki

R' Yoav of Tzelim, see *R' Chaim Shabsai

•**R' Yochanan Aleiman** (40)

R' Yochanan Kremenitzer, see *R' Moshe Isserles

R' Yochanan Luria, antecedent of *R' Eliyahu Loanz

•**R' Yochanan Treves** (87)

R' Yoel, descendant of *R' David HaLevi

R' Yoel ben Gad, grandson of *R' David HaLevi

•**R' Yoel ibn Shuiv** (45)

•**R' Yoel Sirkis** (the *Bach*) (144)

•**R' Yom Tov (Rit) Algazi**, great-great-grandson of *R' Shlomo ben Avraham Algazi I; see also *L.A.*

•**R' Yom Tov Lipman Heller** (154)

•**R' Yom Tov Tzahalon (Maharit Tzahalon)** (127)

Yonah, see R' David Yonah; *R' Shabsai Yonah

•**R' Yonah Landsofer,** see *R' Menachem de Lonzano; *R' Shmuel Eliezer Eidels; see also *L.A.*

•**R' Yonah of Gerona (Gerondi),** see *R' Eliyahu de Vidas; see also *R.*, p. 87

•**R' Yonah Tumim** (179)

•**R' Yonasan Eibeschutz,** see *R' Shabsai HaKohen; see also *L.A.*

•**R' Yosef Albo,** see *R' (Don) Yitzchak Abarbanel; *R' Gedalyah Lipshitz; see also *R.*, p. 112

R' Yosef Almosnino, see *R' Aharon ibn Chaim

R' Yosef Babad, descendant of *R' Yehoshua Heshel of Cracow

•**R' Yosef Bechor Shor**, antecedent of *R' Avraham Shor; see *R.*, p. 157,

R' Yosef ben Aharon Sasson, son of *R' Aharon Sasson

R' Yosef ben Avraham Tzarfati, see *R' Yitzchak Uziel

R' Yosef ben David ibn Yachya, see *R' Gedalyah ibn Yachya

R' Yosef ben Matisyahu Delacrot, see *R' Matisyahu Delacrot

R' Yosef ben Menachem Yisrael, see *R' Mordechai Yafeh

•**R' Yosef ben Shaul Escapa** (164)

R' Yosef ben Yehoshua Falk Katz, son of *R' Yehoshua Falk Katz

•**R' Yosef ben Yehoshua HaKohen** (83)

R' Yosef ben Yitzchak HaLevi, see *R' Yom Tov Lipman Heller

•**R' Yosef ben Yitzchak ibn Ezra** (108)

R' Yosef Benveniste de Segovia, son of R' Meir Benveniste; grandfather of *R' Shlomo ben Avraham Algazi I

•**R' Yosef Caro** (the *Beis Yosef*) (84)

•**R' Yosef Chayon** (38)

•**R' Yosef Colon (Maharik)**, see *R.*, p. 191

R' Yosef Delacrot, son of *R' Matisyahu Delacrot

R' Yosef Dinkeles, see *R' Shlomo Sirilio

R' Yosef Escapa, see *R' Yosef ben Yitzchak ibn Ezra

R' Yosef Firman, teacher of *R' Shlomo HaKohen

R' Yosef Gansu, see *R' Shlomo ben Avraham Algazi I

•**R' Yosef Gikatilia,** see *R.*, p. 98

•**R' Yosef HaDarshan** (200)

R' Yosef HaLavan, see *R' Mordechai Yafeh

•**R' Yosef ibn Lev (Mahari ibn Lev)** (89)

•**R' Yosef ibn Verga,** son *R' Shlomo ibn Verga

•**R' Yosef ibn Zaiach** (or **Zaiat**) (55)

•**R' Yosef Katz** (98)

•**R' Yosef Korkos** (63)

R' Yosef Nasi, see Don Yosef Nasi

R' Yosef Nazir, see *R' Avraham ibn Chananyah